CAMBRIDGE LATIN AMERICAN STUDIES

69

POWER AND THE RULING CLASSES IN NORTHEAST BRAZIL

For a list of other books in the
Cambridge Latin American Studies series,
please see page 384

POWER AND THE RULING CLASSES IN NORTHEAST BRAZIL

JUAZEIRO AND PETROLINA IN TRANSITION

RONALD H. CHILCOTE
University of California, Riverside

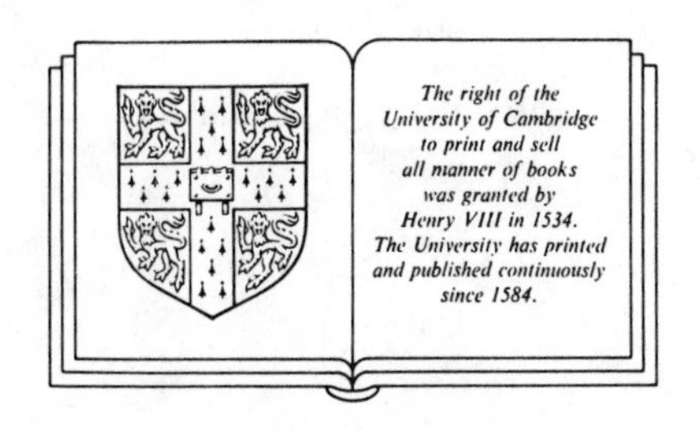
The right of the
University of Cambridge
to print and sell
all manner of books
was granted by
Henry VIII in 1534.
The University has printed
and published continuously
since 1584.

CAMBRIDGE UNIVERSITY PRESS
Cambridge
New York Port Chester Melbourne Sydney

Published by the Press Syndicate of the University of Cambridge
The Pitt Building, Trumpington Street, Cambridge CB2 1RP
40 West 20th Street, New York, NY 10011, USA
10 Stamford Road, Oakleigh, Melbourne 3166, Australia

First published 1990

Printed in the United States of America

Library of Congress Cataloging-in-Publication Data
Chilcote, Ronald H.
Power and the ruling classes in northeast Brazil : Juazeiro and Petrolina in transition / Ronald H. Chilcote.
p. cm. – (Cambridge Latin American studies ; 69)
Bibliography: p.
ISBN 0–521–37384–0
1. Elite (Social sciences) – Brazil – Juazeiro (Bahia) 2. Capitalism – Brazil – Juazeiro (Bahia) 3. Juazeiro (Bahia, Brazil) – Economic conditions. 4. Elite (Social sciences) – Brazil – Petrolina (Pernambuco) 5. Capitalism – Brazil – Petrolina (Pernambuco) 6. Petrolina (Pernambuco, Brazil) – Economic conditions. I. Title. II. Series.
HN290.J83C48 1990
305.5'2'098142 – dc20 89–15797

British Library Cataloguing in Publication Data
Chilcote, Ronald H.
Power and the ruling classes in northeast Brazil : Juazeiro and Petrolina in transition. – (Cambridge Latin American studies; 69).
1. Brazil. Northeast Brazil. Power elites
I. Title
305.5'2'09813

ISBN 0-521-37384-0 hardback

For the people of Northeast Brazil
whose example teaches us how to
struggle, persevere, and commit to
resolving problems of human need.

Contents

Tables and figures

Tables

Unless otherwise indicated the data in the tables date to 1971.

Figures

Preface

The initial idea for this project evolved from discussions with colleagues in about 1964. Originally, the plan was to undertake a comparative study of communities in northeast Brazil, northern Chile, and northwest Mexico. With the completion of the Brazilian work, a portion of the investigation was replicated in Chile and Mexico as originally planned.

Preparatory work was undertaken in Brazil during 1967 with the support of a sabbatical leave from the University of California and a grant from the Rockefeller Foundation, administered through the university's Dry Lands Research Institute. Development of research instruments and some pretesting were done during 1968 and 1969 in Baja California and in the Mexican–American community of South Colton, where I was able to coordinate the activities of two seminars of students. Research in two towns of the backlands or *sertão* of northeast Brazil was first carried out in summer 1969; these towns were Juazeiro and Petrolina, on opposite banks of the São Francisco River, in the states of Bahia and Pernambuco respectively. This investigation consisted of identification of the power structure in each community; initial interviews with leaders, decision makers, and knowledgeable or influential persons; and some background research into the history of the region. Between March and June 1971, with a sabbatical leave from the University of California and a grant from the Organization of American States, I turned to a survey among high school seniors and semiprojective interviews with eleven- and thirteen-year-old sons and daughters of members of the elite ruling classes. From July until October 1971, supported by a grant from the Social Science Research Council, interviews of roughly three hours' duration were conducted with 118 members of the ruling classes. Thereafter effort was devoted to coding and preparing the data for computer processing.

I studied these communities from nearly every conceivable angle. I delved into archives, read newspapers, and conducted interviews in order to understand the history of the region. To assess economic developments, I gathered statistics and data through banks and corporations and the regional census office. I read through municipal records, minutes of municipal council meetings, and budgets in order to gain insight into local and state politics. I explored personal relationships and traced family genealogies so as to comprehend the social life of the area. I used various techniques and approaches to identify the structure of power in each community. I interviewed a universe of persons representing the ruling classes, and I interviewed their sons and daughters as well. In sum, I gathered a tremendous amount of information. I probed for values, attitudes, and views on issues, problems, and needs of each community. During the course of research it became clear to me that in many respects I was becoming more knowledgeable than those who had lived in the communities all their lives. Of course, I would not assume such a pretentious position, but the implications of possessing so much knowledge and realizing the possibility that it could be used in constructive ways by the communities were indeed exciting.

A mass of computer printouts contains my data from the study. I have tried to present as much of it as possible and to do so simply and clearly. Because I interviewed nearly everyone in the universe of rulers, I have not concerned myself with sophisticated manipulation of data and statistical techniques. Instead I have synthesized and presented the data as representative of the perceptions of the people interviewed.

In this short space it is not possible to acknowledge all the persons and institutions who have supported this work, but I shall identify those who were especially helpful in seeing me through the many years of investigation, analysis, and writing. Let me begin with Amaury de Souza of the Instituto Universitário de Pesquisa in Rio de Janeiro, who joined me in 1967 as a researcher in the now defunct Latin American Research Program at the University of California, Riverside, and offered suggestions and ideas. Maria Laura Menezes assisted me in the Biblioteca Pública of Recife, and Lúcia Nery of the Arquivo Público Estadual in Recife was always cooperative and helpful in locating materials. Manuel Correia de Andrade of the Universidade Federal de Pernambuco provided me with insights from his personal experience and investigation. Estanislau Monteiro de Oliveira of the Superintendência de Desenvolvimento do Nordeste (SUDENE) recounted his months of investigation in Juazeiro and Petrolina during 1967 with a team of researchers from the Centro Latinoamericano de Pesquisas em Ciências Sociais of Rio. I am deeply indebted to all these Brazilian specialists. Jean Casimir, who directed the Centro study, was especially helpful in discussions of research problems. Although he showed me his raw data and early writings on Juazeiro and Petrolina, any references to the Centro study (which was not made public) are to copies of the final report in the archives of SUDENE and the Comissão de Desenvolvimento Econômico do São Francisco (CODESF).

Had it not been for the patience, understanding, and counsel of Pedro

Mansueto de Lavor, former director of Petrolina's radio station and now federal senator from Pernambuco, this study probably would not have been completed. From the outset he had a clear perception of my objectives, and he believed that the resulting data and analysis would contribute to the betterment of his community. Such encouragement stimulated my motivation, even in the most difficult of field conditions. I hope that the product meets his expectations. Not only was he able to arrange the interviews, to assist in the administration of a school survey, and to recruit interviewers for the project, but he came to my rescue when the project itself was threatened with termination. For example, near the end of my early field work a military intelligence officer in Juazeiro initiated an inquiry into my activities, the result being an interrogation by local and state military officers both in Bahia and Petrolina. Mansueto immediately arranged an open meeting of major personalities in the two communities and invited me to describe my project and answer questions. My anxiety over a tape recorder brought to the meeting by one of the officers and over two jeeploads of military police at the entrance of the building was alleviated by sympathetic and laudatory statements by several community leaders who even went so far as to invite me to return to the community to present the results of my study.

I wish also to thank my interviewers. Flor de Maria Nascimento Jatobá and Maria José de Souza Carvalho patiently and with great persistence demonstrated remarkable success in seeking interviewees and carefully pursuing every question until completion. Flor de Maria, in particular, was able to move the project along quickly, sometimes obtaining three or four interviews during a day. I was impressed by her determination to complete an interview with a very busy, important, but cautious agency head; realizing the difficulty – sometimes impossibility – of returning to complete an unfinished interview, she did indeed finish the interview but only after a six-hour encounter. When to my dismay both these interviewers were unable to continue for personal reasons, the gap was very ably filled by Rosália de Aráujo Oliveira, a social worker with SUDENE. Jussara Maria Belfort Alemida Saldanha obtained sixty-six interviews with sons and daughters of the ruling class, and Rosângela Rocha Ferrari assisted with coding of most of our interviews. Not only was the work of all those persons efficient and meticulous, but it met every standard of professional rigor and at the same time was carried out with a spirit of enthusiasm and interest probably unique to such tedious research.

I am of course indebted to all persons who gave us their time and shared their thoughts. Their collaboration allowed me to reach all my objectives. In particular, I am appreciative of the assistance of Luiz Augusto Fernandes, who during my first visit to the region in 1967 encouraged me to pursue my study. Upon my return in 1969 he instructed Dr. Giuseppi

Muccini and Honório Rocha to help this project. They provided me with the facilities and services of the Fundação Educacional and CODESF and introduced me to important personalities. The late regional historian Antônio de Santana Padilha recounted events of life in the communities, outlined family genealogies, and read and checked the historical portions of my manuscript. The history of these communities is only partially recorded and not well preserved. But I was able to read newspapers: *O Farol* and *O Sertão* of Petrolina, edited respectively by João Ferreira Gomes since 1915 and by Cid Almeida de Carvalho since 1948. I am appreciative to these gentlemen for letting me delve through their newspaper archives. Also I wish to thank the officers of the Clube Commercial for allowing me to examine their collection of late-nineteenth-century daily newspapers of Juazeiro and Ermi Ferrari Magalhães for assistance in reviewing *Rivale*.

Simão Durando Amorim and the late Américo Tanuri, then mayors of Juazeiro and Petrolina, were receptive and always cooperative in my project. At the outset of my investigation these mayors invited me to meet with town officials and to explain my project; this tended to mitigate a variety of concerns that always are apparent when one asks personal, sometimes sensitive, questions. I also appreciate the cooperation of the former bishops of Juazeiro and Petrolina, respectively Dom Tomás and Dom Antônio Campelo de Aragão, as well as Dom José Rodrigues de Souza, presently bishop of Juazeiro.

Finally, I am especially grateful to the school directors who allowed us to survey and interview students. Because of their efforts, we were also able to survey school teachers. Among these directors were: Nicolau Boscardin, Iêda Nogueira, and Irmã Nazaré Nobrega of Petrolina; and Antonilio de França Cardoso, Edgard Chastinet Guimarães, and Raimundo Medrado Primo of Juazeiro. I am also thankful to students of the Centro de Menores (CEMIC) for their assistance in mimeographing and assembling questionnaires.

Without the intelligent and resourceful effort of Elizabeth Tilly, formerly the Social Science Programmer at the University of California, Riverside, my data would not have been processed so accurately and quickly. She made a very substantial contribution to this study, of which I am most appreciative. Diane Radke, formerly of the Latin American Research Program of the University of California, facilitated the project with typing of questionnaires and coordinating details on campus while I was in the field. Susan Gregory, Danielle Bouvier, and Roseanna Barrón-López also typed portions of the manuscript. My wife, Frances Bunker Chilcote, assisted in many important ways. She helped coordinate interviews with the eleven- to thirteen-year-old students, and she coded those interviews and analyzed some of the data. She checked coding of interviews with high school students as well as with members of the ruling classes. She read and edited the manuscript and suggested revisions. Her help and encouragement always were available when needed, for which my appreciation cannot adequately be expressed in writing.

I am grateful for a critical reading of my manuscript by Professor Charles Adrian of the University of California, Riverside, who looked at Chapter 2; the late Professor Peter Eisenberg of the Universidade Estadual de Campinas, who read all of it; and Barbara Metzger of Laguna Beach, California, who copyedited an early draft. Professor Manuel Correia de Andrade of the Universidade Federal de Pernambuco and Professor André Haguette of the Universidade Federal do Ceará reviewed Chapter 12. Professors Peter McDonough of the University of Michigan and Thomas Skidmore of the University of Wisconsin commented extensively on an early draft of the first ten chapters.

During the review process Professors Arturo Valenzuela of Georgetown University and Simon Collier of the University of Essex were especially encouraging and generous with comments and suggestions. I am appreciative of the Cambridge University Press editorial staff who moved the manuscript toward publication, especially the executive editor, Frank Smith; the production editor, Katharita Lamoza; and Brian MacDonald, who copyedited the manuscript. Claudia Maria Pompan, a doctoral recipient at the University of California, Riverside, provided invaluable assistance in the final revision of the manuscript. Tami Barton prepared the Appendix, and Linda Biro organized the Index.

I wish also to thank the following organizations for financial assistance: the Social Science Research Council; the Rockefeller Foundation for its grant through the Dry Lands Research Institute; and the Organization of American States. I also wish to acknowledge the financial assistance of the Committee on Research, the Computer Center, and the Latin American Research Program of the University of California, Riverside.

PART I

The traditional sertão

1

The background

> Private investors now come to the region, initially prospecting. The visit of Rockefeller, the experience of the Sampaio Ferraz, the grapes of Molina, the onion farmers along the river, the pioneering of the Coelhos . . . are positive indications that "the Valley is good business." . . . In Petrolina alongside the Schumpeterian empire of the Coelhos . . . other investors begin to establish themselves. . . . The former governor of Pernambuco, manly leader of the clan, welcomes and orients these investors almost all of whom are his friends: from the South, the Northeast, and the outside. Rockefeller sends him letters and postcards. Pignatari lunches in the colonial home of Dona Josefa Coelho after having landed his executive plane . . . en route to the copper mines in Caraíbas. The executive president of Heinz – the great agroindustrial complex in California . . . writes him for information about land. . . . Besides the "big shots" of national and foreign industry . . . Nilo Coelho maintains frequent contact with Robert McNamara, president of the World Bank. . . . The agroindustrialists begin to appear. . . . The Simonsens plant alfalfa on the Bahian side. . . . Gustavo Coleço . . . begins experiments with national and foreign varieties of sugarcane. . . . Heinz of California wants to plant tomatoes and process them in order to penetrate the internal market and to export. . . . Pizzamiglio, São Paulo retailer, installs plantations of grapes and tomatoes; the Japanese of Paraná are in fruit; the Bentonite group of Campina Grande . . . wants to produce essential oils; the Pascuale Hermanos are in fruit; Prado Franco expects sugar production along the Bahian side.[1]

This report from a Recife newspaper provides a glimpse of political–economic life in the early 1970s in Juazeiro and Petrolina, neighboring towns of some sixty thousand inhabitants each that are closely linked to each other, to their respective states of Bahia and Pernambuco in the Brazilian Northeast, to the federal government centered in Brasília, and, increasingly, to international capital. Juazeiro is ruled by a paternalistic bureaucracy, and competition for control of this bureaucracy has made it

1 Mário Aurélio Alcântara, "Informativo económico," *Diário de Pernambuco* (June 13, 1972), reprinted in *O Farol* 57 (July 15, 1972): 1. In its early years *O Farol* was published as *O Pharol* but here I use the contemporary spelling.

dependent on the outside world, leaving local merchant capital to survive with difficulty under limited resources. Petrolina is ruled patriarchally, and the concentration of power in a single family has permitted it some autonomous capitalist development and integration into the national and world economy. The ways in which cohesiveness and factionalism within the ruling order have contributed to the development or underdevelopment of these two communities are the subject of this book.

My interest in these two communities of the *sertão*, or backlands, was sparked by Euclides da Cunha's *Rebellion in the Backlands*,[2] the classic account of the heroic resistance of a group of late-nineteenth-century settlers to government efforts to dislodge them. A century ago, Antônio Conselheiro led a band of followers into the heart of the Northeast backlands to a place not far from the São Francisco River they named Canudos. In 1896 Conselheiro contracted with Colonel João Evangelista Pereira e Melo for lumber to build a new church, but when it was not delivered he threatened to descend upon Juazeiro and take the lumber by force. In response to this threat the chief of Juazeiro urgently telegrammed Governor Luiz Viana for military assistance; Viana's family was prominent in the area, and the governor sent troops to prevent Conselheiro and his followers from invading the town. The siege during 1896 and 1897 lasted until "from the last trench the soldiers received the fire of the few last defenders of Canudos, faithful to the death. Two boys, one able-bodied man, and an old veteran still fought on until a volley from the soldiers laid them to rest, their faces turned towards the foe."[3]

The area Cunha described is the oldest and poorest of Brazilian regions and one of the most populous. Its semiarid landscape, home to nearly a third of the nation, gives the impression of suffering, "its skin baked and corroded by the rigors of the climate."[4] Its *caatinga* or scrub brush stifles, blocks the view, strikes the intruder in the face, and "repulses him with its

2 Stefan Zweig described this work as "a great national epic" offering "a complete psychological picture of the Brazilian soil, the people, and the country, such as has never since been achieved with equal insight and psychological comprehension"; *Brazil, Land of the Future* (New York: Viking Press, 1942), pp. 159–160, quoted in Samuel Putnam, "Introduction," in Euclides da Cunha, *Rebellion in the Backlands (Os Sertões)* (Chicago: University of Chicago Press, 1944), p. iii. A valuable contemporary source is Donald Pierson, *O Homem no Vale do São Francisco*, 3 vols. (Rio de Janeiro: Superintendência do Vale do São Francisco, 1972).

3 Quoted in R. B. Cunningham Graham, *A Brazilian Mystic, Being the Life and Miracles of Antônio Conselheiro* (London: William Heinemann, 1920), p. 237. Graham, like most writers, romanticizes the events at Canudos. Edmundo Moniz criticizes such a tendency in a recent novel by the Peruvian, Mario Vargas Llosa, *A guerra do fim do mundo, a saga de Antônio Conselheiro na maior aventura literária de nosso tempo* (Rio de Janeiro: Editora Francisco Alves, 1982). See Moniz, "Canudos: o suicídio literário de Vargas Llosa," *Encontros com a Civilização Brasileira* 29 (1982): 7–20, and his *Canudos: a luta pela terra*, 2d ed. (São Paulo: Global Editora, 1982), and *Guerra social de Canudos* (Rio de Janeiro: Editora Civilização Brasileira, 1978).

4 Josué de Castro, *Death in the Northeast* (New York: Random House, 1966), p. 23

Figure 1.1. "Weneslau Braz," nineteenth-century river steamboat; the principal mode of transportation on the Rio São Francisco. Photo 1967.

Figure 1.2. Wood for the riverboats, brought by traditional means 15 kilometers inland to the edge of the Rio São Francisco, has depleted the sertão of much of its vegetation.

thorns and prickly leaves, its twigs sharp as lances; and it stretches out in front of him, for mile on mile, unchanging in its desolate aspect of leafless trees, of dried and twisted boughs . . . representing, as it would seem, the agonized struggles of a tortured, writhing flora."[5] During the recurrent droughts, "the burning air is sterilized; the ground, parched and cleft, becomes petrified"; yet the plants, "the life within them latent, feed on those reserves which they have stored up in the off seasons and contrive to ride out the ordeal, ready for a transfiguration in the glow of a coming spring."[6]

Since the devastating drought of 1877–79, the area has been recognized as a national problem. Droughts recur at random but average one in every ten years and vary in duration from one to three years. In the annual dry season from about June to December, most of the rivers dry up. The São Francisco, "the river of national unity,"[7] flows 3,200 kilometers to the north year round, but the drop in water level at times brings boat transportation and the rural pastoral and agricultural economy to a halt. The region is semiarid, however, not desert,[8] and receives an annual rainfall of 69 centimeters, although this is low for an area with high rates of evaporation.

In this ravaged and scorched landscape, "death is such a pervasive presence that in some towns . . . the cemetery is the most attractive spot in the community." This fact caught the attention of a poet of the Northeast, who asked:

> Why all these walls? Why isolate the tombs From the more general boneyard,
> The defunct countryside?[9]

Drought brings starvation, and an emigration that has been described as "a veritable death march."[10] The refugee population usually returns, however, with the first rains; the attachment of the *sertanejo,* or backwoodsman, to his land and his way of life is well known.[11]

5 Da Cunha, *Rebellion in the Backlands,* p. 30.

6 Ibid., p. 31.

7 This is the title and theme of Orlando M. Carvalho's *O rio da unidade nacional, o São Francisco* (São Paulo: Companhia Editora Nacional, 1937).

8 This and other misconceptions of the Northeast are discussed in Stefan H. Robock, *Brazil's Developing Northeast: A Study of Regional Planning and Foreign Aid* (Washington, D. C.: Brookings Institution, 1963), pp. 6–8.

9 João Cabral de Mello Neto, "Cemitérios Pernambucanos," 1952, translated and cited in Josué de Castro, *Death in the Northeast,* pp. 24–25.

10 Castro, *Death in the Northeast,* p. 51. Under the Vargas regime the plight of refugees was considered a national problem – see, for example, Ademar Vidal, "Os movimentos nordestinos de emigração," *Cultura Política* 3 (January 1943): 51–56.

11 Albert O. Hirschman, *Journeys toward Progress: Studies of Economic Policy-making in Latin America* (New York: The Twentieth Century Fund, 1963), p. 15.

The sertanejo, says Cunha, "is always tired. He displays this invincible sluggishness, this muscular atony in everything that he does: in his slowness of speech, his forced gestures, his unsteady gait . . . in his constant tendency to immobility and rest." Yet all this is an illusion. Once challenged, "the fellow is transfigured. He straightens up, becomes a new man, with new lines in his posture and bearing; his head held high now, above his massive shoulders; his gaze straightforward and unflinching. Through an instantaneous discharge of nervous energy, he at once corrects all the faults that come from the habitual relaxation of his organs."[12]

Three backlands figures, in particular, have helped shape the history of the region: the *vaqueiro*, the *cangaceiro*, and the *coronel*. The vaqueiro, or cowboy, dressed from head to foot in cowhide or goatskin to ward off the rough caatinga, tended cattle believed to be the descendants of animals brought to Brazil by the colonists in the sixteenth century. According to Cunha:

> He grew to manhood almost without ever having been a child; what should have been the merry hours of childhood were embittered by the specter of the backland droughts. . . . He understood well enough that he was engaged in a conflict that knew no truce, one that imperiously demanded of him the utilization of every last drop of his energies. And so he became strong, expert, resigned, and practical. He was fitting himself for the struggle.[13]

The vaqueiro was traditionally serious and honest; should a stray calf cross his path, it is said, he would return it to the owner or care for it until the owner turned up to claim it. He engaged in some rudimentary farming but considered cattle raising his only dignified work. At roundup time he branded three-fourths of his herd for his patron and took one-fourth for himself.

The cangaceiro, or bandit, lived on the booty from assaults on farms and villages and the proceeds of extortion and the sale of protection. He was as trustworthy as the cowboy even though he was considered a criminal at large.[14] Lampião (1897–1938), the best known of the bandits of the Northeast, was born of a family of small landowners. In the course of a minor dispute he and two brothers murdered a neighbor and member of a rival clan, which brought revenge and the death of their parents. For protection, he and his family joined a renegade band, of which he eventually assumed the leadership.[15] Under Lampião and others, bandits

12 Da Cunha, *Rebellion in the Backlands*, p. 90.

13 Ibid., p. 92.

14 See Estácio de Lima, *O mundo estranho dos cangaceiros: ensaio biosociológico* (Salvador: Editora Itapoã, 1965).

15 There are hundreds of books and articles on Lampião. Among the most useful are Optato Gueiros, *Lampião, memórias de um oficial ex-comandante de forças volantes*, 2d ed. (São Paulo: Linográfica Editora, 1952); Ranulfo Prata, *Lampião, documentário* (São Paulo: Linográfica Editora, 1953); and Algae Lima Oliveira, *Lampião, cangaço e nordeste* (Rio de Janeiro: Edição O Cruzeiro, 1970).

achieved virtual autonomy in the backlands. Through skillful employment of violence, they gained access to power and prestige.[16]

The coronel, or colonel, held a virtual monopoly of political power on the local level. The title sometimes was simply assumed by a person, sometimes bestowed upon him by a municipal or state government in recognition of his position in the community, and sometimes conferred on him by his participation in the Old Republic's national guard. With the establishment of the national guard in August 1831, each municipality maintained a regiment, and the military title of colonel was usually conceded to the local political chief. Thus, the colonel served as commander in chief of the local regiment of the national guard and at the same time dominated political decisions, sometimes dictatorially. Usually he had at least the tacit support of the ruling state government. Victor Nunes Leal has aptly characterized *coronelismo* as "a compromise, a profitable exchange between public power, progressively fortified, and the decadent social influence of the local chiefs, notably the landowners. From this fundamental compromise emanated the secondary characteristics of the coronelista system, such as mandonismo [dominant rule], filhotismo [favoritism], fradulent voting, and the disorganization of local public services."[17]

It was not unusual for these local chieftains to become involved in mobilizing the population. In earlier times, they had led their private troops against bandits and intruders, and the remnants of these troops became their gunmen in battles against rival families. Violence sanctioned by local chieftains was generally accepted as part of sertão life. In the middle of the São Francisco Valley in the 1920s, for example, Colonel Franklin and followers in Pilão Arcado attacked Remanso, which was under the domination of Colonel Leobas, and drove him out of the region. Leobas was able to return and reclaim his property only when Colonel Janjão of nearby Sento Sé warned Franklin to remain in his own domain. The eventual restoration of peace in the area required the direct intervention of the governor of Bahia.[18] Under Vargas during the 1930s, the government moved to disarm the colonels and, once patriarchal and mercenary private violence had been suppressed, turned its attention to eradicating banditry. In the process thousands of bandits were killed or arrested.

Violence, however, still permeates Brazilian life in general and life in

16 One of the best syntheses is Amaury de Souza, "The Cangaço and the Politics of Violence in Northeast Brasil," in *Protest and Resistance in Angola and Brazil: Comparative Studies*, ed. Ronald H Chilcote (Berkeley and Los Angeles: University of California Press, 1972), pp. 109–131.

17 The classic study of the *coronel* is Victor Nunes Leal, *Coronelismo, enxada e voto: o município e o regime representativo no Brasil* (Rio de Janeiro: Livraria Forense, 1949); the quotation is from p. 20. Biographies of four contemporary colonels are in Marcos Vinicius Vilaça and Roberto Cavalcanti de Albuquerque, *Coronel, coronéis* (Rio de Janeiro: Tempo Brasileiro, 1965).

18 Vera Kelsey, *Seven Keys to Brazil* (New York: Funk and Wagnalls, 1941), pp. 186–187.

the backlands in particular. At the local level, violence is evident in the struggle for administrative power. For example, it is not uncommon for private disputes to be settled by gunfights and murders. Violence, too, serves to repress any semblance of popular protest. Márcio Moreira Alves, a former federal deputy, recounts the case of a peasant from the interior of Pernambuco who refused an order to leave a plot of land he had worked on for ten years; his body was found days later without eyes, nose, lips, and the event went unreported in the newspapers.[19] In a brief autobiographical account of his early years in the sertão, economist Celso Furtado referred to a politics that "consisted mainly in rivalries and conflicts between families and groups of families, and usually ended in violence." According to Furtado, his was a "world of men in which power and despotism were more often identified than separated."[20] Law is often premised on the will of landowners. Where there is a police force, it tends to be corrupt and partisan through its integration into the clan structure of society. One writer has astutely observed: "Violence is a tool the ruling classes of Brazil have never ceased to use in defense of their privileges and property."[21] Some writers have linked the traditional violence of the backlands to its periodic droughts and famines.[22] Castro, for example, sees the bandit of the Northeast as "a personality in which the baser impulses released by hunger have won the upper hand over normal restraints."[23]

Violence has been a dominant theme in the popular verse of the hundreds of troubadours who roam the backlands even today.[24] Traveling from fair to fair, these singers recount events of popular resistance; they recall the siege of Canudos and idolize the bandits of the nineteenth and twentieth centuries. They tell of the miracles of messianic figures who challenged the traditional dominant oligarchy. These troubadours function as intermediaries between the outside world and the peasant milieu of the

19 Márcio Moreira Alves, *A Grain of Mustard Seed: The Awakening of the Brazilian Revolution* (Garden City, N.Y.: Doubleday Anchor Press, 1973), pp. 44–45.

20 Celso Furtado, "Adventures of a Brazilian Economist," *International Social Science Journal* 25, nos. 1–2 (1973): 28.

21 Moreira Alves, *Grain of Mustard Seed*, pp. 44–45.

22 For example, Roger Bastide, *Brasil, terra de contrastes*, 2d ed. (São Paulo: Corpo e Alma do Brasil, Difusão Européia do Livro, 1964).

23 Castro, *Death in the Northeast*, p. 61.

24 Analysis of the popular poetry of the troubadours of the Northeast rarely deals with the theme of violence. Among the more useful works in this regard are Renato Carneiro Campos, *Ideologia dos poetas populares do Nordeste* (Recife: Centro Regional de Pesquisas Educacionais do Recife, 1959); Pedro Calmon, *História do Brasil na poesia do povo* (Rio de Janeiro: Editora A Noite, n.d.). Also useful are portions of the classic work of Gustavo Barroso, *Ao som da viola (Folklore)* (Rio de Janeiro: Livraria Editora Leite Ribeiro, 1921); Leonardo Mota, *Violeiros do Norte* (Fortaleza: Imprensa Universitária do Ceará, 1962); and Luís da Câmara Cascudo, *Vaqueiros e cantadores: folclore poético do sertão do Pernambuco, Paraíba, Rio Grande do Norte e Ceará* (Rio de Janeiro: Tecnoprint Gráfica, 1963).

backlands. The themes they stress make explicit the relationship of rulers to ruled, of dominant to dominated, of wealthy to poor. Running through their verse are past and present examples of exploitation and repression and ways of confronting them.

Political power in the backlands, as in Brazil in general,[25] is in the hands of a ruling class and a political elite. The ruling class has traditionally been composed of a small group of families whose power stems from the ownership of property – in the Northeast, mainly sugar plantation owners and cattle ranchers. The political elite consists of persons whose power is generated by their positions in the "patrimonial state" – the bureaucracy, the church, and the military. The political elite is concerned primarily with achieving public office and manipulating the patronage associated with it. It receives at least the tacit support of the ruling class through a quid pro quo arrangement in which the latter's hegemony is guaranteed not to be disturbed by, for example, land-tenure reform.[26] The ruling class and the political elite may be separate from each other or closely intertwined. In contemporary Juazeiro, the former is the case; in Petrolina, the latter.

The power of the ruling class is rooted in the patriarchal family, whose values of loyalty, respect for authority, hospitality, and reserve are "reflected in a general way in the psychology of the man of the Northeast, transmitted from generation to generation."[27] Historically, the big house on the large landed estate of the region was "the center of patriarchal and religious cohesion, the point of support for the organized society of the nation."[28] It represented an entire economic, social, and political system, including a latifundiary monoculture, a system of labor, a system of religion, and a system of politics based on *compradismo,* or political patronage and favoritism. Thus it was "at one and the same time a fortress, a bank, a cemetery, a hospital, a school, and a house of charity giving shelter to the aged, the widow, and the orphan."[29] Power was concentrated in the patriarchs who ruled over this system: "They were the lords of the earth and of men. The lords of women also."[30]

The power of the patriarchs resided in a family system consisting of the clan with the married couple, their offspring, and relatives at the center

25 Riorden Roett, *Brazil: Politics in a Patrimonial Society* (Boston: Allyn and Bacon, 1972), p. 53.

26 For a helpful discussion, see Reinhard Bendix, *Max Weber: An Intellectual Portrait* (Garden City, N.Y.: Doubleday Anchor, 1962), esp. chap. 11, "Traditional Domination," pp. 329–359.

27 M. Rodrigues de Melo, *Patriarcas e carreiros: influência do coronel e do carro de boi na sociedade rural do Nordeste,* 2d ed. (Rio de Janeiro: Irmãos Pongetti Editores, 1954), p. 23.

28 Gilberto Freyre, *The Masters and the Slaves (Casa Grande e Senzala): A Study in the Development of Brazilian Civilization* (New York: Alfred A. Knopf, 1964), p. 7.

29 Ibid.

30 Ibid., p. 8.

and extending to a periphery of godsons and rural tenants. Male supremacy served as the basis for decision making and the arbitration of disputes within the clan. Family solidarity and nepotism were the principles of its operation as a political institution.[31] The clan flourished during the colonial period, and during the nineteenth-century empire it became the basis of the "electoral clans" that dominated municipal politics. The power of these clans was diminished somewhat in the Old Republic by the abolition of slavery, but they remained a force in backlands politics.

Especially in colonial and imperial Brazil but also during the twentieth century, relations among the clans were dominated by struggles for power and prestige that amounted to blood feuds. The desire for more land was at the root of many of these struggles in the early period; the dispute in the backlands of Ceará between the clans of the Montes and the Feitosas is one example. By the nineteenth century, these conflicts were tied to the struggle to gain control over municipal councils; the dispute between the Carvalhos and the Pereiras began in 1849, when the former lost local elections but prevented the latter from assuming office, and lasted into the 1920s (by which time the aims of electoral victory had been replaced by the objective of mutual extermination).[32] These struggles for control of land and of towns resulted in the large landed estates' becoming not only powerful economic institutions, but also military ones: The economic and social structure was "guaranteed and protected by the resistant shield of its warring clans."[33]

Because the political economy of the colonial period was based on agriculture, rural landowners were able to establish a modus vivendi with the central government that favored their private interests. Thus, the development of the nation became tied to the pride, individualism, and independence of property owners. Consequently, there was more interest in political struggles at the municipal level than in those at the state and national levels. The social organization of the nation tended to support the latifundio and the nepotism that derived from it.[34] Under the Republic

31 Francisco José Oliveira Vianna, *Instituições políticas brasileiras*, vol. 1 (São Paulo: Livraria José Olympio Editora, 1949), p. 197.

32 These two family feuds are described in detail in L. A. Costa Pinto, *Lutas de famílias no Brasil: introdução ao seu estudo* (São Paulo: Companhia Editora Nacional, 1949), esp. chaps. 4 and 5. See also the appendix of Ulysses Lins de Albuquerque, *Un sertanejo e o sertão* (Rio de Janeiro: Livraria José Olympio Editora, 1957). For a useful discussion of family life in the sertão, see Billy Jaynes Chandler, *The Feitosas and the Sertão dos Inhamuns: The History of a Family and a Community in Northeast Brazil, 1700–1930* (Gainesville: University of Florida Press, 1972).

33 Francisco José Oliveira Vianna, *Recenseamento realizado em 1 de setembro de 1920* (Rio de Janeiro, 1922), p. 293.

34 Maria Isaura Pereira de Queiroz, "O mandonismo local na vida política brasileira," in *Estudos de sociologia e história*, ed. M. I. Pereira de Queiroz et al. (São Paulo: Editora Anhembi, 1957), pp. 299–300. Published separately as *O mandonismo local navida política brasileira* (São Paulo, 1969).

and especially after the Revolution of 1930, a federal system gradually began to absorb some of the power and autonomy of the municipalities, and at the same time the state executive began to preempt local legislative and judicial functions.[35] These changes in the structure of power were a challenge to the traditional ruling classes at the local level, and we shall examine their implications for the leaders of Juazeiro and Petrolina. They came at a time when the position of these rural property owners were being challenged in another way – by an incipient economic development bringing national and, to some extent, international capital into the region. This development is a more or less direct outgrowth of federal government efforts to solve the climatic problems of the Northeast.[36]

Government efforts to deal with the dry spells and droughts of the backlands date to the early years of this century, with the establishment in 1909 of the Departamento Nacional de Obras Contra Sêcas (DNOCS). Its task was to plan specific projects such as dams. Article 177 of the Constitution of 1934 provided that 4 percent of federal tax revenues be annually allocated to resolving the drought problems of the Northeast, but this provision was omitted in legislation establishing the New State under Getúlio Vargas in 1937.

Because of waste, paternalism, and corruption, the activities of the DNOCS proved not to be very effective. In 1948 the Comissão do Vale do São Francisco (CVSF), today known as the Superintendência do Vale do São Francisco (SUVALE), was established and assigned the broad task of promoting development in the valley. About the same time, the Companhia Hidroelétrica do São Francisco (CHESF) was charged with harnessing the power of the Paulo Afonso Falls.

The CVSF of these early years was short on technical expertise and incapable of aggressively attacking the problems of the region. The small dam and locks it constructed at Sobradinho, just south of Juazeiro and Petrolina, collapsed in December 1954 some two weeks after their inauguration, and were not rebuilt until the mid-1970s. In 1956 President Juscelino Kubitschek decided to build a dam at Três Marias, at the head-

35 Vianna, *Recenseamento*, pp. 391–392. For an analysis of changing political conditions, see also Moacir Palmeira, "Nordeste: mudanças políticas no século XX," *Cadernos Brasileiros* 37 (September–October 1966): 67–78.

36 A case study of these efforts is in Hirschman, *Journeys toward Progress*, pt. 1, chap. 1, "Brazil's Northeast," pp. 11–91. There are several hundred volumes on drought in the Northeast in the library of the University of California, Riverside. Three works illustrative of the concern for the area are P. Saturnino Rodrigues de Brito, *As sêccas do norte* (Recife: Imprensa Industrial, 1913); Joanny Bouchardet, *Sêccas e irrigação: solução scientífica e radical do problema nordestino brasileiro, geralmente intitulado 'O problema do Norte'* (Rio Branco, Minas Gerais: Officinas Graphs. da Papelaria Império, 1938); and J. G. Duque, *Solo e água no polígono das sêcas* (Fortaleza: Tipografia Minerva, 1949).

waters of the river in the state of Minas Gerais, for flood control and the generation of power. The project was entrusted to the Minas Gerais state power utility company, thereby relegating the CVSF to an insignificant role. Although the CVSF was not affected by the failures and scandals of the DNOCS a generation earlier, it was the victim of indecision and lack of planning that made it vulnerable to manipulation by rural politicians. Manoel Novais, a federal deputy from Bahia, in particular, influenced appointments and projects within the agency, until he antagonized the Kubitschek administration during the 1960 presidential campaign.[37]

When in 1951 another drought, the first in nineteen years, struck the Northeast, the Banco do Nordeste do Brasil (BNB) was established. This bank represented a new approach to the problems of the region, a response to the failure of past hydroelectric schemes and reforestation efforts and to recognition of the need for credit to build industry supplied with hydroelectric power from the Paulo Afonso dam.[38] In contrast to the DNOCS, CVSF, and CHESF, which were headquartered in Rio de Janeiro, the BNB was located in the Northeast, in Fortaleza. Initially the bank emphasized credit for agriculture, but eventually it became involved in the full spectrum of banking operations. Concentrating on short-term credit, however, the BNB tended to assume the role of a commercial bank rather than that of a developmental institution oriented to long-range activities in agriculture and industry. New legislation in 1959 altered this orientation, and the BNB shifted a majority of its operations to financing through medium- and long-term credits.[39] Unlike the other agencies previously set up to deal with the problems of the Northeast, the BNB managed to avoid assuming a patronage character; it made efforts to form a qualified staff, and a special research office operating autonomously within the bank produced a series of useful monographs on the region.[40]

Drought in 1959 prompted the creation of the Superintendência do Desenvolvimento do Nordeste (SUDENE). The impetus for the new agency came from Celso Furtado, a Northeasterner who in 1958 had become director of the BNB and a year later had submitted to Kubitschek

37 Nelson de Souza Sampaio, *O diálogo democrático na Bahia* (Belo Horizonte: Edições RBEP, 1960), p. 85, cited in Hirschman, *Journeys toward Progress*, p. 53.

38 Especially critical of past efforts was the geographer Hilgard O'Reilly Sternberg. Three of his studies are "Aspectos da sêca de 1951, no Ceará," *Revista Brasileira de Geografia* 13 (July–September 1951): 327–369; "Sêca: causas e soluções," *Boletim Geográfico* 16 (September–October 1958): 638–643; and "Não existe ainda um plano para o problema das sêcas," *Boletim Geográfico* 16 (May–June 1958): 377–384.

39 The legislation and some analysis of the shift in the BNB operations is in Hirschman, *Journeys toward Progress*, pp. 64–65.

40 One such study is Banco do Nordeste do Brasil, *Petrolina–Juàzeiro: aspectos sócio-econômicos e área de influência comercial* (Fortaleza, 1968).

an analysis of the region's problems and a plan for action.[41] Furtado was particularly concerned about the disparity in levels of income between the Northeast and the Center-South. He attributed this disparity to a system of exchange allocation that provided the Center-South with economic advantages and argued for establishing the Northeast as a new dynamic center of growth and investment. He proposed moving in three directions: expanding irrigation using the reserves of water held by the dams, encouraging colonization in the humid lands of the state of Maranhão, and utilizing more efficiently the rich lands in the *mata* zone along the coast. These proposals were incorporated into SUDENE. In its early years, SUDENE was backed by the "reformist" governors of the Northeast, who served on its board of directors and also had the support of social-minded Catholic bishops in the Northeast and of congressmen from Rio and São Paulo. An assessment of the program in 1962 was optimistic:

> On the one hand, an upsurge in public investment and private industrial activity was definitely under way. On the other, the region's traditional elites were subjected to a wide range of pressures, from revolutionary threats and direct local actions to gentle, face-saving persuasion and advice. Investment boom and profound social transformation were seemingly both in the making, and both were promoted and "administered" in various ways by the same agency, SUDENE.[42]

Thus the climatic problems of the backlands had provoked a series of actions designed to transform the Northeast, eliminating its backwardness and in the process possibly undermining the position of its ruling oligarchies.

Once economically powerful because of income generated by sugar and gold exports, the Northeast has declined since the turn of the century and today is dependent on the industrial Center-South region and, in particular, such cities as Rio de Janeiro and São Paulo. Within the Northeast, two states predominate; Pernambuco and Bahia are central, while the other (generally smaller) states remain peripheral. Recife and Salvador, the state capitals, dominate the outlying and rural areas, including Juazeiro and Petrolina, communities dependent on farming and cattle raising and the economic activities of a few wealthy families. Although these communities have long provided a marketplace for trade between the coast and the interior and along the São Francisco River as far south as Minas Gerais, much of their economic activity has been based on internal capitalization.

41 The substance of Furtado's report is found in two books: *Perspectivas da economia brasileira* (Rio de Janeiro: Instituto Superior de Estudos Brasileiros, 1958) and *A Operação Nordeste* (Rio de Janeiro: Instituto Superior de Estudos Brasileiros, 1959).

42 Hirschman, *Journeys toward Progress*, p. 91. A similar assessment is offered by Heitor Ferreira Lima, "Soluções para os problemas do Nordeste," *Revista Brasiliense* 34 (March–April 1961): 8–22.

After World War II, the ruling families established plants for processing the agricultural products of their land. Somewhat secure politically and economically, they tended to invest their profits and income in these new enterprises. Their isolation was ensured by a lack of communication with the coastal cities; only inferior dirt roads and direct communication via the few wireless radios owned by a family or a government agency existed. The ruling families also turned to outside capital (public, wherever possible) to enhance their hold over the local economies. At the same time, monopoly over the commerce of the area and the prospects of rapid profits attracted outside investors, resulting either in new alliances between local and outside capitalists or, occasionally, in competition. Although the beginnings of some development were apparent at the time of my study – with Juazeiro and Petrolina being viewed as "poles of development," locales in which geography and human and physical resources offered some prospect of economic growth and change[43] – the economic life of these communities still bore all the earmarks of underdevelopment: profitable exploitation through monoculturative or monoextractive enterprises, dependence on foreign markets and financial interests, inadequate communication and transportation, low productivity, low per capita income, unequal distribution of income, monopolization of markets, unskilled labor, concentration of land ownership, unemployment and underemployment, and low level of technology, all against the background of climatic stress, depleted forest resources, low natural fertility and shallow soils, and the like.

The study of communities like these provides an opportunity to test some hypotheses about capitalist development and underdevelopment. The activist reformer Celso Furtado and the Marxist critic Caio Prado Júnior have documented the decline of the Northeast economy and analyzed the region's underdevelopment as a consequence of cycles of capitalist development based on fluctuating demand for such commodities as sugar and gold.[44] From a broader perspective, André Gunder Frank has also seen underdevelopment as the result of capitalist development; he has argued that capitalism produces a developing metropolis and an underdeveloped periphery both on a worldwide scale and within nations, between

43 The concept of "poles of development" derives from the work of F. Perroux, *L'économie du XXème siècle*, 2d ed. (Paris: Presses Universitaires de France, 1964). In relation to the Brazilian Northeast, the concept has been elaborated by Manoel Correia de Andrade, *Espaço, polarização e desenvolvimento: a teoria dos polos de desenvolvimento e a realidade nordestina* (Recife: Centro Regional de Administração Municipal, 1967).

44 Celso Furtado, *Economic Growth of Brazil: A Survey from Colonial to Modern Times* (Berkeley and Los Angeles: University of California Press, 1963); Caio Prado Júnior, *The Colonial Background of Modern Brazil*, trans. Suzette Macedo (Berkeley and Los Angeles: University of California Press, 1969).

a domestic metropolis and the surrounding cities and regions.[45] These writers and others tend to focus on the capitalist roots of underdevelopment at the expense of evidence that the persistence of precapitalist modes of production also plays a role. Obviously, the industrial metropolises of Rio de Janeiro and São Paulo are representative of essentially capitalist urban life; even in the smaller cities the prevalence of banks and import–export firms gives the appearance of the dominance of the capitalist mode of production. In Juazeiro and Petrolina, new technology and local capital along with some outside capital have been infused into the traditional agrarian economy, and capital investment by Petrolina's ruling Coelho family has stimulated some local industry. Furthermore, mercantile or commercial capital has prevailed since the end of World War II, and all this has led some observers to consider life in the backlands essentially capitalist. At issue here is whether a social formation may contain contradictory modes of production, capitalist and precapitalist.

This question was raised in a broader context during a debate between economists Paul Sweezy and Maurice Dobb.[46] Sweezy argued that in the late medieval period of western Europe expansion of trade brought about the decay of feudalism as capitalist production for exchange replaced feudal production for use. Dobb countered that although trade affected the existing relations of production, it was not decisive in the breakdown of feudalism. This debate has implications for the accumulation of mercantile capital and its impact on precapitalist modes of production in less developed areas of the world today. John G. Taylor suggests that merchants' capital supported an agrarian heritage and served as a barrier to capitalist development in Latin America. Expansion of exports and external markets during the eighteenth and nineteenth centuries did not disintegrate the system of large estates but consolidated it. Thus a small class with ownership and control of the fertile areas emerged, and the result was both exploitation of low-paid labor and the perpetuation of subsistence farming. The class of landowners was able to expropriate a large surplus from a labor force with low productivity; its estates "constituted a series of isolated and rigidly stratified units, dominated by what can only be termed an extremely paternalistic ideology."[47] These "feudal economic and political forms," says Taylor, "were increasingly forced to exist alongside a developing capitalist sector whose penetration gradually threatened their economic dominance in the agrarian sector."[48]

45 The thesis is elaborated in André Gunder Frank, *Capitalism and Underdevelopment in Latin America: Historical Studies of Chile and Brazil* (New York: Monthly Review Press, 1967).

46 Paul M. Sweezy, "A Critique," and Maurice Dobb, "A Reply," in *The Transition from Feudalism to Capitalism*, ed. P. M. Sweezy, M. Dobb, et al. (London: Verso Edition, 1978), pp. 33–56, 57–67.

47 John G. Taylor, *From Modernization to Modes of Production: A Critique of the Sociologues of Development and Underdevelopment* (New York: Macmillan, 1979), p. 191.

48 Ibid.

Brazil's path toward capitalist development was different from those of western and eastern Europe. According to Teresa Meade's view of these developments, the expansion of trade and exchange of goods under precapitalist conditions contributed to the dissolution of the feudal system in England and western Europe during the fourteenth century. The ownership of the means of production was transferred to the emerging small-commodity producers who employed and extracted surplus labor from the developing proletariat, while the big merchants remained tied to the previous mode of production because of their dependence on feudal landowners for commodities produced by the estates. In eastern Europe, in contrast, the peasant was not permitted to leave the estate but instead was resubjugated to the feudal order by an alliance between merchants and lords that repressed peasant resistance to taxation and surplus production for the owners. While feudal production continued in the countryside, merchants took possession of production destined for the West: "Medieval relations of landowning were not liquidated but were gradually adapted to capitalism, which retained semi-feudal features."[49] The Brazilian road to capitalism was similar to the eastern European in that an alliance between merchants and landowners ensured the maintenance of precapitalist relations of production in the transition from precapitalist production. However, "the subordinate position that Brazil assumed from the outset in the world capitalist market caused variations in the forms of primitive accumulation and class formation."[50]

In Juazeiro and Petrolina, individuals tended to fall into relationships dependent upon the dominant landowners, through debt peonage, sharecropping, and service in militias. As Meade puts it, these were distortions in the primitive accumulation process that became obstacles to any emergence of capitalist relations of production: "After abolition, previous relations of production were restructured into other pre-capitalist forms."[51] The merchants who became prominent in the towns maintained ties with the large landowners, thus ensuring some production of commodities from the estates for sale in the market as well as continued subjugation of peasants, who remained tied to the old order. When merchant capital was invested in local industry, it contributed to a transition to capitalism.

Fernando Henrique Cardoso and Enzo Faletto, describing the transition to capitalism in Latin America as a whole, point out that "peripheral economies, even when they are no longer restricted to the production of raw material, remain dependent in a very specific form: their capital goods productive sectors are not strong enough to ensure continuous advance of

49 Teresa Meade, "The Transition to Capitalism in Brazil: Notes on a Third Road," *Latin American Perspectives* 5 (Summer 1978): 12.

50 Ibid., p. 13.

51 Ibid., p. 20.

the system, in financial as well as in technological and organizational terms."[52] In countries like Brazil, the accumulation and expansion of capital is not great enough to allow for the reproduction of capital, and this leads to dependency. Dependency is the consequence of links between external and internal forces "rooted in coincidences of interests between local dominant classes and international ones, and . . . challenged by local dominated groups and classes."[53] In the period of the transition to capitalism, they assert, the export economy is diversified, and this is accompanied by the appearance of an industrial bourgeoisie, trained professionals, white-collar workers, and a military bureaucracy. Foreign capital may be invested in local processes and transformed into wages and taxes: "Its value is increased by the exploitation of local labor forces, which transform nature and produce goods that *realize* again the life of this capital when staples . . . are sold in the *external* market." Where the economy is controlled by the local bourgeoisie, in contrast, "accumulation is the result of the appropriation of natural resources by local entrepreneurs and the exploitation of the labor force by this same group."[54] Accumulation is internal, although some products may be oriented to the international market. This latter situation is more typical of Juazeiro and Petrolina.

In societies in which production is under national control, a bourgeoisie assumes a dominant role in an expanding capitalist sector, and this ensures the formation of a national state. Alliances between this bourgeoisie and owners of less productive estates and military and bureaucratic elements eventually produce a national bourgeoisie. In some instances, agrocommercial exporting sectors run the financial system and monopolize external relations through control over customs or an essential position in the external market; one example is the control by the Buenos Aires bourgeoisie of regional bourgeoisies and latifundistas. These sectors exhibit a semblance of unity and dominate both the ruling classes and the producing sectors of local economies. Where the leading segment of the bourgeoisie is unable to achieve class unity, an oligarchic, latifundist group may dominate, thereby disguising the capitalist nature of the system. Cardoso and Faletto consider this to have been the situation in Brazil prior to 1930. Although they are concerned with the national level, their distinction might be extended, with caution, to the cases of Petrolina and Juazeiro, with the former displaying a coherent bourgeoisie dominant over all sectors of the ruling class as well as the producing sectors of the local

52 Fernando Henrique Cardoso and Enzo Faletto, *Dependency and Development in Latin America*, trans. Marjory Mattingly Urquidi (Berkeley: University of California Press, 1979), p. xxi.

53 Ibid., p. xvi.

54 Ibid., p. xix.

economy and the latter exemplifying a bourgeoisie unable to establish hegemony.

According to Peter Evans, who has examined the interrelationship of foreign capital, local capital, and the state in Brazil:

> The end result of the incorporation of the periphery into the international capitalist system, as far as the elite is concerned, is to create a complex alliance between elite local capital, international capital, and state capital, which I have called "the triple alliance." . . . all members of the alliance will benefit from the accumulation of industrial capital within Brazil.[55]

Evans distinguishes between classic dependency and dependent development. Classic dependency appears in the periphery with the export of primary products in exchange for manufactured goods. Dependent development occurs where, as in Brazil, industrialization involving foreign as well as local capital brings about new accumulation, a more complex internal division of labor, and increased productivity. Whereas classic dependency is associated with weak states, dependent development is linked with the emergence of a strong state in a position to bargain with the multinationals.[56] The multinationals must create a market for their products among local elites, and to do this they combine international with local capital and that of the national industrial bourgeoisie. This bourgeoisie, the "stepchild of imperialism," has "no opening for either political domination or economic hegemony."[57] Consequently, the state must promote peripheral industrialization through local accumulation and local markets: "The problem is to redirect the global rationality of the multinational when it conflicts with the necessities of local accumulation. The state must continually coerce or cajole the multinationals into undertaking roles that they would otherwise abdicate."[58]

At the time of my study it was clear that although multinational capital had combined with national capital in Brazil, it had not yet become consequential for local capital in Juazeiro and Petrolina. Such industrialization as had taken place in the communities had been stimulated by local merchant capital and agricultural resources and was controlled by a few individuals. These local industrialists maintained relationships with capitalists in the large cities and even abroad, but they had not yet formulated any capital alliances. Indeed, they were suspicious of such connections. Yet, one could speculate on the probability of a change in this attitude and

55 Peter Evans, *Dependent Development: The Alliance of Multinational, State, and Local Capital in Brazil* (Princeton: Princeton University Press, 1979), pp. 11–12.

56 Ibid.

57 Ibid., p. 39.

58 Ibid., p. 44.

a necessary alliance with outside capital predicated on the projects of the state for irrigating and farming in the region and the quite likely appearance of large foreign firms. Thus, Evans's historical overview and analysis of the role of local and foreign capital in Brazil may prove helpful in understanding future changes in the interior Northeast.

His and other recent studies on Brazil[59] make it clear that attention to the capitalist transition, the role of the state, and the activities of the multinationals must not ignore questions of class rule. No single study has effectively analyzed the Brazilian ruling classes. That task has been beyond the scope and probably the comprehension of most investigation to date, yet one study in particular should be mentioned. Beginning with the premise that the Brazilian system is avowedly "elitist," Peter McDonough focuses on the structure of power and the nature of elite ideology and employs the notion of "limited pluralism" to describe the balance between those in power and their opposition. His study assumes that the identity of elites is obvious: The nationally powerful elites reside in Brasília, Rio de Janeiro, and São Paulo; top civil servants, including executives of state enterprises, and directors of the leading industrial and financial institutions, including the multinationals, are on his list. Politicians from government and opposition parties as well as labor leaders are included. Omitted because of lack of access are leaders in the military and security agencies.[60]

Although my study differs substantially from that of McDonough, notably in its conception of class, it shares a concern with the structure of power. Both of us look for major cleavages and conflicts within the power structure, kinship and family ties, interclass marriage, and class alliances. We also focus on the sociometry of rulers or elites – the depiction of the axes of power around which powerful persons revolve. Further, McDonough is concerned with the form and substance of political beliefs,

59 See, for example, David R. Dye and Carlos Eduardo de Souza e Silva, "A Perspective on the Brazilian State," *Latin American Research Review* 14 (Winter 1979): 81–98; Werner Baer, Richard Newfarmer, and Thomas Trebat, "On State Capitalism in Brazil: Some New Issues and Questions," *Inter-American Economic Affairs* 30 (Winter 1976): 69–91; Jonathan Fox, "Has Brazil Moved toward State Capitalism?" *Latin American Perspectives* 7 (Winter 1980): 64–86; Herbet Souza and Carlos A. Afonso, *The Role of the State in the Capitalist Development in Brazil: The Fiscal Crisis of the Brazilian State* (Toronto: Brazilian Studies 7, 1975).

60 Peter McDonough, *Power and Ideology in Brazil* (Princeton: Princeton University Press, 1981). Related studies of elites in Brazil include Renato Raul Boschi, *Elites industriais e democracia: hegemonia burguesa e mudança política no Brazil* (Rio de Janeiro: Edições Graal, 1979). The first four chapters synthesize historical origins and evolution of the industrial bourgeoisie at a national level. Emphasis on the industrial bourgeoisie during the Vargas period is in Eli Diniz, *Empresário, estado e capitalismo no Brazil, 1930–1945* (Rio de Janeiro: Paz e Terra, 1978). Luciano Martins, *Pouvoir et développment économique* (Paris: Editions Anthropos, 1976), looks at the state and industrial enterprise. Finally, there is the classical empirical study by Fernando Henrique Cardoso, *Empresariado industrial e desenvolvimento econômico no Brasil* (São Paulo: Difel, 1972).

the degree of consensus on specific policy issues, and priorities regarding developmental strategies – all matters examined in my study. He notes the reluctance of Brazilian elites to fight it out among themselves, to cultivate extremist ideologies, and to oppose strong authoritarianism. He attributes this to the separation of religious controversies from other political issues, arguing that absolutist modes of thinking are not prevalent. Although examples can be found to support this proposition, it seems to me that the interior communities of the Northeast have experienced a considerable degree of personal and family struggle for power, that they have traditionally leaned toward the authoritarian tendencies of the Church, and that political, economic, and religious activities were for the most part closely intertwined.

In their size, location, interrelations, and histories, Juazeiro and Petrolina are especially interesting cases for study of the traditions depicted by Euclides da Cunha and the changes brought about by an emerging capitalism. This introductory chapter provides the backdrop for an analysis of political–economic life in these communities. An initial task will be the identification of the structure of power and ruling classes in the two communities.

2

The structure of power and the ruling class

Studies of local or community politics are often primarily concerned with the functions or goals of local government, the degree of autonomy or integration of local government with national politics, and power structure or the distribution of power within the community.[1] They tend to focus on policy formulation and on decision making, the results often being presented in the form of case studies.[2] "Power" suggests control, whether arbitrary or based on traditional rights; it involves the ability to control the decision-making process or to mobilize resources. It may be distinguished from influence, the ability to persuade those who control.[3] John Walton has defined "power structure" as the "pattern within a social organization whereby resources are mobilized and sanctions employed in ways that affect the organization as a whole."[4] G. William Domhoff has distinguished three types of power indicators: "who benefits from the system, who directs or governs important institutions, and who wins on

1 Charles R. Adrian, "Local Politics," in *International Encyclopedia of the Social Sciences* (New York: Macmillan/Free Press, 1968), 9:460.

2 See Richard M. Morse, "Recent Research on Latin American Urbanization: A Selective Survey with Commentary," *Latin American Research Review* 1 (Fall 1975: 35–74. Morse refers to the colonial tradition in Brazil and much of South America where municipalities incorporated rural lands so that "more typical than the struggle between burgher and feudal groups was the conflict between local rural–urban oligarchies and agents of the royal bureaucracy" (p. 38). Morse updated his survey in "Trends and Issues in Latin American Urban Research, 1965–1970," parts 1 and 2, *Latin American Research Review* 6 (Spring 1971): 3–52, and (Summer 1971): 19–75. During the 1970s Sage Publications sponsored an annual series, *Latin American Urban Research*. See also the review by John Walton, "From Cities to Systems: Recent Research on Latin American Urbanization," *Latin American Research Review* 14, no. 1 (1979): 159–169, as well as Alejandro Portes and John Walton, *Urban Latin America: The Political Condition from Above and Below* (Austin: University of Texas Press, 1976).

3 The literature is replete with references to definitions of power, and I shall not offer a survey, but one might begin with a provocative essay in which power is placed in a historical context – Barrington Moore, Jr., "Notes on the Process of Acquiring Power," *World Politics* 8 (October 1955): 1–19. Richard N. Adams has attempted to define power for students of Latin America in "Power and Domains," *América Latina* 9 (April–June 1966): 3–21, and in "Political Power and Social Structures," in *The Politics of Conformity in Latin America*, ed. Claudio Veliz (London: Oxford University Press, 1967), pp. 15–42.

4 John Walton, quoted in *The Search for Community Power*, ed. Willis P. Hawley and Frederick M. Wirt (Englewood Cliffs, N.J.: Prentice-Hall, 1968), p. 359.

important decisions."[5] Agger, Goldrich, and Swanson have offered a typology of power structures based on "the extent to which political power is distributed broadly or narrowly over the citizenry, and the extent to which the ideology of political leadership is convergent and compatible or divergent and conflicting."[6]

The pioneering community studies of Robert and Helen Lynd during the 1920s and 1930s and W. Lloyd Warner in the late 1930s and Hunter's work on power structure in Atlanta during the 1940s provided a framework for what became known as the "elitist" school.[7] These and other early studies, primarily by sociologists, indicated that relatively few persons dominated local decision making for the benefit of business and political leaders. The power structure tended to be viewed as monolithic and based on economic resources. Later studies, particularly in political science, found that power holders compete with one another, operating from special interests based on business, industry, organized labor, education, religion, and politics. The political science viewpoint came to be called "pluralist" for its stress on the distribution of power among many bases. Robert A. Dahl was an early advocate of this position and a sharp critic of the work of Hunter and his followers for overlooking the fact that the same persons do not necessarily control a wide variety of issues in any particular society.[8] Robert Presthus, however, found that democracy under pluralism was possible even when the major decisions of a community were made by a small group of people,[9] and Domhoff later replicated Dahl's study of New Haven to show that the pattern of power was more "elitist" and Dahl's findings were largely a reflection of research methods.[10] Today in the United States community studies are of less interest because social scientists have put aside the elitist–pluralist debate and turned to ques-

5 G. William Domhoff, *The Powers That Be: Processes of Ruling Class Domination in America* (New York: Vintage Books, 1978), p. 132.

6 Robert E. Agger, Daniel Goldrich, and Bert E. Swanson, *The Rulers and the Ruled: Political Power and Impotence in American Communities* (New York: John Wiley, 1964), p. 73.

7 Robert S. Lynd and Helen Merrell Lynd, *Middletown: A Study in Contemporary American Culture* (New York: Harcourt, Brace, and World, 1929), and *Middletown in Transition: A Study in Cultural Conflicts* (New York: Harcourt, Brace, and World, 1937): W. Lloyd Warner and Paul S. Lunt, *The Status System of a Modern Community* (New Haven: Yale University Press, 1942).

8 Robert A. Dahl, "A Critique of the Ruling Elite Model," *American Political Science Review* 52 (June 1958): 463–469.

9 Robert Presthus, *Men at the Top: A Study in Community Power* (New York: Oxford University Press, 1964). A more critical assessment of pluralism is Todd Gitlin, "Local Pluralism as Theory and Ideology," *Studies on the Left* 5 (1965): 21–45.

10 G. William Domhoff, *Who Really Rules? New Haven and Community Power Reexamined* (New Brunswick, N.J.: Transaction Books, 1978). Very few replication studies exist; one that confirms earlier findings is David A. Booth and Charles R. Adrian, "Power Structure and Community Change: A Replication Study of Community A," *Midwest Journal of Political Science* 6 (August 1962): 277–296.

tions relating intergovernmental relations to state and national as well as local levels.

Marxists, especially in Latin America, have been critical of power-structure research. The "pluralist" view suggests to them all the negative images of a manipulative democratic society, whereas the "elitist" one seems to them to imply a neglect of the exploitative impact of capitalism upon the masses of workers and peasants. Domhoff argues, however, that Marxists who are concerned with showing the existence of a ruling class in a society do not necessarily neglect analyses of other classes and must become involved "in the development of power indicators and class-membership criteria" and "show how this ruling class controls economic institutions and maintains its domination over other groups in society."[11] Marxist work on these questions in Latin America tends to be theoretical rather than empirical. For example, Marcelo Cavarozzi has characterized "oligarchic capitalism" as of two types, one in which the ruling class and the state are indirectly involved in the control of productive activities and integrated with the civil society and the other in which the state is opposed to civil society so that other classes come into conflict with the state and politics are subject to manipulation and favoritism.[12] For the most part, the studies of power structure in Latin America have been the product of efforts by North American scholars. They range from a focus on a cohesive oligarchy to a focus on clusters of power in which a power structure is not even discernible. Among the two dozen or so prominent studies are the work by Drake, Ocampo, and Ogliastri on towns in Colombia; Fagen and Tuohy on Jalapa, Mexico; D'Antonio and Form on El Paso, Texas, and Ciudad Juárez, Mexico; Hoskin on San Cristóbal, Venezuela; Ugalde on Ensenada, Mexico; Klapp and Padget on Tijuana, Mexico; and Miller on Córdoba, Argentina, and Lima, Peru. Except for those of Drake, Ocampo, Ogliastri, and Fagen and Tuohy, who see power as largely monolithic, these studies suggest that competitive and coalition power structures prevail in Latin America.[13] In his comparative study of four commu-

11 Domhoff, *The Powers That Be*, p. 125.

12 Marcelo Cavarozzi, "Elementos para una caracterización del capitalismo oligárquico," mimeographed copy, Buenos Aires: Documentos CEDES-CLACSO (12), Centro de Estudios de Estado y Sociedad, June 1978.

13 See George F. Drake, *Elites and Voluntary Associations: A Study of Community Power in Manizales, Colombia* (Madison: Land Tenure Center, University of Wisconsin, 1970); José Fernando Ocampo, *Dominio de clase en la ciudad colombiana* (Medellín: Oveja Negra, 1972); Enrique Ogliastri U., "Elites, Class, Power and Social Consciousness in the Economic Development of a Colombian City: Bucaramanga" (Chicago: Ph.D. dissertation, Northwestern University, 1973). Richard R. Fagan and William S. Tuohy, *Politics and Privilege in a Mexican City* (Stanford: Stanford University Press, 1972); William V. D'Antonio and William H. Form, *Influentials in Two Border Cities: A Study in Community Decision-Making* (Notre Dame: University of Notre Dame, 1965); Gary Hoskin, "Power Structure in a Venezuelan Town: The Case of San Cristóbal," in *Case Studies in*

nities, Walton finds both types, with a tightly knit elite dominating in Cali, Colombia, and Monterrey, Mexico, and coalitions prevailing in Medellín, Colombia, and Guadalajara, Mexico.[14]

Power and class: theoretical approaches

Surveys of power-structure literature have indicated that different methods result in different findings. Three major methods of identifying leaders have been employed – reputational, positional, and decision making – and whether a power structure looks monolithic has been shown to depend on the method used.

The reputational method, developed by Hunter, began with the premise that persons of authority are "power and influence leaders."[15] Hunter asked judges to choose ten top leaders from a list of forty, and his findings showed that there were pyramids of power in Atlanta. He found that at the top there was cohesion and rapport among leaders who operate at a very high level of decision making in the community. He constructed a sociogram to show the interrelationships among the persons chosen. D'Antonio and Form used a similar approach in their study of El Paso and Juárez.

In his study of New Haven, Dahl was critical of the reputational approach: "No matter how precisely one defines influence and no matter how elegant the measures and methods one proposes, the data within reach even of the most assiduous researcher require the use of the operational measures that are at best somewhat unsatisfactory."[16] Nevertheless, Dahl was interested in the identification of influentials, so he used a variety of techniques, including the study of changes in socioeconomic characteristics of incumbents of city offices; determination of the extent of participa-

Social Power, ed. Hans-Dieter Evers (Leiden: Brill, 1969), pp. 28–47; Antonio Ugalde, *Power and Conflict in a Mexican Community: A Study of Political Integration* (Albuquerque: University of New Mexico Press, 1970); Orrin E. Klapp and Vincent L. Padgett, "Power and Decision-Making in a Mexican Border City," *American Journal of Sociology* 65 (January 1960): 400–406; and Delbert C. Miller, *International Community Power Structure: Comparative Studies in Four World Cities* (Bloomington: Indiana University Press, 1970). One of the earliest comparative studies was Andrew H. Whiteford, *Two Cities of Latin America: A Comparative Description of Social Classes* (New York: Doubleday, 1964); based on research in 1949, 1952, and 1958, this study focuses on Queretero, Mexico, and Popayán, Colombia. Arturo Valenzuela, in *Political Brokers in Chile: Local Government in a Centralized Polity* (Durham, N.C.: Duke University Press, 1977), examines issues of power and oligarchy through interviews with municipal mayors and council members in Chile.

14 John Walton, *Elites and Economic Development: Comparative Studies on the Political Economy of Latin American Cities* (Austin: Institute of Latin American Studies, University of Texas, 1977).

15 Floyd Hunter, *Community Power Structure: A Study of Decision Makers* (New York: Doubleday Anchor Books, 1963), p. 2.

16 Robert A. Dahl, *Who Governs? Democracy and Power in an American City* (New Haven: Yale University Press, 1961), p. 330.

tion of persons in local affairs; examinations of decisions in issue areas in which persons were influential; and interviews of voters to determine the nature of their participation.[17]

The positional method relies on the identification of persons in positions of power. E. Digby Baltzell, for example, examined the wealthiest people of Philadelphia and related their upper-class position to listings in the *Social Register.*[18] In designating leaders of the power elite within the corporate, military, and governmental bureaucracies, C. Wright Mills relied on the positional method on the assumption that "no one can be truly powerful unless he has access to the command of institutions."[19] G. William Domhoff employed the positional method as part of his mapping the network of important people and institutions in the United States.[20] Thomas R. Dye also used network analysis, emphasizing institutional position.[21] Robert Perrucci and Marc Pilisuk relied on identification of people in decision-making positions in multiple community organizations to determine the pattern of interlocking relationships.[22] Studies of power structure outside the United States also have emphasized the positional approach. For example, Lewis Edinger and Donald Searing examined the social background of national leaders in France and Germany, and Frederick Frey focused on legislators in Turkey.[23]

The problem with all these studies is the reconciliation of contradictions between theory and quantitative analysis based on field research. This problem was described by Maurice Zeitlin and Richard Ratcliff in their study of Chile. They began with Marx's recognition of the three great classes – wage laborers, capitalists, and landlords – and compared theories of development in Latin America that accept the premise of two ruling or dominant classes. They showed the similarities between, on the one hand, studies by John Guillen and Federico Gil, who focused on the landowning aristocracy and a new upper class of self-made men whose interests are opposed and, on the other hand, the analysis by Rodolfo

17 Ibid., pp. 330–340.

18 E. Digby Baltzell, *Philadelphia Gentlemen: The Making of a National Upper Class* (New York: Free Press, 1958).

19 C. Wright Mills, *The Power Elite* (New York: Oxford University Press, 1956), p. 9.

20 Domhoff, *The Powers That Be.*

21 Thomas R. Dye, *Who's Running America?* (Englewood Cliffs, N.J.: Prentice-Hall, 1976). With John W. Pickering, Dye, in "Government and Corporate Elites: Convergence and Differentiation," *Journal of Politics* 36 (November 1974): 900–925, divides society into corporate, governmental, and public interest sectors and identifies positions of authority in each.

22 Robert Perrucci and Marc Pilisuk, "Leaders and Ruling Elites: The Interorganizational Bases of Community Power," *American Sociological Review* 35 (December 1970): 1040–1057.

23 Lewis J. Edinger and Donald D. Searing, "Social Background in Elite Analysis: A Methodological Inquiry," *American Political Science Review* 61 (June 1967): 428–445; Frederick W. Frey, *The Turkish Political Elite* (Cambridge, Mass.: MIT Press, 1965).

Stavenhagen and Luis Vitale, who argued that agricultural, financial, and industrial interests are found in the same class, economic group, or set of families. Zeitlin and Ratcliff attempted to demonstrate the latter case for contemporary Chile and argued that quantitative analysis that freezes class relationships in constant flux is necessary and informative; at the same time they acknowledged the criticism of Barrington Moore, Jr., that quantitative measures may be misleading in the study of ruling classes. They also recognized that classes, unlike strata by occupation or income, do not have precise boundaries, so they identified leaders according to position in large corporations and banks and among landowners. They found that "the overwhelming majority of the corporate executives in the central core were closely related simultaneously to large owners of capital and to large landowners.[24]

The decision-making method calls for attention to participation in community affairs. Robert Alford has defined a decision as "a particular act by a local government agency or other authoritative group."[25] Edward O. Laumann and Franz Urban Pappi posited "an open-ended system, input–throughput–output model" of community decision making.[26] Antonio Ugalde suggested that a series of decisions be the basic unit of study of decision making in public bureaucracies.[27] Agger, Goldrich, and Swanson proposed a decision-making model of stages involving policy formulation and deliberation, organization of public support, authoritative consideration, promulgation of the decisional outcome, and policy implementation.[28]

In monolithic power structures such as those identified by Hunter, the values and attitudes of the powerful conform to their common interests and are applied unilaterally to decisions of the community. In the fragmented or pluralistic power structure, no single interest dominates, and various positions are taken in the effort to resolve problems. D'Antonio and Form have suggested that where members of the power structure share similar backgrounds and views, they are likely to experience similar pat-

24 Maurice Zeitlin and Richard Earl Ratcliff, "Research Methods for the Analysis of the Internal Structure of Dominant Classes: The Case of Landlords and Capitalists in Chile," *Latin American Research Review* 10 (Fall 1975): 5–61. See also Maurice Zeitlin, W. Lawrence Newman, and Richard Earl Ratcliff, "Class Segments: Agrarian Property and Political Leadership in the Capitalist Class of Chile," *American Sociological Review* 41 (December 1976): 1006–1029.

25 Robert R. Alford, "The Comparative Study of Urban Politics," in *Urban Research and Policy Planning*, ed. Leo F. Schnore and Henry Fagin (Beverly Hills, Calif.: Sage Publications, 1967), p. 263.

26 Edward O. Laumann and Franz Urban Pappi, "New Directions in the Study of Community Elites," *American Sociological Review* 38 (April 1973): 212–230.

27 Antonio Ugalde, "A Decision Model for the Study of Public Bureaucracies," *Policy Sciences* 4 (1973): 75–84.

28 Agger, Goldrich, and Swanson, *The Rulers and the Ruled*, pp. 40–51.

terns of participation and find agreement on how to solve community problems. Where business leaders are dominant in the power structure, they are also likely to be influential in politics. Where decision making follows different spheres of influence, say in business and politics, a division of interest is evident.[29]

The focus on decision makers and participation has not been without its critics. Domhoff has argued that the approach encounters difficulty in identifying important political issues and the real interests of the opposition and does not deal with long-run consequences.[30] Peter Bachrach and Morton S. Baratz have suggested that Dahl and others who emphasized decision making in their community studies ignored the possibility that the dominant rulers control the agenda of political dialogue and thus are able to limit or prevent decision making.[31] A number of other difficulties can be suggested. The approach is overly concerned with political issues and thus may ignore economic, educational, and cultural decisions. In a monolithic power structure, political issues may not be perceived as important by rulers. Further, the real nature of the decision-making process may not be known over the short run; many aspects of a situation may remain secret, forgotten, or repressed; and the participants may not be able to assess accurately the roles of others.

Walton, in an examination of the relationship between research methods and findings in thirty-three studies of fifty-five communities, found that the reputational method tends to identify pyramidal structures and the decision-making method reveals factional and coalitional power structures. He linked reputational, positional, and decision-making methods with pyramidal, factional, coalitional, and amorphous structures of power.[32] Douglas Fox distinguished between sociologists, who use the reputational method and find monolithic power structures, and political scientists, who rely on decision-making methods and find pluralistic power structures. He also found that within each method different kinds of questions may result in different patterns of power.[33] With this in mind, I have used all three methods to identify the power structures of Juazeiro and Petrolina.

The power-structure literature employs a variety of terms for power

29 D'Antonio and Form, *Influentials in Two Border Cities*, pp. 89–102.

30 Domhoff, *Who Rules America?*, p. 145.

31 Peter Bachrach and Morton S. Baratz, "Two Faces of Power," *American Political Science Review* 56 (December 1962): 947–952. See also the reply by Raymond E. Wolfinger, "Nondecisions and the Study of Local Politics," *American Political Science Review* 65 (December 1971): 1063–1080.

32 John Walton, "Structures and Artifact: The Current Status of Research on Community Power Structure," *American Journal of Sociology* 71 (January 1966): 430–438.

33 Douglas M. Fox, "Methods within Methods: The Case of Community Power Studies," *Western Political Quarterly* 24 (March 1971): 5–11. See also Claire W. Gilbert, "Communities, Power Structures and Research Bias," *Polity* 4 (Winter 1972): 218–235.

holders. "Leaders" is one of these, and the leader is viewed in many ways. For Floyd Hunter, "men of authority are called power and influence leaders."[34] Max Weber was concerned with different types of authority as related to leadership; his notion of charisma, for instance, was found in persons "endowed with supernatural, superhuman, or at least specifically exceptional powers or qualities . . . and on the basis of them the individual concerned is treated as a leader."[35] Robert Merton referred to local and cosmopolitan leaders, the local leader being one who has lived in a community most of his life and whose "influence in the community power structure is a function of whom he knows rather that what he knows," whereas the cosmopolitan leader is highly mobile and a trained specialist who "predominates in appointive positions in the community and socialized fundamentally with those who share his own particular interests and perspectives."[36] Robert Dahl suggested five patterns of leadership: top leaders who arrive at agreements by covert negotiations and discussions; a coalition of public officials and private individuals who reflect the interests and concerns of different segments of a community; a coalition of chieftains; top leaders whose goals and strategies relate to issues of particular segments of the community; and rivalry among sovereignties of such leaders.[37] Agger, Goldrich, and Swanson have differentiated between manifest and latent leaders.[38] Donald Searing has identified two alternative images of leadership, mechanistic and organismic.[39]

There has been little effort to deal theoretically with leadership in Latin America, although there are specialized studies of specific types of rulers.[40] Kalmon Silvert has identified seven types of leadership in Latin America: caudillo, oligarch, middle-class professional, ad hoc military amateur, populist conservative, totalitarian of the left, and totalitarian of

34 Hunter, *Community Power Structure*, p. 2.

35 Max Weber, *The Theory of Social and Economic Organization* (Glencoe, Ill.: Free Press, 1964), p. 359. For a treatment of Weber's concept of charisma, see D. L. Cohen, "The Concept of Charisma and the Analysis of Leadership," *Political Science* 20 (September 1972): 299–305. Richard R. Fagen has related hypotheses of charisma, drawn from Weber, to a study of Fidel Castro; see his "Charismatic Authority and Leadership of Fidel Castro," *Western Political Quarterly* 18 (June 1965): 275–284.

36 Quoted from Ritchie P. Lowry, *Who's Running This Town?* (New York: Harper Torchbook, 1968), pp. 121–122; see also Robert K. Merton, *Social Theory and Social Structure* (New York: Free Press, 1957), pp. 387–436.

37 Dahl, *Who Governs?*, pp. 184–189.

38 Agger,Goldrich, and Swanson, *The Rulers and the Ruled*, pp. 324–326.

39 Donald D. Searing, "Models and Images of Man and Society in Leadership Theory," *The Journal of Politics* 31 (February 1969): 3–31.

40 For example, on the role of caciques in Mexico, see Paul Friedrich, "A Mexican Cacicazgo," *Ethnology* 4 (April 1965): 190–209. On the *coronéis* of Brazil, see the classic study by Victor Nunes Leal, *Coronelismo, enxada e voto: o munícipio e o regime representativo no Brasil* (Rio de Janeiro: Livraria Forense, 1949).

the right.[41] Although these categories allow for an identification of characteristics, they nevertheless remain imprecise.[42]

Murray Edelman suggests that "leadership" may be the wrong word because it "connotes an individual free to choose his course of action and able to induce others to follow his lead because of superior intelligence, knowledge, skill, and the force of personality." Leadership is not understood as something an individual has or does not have at all times and places, he argues; "it is always defined by a specific situation and is recognized in the response of followers. . . . If they respond favorably and follow, there is leadership."[43] Domhoff believes that leaders do not necessarily come from the ruling class, although they may be selected, trained, and employed in institutions that function for the benefit of members of the ruling class.[44]

Other terms of power holders have been suggested. "Power elite" is Mills's term for persons with power derived from the institutional hierarchies they command – corporate, military, and political leaders.[45] Domhoff restricts the term to persons who come from the upper class or hold positions in institutions controlled by the upper class.[46] "Ruling elite" is the term used by Thomas B. Bottomore,[47] and it has been used by Dahl to characterize the model of power emanating from studies by Hunter and Mills.[48] Domhoff has distinguished a "governing class" as "a social upper class which owns a disproportionate amount of a country's wealth, receives a disproportionate amount of a country's yearly income, and contributes a disproportionate number of its members to the controlling institutions and key decision-making groups of the country."[49] Finally, a "ruling class" as Marx defined it is a group of families and individuals, related through intermarriage, similarity of wealth and income, values, style of life, and so on, who controls the means of production and rule politically. A ruling class is typically hereditary and thus maintains its

41 Kalman H. Silvert, "Leadership Formation and Modernization in Latin America," *Journal of International Affairs* 20, no. 2 (1966): 318–331.

42 William A. Welsh, "Methodological Problems in the Study of Political Leadership in Latin America." Mimeographed, Iowa City: Laboratory for Political Research, University of Iowa, October 1969.

43 Murray Edelman, *The Symbolic Uses of Politics* (Champaign: University of Illinois Press, 1967), pp. 73–75.

44 Domhoff, *Who Rules America?* p. 143.

45 Mills, *The Power Elite.*

46 Domhoff, *Who Rules America?*, pp. 8–9.

47 Thomas B. Bottomore, *Elites and Society* (New York: Basic Books, 1964).

48 Dahl, "A Critique of the Ruling Elite Model."

49 Domhoff, *Who Rules America?*, p. 5.

control over the polity, economy, army, and other institutions from generation to generation. Because of its focus on political economy, I prefer ruling class to the other terms identified here.

Marx viewed all but the most primitive society as characterized by a ruling class and one or more subject classes. In capitalist society the ruling class is that class that owns and controls the means of production and through its economic power uses the state to dominate society.[50] Marx and Engels articulate this position in the *Communist Manifesto:* "The executive of the modern state is but a committee for managing the common affairs of the whole bourgeoisie."[51] According to Engels, the state is an "organization of the exploiting class in each period for preserving the external conditions of production, and particularly for holding down by force the exploited class in the condition of oppression (slavery, serfdom or unfree tenure, wage labour) required by the existing mode of production."[52] Thus the concept of class becomes inseparable from the concept of exploitation. In Marxist theory, an exploiting class is a "group of individuals whose ownership of the means of production enables them to appropriate products of the others' labour." An exploited class is "a group of individuals whose use of the means of production involves appropriation of their products by members of an exploiting class." In contrast, in a classless

50 This view of the ruling class as manipulator of the state is classified as "instrumentalist" and is advocated by Ralph Miliband in his *The State in Capitalist Society* (New York: Basic Books, 1969), p. 23. Miliband prefers "dominant class" to "ruling class" and acknowledges an opposing view to his conception of dominant class, that of proponents of liberal and sometimes social democracy who argue that it is impossible to identify any meaningful capitalist dominant or ruling class because power in capitalist society is diffused and fragmented. Miliband admits the possibility of competitive pluralism among elites, which in turn might prevent the formation of a dominant class. He argues that, first, it is important to determine if a dominant class exists at all. If so, then it is useful to assess its power in society. A critique of pluralism and a testing of the pluralist hypothesis is found in Robert Presthus, *Men at the Top: A Study in Community Power* (New York: Oxford University Press, 1964), esp. chaps. 1 and 2. Miliband's instrumentalist stance was opposed by French structuralist Nicos Poulantzas who analyzed the capitalist state in terms of its structures that permit policy making in the interests of the ruling classes. See the debate between the two in Miliband's "Poulantzas and the Capitalist State," *New Left Review* 82 (November–December 1973): 83–92, and in Poulantzas's "The Problem of the Capitalist State," *New Left Review* 58 (November–December 1969): 67–78. The instrumentalist interpretation is especially relevant to analysis of Petrolina, the structuralist interpretation to understanding Juazeiro. For an updating of this debate and an imaginative overview and positing of a theory of the "Local State," see M. Gottdienner, *The Decline of Urban Politics: Political Theory and the Crisis of the Local State* (Beverly Hills, Calif.: Sage Publications, 1987).

51 Quoted in Karl Marx and Frederick Engels, *Selected Works in Two Volumes* (Moscow: Foreign Language Publishing House, 1958), 1:36.

52 Frederick Engels, cited in Stanley W. Moore, *The Critique of Capitalist Democracy: An Introduction to the Theory of the State in Marx, Engels, and Lenin* (New York: Paine-Whitman, 1957), p. 21.

society, "where the means of production are owned by the community as a whole, it is impossible for one group to exploit another."[53]

The dominant position of a ruling class is based on its possession of the major means of economic production and of political power. This suggests an analysis of rulers and exploiters, on the one hand, and ruled and exploited, on the other. My own conception of ruling or dominant class is not monolithic, but represents a coalescence of varied interests. I view "class" as an economic term and "rule" as a political term; thus for me a ruling class is an economic class that rules politically.[54] Members of such a class share interests. Its power may be concentrated, with decisive control over such resources as expertise, status, or wealth. Usually its monopolization of power is intimately related to capitalism and the ownership of the means of production; it dominates the economy through control over the corporations and financial institutions. Further, it may dominate the government because it occupies a key position at the executive center of the state, controls the national media, and finances the electoral process. Through its reliance on capitalism, the ruling class in Latin America may be tied to foreign capital; in fact its interests may be internationally oriented and unrelated to national ideals of autonomy, self-determination, and domestic development.

The interests that a ruling class incorporates are those of persons owning capital, called capitalists or the bourgeoisie. These persons are distinguishable by property relationships (they may be monopolistic or nonmonopolistic bourgeoisie), by the type of capital or means of production they possess (they may be agrarian, mining, commercial, manufacturing, or banking bourgeoisie), and by the amount of capital they own (they may be large, medium, or small bourgeoisie).

A monopolistic bourgeoisie consists of the large owners of industry and banking, with capital controlled by the latter. These owners group into economic clans and may have ties with capitalists of other countries. Constituting a small minority of the bourgeoisie, they own factories, insurance companies, banks, and large commercial companies. They may

53 Quoted in Moore, *Critique of Capitalist Democracy*, p. 22. In recent years there has been considerable effort by Marxist scholars to delineate a theory of class and class struggle. While the concept "class" is essential to Marxist theory, it was used by theorists before Marx and Engels. Further, Marx never fully conceptualized class in any elaborate way, although in the *Eighteenth Brumaire* he presented an excellent class analysis of mid-nineteenth century French society. In addition, there is a two-page sketch in the last chapter of the third volume of *Capital*. A useful discussion of this problem is in Theotonio dos Santos, "The Concept of Social Classes," *Science and Society* 34 (Summer 1970): 166–193. A review of early research on social classes in Latin America is Sugiyama Iutaka, "Social Stratification Research in Latin America," *Latin American Research Review* 1 (Fall 1965): 7–21.

54 David Nichols, "Ruling Class as a Scientific Concept," *Review of Radical Political Economics* 4 (Fall 1972): 35–69.

also be large landowners. The monopolistic bourgeoisie depends on the foreign bourgeoisie for its business activities, and as a consequence its interests tend to overlap with those of the foreign bourgeoisie; it is not much interested in the destiny of its nation.

Closely associated with the monopolistic bourgeoisie are the agrarian capitalists. Two types prevail, the modern and the traditional. The modern capitalists run farms with machinery and modern means of production; they pay salaries to their workers, and they make profits. Usually they hold property in urban industry, and their interests are similar to those of the monopolistic bourgeoisie. They also may be close to the traditional large landowners, who operate large estates. These traditional landowners enjoy the life of the cities and make little or no investment in their land. Their land lies idle or in the hands of an administrator, with tenant farmers and sharecroppers exchanging their labor for the use of it.

The bourgeoisie who do not pertain to the monopolistic sector of an economy usually comprise owners of certain industrial and commercial firms. Those owning large firms sometimes ally themselves with the monopolistic or foreign bourgeoisie. Others are owners of small industrial and commercial enterprises whose taxes often are high, whose credit is limited, and whose markets are restricted. These problems make them potential enemies of the monopolistic bourgeoisie, according to some observers, yet when threatened by drastic change (such as that which occurred in Chile during the early 1970s) they are likely to adhere to traditional bourgeois values. There may also be the middle and small owners of farms, dependent on large producers and merchants for credit and marketing of their products.

Another social class is the petty bourgeoisie, comprising persons who directly or indirectly control the means of production but do not possess capital. Their interests are contradictory. On the one hand, they may desire to acquire capital and become wealthy; on the other, they may feel oppressed by the bourgeoisie. In the urban areas the petty bourgeoisie comprises owners or tenants of small artisan industries or businesses that yield what is necessary for life. In rural areas they may consist of sharecroppers, tenant farmers, and so on, who live off the land of the large landowners. Sometimes the petty bourgeoisie includes independent professionals – attorneys, some physicians and architects, engineers, artists, writers – or the intelligentsia. Although this petty bourgeoisie enjoys a privileged status, it also sometimes understands the values of bourgeois society and is willing to change those values.

The positions of some professionals, bureaucrats, and managers may place them in a "middle class" that appears distinct from workers and capitalists. Various approaches are employed in the literature to relate these groups to a class: They may be assigned to the working class; to a segment of the small or petty bourgeoisie called the "new petty bourgeoisie," distinguishable from artisans, shopkeepers, and independent professionals; or to a professional and managerial class.[55]

There is also the proletariat, or the working class, which does not own the means of production, sells its labor power for money, and is obliged to work for the bourgeoisie. The proletariat, it is believed, has no interests linking it to private property and therefore is opposed to the bourgeoisie. It is thus the only class in a position to carry out a revolution resulting in the collective appropriation of the means of production on behalf of all workers. This class includes workers in monopolistic and nonmonopolistic industries, farmhands and sharecroppers, white-collar employees of private or public industry and banks, and even some professionals. Beyond the proletariat is a class of peasants, who usually do not own their land and whose social relations are associated more with precapitalist modes of production than with the capitalist one. Peasants may be squatters, renters, unpaid family workers, and so on. With expansion of economic activities and services to rural areas, they may be assimilated as wage-earning members of the rural proletariat.

According to some Brazilian observers, the power of the ruling class in Brazil has traditionally been based on patrimonial relationships.[56] Raymundo Faoro, for example, argues that Brazil is ruled by a minority that is unresponsive to the majority it purports to represent. This minority, an aristocratic stratum with privileges and position, rules through an unchanging patrimonial order. Although it is conditioned by social and economic forces, it is above the nation, which cannot dominate or eliminate it, and is the motive force of governmental activity.[57] A variant of this interpretation identifies two styles of political rule: One is found in the system of political representation of pre-1964 São Paulo, and the other is the system of patronage and cooptation that still prevails (having thrown its weight behind the armed forces in 1964) especially in the Northeast.[58]

55 Erik Olin Wright identifies these approaches as well as his own preference to locate these groups "in terms of *contradictory structural relations* of domination and subordination within production." See his "Varieties of Marxist Conceptions of Class Structure," *Politics and Society* 9, no. 3 (1980): 327.

56 The following discussion does not focus on the interpretations of class rule, authoritarianism, and underdevelopment that permeate recent North American writings on Brazil, but Peter Flynn provides a critical overview in his "Brazil: Authoritarianism and Class Control," *Journal of Latin American Studies* 6 (November 1974): 315–333.

57 Raymundo Faoro, *Os donos do poder: formação do patronato político brasileiro* (Rio de Janeiro: Editora Globo, 1958), pp. 261–263. See also a new and enlarged edition of this work, Porto Alegre and São Paulo: Globo and USP, 1975, 2 vols.

58 Simon Schwartzman, "Representação e cooptação política no Brasil," *Dados* 7 (1970): 9–41. See also Gentil Martins Dias, "New Patterns of Domination in Rural Brazil: A Case Study of Agriculture in the Brazilian Northeast," *Economic Development and Cultural Change* 27 (October 1978):

Economically dominant, the ruling class exercises coercion through political activity. Until 1930 it simply appointed its representatives "to various offices, including the presidency, according to the accustomed formalities."[59] Historically, the ruling class was composed of oligarchical regional or state groups whose power was based on the control of large expanses of land. The interests of these groups depended on influence in a state government. At the head of these groups were the colonels who dominated the rural population but in turn were subject to state oligarchical groups, "the real protagonists of political life."[60] National politics, in turn, was the consequence of adjustment and compromise among the state oligarchies.

After World War I, industrialization evolved and an urban working class emerged. The federal government benefited from a shift in capital from the Northeast to the Center-South and an emphasis on coffee as a major export. At the same time, the state oligarchies in São Paulo and Minas Gerais became powerful. Later, under Getúlio Vargas from 1930 to 1945, Rio Grande do Sul also shared in that power. Thus, although *coronelismo* persists in many rural areas, new forms of political and economic control were evolving. Paul Singer distinguishes three representatives of the dominant or ruling classes in Brazilian politics after World War II: the colonel, the representative of an economic group, and the representative of a clientele. The colonel could deliver blocs of votes, ensuring the election of his candidates at all levels. So too could the representative of an economic group (e.g., industrial or mining interests), who could exchange votes for governmental services. The clientele politician likewise could secure support from an ethnic group or some urban constituency willing to trade its votes for some favor. In many instances, these representatives combined forces to take advantage of situations resulting in windfall profits through investment in capitalist enterprise. Such activity tended to blur ideological lines and undermine political commitments, and this had several consequences. First, elected and appointed officials at the municipal, state, and federal levels of government became

169–182. Dias suggests an alternative view, based on a recent study in Bahia, that "traditional forms of social control used by the fazendeiro – mainly patron–client relationships – are being weakened" by workers, who seek the protection of law in the towns, and by merchants, who constitute the wealthiest and most influential group in the market centers. He sees the apathy of the peasant as related to the socioeconomic structure of Brazil: "While the rural masses seem to be immobilized in an apparently stable order, the rest of society is going through a process of rapid change" (p. 182).

59 Miguel Arraes, *Brazil: The People and the Power* (Baltimore: Penguin Books, 1972), p. 97.

60 Juarez R. B. Lopes. "Some Basic Developments in Brazilian Politics and Society, " in *New Perspectives of Brazil*, ed. Eric N. Baklanoff (Nashville: Vanderbilt University Press, 1966), p. 61. See also Linda Lewin, *Politics and Parentela in Paraíba: A Case Study of Family-Based Oligarchy in Brazil* (Princeton: Princeton University Press, 1987).

interlinked. Second, the distribution of positions in the executive branch to ensure legislative support tended to tie legislators to the bureaucratic apparatus. Third, local power became more dependent on regional and other alliances. Although the Brazilian ruling class quite obviously experienced change in these decades and their rank and file became more cohesive, these relationships ensured their continued consolidation in the political economy.[61]

With the emergence of popular demands after 1930, the privileges of the ruling class were threatened, however, and it became incumbent upon it to strengthen its position in the life of the country. Thus, for example, the coup of 1964 was quickly followed by the coming to power of presidents indirectly elected through a congress, which itself had been purged of most opposing tendencies. The old rule of force was brought into play. Whether in the past or in the present, force served the ends of the ruling classes:

> Ever since the colonial period the machinery enabling the country to be ruled by force functioned at national, regional and local levels. There was no inherent contradiction in this method of organization; the purpose common to the three levels was the maintenance of order. But they were governed by a different principle, since each evolved with the ruling class to which it was bound and from which it derived its relative importance. The predominance of the big landowners, for example, brought the local and regional forces to the fore; the national army was only to emerge later with the appearance on the political scene of other economic forces.[62]

The central government, then, has been in the hands of various groups, all related to the ruling class. At the same time the dominant interests inside and outside the country acted in concert. The result, according to Miguel Arraes, was the abandonment of efforts to win national autonomy. Within the country the various groups of the ruling class created an illusion of competition and diversity. In reality, they "made use of the institutions of the country and of political action to maintain control by sharing among themselves the various offices to which power was attached. . . . they were able to consolidate their authority . . . and also, of course, to establish dialogue with the various competing interests."[63]

Theory and the study of Juazeiro and Petrolina

My study attempts to assess these generalizations about the ruling class in the light of findings in Juazeiro and Petrolina – to examine the degree of its economic and political power, the local impact of that power, and the

61 Paul Singer, "A política das classes dominantes," in *Política e revolução social no Brasil*, ed. Octavio Ianni et al. (Rio de Janeiro: Editora Civilização Brasileira, 1965), pp. 72–78.

62 Arraes, *Brazil*, p. 107.

63 Ibid., p. 77.

Table 2.1. *Occupations of randomly selected persons in Juazeiro and Petrolina, 1967*

Occupation	Juazeiro	Petrolina
Liberal professions and high administrative posts	4	1
Management position	5	2
High positions of supervision, inspection, etc. (nonmanual)	20	10
Lower positions of supervision, inspection, etc. (nonmanual)	49	39
Manual occupation, skilled	111	79
Manual occupation, semiskilled	85	71
Small farmers, agricultural workers	7	12
Other	0	0
Total	281	215

Source: Centro Latinoamericano de Pesquisas em Ciências Sociais, "Juazeiro e Petrolina, um polo de crescimento?" (Rio de Janeiro, 1967), p. 97 (from files of CODESF).

Table 2.2. *Social-class membership of randomly selected persons in Juazeiro and Petrolina, 1967 (%)*

Social class	Juazeiro (N = 281)	Petrolina (N = 215)
Upper	3.2	1.4
Middle	24.6	22.8
Lower	72.2	75.8
Total	100.0	100.0

Source: Centro Latinoamericano de Pesquisas em Ciências Sociais, "Juazeiro e Petrolina, um polo de crescimento?" (Rio de Janeiro, 1967), p. 97 (from files of CODESF).

influence of their relations with the outside world on their everyday activities.

Some information on the ruling classes of Juazeiro and Petrolina may be found in a 1967 report by a group of investigators from Rio de Janeiro. Using a random sample, they interviewed 281 persons in Juazeiro and 215 in Petrolina. A classification of these respondents according to occupation is shown in Table 2.1 and their distribution by social class membership in Table 2.2.

The study offered the following portrait of the ruling classes:

1 With the exception of some "traditional" groups, most elements in this class had enriched themselves substantially during the 1950s and 1960s through "speculative commerce," "directed credit," and "dishonest concealment of imports."

2 Petrolina's ruling class was divided into two clanlike groups between which there was intense rivalry and ill will. In Juazeiro, economic leadership was held by businessmen from other parts of Brazil who were able to operate without intruding upon the rivalry of traditional families.
3 The most important members of the ruling classes held agricultural property while maintaining business interests in the cities. Half-entrepreneur, half-latifundista, and semifeudal, they were traditional in their understanding of the problems of the lower classes.
4 The ruling classes collaborated with elites in other local and regional centers to effect political decisions through "exchange of favors and obligations." Their relations with the lower classes manifested "a paternalistic spirit, a spirit of patronage."
5 The ruling classes considered themselves subordinate to the "supreme" power of the state. That feeling of subordination was characteristic "of the political structure of various underdeveloped countries."

The researchers argued that elements of the ruling classes that continued to operate with traditional values had impeded the development of the interior. In contrast, the dynamic business sector had demonstrated the potential typical of mature capitalist societies. The important persons in the ruling classes tended to display entrepreneurial capabilities.[64]

My own study bears out most of these observations. However, it elaborates in considerable detail not only on the composition and behavior of the ruling classes but also on their relationship with the outside world. Understandings of ruling-class activities and explanations of why development and underdevelopment occur are especially important.

My field investigation incorporated but attempted to move beyond traditional approaches to the study of community power structure, employing methods designed to avoid some of the problems of past studies.[65] Assuming that development and community power are intricately related, I felt that empirical inquiry might shed new light on theories of development and underdevelopment. Further, I believed that it might be possible to transcend the limitations of studies focused on the city by examining a municipality, which incorporates a rural area as well as the urban center; here the flow of capital from city to countryside could be noted in mining activities, the processing of agricultural commodities, and so on, and assumptions about feudal and semifeudal conditions could be critically assessed alongside observations about modernizing urban life. Finally, I considered it essential to combine the positional, reputational, and decision-making approaches of other community studies with other data-gathering methods and to consider not only those who govern through

64 Centro Latinoamericano de Pesquisas em Ciências Sociais, "Juazeiro e Petrolina, um polo de crescimento?" (Rio de Janeiro, 1967), pp. 129–135, from files of CODESF.

65 See Francine F. Rabinowitz, "Sound and Fury Signifying Nothing? A Review of Community Power Research in Latin America," *Urban Affairs Quarterly* 3 (March 1968): 120.

elected or appointed position, but also those with influence in the economy, with social status, or with wealth and class position.[66]

A first task was the compilation of lists of persons occupying positions of prominence in civic organizations, business establishments, educational institutions, and public service. This was accomplished through informal interviews, reading newspapers, and visits to municipal, state, and federal offices, to service and social clubs, and so on. A chart was then prepared on which the name of each person was associated with a type of occupation (e.g., banking, finance, insurance, commerce, government, labor, industry, profession), organizational affiliation, and position. In this way prominent persons could be related to important occupational areas and organizations. In this task I relied upon some assumptions drawn from other studies, among them Hunter's assumption that persons occupying offices and public positions of trust will be involved in some way in the power relations of the community[67] and D'Antonio and Form's assumptions that a small number of persons in business and politics participate in the decision making of a community, that there are likely to be close links among these leaders, that the analysis of power in the political arena is easier than in the business world (where decisions can be made without formal authority), and that persons in the business community may actually have more influence over governmental decisions than elected or appointed officials.[68]

A second task was the formation of a panel of persons in each community that would tell me who the most reputable people were. I approached this task with the modest objective of identifying potentially useful persons to interview, sharing Raymond Wolfinger's view that "the reputational method should be regarded as merely a systematic first step in studying a city's political system rather than a comprehensive technique for discovering the distribution of power."[69] I was interested in locating individuals capable of initiating, carrying out, or blocking programs of significance to the community – people whose actions were manifest and identifiable in relation to known problems, issues, and needs of the community. It was clear that reputational selection might not yield informa-

66 Emphasis on the ruling class of course limits the possibility of a dynamic analysis of all classes. A detailed examination of all classes in Juazeiro and Petrolina was not possible because of constraints of time and financial resources. Other classes are, however, taken into account. While I have tried to avoid the problems of stratification studies carried out by many social scientists and to correct the deficiencies of static studies of power such as Hunter's, my study does not fully resolve the methodological problems of studies of power that fail to analyze the dynamic relations among all social classes.

67 Hunter, *Community Power Structure*, p. 256.

68 D'Antonio and Form, *Influentials in Two Border Cities*, pp. 58–59, 83.

69 Raymond E. Wolfinger, "Reputation and Reality in the Study of 'Community Power,' " *American Sociological Review* 25 (October 1960): 637.

tion about the inner workings of the communities and that some significant persons would not be identifiable from their leadership activities in the community.

Utilizing the panel selection technique of Miller and Form and reviewing the chart of holders of significant positions, I attempted to select panels that would include persons in different sectors of community life: press (editor or publisher), local government (mayor or vice mayor), clergy (bishop or priest), finance (banker), commerce (merchant), civic leader (head of a service club), and outside developmental agency (official). In Juazeiro the panel comprised eight persons, including the head of a local development center, a prominent physician, a state deputy and former councilman, the head of a regional agency through which federal funds were allocated for projects, the municipal director of schools, a merchant and former mayor, a priest, and an engineer. In Petrolina the panel was made up of ten persons, including a former mayor and engineer, a councilman and farmer, a former councilman, member of the opposition and owner of a large pharmacy, the mayor, a social worker, a soils engineer, the two editors of local newspapers who were former councilmen, the director of the radio station, and the director of the educational foundation.

Interviews were exploratory, and respondents were asked to identify five leaders (*dirigentes*) in each of the following areas: politics, business–finance–commerce, professional life, and high society. They also were asked to identify the five most important persons in the neighboring community, to select ten civic and voluntary organizations of importance to their community, and to list the major socioeconomic problems and basic needs of their community. Some of the results are shown in Table 2.3.

Synthesis of information from these interviews resulted in a list of prominent persons in each community. This list was compared with the positional chart, and a small number of prominent persons were added, among them persons identified in the press during the previous decade (especially members of important families not now as active as in the past) and some past councilmen and mayors. In all, the new lists totaled forty-seven persons from Juazeiro and forty-six from Petrolina.

These lists were used in a follow-up set of interviews conducted with the thirty-nine persons named – twenty-three in Juazeiro and sixteen in Petrolina – in which respondents were asked to name the most important person in each community, to identify ten persons who would be acceptable to a majority of the residents in the community if there were a project that necessitated a decision by a group of leaders, and to assess the degree of participation in the affairs of the community. Their choices are also shown in Table 2.1. Responses to the latter question led to the addition of several persons to the Juazeiro list, including four who had received only one vote each and three who had received two votes from each panel (prior to this comparison I had eliminated all persons receiving fewer than four votes). The nature of the question had yielded different choices because respondents were now asked to identify not only reputable persons, but ones who were cooperative, responsible, and involved in community affairs.

The choices of most important person reveal a very strong recognition of the bishop and the mayor in Juazeiro and two of the Coelho brothers in Petrolina, and the total number of choices also places these persons at the tops of their communities. The overall rankings of these persons tend to reflect their local political power; members of the political faction in power rank higher than members of the opposition. Power holders residing outside their communities are generally ranked lower than resident ones. For example, Governor Nilo Coelho and his brother Senator Osvaldo Coelho were prominent in Pernambucan and national affairs, and although they frequently returned to Petrolina, they were ranked lower than resident members of their family. However, Luiz Augusto Fernandes, married to a niece of Nilo Coelho, a former mayor of the town but during the time of the study residing in Recife and Brasília, where he held governmental posts, appeared to be very influential in the community despite his absence. In Juazeiro, Ana Oliveira and Raulino Queiroz, both state deputies, received only two and one votes from the panel of judges but were deemed persons who should be involved in a community project by a half-dozen or so persons; they ranked low within the power structure. In contrast, Rinaldo Oliveira, a merchant residing in Salvador and a relative of Ana, was recognized in nearly half of the follow-up interviews but received only a single vote from the panel judges.

In addition to naming persons, respondents in the follow-up interviews also revealed their involvement on committees in which persons on the lists were members. Then they were requested to describe their relationship, if any, with each person on the list and to assess the degree of involvement of each in the affairs of the community. These responses are reflected in Table 2.4. The responses show a rough correlation between ranking in the power structure and degree of involvement as perceived by others. In Petrolina, those most involved are members of the Coelho family; in Juazeiro, participation appears to be more diffuse.

Next, using the responses of the panels listing the major socioeconomic problems and basic needs of their communities and information in the local newspapers over the period, I identified eleven problem areas. I then explored these areas in my interviews with the twenty-three Juazeiro and sixteen Petrolina leaders, asking them about their own participation in community efforts to resolve such problems as hydroelectric power, paving of roads, rural electrification, sewage, river transportation, schools, housing for the poor, water treatment, health assistance, and water sup-

Table 2.3. *Power holders in Juazeiro and Petrolina, as identified by panels of community members and each other*

	Nominations by panel[a]						Nominations by identified leaders[b]			
	Politics	Business	Financial	Professional	Social	Total	Most important in Juazeiro	Most important in Petrolina	Most acceptable to community	Total
Juazeiro										
Bishop Tomás Murphy			7		4	11	11	11	19	52
Américo Tanuri	6	2			8	16	7	3	15	41
Joca de Souza Oliveira	7	3			8	18	2	1	13	34
Guiseppe Muccini			4		6	10	1		13	24
Flávio Silva	2	4			6	12	1		10	23
Niator Sampaio Dantas		1				1			16	17
Antônio Carlos de Andrade e Silva		3			1	4			11	15
Francisco Etelvir Dantas		4				4			9	13
Humberto G. Pereira			2		2	4			8	12
Rinaldo Oliveira	1					1			11	12
Pedro Borges Viana		5			1	6			6	12
Raimundo Medrado Primo			1			1			9	10
Maria Isabel Pontes			1			1			9	10
João Cordeiro Neves		3			2	5			5	10
Judith Costa Leal			2			2			8	10
Paulo Campelo		5			2	7			2	9
Luiz Libório	2	4			1	7			2	9
Orlando Pontes	5				1	6			3	9
José Rodrigues Lima	6				1	7			2	9
Raulino Queiroz	2					2			7	9
João Nelly de Menezes Régis			1		1	2			6	8
Ana Oliveira Menezes					1	1			6	7

Petrolina										
Arnold de Souze Oliveira	1	2			1	4			2	6
José de Souza Coelho	10	7			7	24	5	8	10	47
Paulo de Souza Coelho	5	9			6	20	11	2	11	44
Geraldo de Souza Coelho	8	8			5	21			9	30
Luiz Augusto Fernandes	1				7	8	2	2	12	24
Honório Rocha	1		9		1	11			10	21
Washington Barros	2		9		1	12			8	20
Díniz Cavalcanti	4	6			3	13			5	18
Nilo de Souza Coelho	1				6	7	1	2	7	17
Augusto de Souza Coelho	3	2	1		5	11			4	15
Simão Durando	6				4	10			5	15
Osvaldo de Souza Coelho	1				6	7			7	14
Padre Mansueto de Lavor			5		3	8	1	1	4	14
João Batista Cavalcanti		2		2	3	7			4	11
Bishop Campelo de Aragão			5	1	1	7	1	1		9
Antônio de Santana Padilha			3	2	1	6			2	8
João Ferreira da Silva	2	2		1		5			3	8

[a]The panel for Juazeiro consisted of eight persons. The panel for Petrolina consisted of ten persons. Not all respondents used all their five possible choices in each category; some used more than five in a category, and in these cases all were accepted and are included here. Data are based on interviews during 1969.

[b]The follow-up interviews were conducted with the twenty-three persons in Juazeiro and sixteen in Petrolina identified as leaders by the panels.

Table 2.4. *Social relationships among power holders and perceptions of each other's participation*

	Social Relationship								Participation in Community				
	Relative	Source of special counsel	Very close	Knows socially	Knows a little	Has heard of	Does not know	Other	Very involved	Involved	More or less	Not involved	Other
Juazeiro													
Bishop		13	2	6	1			1	13	3	5	1	1
Small merchant, mayor		4	7	9	2			1	12	8	2		1
Merchant, ex-mayor	1	3	5	9	4			1	5	5	9	1	3
Physician		2	4	11	5			1	13	7	2		1
Merchant		4	3	10	5			1	5	5	9	1	3
Merchant	1		4	11	6			1	7	7	8		1
Merchant	1	1	4	12	1	2	1	1	9	9	3	1	1
Merchant	1	1	4	11	6			1	7	7	8		1
Physician		1	6	14		1		1	7	5	11		
Merchant	2	1	6	11	3				5	14	2	2	
Physician			4	13	4	1		1	5	5	8	1	4
School principal		1	5	13	3			1	6	7	8	1	1
Director, municipality	1		1	15	3	2		1	3	3	16		1
Merchant	1		2	11	5	2	1	1	4	4	8	4	3
Director, regional education		2	2	9	7	2		1	4	5	13		1
Industrialist	1		4	6	10	1		1	4	4	10	4	1
Merchant		1	1	15	4	1		1	5	5	7	4	2
Small merchant, councilman	1		3	13	4	1		1	5	11	3	3	1
Bureaucrat, state deputy	1		2	11	8			1	3	9	6	4	1
Military police, state deputy		1	2	11	8			1	4	13	3	1	2
Bureaucrat		1		8	10	1	2	1	3	8	9	1	2
State Deputy	1	1	3	8	8	1	1	1	1	8	10	2	2
Attorney	1	1	1	10	7	2		1	7	5	6	1	4

Petrolina											
Merchant, ex-mayor	6	4	1	3	1	1	12	2	1		1
Industrialist	6	4	1	3	1	1	12	2	1		1
Engineer, mayor	6	1	4	3	1	1	11	4			1
Engineer, ex-mayor	6	3	1	4	1	1	13	2			1
Priest, state deputy		7	2	6		1	10	2	3		1
Physician, vice mayor	6	1		7	1	1	8	1	4	2	1
Merchant		1	5	8	1	1	4	9	2		1
Governor of state	7			7	2		11	4		1	
Physician	6	2	6	1		1	6	7	2		1
Salesman, mayor		1	2	11	1	1	5	8	2		1
Federal senator	6	1		6	2	1	10	2	2	1	1
Priest, radio station director		5		6	3	1	6	3	6		1
Merchant			3	6	6	1	3	4	3	3	3
Bishop			2	7	6	1	1	5	4	4	2
Accountant, ex-mayor		2	3	6	4	1	5	3	5	1	2
Merchant, ex-mayor	1			7	7	1	2	1	1	9	3

ply. The results are shown in Table 2.5. Responses for the two communities are combined here because the problems are regional. For example, although the problem of highways affected each community in a different way, the concern of Juazeiro that the road to Salvador be paved was also a concern of Petrolina because that was the normal direction of most commerce. Again, when Nilo Coelho became governor of Pernambuco, a paved road to Recife suddenly became a priority, and involvement in the project was high in both communities. The patterns of participation in the two communities did differ, however. In Petrolina involvement tended to be limited to the Coelho family and those close to it; about half of the Petrolina respondents were not involved in any way. In Juazeiro participation in solving the problems was more uniformly distributed.

The data, correlated for all respondents across the eleven problem areas, showed that four power holders were very much involved, twenty-one involved, eight slightly involved, and six not involved at all. Most of those involved tended to be so as members of committees, often regional in scope. This was the usual way of mobilizing people to attack problems in Petrolina. In Juazeiro, the approach to problems was more often through a political party or some other organization. Participation by the power holders was diffuse and indirect in the latter community, concentrated and direct in the former.

These patterns of participation may be understood in terms of the social relationships among power holders. Each of the persons interviewed was asked to identify his or her relationship to the others from his or her community. George Lundberg and Margaret Lawsing have called this technique the "sociography" of relations. They canvassed families in a small Vermont village, observing and measuring socioeconomic status, seeking information on occupation, family size, and general housing conditions, and asking the person interviewed to name his or her most intimate friends in the community. Friendship relationships were identified and charted.[70] The data in Table 2.4 could be charted in various ways to show how each individual relates to every other individual or to suggest clusters of relationships among individuals, but, given the obvious patterns in the data, a more graphic presentation is unnecessary. It is immediately clear that half of the Petrolina power holders are related to each other by blood or marriage, whereas those in Juazeiro tend not to be related to more than one person. Likewise, the powerful in Petrolina seek special counsel among relatives, with the exception of two priests who are prominent in community affairs; in Juazeiro there is an inclination to look to the top five power holders for special counsel and in particular to the local bishop. In

70 George A. Lundberg and Margaret Lawsing, "The Sociography of Some Community Relations," *American Sociological Review* 2 (1937): 318–335.

Table 2.5. *Power holders' assessments of their own participation in resolving major community problems*

	Degree of participation (%)			Manner of participation (N = 39)						
Project	Very involved	Slightly involved	Uninvolved	Personal interest	Committee	Politics	Other organization	Two ways	Three or more ways	Uninvolved
Highways	51	26	23	3	18	1	4	3	1	9
Rural power	54	18	28	3	6	7	8	4		11
Sewage	51	13	36		3	10	9	2	1	14
River transportation	26	5	69	1	2	3	5	1		27
Schools	59	10	31		7	8	12			12
Housing	44	15	41	1	5	8	7	2		16
Water treatment	39	5	56	2		6	9			22
Hospitals	44	12	44	4	1	5	11	1		17
Water supply	33	5	62	2	1	3	8	1		24
University	69	13	18	2	18	3	8	1		7
Urban planning	28	16	56	2	1	9	5			22

Petrolina, a tight network operates among all persons with the exception of the bishop, who was somewhat isolated from the Coelho family, and a merchant whose political ambitions had been destroyed by the Coelhos. In Juazeiro, relationships were also close; most of the powerful were known socially or intimately by a majority of their compatriots. That a good share of Juazeiro respondents did not know very well or only had heard of others was likely attributable to the factionalism endemic to this community.

This first phase of research, then, involved the use of several well-known, tested techniques to identify a power structure in each community. In the course of it, I became aware of a number of other persons – secondary leaders, influentials, decision makers, and knowledgeables – who were connected socially, economically, or politically to those in the power structure. In the second phase, I interviewed many of these persons as well.

For the interviews of this phase, the lists were refined, some names being deleted and others added. A few new individuals had assumed conspicuous positions in the interim; for example, due to Coelho influence, a formerly little-known lawyer had become a state deputy. I also included all the mayors since 1945 and the names of all persons on the executive committee of the political parties at the time of my interviews. The new lists consisted of 120 persons, 66 from Juazeiro and 54 from Petrolina. The lists included the 39 power holders, another 28 identified as power holders at a secondary level, 12 additional persons considered influentials by reputation, and 40 other power holders identifiable by position. All of these were formally interviewed except 2 (who were interviewed only in the earlier phase).

Most of those interviewed resided in the two communities, although 4 lived in Recife and 7 in Salvador, where they served as political representatives or coordinated the commercial activities of their family businesses. Table 2.6 shows that more than half of the respondents were born in their communities and nearly all in either Bahia or Pernambuco. Nearly 90 percent had lived in their communities more than a decade and about half a generation or more.

Only 12 of the interviewees were women (see Table 2.7). All but 3 of them were over the age of twenty-five years. Sixty percent were between thirty-five and fifty-four years, 20 percent were between fifty-five and sixty-four years, and 9 percent were over sixty-five. Eighty percent were married. Nearly a quarter had five or six children, another quarter more than seven children. Nearly half had more than seven brothers and sisters. The respondents were preponderantly Catholic (107 of them, or 91 percent); 4 were Protestant and 4 professed no religion.

The level of education of the ruling classes was high for the hinterland of Brazil (see Table 2.8). Only 4 had had no education, a third had some

Table 2.6. *Birthplaces and years of residence of members of the ruling classes in Juazeiro and Petrolina*

	Juazeiro (N = 66)	Petrolina (N = 52)	Total (N = 118)
Birthplace			
Juazeiro	24	0	24
Petrolina	4	28	32
Elsewhere in Bahia	25	5	30
Elsewhere in Pernambuco	5	11	16
Other	8	8	16
Years of residence			
< 3	0	2	2
3–10	6	7	13
11–20	12	9	21
21–30	20	12	32
31–40	12	8	20
41–50	8	9	17
51–60	4	2	6
> 60	4	3	7

Table 2.7. *Sex, age, and marital status of members of the ruling classes in Juazeiro and Petrolina*

	Juazeiro (N = 66)	Petrolina (N = 52)	Total (N = 118)
Sex			
Male	61	45	106
Female	5	7	12
Age			
< 25	2	1	3
25–35	4	7	11
35–44	19	14	33
45–54	20	15	35
55–64	13	10	23
> 64	7	6	13
Marital status			
Single	8	12	20
Married	53	39	92
Widowed	1	1	2
Divorced	3	0	3

Table 2.8. *Level of education of members of the ruling classes in Juazeiro and Petrolina*

	Juazeiro (N = 66)	Petrolina (N = 52)	Total (N = 118)
None	3	1	4
Primary, 1–4 years	17	10	27
Primary, 5–6 years	7	6	13
9 years	5	2	7
High school degree	6	6	12
Some university	4	1	5
University degree	16	23	39
Vocational	7	3	10
Other	1	0	1

Table 2.9. *Occupations (and fathers' occupations) of members of the ruling classes in Juazeiro and Petrolina*

	Juazeiro (N = 66)	Petrolina (N = 52)	Total (N = 118)
Professional	13 (2)	18 (4)	31 (6)
Merchant	28 (28)	13 (22)	41 (50)
Industrialist	0 (1)	2	2 (1)
Farmer	4 (13)	2 (14)	6 (27)
Bureaucrat	17 (13)	14 (4)	31 (17)
Worker	0 (5)	0 (2)	0 (7)
Military	1 (2)	0	1 (2)
Religious	1 (1)	3	4 (1)
Unemployed mother	1 (1)	0 (6)	1 (7)
Not identified	1	0 (2)	1

exposure at the primary level, and nearly a fifth had reached the secondary level. One-third of the respondents had graduated from a university, including eight in Recife and twenty-two in Salvador. Nearly a quarter of the respondents had attended private schools in Juazeiro and Petrolina.

Table 2.9 gives the occupations of respondents and their fathers. Nearly half of their fathers had been merchants, and many of the respondents continued in this tradition. That only 2 became industrialists is a reflection of the incipient character of industry in the area. In contrast to their fathers, one-fourth of them had become professionals – doctors, lawyers, engineers, and so on. Of their fathers, 27 had been farmers and another 7 workers, while only 6 of the respondents were now farmers and none of them workers. The fathers had often been functionaries in the towns, and so were their sons and daughters. Three-fourths of their mothers had been housewives.

Many respondents were politically active. Forty persons were on executive committees of political parties, 46 were former or present council persons, 15 were former or present mayors or vice mayors, 7 were former or present state deputies, and 1 had served as federal deputy.

When asked their social class position, 5 respondents said that they were "rich" and 28 that they were "poor," while the others believed they were "modestly average." Fifteen persons identified with the upper class, 100 with the middle class, and 1 with the lower class. Responses to different questions revealed that nearly half thought of themselves as members of the "proletariat" while only 1 considered himself a member of the "upper bourgeoisie." These responses probably reflect the pejorative connotation of the word "bourgeoisie" in many parts of Latin America.

Diversity of interests among members of the ruling classes of Juazeiro and Petrolina is evident at a glance. Commenting on a similar diversity in late-nineteenth-century Brazil, Prado has spoken of "an urban bourgeoisie that sheltered foreigners of the most varied origin in the country along with Brazilians of the greatest chronological diversity in terms of their family tradition" but was "nevertheless perfectly homogeneous with respect to the nature of its business and interests and in the essential manner in which they are conducted." He attributed this homogeneity to the absence of the noncapitalist structures that had emerged from feudalism in Europe. Far from opposing each other, agrarian and industrial sectors are tied together and support each other, even though among them "one can find the whole gamut of political opinion – from conservatives to those more or less tolerant of popular rights and aspirations."[71] The present study shows that agricultural, financial, and industrial interests are often found in the same economic groups, the same firms, and the same families; an alignment of landowning, urban commercial, and manufacturing bourgeoisies certainly exists in Juazeiro and Petrolina.

Given the diversity and, at the same time, homogeneity of these ruling classes, it seemed necessary to examine the ideologies underlying them. The behavior of a ruling class may be a reflection of its positions on certain local, national, and international issues. Respondents were asked for their views on income distribution, care for the sick, education, property, private enterprise, and government planning. Other questions attempted to assess to what extent they were motivated by local rather than national or international considerations. Tendencies toward patriotism and nationalism were

71 Caio Prado Júnior, *A revolução brasileira* (São Paulo: Editôra Brasiliense, 1966), pp. 178–180, quoted in Philippe C. Schmitter, *Interest Conflict and Political Change in Brazil* (Stanford: Stanford University Press, 1971), pp. 374–375.

Table 2.10. *Views of members of the ruling classes in Juazeiro and Petrolina about relationships of political and economic sectors (%)*

	Juazeiro	Petrolina
Degree of cooperation between sectors		
Excessive		3
Enough cooperation	3	19
Need more cooperation	62	24
Cooperation not necessary	1	
Other		6
Total	66	52
Degree of dominance		
Economy dominates polity	28	26
Polity dominates economy	13	5
No difference between the two	20	9
Other	5	12
Total	66	52

examined, and so were beliefs and attitudes on development and underdevelopment. In response to other questions, three-quarters of these leaders, influentials, and decision makers said their community was a good one to live in. Of those who thought it a poor community to live in, a majority resided in Juazeiro (31.8 percent of the Juazeiro sample in contrast to 13.4 percent of those in Petrolina). Asked to rate the communities on a number of aspects, 9 judged opportunities for economic advancement good or excellent, and a similar proportion felt positively about their community schools. Half of them were concerned about the availability of adequate housing. Two-thirds said that there was pride among the people of their community, and nearly three-fourths said that the people of the community were willing to undertake action to meet community needs and problems. Four-fifths acknowledged the friendliness of the people, and two-thirds thought that the municipal government was responsive to the people's wishes and that the big firms were in line with community spirit.

Finally, respondents were asked what they believed to be the relationship between the political and economic sectors of their communities. Identification of prominent persons by position had shown great overlap among political leaders and businessmen. Identification of persons by reputation had revealed some differentiation of political, economic, and social segments of the communities but also substantial linkage among influentials. Identification of persons participating in community decision making had revealed a tight network of relationships. Thus, my questions sought to discover if distinctions between political and economic sectors were meaningful. The results are shown in Table 2.10. In Juazeiro, where politics was splintered among several factions and economic issues were accorded special significance, a sharp difference was perceived between the political and economic sectors. In Petrolina, whatever dissatisfaction was expressed probably emanated from persons politically outside the Coelho control of community affairs; at the same time, there was a clear recognition that economic affairs dominated politics. These results did not imply a lack of interest in government, however, as a large majority of persons in both communities (71.2 percent) responded that they followed what was happening in government most of the time; others (19.5 percent) felt they paid attention some of the time, a small number (5.9 percent) thought about government only now and then, and a handful were little interested. The biographical data also show that the ruling classes share both political and economic interests and that, regardless of their infighting, they desire to preserve and enhance their wealth and dominant position. In large measure their existence and success are a reflection of the emerging capitalism of their economies.

Figure 3.1. Petrolina in the foreground and Juazeiro on the far bank of the São Francisco; the two towns are linked by the bridge. Photo 1971.

Figure 3.2. View of Juazeiro commercial houses fronting the São Francisco. Photo 1971.

3

Juazeiro: cohesion and factionalism

The first European to reach Juazeiro was probably Belchior Dias Moréa; he had left Rio Real for Barra do Rio Grande in 1593 and from there descended the São Francisco River to Juazeiro, arriving some three years later. By the early seventeenth century most of the backlands were under the control of the García d'Avila family. In 1658 the head of the family, Francisco Dias d'Avila, and his uncle, Father Antônio Pereira, obtained land grants including the present municipality of Juazeiro along the São Francisco River.[1] Effective control and colonization of the area, however, were possible only after years of struggle with the Indian inhabitants. The second Francisco Dias d'Avila was able to repress Indian resistance by June 1676. By the end of the seventeenth century, Juazeiro had emerged as the center of the lower and middle segments of the São Francisco Valley because of its strategic location at the crossroads of two old passageways of the interior: the river and the land route of the early explorers, including Paulistas under the domination of Domingos Sertão, Bahians under García d'Avila, Pernambucans under Francisco Caldas, and Portuguese under Manuel Nunes.[2]

In 1766 Juazeiro was classified a *vila* or town under the jurisdiction of the *comarca,* or judicial district, of Jacobina (and in 1857 under the comarca of Juazeiro). This important step in Juazeiro's political and administrative evolution was the result of the efforts of Captain General Antônio Rolim de Moura Tavares, count of Azambuja. With continued growth

1 The land grant was made on July 22, 1658, in a letter from Olinda, according to Barbosa Lima Sobrinho (*Pernambuco e o São Francisco* [Recife: Imprenta Oficial, 1929], pp. 106–107). This fact is confirmed in the writings of Pedro Calmon; see, for example, his *História da fundação da Bahia.* (Salvador: Museu do Estado [Publication No. 9], 1949). These writers differ in interpretation over which state, Bahia or Pernambuco, has jurisdiction over this region of the São Francisco River. Their debate was published by Calmon in *Jornal do Commercio* and Barbosa Lima Sobrinho in *Jornal do Brasil;* the latter's views were contained in "A Bahia e o Rio São Francisco," *Revista do Instituto Archeológico Histórico e Geográphico Pernambucano* 30, nos. 143–146 (1930): 127–174. Such debate is found in the writings of many other historians of Bahia and Pernambuco.

2 Edson Ribeiro, *Juazeiro na esteira do tempo: Juazeiro-Bahia, suas origens, sua política administrativa e social* (Salvador: Editora Mensageiro da Fé, 1968), pp. 13–14. See similar information on João Fernandes da Cunha, *Memória histórica de Juazeiro,* 2d ed. (Juazeiro, 1978).

throughout the eighteenth and early nineteenth centuries, Juazeiro was elevated to the status of a municipality on June 11, 1834. An aggressive municipal council thereafter divided it into three administrative districts and established an administrative code, a national guard unit, judicial and educational systems, a revenue service, a postal agency, a religious center, and a budget providing for public works, roads, and protection of small farmers.[3]

Evolution of the community

Subsequent to Juazeiro's rise to a municipality, the following periods of its history call for discussion: the imperial period, ending in 1889; the Old Republic, from 1889 to 1930; and the Vargas regime and subsequent years up to the present.

During its initial period as a municipality, from 1834 to the end of the empire in 1889, Juazeiro emerged as a major economic center in the interior, dominating navigation and commerce on the river, which extended into Bahia and Minas Gerais. The economy of the interior of Piauí and Pernambuco also became dependent on Juazeiro, through which agricultural products, minerals, and other commodities tended to filter en route to Salvador and other coastal points. A rail link between Salvador and Juazeiro, established at the end of the nineteenth century, served to consolidate Juazeiro's dominance. The consequences of Juazeiro's strategic position were severe for neighboring Petrolina. The renowned Pernambucan geographer Mário Melo once complained that Juazeiro's control of the river commerce and its taxation of commodities from Petrolina were the result of poor communications between Recife and Petrolina: "We risk the loss of this desert oasis . . . which in every respect is absorbed by Bahia. We lose what is ours and what comes to us from Piauí."[4]

Reinforcing and maintaining this dominance over the region was a clique of ruling families whose control over the local political economy seemed assured by its position in government and commerce. The seven municipal councilmen during the period 1834 to 1836 included a Costa, a Duarte, a Ferreira, and a Melo. The first municipal judge was a Duarte, the first municipal attorney a Pereira, and among a variety of other judicial positions (many of them probably honorary) the name Pereira appears six times, Ferreira four times, Souza and Barbosa each twice, and Duarte

3 Ibid., pp. 16–17; for details of this early legislation, see pp. 17–53.

4 Mário Melo, "Como Mário Melo viu Petrolina," *O Farol* 16 (July 4, 1931): 1, and 16 (July 11, 1931): 1, reprinted from *Diário de Pernambuco*. The role of Juazeiro commerce is emphasized in the historical account of Ermí Ferrari Magalhães, "O comércio e suas origens em Juazeiro," *Rivale* 7 (July 15, 1978): 14.

and Silva each one. The first postal administrator was a Pereira, the second a Ferreira. A Duarte, a Melo, and a Pereira were three of the four members of a special commission appointed by the municipal council in 1835 to plan and supervise the construction of a building for the council and a municipal jail.[5]

There was, however, a constant shuffling of positions among members of the ruling families. In the elections of September 7, 1836, a Duarte, a Ferreira, and a Souza won three of the seven council seats, and no incumbent was reelected. Whereas in 1837 the municipal judgeship remained with the same Duarte and the municipal attorney position with the same Pereira, three new Pereiras were appointed to judicial positions. A five-man commission appointed in 1838 to propose a plan of public works included an Amorim, a Duarte, a Ferreira, and a Silva.[6] The electorate seems to have been small; in the 1836 elections the vote totals of councilmen ranged from twenty-four to fifty-seven. The wide range of voting totals among the seven councilmen elected[7] suggests differences in power among the ruling families. No single family appears to have monopolized politics.

The data in Table 3.1 support this interpretation. Of the ten family names that appear most frequently, five (Amorim, Araújo, Barbosa, Costa, and Viana or Vianna [see n. 27]) seem relatively unimportant and are included because of their prominence in the twentieth century. Members of these five families occupied less than 18 percent of the positions held by the ten families and less than 12 percent of the total governmental positions during the period. The other five families (Duarte, Ferreira, Melo e Pereira, Silva, and Souza) held more than 40 percent of the positions during the period. (The Melo and Pereira families are often combined because of extensive intermarriage between them.) The pivotal presidency of the municipal council rotated among the Duarte, Ferreira, and Melo e Pereira families. These families also wielded considerable influence as councilmen or council secretary, and occasionally they also held influential posts in the judiciary.

Table 3.1 shows that no single family held absolute dominance and that a division of power existed throughout the imperial period. We know that there were frequent differences and minor power struggles among these families. One might conclude that a sort of pluralism prevailed in the politics of the period. At the same time, these families collectively dominated the polity and the economy; as we have seen (Table 3.1), they

5 Ribeiro, *Juazeiro*, pp. 19–21, 24, 28–30.

6 Ibid., pp. 30–32.

7 Joaquim José Ribeiro de Magalhães (57 votes); João Antônio Ferreira (52); José Batista de Souza (52); Jerónimo Rodrigues Infante da Câmara (45); José Luiz da Rocha (27); Felipe Barroso de Santiago (27); and Raimundo de Souza Duarte (24) (ibid., pp. 54–56).

Table 3.1. *Governmental representation of prominent families in Juazeiro, 1834–90*

Family	President of municipal council	Councilmen	Alternate councilmen	Secretary of council	Judge	Municipal attorney	Total positions	% of total family positions	% of total positions
Amorim	0	5	1	0	0	0	6	4	2
Araújo	0	1	1	0	0	0	2	1	<1
Barbosa	0	4	4	0	0	0	8	5	3
Costa	0	4	6	2	0	0	12	7	5
Duarte	3	9	9	0	2	0	23	14	9
Ferreira	6	11	5	3	0	1	26	16	10
Melo e Pereira	3	14	5	4	1	3	30	19	11
Silva	1	13	10	2	1	0	27	17	7
Souza	0	10	15	0	0	2	27	17	7
Viana or Vianna	0	1	0	0	0	0	1	<1	<1
Total family positions	13	72	56	11	4	6	162		
Total positions	15	114	84	20	9	11	253		
Family positions/total positions (%)	87	62	67	55	44	55	64		

Source: Adapted from lists of names of Edson Ribeiro, *Juazeiro na esteira do tempo* (Salvador: Editora Mensageiro da Fé, 1968). Selection based on identification of maternal and paternal names. Because of the small population, it is assumed that most names elected have a kin relationship to one of the ten families.

controlled the council presidency (87 percent of the positions), the council itself (62 percent), alternate council positions (67 percent), the council secretariat (55 percent), the municipal judgeship (44 percent), and the post of municipal attorney (64 percent).

The rivalry among these families was sometimes intense, but generally consensus prevailed. One explanation for this phenomenon was the early establishment of an administrative foundation. Despite the municipality's small size, an elaborate administrative structure was created at the outset. For example, each of its three districts had its administrative staff and functions. Again, besides the municipal judgeship and attorney posts there were twelve justices of peace, a judge for orphans, and four judicial inspectors. The post office had numerous employees, foreshadowing today's enormous staff and physical plant relative to the size of the municipality.[8] With this rapid expansion of administration, Juazeiro quickly became identifiable as a city of civil servants.

In 1838, the municipal authorities quickly responded to an order of the Bahian state government and organized security forces to deal with elements of Sabinada revolt, which had broken out near Salvador a few years earlier. The municipality suffered smallpox epidemics in 1838 and 1862. Frequently recurring droughts and severe floods, such as those of 1838 and 1865, devastated the community. From the outset the municipality suffered from its burgeoning administration. In 1835 the municipal council appealed for outside public funds to alleviate a financial crisis, but the appeal was to little avail and municipal employees failed to receive salary payments throughout most of the year.[9]

Under the Old Republic, from the fall of the empire to the Revolution of 1930, a clique of families continued to dominate political life in Juazeiro (Table 3.2). Especially significant in this period were the Duarte, Pereira e Melo, Ribeiro, and Souza families, which collectively represented about 51 percent of the positions held by the ten major families and about a third of all government positions identifiable during the period. Together these ten families held more than half of all government positions and were represented by 9 of the 10 intendents or mayors, 11 of the 15 council presidents, 7 of 10 council secretaries, and 71 of 151 councilmen.

The shift from an imperial to a republican government was achieved smoothly in Juazeiro. In early 1890 a new municipal council was named under the presidency of long-time political chief Colonel Francisco Mar-

8 More than fifty employees staffed the Juazeiro postal service in 1977. The building was constructed with funds originally allocated for Curitiba, a city more than ten times the size of Juazeiro. This was the result of political manipulation (interview with Aurelio Pereira da Silva, June 7, 1971).

9 Ribeiro, *Juazeiro*, pp. 46–50. Again, in 1836, the council appealed to the provincial president for funds, an early indication of the municipality's dependent status.

Table 3.2. *Governmental representation of prominent families in Juazeiro, 1890–1930*

Family	Intendent or mayor	President of council	Secretary of council	Councilmen	Total positions	% of total family positions	% of total positions
Araújo	0	0	0	3	3	3	2
Duarte	3	2	2	7	14	14	8
Ferreira	0	0	0	9	9	9	5
Oliveira	0	1	3	4	8	8	4
Pereira e Melo	1	4	1	15	21	20	11
Ribeiro	2	2	1	8	13	13	7
Silva	1	1	0	3	5	5	3
Siqueira	1	1	0	5	7	7	4
Souza	0	0	0	13	13	13	7
Vianna or Viana	1	0	0	4	5	5	3
Total family positions	9	11	7	71	98		
Total positions in government	10	15	10	151	186		
Family positions/(%) total positions	90	73	70	47	53		

Source: Adapted from lists of names in Ribeiro, *Juazeiro*, pp. 130–135.

tins Duarte. Not one of the new appointees had served on the previous council, although the family names Duarte, Silva, and Souza were represented. The first elected council under the republic, which served from 1893 to 1896, included two Silvas and one Viana as well as three of the eight appointees of the period 1890 to 1893. José Inácio da Silva, a popular administrator who had served the municipal council as president in the last year of the empire, received the most votes in the elections of December 18, 1892. Only one other councilman, Antônio Luiz Vianna, had also served as a councilman during the empire (from 1883 to 1887). With the notable exception of José Inácio da Silva, no other local politician of the imperial period reemerged as an elected councilman after 1896. New personalities representing the old families became prominent, however.

With little historical information available, it appears that the first elections under the republic were democratic in nature, allowing participation that was extensive relative to elections of both the earlier imperial and the later republican periods. In the elections for state deputy in July 1892, José Inácio da Silva received the most votes (691) among forty-six candidates, and in the local elections of December 1892, Ramiro Antônio Ribeiro, an unopposed candidate for mayor, was elected with 853 votes. The total electorate was probably 1,000 at that time. That there was indeed some choice was evidenced by vote totals among the ten elected councilmen ranging from 710 votes for Inácio da Silva to 134 for Cirilio de Sales.[10] The appearance of representatives of the Duarte and Pereira e Melo families in the local elections of March 1896, however, suggests a partial return to the dominance of prominent families in municipal politics. At the same time, the electorate was reduced to fewer than 150. While vote totals ranged from 101 to 30 (there were sixteen candidates for ten municipal council seats), some degree of control by the ruling class is apparent in the vote distribution: 101 votes for three candidates, 35 for two candidates, and 30 for two others.[11]

Early in the republic, Juazeiro's governments produced some accomplishments. Under Ramiro Antônio Ribeiro from 1893 to 1896 a new railroad station was inaugurated, and legislation to establish the first municipal public school was approved. In May 1894 Juazeiro armed itself against an imminent attack by groups of bandits in Pernambuco, but no attack occurred.[12] In October two years later, in anticipation of an attack by Antônio Conselheiro, the messianic leader of nearby Canudos, large numbers of panicked inhabitants of Juazeiro sought ref-

10 Ibid., p. 83.
11 Ibid., p. 86.
12 Ibid., p. 83.

uge in Petrolina.[13] During the administration of Colonel Henrique José da Rocha (1896 to 1900), who was elected without opposition by a coalition of parties and the support of the municipal council, the major accomplishment was the erection of a town hall. Under Antônio da Cunha Melo, a physician, prominent rancher, and provincial deputy during the empire, the succeeding government was stalemated by an interfamily split in the coalition. José Inácio da Silva assumed the leadership of the opposition to the Cunha Melo family, whose candidate for the intendency was Colonel Antônio Evangelista Pereira e Melo. Both Inácio da Silva and Pereira e Melo claimed victory in the November 15, 1903, elections, and both held office until the Bahian state senate recognized Inácio da Silva as the victor six months later. Serving a dual role as mayor and state deputy, Inácio da Silva devoted little attention to municipal affairs, although he was able to mobilize state resources for the relief of flood victims in early 1906, when one-third of the city's homes were destroyed.[14]

Thereafter rivalry between families continued to plague the municipality. Colonel Aprígio Duarte Filho emerged as a candidate opposed to Inácio da Silva, whose candidate for the mayorship, Colonel Ramiro Antônio Ribeiro, was nevertheless elected and served as head of the local government from 1908 until his death in 1910. He initiated a number of public works, including a municipal slaughterhouse, a market, and a new school building. Two candidates also contested the election results of November 15, 1911. Inácio da Silva's choice, Manoel Francisco de Souza Filho (who later achieved prestige as a federal deputy from Pernambuco) was defeated by Aprígio Duarte Filho, candidate of political forces led by Colonel João Evangelista Pereira e Melo.[15] As in the 1903 elections, both candidates claimed victory, but a shift in Bahian politics and Inácio da Silva's subsequent defeat for the state assembly tipped the balance in favor of Pereira e Melo, resulting in the recognition of Duarte Filho as mayor in 1913.

This first of Duarte Filho's two mayorships, from 1912 to 1924, was marked by the construction of public buildings, the widening of streets, and the planting of trees throughout the city. A new public market was built, and construction of a new school was initiated. An electric lighting

13 *Cidade do Joazeiro* 1 (November 1, 1896): 2 (November 8, 1896): 2; and (November 29, 1896): 1. Also in Euclides da Cunha, *Rebellion in the Backlands* (Chicago: University of Chicago Press, 1944), pp. 178–180. See a recent account by local historian, Walter Dourado, "Canudos: trincheira sagrada," *Rivale* 7 (April 29, 1978): 5.

14 This and subsequent historical details, except where otherwise noted, are drawn from Ribeiro, *Juazeiro*, pp. 83–110.

15 Souza Filho was one of only a few Petrolina politicians to run for office in Juazeiro. Filgueiras Cavalcanti unsuccessfully ran for a municipal council seat in 1903, and José Padilha de Souza lost in the races for mayor in 1947 and 1950 before emerging victorious in 1955.

system for the city was inaugurated in 1917. An epidemic of bubonic plague swept the city in 1916, and flooding of the São Francisco River in 1919 destroyed more than a thousand buildings. An effort to increase taxes in order to build a new wharf for the port of Juazeiro was stalled by the refusal of Octacilio Nunes de Souza, one of the region's important merchants, to pay the tax; a court decision in his favor delayed the project twenty years. Financially, the government suffered from deficits and excessive expenditures, the consequence of the ambitious public works program. While school buildings were constructed or improved, for example, teachers frequently were not paid salaries for lack of sufficient funds. An anonymous letter published in the Petrolina press alleged administrative incompetence and corruption in the Duarte Filho government. Further, the government imposed censorship on the local press and so dominated Juazeiro politics as to permit Duarte Filho's reelection unopposed in 1916, 1920, and 1922.

Unable for personal reasons to continue in office in 1924, Duarte Filho presented Tito Nunes de Souza as his candidate and successor. Souza assumed office in January 1924 despite having been defeated by Adolpho Vianna.[16] However, Bahian politics had again shifted, and by May Vianna's victory was recognized by the state senate.[17] Vianna, however, resigned immediately thereafter, possibly because of the large debt left him by the Duarte administration. His successor, Leônidas Gonçalves Tôrres, built a bridge over the Salitre River and then, as an unopposed candidate, was elected mayor for the period 1926 and 1927. As a result of the São Paulo uprising of 1924 and the march of the Prestes Column through the Northeast, the municipality of Juazeiro was occupied by military forces for a brief period during Tôrres's term but did not come under attack.[18] Some nine hundred homes and the slaughterhouse were lost in a 1926 flood.

The last government under the Old Republic was that of Colonel Miguel Lopes de Siqueira from 1928 until the Revolution of 1930. Siqueira, the candidate of local forces under the aegis of José Cordeiro de Miranda and supported by the state government in power, took office on

16 Ribeiro, *Juazeiro*, pp. 100–101; also "Por conta alheia, município de Juazeiro, carta à opinião pública," *O Farol* 9 (May 15, 1924): 1–2. The letter claimed that salaries for schoolteachers had not been paid over a period of eighty months. Duarte Filho's manipulation was accompanied, according to the letter, by an emptying of the public treasury and disbursing of monies to the poor and others in exchange for their support.

17 *O Farol* 9 (November 9, 1924): 1; (November 15, 1923): 1; and (May 25, 1925): 1–2. Vianna was the victor with a majority of 89 votes. Some descriptive notes on Adolpho Vianna are in Pedro Diamantino, *Juazeiro de minha infância: memórias* (Rio de Janeiro: Imprensa Nacional, 1959), pp. 113–117.

18 The Prestes Column actually penetrated the municipality of Juazeiro (*O Farol* 9 [March 20, 1926]: 1), resulting in many persons' fleeing to Petrolina.

January 1, 1928, despite his actually having been defeated by Duarte Filho. Duarte therefore also took office on January 1. The Bahian senate confirmed the election of Siqueira in March 1928.[19]

Siqueira proved to be an able administrator and initiated construction of a new school, the paving of the city's streets, and the building of new roads.[20] A feud between the Souza and Evangelista families marred the otherwise peaceful years of the Siqueira regime, which was also threatened by a brief invasion of the municipality by bandits under the leadership of Virgulino Ferreira or Lampião.[21] Siqueira resigned upon the seizure of Juazeiro by revolutionaries in October 1930.[22]

The 1930 Revolution signified a transition in politics. Whereas the old-style oligarchic rule that had pervaded the Old Republic had resulted in some municipal autonomy for Juazeiro, the Revolution emphasized decision making at the national rather than the state or municipal levels. Oriented to national problems, the government often ignored the demands of the municipality. Juazeiro, with its ever increasing bureaucracy, actually had long been dependent on decisions at the state and federal levels, especially those affecting the allocation of funds and resources for public services. Its dependency was maintained and reinforced by the events of 1930 and thereafter. While Petrolina was occupied without resistance by revolutionary forces on October 15, Juazeiro resisted under the command of federal deputy Colonel José Cordeiro de Miranda and fellow political chiefs Franklin Lins de Albuquerque (of Pilão Arcado) and Francisco Leobas (of Remanso). Albuquerque beat back a revolutionary force in the interior of Juazeiro. Not until President Washington Luiz was deposed on October 24 did revolutionary forces cross the river to occupy Juazeiro.[23] For its resistance, Juazeiro suffered the suppression of its postal administration, the transfer of a school for poor children to another city, and the loss of a health center.[24]

The Bahian state intervenor under the Revolution named a local merchant, Rodolfo Araújo, mayor of Juazeiro on December 4, 1930. Inherit-

19 *O Farol* 13 (January 12, 1928): 1, 4; Ribeiro, *Juazeiro*, p. 105. On local parties during the Old Republic, see Walter Dourado, "História da política partidária Juazeirense e sua evolução no passado," *Rivale* 1 (November 12, 1972): 6.

20 Praise of Siqueira appeared in *O Echo* of Juazeiro in articles reprinted in *O Farol:* see, for example, *O Farol* 14 (March 31, 1929).

21 On the family feud, see *O Farol*, 13 (April 26, 1928): 1; on Lampião, see *O Farol* 15 (March 25, 1930): 4.

22 In an interview on June 18, 1971, Siqueira denied that he was "deposed," as is stated by Ribeiro, *Juazeiro*. p. 108.

23 *O Farol* 16 (October 30, 1930): 1, 4; *O Echo* 5 (February 14, 1930): 1.

24 These changes apparently were ordered by the head of the revolutionary forces in Juazeiro, Captain Nelson C. Xavier, who, according to Ribeiro (*Juazeiro*, p. 110), became a political chief of the São Francisco.

ing a substantial deficit from his predecessor, Araújo nevertheless initiated several projects, including a new wharf, a school, the remodeling of the municipal slaughterhouse, and construction of a small airport. In late February 1933 Araújo resigned, and Aprígio Duarte Filho was named in his place. Among the accomplishments of this second Duarte Filho regime were the remodeling of the town hall and construction of a school. In mid-1937, Duarte Filho was removed from office by the Superior Electoral Court, which ruled that he had illegally held the mayorship since January 1936. Colonel Alfredo Vianna, who after a bitter and sometimes violent struggle in 1935 had been elected mayor, assumed the post on September 20, 1937, but was ousted two months later as a result of the November 10 Vargas coup.[25] Duarte Filho reassumed office to inaugurate a bridge across the Salitre and several municipal buildings. After Vargas was pressured to step down and in line with the "democratization" of national politics and the appearance of parties in 1945, Duarte Filho was removed from office on October 29. His temporary successor was Ademoar Raimundo da Silva, who after twenty days in office was replaced by Edson Ribeiro.

In office from December 1945 until November 1946, Ribeiro, linked politically with Vianna influence, implemented a variety of projects, including the establishment of a commission to reorganize the municipal administration and the construction of a public market in an outlying suburb and in the town of Macaroca. Ribeiro resigned to run for state deputy and was replaced by Ludgero de Souza Costa, who held office until January 10, 1948, when freely elected Alfredo Vianna assumed the post.

Vianna, of the União Democrática Nacional (UDN), had easily defeated (with 2,777 votes) Aprígio Duarte Filho (1,774 votes) of the Partido Trabalhista Brasileiro (PTB) in the December 1947 municipal elections.[26] These parties obtained registration on the municipal council, with the UDN controlling a majority of seven seats (see Table 3.3) UDN representation included a woman, Ana Oliveira, who later won a seat in the state legislature, and José Rodrigues Lima, who was to remain in office until the early 1970s. The four Partido Social Democrático (PSD) representatives included the well-known community leaders Dr. Lauro Lustosa Natalino Aragão, Dr. Balbino Oliveira, and Manoel de Souza Duarte. The PSD was also supported by a newspaper, *O São Francisco,* which appeared briefly under the direction of Nestor de Souza (who was later to represent Petrolina in the Pernambuco state legislature).

In the October 3, 1950, elections, the Juazeiro electorate cast 60 percent of its votes for presidential victor Getúlio Vargas, while giving a

25 The Vianna opposition emerged in March 1933 within the Partido Democrata Juàzeirense, which was headed by Adolpho Vianna and included Alfredo Vianna and Rodolfo Araújo on its executive committee (*O Farol* 18 [April 6, 1933]: 4).

26 *O Farol* 33 (January 1947): 1.

Table 3.3. *Party representation in Juazeiro municipal council, 1947–70*

Party	Election						
	December 27, 1947	October 3, 1950	October 3, 1954	October 3, 1958	October 12, 1962	December 16, 1966	November 25, 1970
UDN	7[a]		1				
PSD	4	1	1	4			
PTB	1	3	2[a]		2		
PL		4[a]	5		3		
AD		4					
PR			3	2			
AULD				4[a]			
PSB				1			
PDC				1			
ACP					3[a]		
AP					4[a]		
$ARENA_1$						6	5[a]
$ARENA_2$						4[a]	6
MDB						3	2

[a]Political party of the mayor.

plurality of votes to Luiz Viana Filho for federal deputy and 1,630 votes to Alfredo Vianna for state deputy.[27] These votes and the reemergence of Edson Ribeiro as mayor reflected the prevailing Viana and Vianna influence in Juazeiro politics. While Ribeiro (with 2,347 votes) defeated Ludgero de Souza Costa (1,733 votes), José Padilha de Souza (1,516 votes), and José Costa Lima (1,009 votes), his support on the municipal council was now limited. Representation was divided among four parties. Ana Oliveira and two former UDN colleagues were reelected under the Partido Libertador (PL), which held four seats, while former UDN councilmen José Rodrigues Lima and Severino Bernardino Silva and former PSD councilman Manoel de Souza Duarte were reelected under the Aliança Democrática, which also held four. The strength of the PTB increased from one to three seats, and the devastated PSD managed to retain only one. Ribeiro, by his own admission, was stymied by the council, which persistently opposed his policies, in part because of his veto of their legislation granting salaries to councilmen.[28]

In the elections of October 1954, twice-defeated mayoral candidate José Padilha de Souza won by a margin of 653 votes over Alfredo Vianna. The council contained representatives of five parties, including the Partido Trabalhista (PT) with five seats, the Partido Republicano (PR) representing Vianna interests with three, the PTB with two, and the UDN with one each. The PTB councilmen were Américo Tanuri, who nearly a decade later emerged as mayor, and Souza Costa, who in 1958 ran under the Partido Socialista Brasileiro (PSB).[29]

In October 1958, with the support of the coalition Aliança União Libertadora Democrática (AULD), with four seats, and the PR, with two seats, Alfredo Vianna was reelected. The PSD took four seats and the Partido Democrata Cristão (PDC) one, that of Raulino Franklin de Queiroz, a military officer and later a state deputy. Representing the Vianna and Viana interests now and for many years thereafter were Ivan de Araújo Amorim and Rinaldo Oliveira de Menezes (a relative of then alternate state deputy Ana Oliveira).[30]

Américo Tanuri (4,879 votes) defeated the Vianna (Viana) family candidate, José de Araújo Souza (3,018 votes), in the October 1962 elections, thus ensuring the dominance of "popular" or less family-oriented elements during the succeeding decade. Again the council was split among four

27 *O Farol* 36 (November 11, 1950): 4. The core of the Vianna family's political–economic power was in the nearby municipality of Casa Nova. The difference in spelling (Viana or Vianna) is due to old and new orthography; some members of the family, such as Alfredo, continued to use the old spelling. Alfredo and Luiz were distantly related.

28 Ribeiro, *Juazeiro*, p. 122; see pp. 122–125 for his description of his accomplishments.

29 Câmara de Vereadores, Juazeiro, minutes, April 1955; *O Farol* 40 (October 9, 1954): 1.

30 Câmara de Vereadores, Juazeiro, minutes, April 7, 1959.

parties. Tanuri enjoyed the support of the PTB (three seats) and the Aliança Popular (AP), which included elements of the PSD (four seats). Opposed to him were Juazeiro's representatives in the state legislature, Ana Oliveira and Durval Barbosa da Cunha.[31]

Under military rule after March 1964 the Brazilian party system was reconstituted into the progovernment Aliança Renovadora Nacional (ARENA) and the opposition Movimento Democrático Brasileiro (MDB). Most of Juazeiro's politicians ended up in ARENA, where elements opposed to and allied with the interests of the Vianna family found themselves uncomfortably united. The ruling party had split into two factions by the December 1966 election, with $ARENA_1$ favoring Vianna interests and mayoral candidate Rinaldo Oliveira de Menezes and $ARENA_2$ favoring the group around Américo Tanuri and mayoral candidate Joca de Souza Oliveira. $ARENA_2$ emerged victorious, capturing the mayorship (5,460 to 4,477 votes) and four seats on the council ($ARENA_1$ won six and the MDB three). The municipality's representation at the state level divided, with Ana Oliveira aligning with $ARENA_1$ and Raulino Queiroz embracing both ARENA factions but leaning toward Tanuri's $ARENA_2$. Although Ana Oliveira was close to Bahian Governor Luiz Viana Filho, the differences within the municipality and the declining interests of the Vianna family contributed to state government's inattention to pressing local needs in Juazeiro.

Juazeiro politics were splintered by factionalism in the ARENA party during the campaign for the November 1970 elections. Américo Tanuri (7,552 votes) defeated the Vianna candidate Jaime Badeca de Oliveira (5,276 votes) for mayor. With five councilmen in support of $ARENA_2$, the Tanuri faction continued dominant. But the deep-rooted divisions, the opportunistic shifting of politicians from one faction to another, the dependence of the local factions on divided state politics, and the opposition of the Tanuri group to Governor Antônio Carlos Magalhães were indicators of a rough road ahead. These pressures were evident in the elections for mayor of November 1972, when the Tanuri-supported candidate, Arnoldo Vieira do Nascimento (6,838 votes), narrowly lost to former state deputy Durval Barbosa da Cunha (6,879).

Styles of politics

Varying styles of politics have affected developments in Juazeiro over the past hundred years. Especially in evidence was the dominance of a few

31 Electoral data for 1962 through 1970 from Tribuna Eleitoral de Juazeiro, *Livro dos atos eleitorais*. A description of each in the Tanuri government of 1963–67 is found in annual addresses to the city council entitled *Mensagem do Prefeito Américo Tanuri à câmara de Vereadores*. Juazeiro, 1964, 1965, 1966, 1967.

families whose destiny was directly tied to the deep-rooted economic life of the municipality. Traditionally two factions vied for power. After 1945, the Brazilian multiparty system injected at least a semblance of pluralism into the politics of Juazeiro. The local political economy has long been dependent on outside influences and decisions, especially at the state and national levels, and this has tended to increase local factionalism.

During the imperial period, Juazeiro politics were characterized by a division of power among several families, with no single family holding absolute dominance and frequent minor struggles for political and economic influence. Although rivalry among the families was sometimes intense, a patriarchy held together by common interests and interfamily marriages was clearly evident. This tendency extended well into the Old Republic, a period in which Juazeiro professed a politics of democracy based on a broad electorate, open elections with many candidates vying for office, and a free and culturally sensitive press. For example, examination of a list of 911 persons eligible to vote in state elections during 1903 reveals that 39 percent belonged to ten major families, including the Silvas (101), Souzas (61), Oliveiras (44), Pereira e Melos (33), Ferreiras (33), and Duartes (21).[32] The list of 1,018 persons eligible to vote in federal elections in that year revealed a similar pattern, with ten families representing 40 percent of the total.[33] Furthermore, in the municipal elections of November 1903 only about a third of these voters cast ballots, despite the fact that two major factions had emerged to contest political power. The appearance of two factions was the consequence of interfamily differences and the termination of a modus vivendi that had been established by the Pereira e Melo family in 1896. The vote totals of the 1903 elections suggest manipulation of the electorate, for the challenge of political chieftain Colonel João Evangelista Pereira e Melo resulted in 68 votes for his mayoral candidate, Colonel Antônio Evangelista Pereira e Melo, and 67 votes for each of his candidates for municipal council. In contrast, the other faction obtained 233 votes for its mayoral candidate, Dr. José Inácio da Silva, and between 272 and 277 votes for each of eight candidates for the council.[34]

Examination of tax records at the turn of the century also tends to confirm the impression that Juazeiro was ruled by a clique of families. Table 3.4 lists the major taxpayers in 1903. Octacilio Nunes de Souza and José Rabelo Padilha were the prominent economic and political personalities of Petrolina; they also controlled much of the commerce, although their role in Juazeiro politics is unclear. José Filgueiras Cavalcanti, elected

32 *Correio do São Francisco* (Juazeiro) 2 (May 3, 1903): 3; (May 10, 1903): 3; and (May 17, 1903): 3.

33 *Correio do São Francisco* 2 (May 31, 1903): 3; (June 7, 1903): 3; and (July 12, 1903): 3–4.

34 A ninth candidate received 264 votes. See analysis of the 1903 elections in *Correio do São Francisco* 2 (November 9, 1903): 3; and 3 (November 29, 1903): 2.

Table 3.4. *Major tax contributors in Juazeiro, 1903 (in Reis)*

Contributors	Tax on industry and profession		State taxes
Octacilio Nunes de Souza	3,500	(commerce)	1,667
José Rabelo Padilha	2,300	(skins, leather)	1,417
Duarte and Dias	1,416	(skins, leather)	2,167
Antônio Luiz Vianna	1,000	(cattle, commerce)	
José Filgueiras Cavalcanti	1,000	(commerce)	325
Josino Antônio Pereira	433	(commerce)	
Adolpho Vianna	50	(pharmacy)	150
João Evangelista Pereira e Melo		(skins)	100
Antônio Evangelista Pereira e Melo	50	(bakery)	
José Inácio da Silva	50	(medical service)	

Sources: Industrial-professional tax contributors from tax lists published in *Correio de São Francisco* 2 (March 22, 1903): 3 and (April 5, 1903): 3. State tax contributors from lists published in *Correio de São Francisco* 4 (February 19, 1905): 3 and (February 26, 1905): 3. It is likely that these figures are incomplete, but they give a relative indication of the economic importance of the major politicians of the time.

a councilman in November 1903, later served as mayor (1907–10) of Petrolina.

The political divisions of the Old Republic brought a significant transformation to Juazeiro politics. The schism evident at the turn of the century was to perpetuate itself long thereafter. The Inácio da Silva faction incorporated the Ribeiros, while the Pereira e Melo faction aligned with the Duartes. Colonel Aprígio Duarte Filho's rise to mayor in 1913 restored power to the latter faction, which ruled throughout much of the last half of the Old Republic. The opposition, from 1924 on led by Adolpho Vianna (whose rise was conditioned by a change in state politics) was dominated by Colonel José Cordeiro de Miranda, head of the Partido Republicano de Juazeiro, whose political influence was ensured by his election as federal deputy in early 1930. The Juazeiro vote for federal deputy, in which Miranda's vote total was second among the candidates, and the fact that the Juazeiro electorate gave 2,285 votes to Júlio Prestes and only 352 votes to Getúlio Vargas made a change in local politics after the October 1930 Revolution inevitable.[35] It was not surprising, therefore, that Aprígio Duarte Filho was restored to power after a temporary transition in which Rodolfo Araújo, later a supporter of Adolpho Vianna, held office by appointment. It was Vianna forces, however, that were to remain significant after World War II.

35 *O Echo* (Juazeiro) 5 (March 6, 1930): 1.

Theoretically, the Vargas revolution consolidated Brazilian politics at the national level and undermined the strength of the patriarchy in local affairs. The real impact of the Vargas period upon Juazeiro politics is difficult to assess, for the traditional families continued to prevail. It is clear, though, that the patriarchy had long been plagued by factionalism. As early as 1907, in a critical review of "the Liverpool of the São Francisco," the Duarte family's weekly, the *Correio do São Francisco,* had editorialized that "local politics is abundant in factions and consequently detrimental . . . each [politician] prefers to struggle for the absorption of the opposition's influence rather than for the benefit of public affairs."[36]

The intense rivalry between factions of the ruling families gave Juazeiro an aura of political democracy. This was particularly evident in a variety of newspapers, among which were *Cidade de Joazeiro,* published late in the nineteenth century, and *Correio do São Francisco,* first published by José Martins Duarte on November 15, 1899, and still being published fifteen years later. During the early years of the present century the small municipality had a prolific and critical press. Besides the *Correio,* there were the *Fôlha de São Francisco,* replaced in 1916 by *Fôlha do Povo,* and the *Diário de Juàzeiro,* which in 1918 ceased publication "for lack of paper."[37] This journalistic tradition persisted into the 1930s. *O Echo,* owned and founded by Aprígio Duarte Filho in 1926, represented one political faction, while *O Trabalho,* founded and edited briefly by Edson Ribeiro, reflected the views of another.[38] There also was the hard-hitting *A Luta,* which moved to Pirapora in June 1933,[39] and *O Momento,* published in 1928.[40] Whatever the impact of this press upon political affairs, it is clear that these partisan newspapers were able to alert the reading public to particular problems. One editorial in 1896, for example, denounced the local government "for hiding their actions in impenetrable mystery, even though the law requires publication of municipal resolutions."[41] The press also provided a forum for the party platform; thus in 1907 the Partido Republicano de Juàzeiro was able to disseminate its demands for reforms of the tax system, improvements and expansion of public education, city lighting, and health services, as well as the establishment of developmental planning.[42]

With World War II, Juazeiro's tradition of a press had come to an end, probably for financial reasons. There were abortive efforts to revive it, but

36 *Correio do São Francisco* 6 (September 15, 1907): 1.
37 *O Farol* 1 (June 10, 1916): 2; 4 (September 17, 1918): 1.
38 *O Farol* 11 (March 20, 1926): 1.
39 *O Farol* 18 (June 23, 1933): 1.
40 *O Farol* 13 (January 28, 1928): 1.
41 *Cidade de Joazeiro* 1 (June 1, 1896): 1; (October 4, 1896): 1; and (June 7, 1896): 1.
42 *Correio do São Francisco* 6 (September 29, 1907): 1.

to little avail.[43] There was no end to factionalism, however. New electoral legislation encouraged the emergence of many parties and political orientations. At first the factionalized politics of the many parties benefited the remnants of the patriarchal order, now fully dominated by the Vianna family. Alfredo Vianna and Edson Ribeiro dominated municipal politics from 1945 to 1955 and from 1959 to 1963, but the strength of patriarchal politics also gradually eroded during the period. The first significant indication of a decline in the prestige of the Vianna family was the mayoral election in 1954 of José Padilha de Souza under the left nationalist and populist PTB. The demise of family dominance in Juazeiro politics seemed assured by the victory of populist Américo Tanuri in 1962. The destiny of local populism also seemed somewhat in doubt with military intervention in April 1964. The pragmatic populists gradually adapted to the military presence, and by the early 1970s it was clear that many decisions in Juazeiro politics reflected in large measure the will of the local military authority.[44]

This tactic of collaboration allowed such populists as Américo Tanuri and Joca de Souza Oliveira to maintain political power. At the same time elected Vianna or Viana supporters, such as councilman Raimundo Medrado Primo and state deputy Ana Oliveira, were close to gubernatorial decision making. Municipal politics became particularly complicated by the indirect election of Bahian governor Luiz Viana Filho.[45] The opposition of local populists to the local Vianna and state Viana forces had disastrous consequences for the municipality, particularly in the economy, where state projects were often halted or not implemented, credit was stifled, and local industry and commerce fell into severe depression.[46]

Especially important in the analysis of political life in Juazeiro is the realization that local politics is directly dependent upon ties with politicians and party factions at the state level. Whereas in 1966 the majority

43 One issue of *Tribuna do São Francisco* was published in November 1970, for example.

44 In July to September 1971, commemorations were dominated by the activities of the local battalion. A week of festivities on behalf of the army in late August was followed by another in celebration of Brazilian independence in early September. In the past, such celebrations normally had been limited to September 7, but in 1971 a full week was allocated to marching schoolchildren and soldiers. The Superintendência do Vale do São Francisco (SUVALE), headed by an army colonel, organized many of the activities. The military in Juazeiro also developed a new traffic system for the city's streets.

45 Luiz Viana Filho had served in the cabinet of President Humberto Castelo Branco, and his election in 1966 was supported by the president. After leaving office in 1971, Viana turned his attention to the writing of a book on Castelo Branco. See analysis of his relations with the president in *Veja* (March 3, 1971): 17.

46 For example, by mid-1971 all but one major industry had shut down. Construction of a new luxury hotel was initiated by the Viana government as Bahia's response to the construction of a hotel in Petrolina by the Pernambucan government, but completion was delayed until 1972. A Faculty of Philosophy was forced to close temporarily due to lack of state funds.

faction, ARENA$_1$, lined up behind Governor Luiz Viana Filho, the minority faction, ARENA$_2$, found itself ostracized in state affairs, as a result of its opposition to Vianna interests in Juazeiro. With the exit from office of Viana Filho in March 1971, both ARENA factions suffered defections. With his reelection as mayor in 1970, Américo Tanuri established his faction, ARENA$_2$, as the majority faction. The internal maneuvering of councilmen from one faction to another was typical of the pragmatic politics long familiar to Juazeiro. Five of the reelected councilmen had changed their positions. Orlando Pontes and Alvaro Correia da Silva aligned with Tanuri (and subsequently were elected president and vice president of the council) and were joined by former alternate and newly elected councilman Raimundo Clementino de Souza. Four of the councilmen elected in 1966 with the minority faction that had supported Tanuri's candidate, Joca de Souza Oliveira, now joined the opposition; one of these, Jayme Badeca de Oliveira, ran unsuccessfully against Tanuri, with the strong backing of Viana interests. João Bernardino Irmão was elected an alternate. Only Manoel de Souza Duarte and José Rodrigues Lima were reelected.[47]

As Table 3.5 shows, the Tanuri faction (ARENA$_1$), composed of five of the thirteen councilmen and ten of the eighteen members of the ARENA executive committee, also opposed Viana Filho's successor, Governor Antônio Carlos Magalhães. Tanuri enjoyed the support of the MDB as well. A plurality of councilmen constituted the minority faction of ARENA, but this faction was split into three groups. One local group of three councilmen and four members of the executive committee continued to support the state-level ARENA faction (four state deputies and two federal deputies) behind Viana Filho. Another group of two councilmen and three members of the executive committee supported the faction of Federal Deputy Manoel Novais (three state deputies and three federal deputies), who had not fared well among Juazeiro voters in 1970.[48] A third group,

47 Splintered politics in Juazeiro tended to promote manipulation of the electorate through the purchased vote, a practice not unknown in Juazeiro or, indeed, most of the *sertão*. The 1970 campaign was no exception to this practice. According to one of the ARENA leaders I interviewed, money to buy votes was donated by local merchants and industrialists. One of these divided his donations between the two ARENA factions, generally supporting the Tanuri faction locally and the Viana faction at the state level, where deputy Ana Oliveira maintained strong influence with the secretary of finance, which in turn could ease the tax situation of local merchants. With the cruzeiro rate at about five to the dollar, a vote for state deputy cost two cruzeiros; for federal deputy, three cruzeiros; for municipal councilman, one cruzeiro; and mayor, five cruzeiros. These differences related to the degree of impact on Juazeiro of respective spheres of government. At the state level, the Tanuri faction aligned with Federal Deputy (representing Bahia) Antônio Lomanto Júnior, who had managed in past years to direct several federal projects to Juazeiro and who was popular among the municipality's electorate.

48 In the November 15, 1970, election, Lomanto Júnior received 2,159 votes in contrast to 215 votes for Manoel Novais (*Tribunal Electoral de Juazeiro*. "Atos Electorais," June 25, 1971).

Table 3.5. *Political allegiances of Juazeiro politicians to state-level factions, June 1971*

	Local council			Local party executive committee		
	ARENA$_1$[a]	ARENA$_2$[a]	MDB	ARENA$_1$	ARENA$_2$	MDB
State-level faction						
Luiz Viana Filho		3			4	
Jutahy and Juracy Magalhães		1			1	
Manoel Novais		2			3	
Lomanto Júnior	5[b]		1	10[b]		1
Other			1[c]			3[c]
Total	5	6	2	10	8	4

[a]ARENA$_1$ = majority faction; ARENA$_2$ = minority faction.
[b]Including one councilman who shifted from the Novais faction after the November 1970 elections.
[c]During the 1970 campaign and even thereafter, the MDB generally supported the Lomanto or Tanuri faction. One councilman and three of the four members of the MDB executive committee are here classified as outside any ARENA faction, although in reality, as one MDB leader has said, "There is no opposition party in Juazeiro."

made up of one councilman and one member of the executive committee, stood behind state deputy Jutahy Magalhães and his father, former governor and ambassador to the United States, Juracy Magalhães, whose support included at least six state deputies.[49] It was this latter faction that represented the real opposition to the governor.[50]

Lack of consensus in local politics resulted in greater reliance on political decisions at the state level. The persistence and growth of its nepotistic bureaucracy have also tended to be directly dependent on decisions and allocations of material and human resources at the state and federal levels. Typical of most municipalities, the local administration has generally been

49 Before the reconstruction of the Brazilian party system after the 1964 Revolution, Viana Filho, Juracy Magalhães, Lomanto Júnior, and Novais had all been members of the UDN. Their respective factions were partially a reflection of divisions that had developed many years earlier in the ranks of the UDN. Local delegates to the state convention were Councilman José Rodrigues Lima and mayoral candidate Jaime Badeca de Oliveira (representing the Novais faction); Councilman Orlando Pontes (Lomanto faction); and Luiz Libório (Jutahy Magalhães faction, apparently formerly of Viana faction). This analysis of state politics is based on an interview with Dr. Pedro Borges, president of the ARENA in Juazeiro, April 25, 1971.

50 In early August an exchange of letters between Antônio Carlos and Juracy provoked an open break and a "crisis" in the ARENA of Bahia. According to the new governor, Juracy was angry that state concessions had not been granted to particular private firms. See the letters in *Tribuna da Bahia* (August 10, 1971): 2.

subject to outside pressures and decisions. Often, political infighting led to outside sanctions.[51]

Juazeiro politicians have not been oblivious to their dependent status. While their municipality was economically dominant over the São Francisco region, they sought autonomy. As early as 1896 there was a call for a new state of São Francisco, incorporating and uniting Juazeiro and Petrolina into a single capital.[52] In fact, the idea of a new state was included in the constitutions of 1934, 1937, and 1946. According to the 1946 constitution, such a state was to be created with the approval of the respective state assemblies, the people of the designated state, and the national congress. Legislation prepared in 1964 and 1967 called for a state of nearly six hundred thousand square kilometers in size and 5 million in population and including territory of the states of Alagôas, Bahia, Minas Gerais, Pernambuco, and Sergipe. The capital of the new state was to be called Joalina, combining the present municipalities of Juazeiro and Petrolina.[53]

With the construction of a bridge across the São Francisco and a paved road to Recife, Juazeiro came to be dependent not only on Salvador, but on neighboring Petrolina as well. Local politicians were quick to recognize the advantages that the election of Nilo Coelho as governor promised for Petrolina and appealed to Luiz Viana Filho, governor of Bahia, not to ignore the interior municipality.[54] Their position was manifested in a letter to the governor in September 1967: "The election of Governor Nilo Coelho in Pernambuco will bring Petrolina . . . a wave of progress never before attained. This will create serious disequilibrium for Juazeiro if there is no commensurate compensation from the Bahian government, from you, a man of conviction who also is tied to Juazeiro through family relations."[55] With local politics controlled by a fraction opposed to Viana interests, Viana Filho generally ignored Juazeiro. A year later Mayor Joca de Souza Oliveira warned that Bahia had effectively lost its influence over the São Francisco region from Juazeiro to Paulo Afonso. He lamented that Juazeiro "was integrating itself to the economic system of Pernambuco and slowly withdrawing from Bahia."[56]

51 An early critique of local bureaucracy appeared in "Govêrno Municipal," *Correio do São Francisco* 6 (September 15, 1907): 1.

52 Arvonymo Uzeda, "Estado do São Francisco," *Cidade de Joazeiro* 1 (July 23, 1896): 1.

53 Document in the files of the Comissão de Desenvolvimento Econômico do São Francisco (CODESF) based on extracts from *Diário Oficial* of April 24, 1967, including a bill (no. 2802-64) presented by deputies Juarez de Souza and Adão Souza and a Bahian state law approved on June 15, 1964.

54 See, for example, J. Antônio d'Avila, "Um 'parisiense' em Juazeiro-das lordezas," *O Farol* 52 (April 14, 1967): 1.

55 Orlando Pontes, "Carta de Juazeiro ao seu governador," approved by the city council on August 28, 1967, and published in *O Farol* 53 (September 7, 1967): 1.

56 "Bahia poderá perder a região do baixo-médio São Francisco diz prefeito," *O Farol* 53 (June 8, 1968): 1; interview with Joca de Souza Oliveira.

Figure 4.1. A view of the São Francisco, looking down on the principal street of Petrolina, with its commercial houses and the open market. Photo 1971.

Figure 4.2. The Catholic church of Petrolina, with the Edificio Borges and its Coca Cola advertisement in the foreground. Photo 1982.

4

Petrolina: patriarchy and family dominance

From its inception, certainly as early as 1730, until well into the nineteenth century, Petrolina was known for its function as the place where travelers from the dry interior (the states of Ceará, Maranhão, and Piauí and the Pernambucan municipality of Ouricuri) crossed the São Francisco River to reach Juazeiro and other points in the states of Bahia or Minas Gerais. By 1860, it had become a *povoada*, or village; on June 7, 1862, it was classified as a *freguesia* (an ecclesiastical administrative unit) and named Petrolina (a reference either to Emperor Dom Pedro II or to the local abundance of stones [*pedras*]). In the same year its first church was erected, and two years later its first parish priest, Manoel Joaquim da Silva, was appointed. In June 1879 Petrolina officially became a *vila*, or town, and on April 25, 1893, it was constituted as a municipality. Having been separated from the muncipality of Santa Maria de Boa Vista to the east, it now also adjoined the municipalities of Ouricuri to the north and Afrânio to the west and touched the state of Bahia to the south along the São Francisco River. In 1895 the classification of the muncipality's urban center was changed from "town" to "city" and September 25 is now celebrated as its anniversary. Situated in the area now known as the "drought polygon," Petrolina was some 650 kilometers from Recife, the state capital.[1]

1 Although very little has been written about the early history of Petrolina, a perspective can be gleaned from a few major works that deal with the penetration and colonization of the interior since the sixteenth century. Among these are Aroldo de Azevedo, *Regiões e paisagens do Brasil*. 2d ed. (São Paulo: Companhia Editora Nacional, 1954); Vicente Licinio Cardoso, *À margem da história do Brasil (Livro póstumo)* (São Paulo: Companhia Editora Nacional, 1933); Orlando M. Carvalho, *O rio da unidade nacional: o São Francisco* (São Paulo: Companhia Editora Nacional, 1937); Barbosa Lima Sobrinho, *Pernambuco e o São Francisco* (Recife: Imprenta Official, 1929); and Agenor Augusto de Miranda, *O Rio São Francisco: como base de desenvolvimento econômico do nosso vasto interior* (São Paulo: Companhia Editora Nacional, 1936). Robert Levine's *Pernambuco in the Brazilian Federation. 1889–1937* (Stanford: Stanford University Press, 1978) focuses on the political elite of Pernambuco, mainly in Recife, but contains only two brief references to Petrolina. It is possible that the name Petrolina resulted from Dom Pedro II's travels to the Northeast in 1859 to 1860 when he may have passed through the region; see Dom Pedro II, *Diário de uma viagem ao norte de Brasil* (Salvador: Progresso, 1959). José Raulino Sampaio accepts this interpretation in "Petrolina e o seu dia maior,"

Evolution of the community

From the late nineteenth century until World War I, Petrolina remained geographically isolated from the state capital, without means of communication, and suffered from incessant drought. State and federal authorities paid little attention to the municipality's thirty-five hundred inhabitants, who "lived under a patriarchal regime . . . absolutely dependent on Juazeiro, which always treated [Petrolina] as a mere tributary."[2] Constituting the patriarchy were the Amorim, Cavalcanti, Coelho, Padilha, and Santana Souza families, each led by its colonel. The major political chiefs of the late nineteenth and early twentieth centuries were Antônio Correia de Amorim, who ruled for some twenty years in alliance with state senator Francisco de Assis Rosa e Silva, and José Rabelo Padilha (see Figure 4.4), whose influence was strengthened by the marriage of five of his daughters into prominent families. His daughter Antónia Amelia married Colonel Octacilio Nunes de Souza, who served as mayor of Petrolina from 1916 to 1919. Nunes de Souza assumed political power partially as a consequence of being aligned with statewide political forces that broke with Rosismo (the tendency supporting Rosa e Silva) and made Dantas Barreto governor in 1911.[3] His power base was economic as well; press reports described him as the region's eminent "capitalist" and "political chief," a "figure of

O Farol 62 (September 30, 1977): 1. For the most part this overview of Petrolina's early history is drawn from conversations with several persons who have lived in the community since the turn of the century and from interviews with and notes of Antônio de Santana Padilha, the town's major literary figure. Also important and useful in reviewing the community's evolution has been the weekly and sometimes biweekly *O Farol*, edited by João Ferreira Gomes since 1915.

The previous reference to the date 1730 is documented in a letter by captain general of Pernambuco, Duarte Sodré Pereira, to the king of Portugal, December 18, 1730, and is cited by Nestor Cavalcanti, "Freguesia de Santa Maria Rainha dos Anjos de Petrolina," *O Farol* 47 (June 5, 1962): 1. This source apparently was part of the author's unpublished manuscript on the history of Petrolina. A general source with some of these historical details is Azevedo, *Regiões e paisagens do Brasil*, pp. 109–120. References to the historical notes of Antônio de Santana Padilha are from his unpublished manuscript, "Petrolina – súmula histórica, cronológica do seu passado político, religioso, social, administrativo e cultural." Padilha is the author of several plays presented in Petrolina: "Paulo e Alice" (1925) and "A beiradeira, pescadores do São Francisco" (1932). He has published *Album de Suadações* (Petrolina, 1964), a collection of speeches greeting important visitors to the city; *Corre um rio de lágrimas (contos)* (Recife: Coleção Concórdia, 1965), essays on the region; *Superfície (versos)* (Bahia, 1967); and *Ribeiril do São Francisco* (Recife: Companhia Editora de Pernambuco, 1970). His last work was *Pedro e Lina. Romance* (Recife: Companhia Editora de Pernambuco, 1980). A brief historical account is in "Memórias de nossa terra, Petrolina de hontem e de hoje," *O Farol* 11 (September 7, 1925): 1, 3. See also Tadeu Rocha, "Roteiro de Petrolina," *O Farol* 36 (October 28, 1950): 1, 3, and (November 11, 1950): 1.

2 J. Avila, "Petrolina de hontem, de hoje e de amanhã," *O Farol* 6 (October 24, 1920): 1.

3 *O Farol* 9 (September 7, 1923): 3 briefly describes the campaign that successfully challenged Rosa e Silva's dominance over Pernambucan politics.

indisputable prestige" in Juazeiro and Petrolina and a respected member of "Bahian high society."[4] One of his sons, José Padilha de Souza, was mayor of Juazeiro from 1955 to 1959. Another daughter of Colonel José Rabelo Padilha, Bernardina, married a prominent physician, Pacífico da Luz, who later became mayor of Petrolina and a state deputy. After her death, in 1920, Pacífico da Luz married Maria das Dores, yet another daughter of Colonel Padilha; their offspring all became prominent in Petrolina society. A fourth daughter, Joana, married Alcides Padilha, a businessman who served as mayor of Petrolina from 1922 to 1927.[5] A fifth daughter, Daria, married João Francisco de Souza Filho, a nationally known politician and mayor of Petrolina in 1927 and 1928.

The Cavalcanti, Coelho, and Souza families were important in this early period. Manoel Francisco de Souza Júnior, father of the federal deputy Souza Filho, was Petrolina's first mayor, from 1893 to 1895. He was succeeded by a Cavalcanti, who in turn was replaced by a Coelho. The Cavalcanti family, with ties to the nearby towns of Afrânio and Cabrobró, emerged from time to time to play a major role in Petrolina politics. Colonel Clementino de Souza Coelho (Quelé), a descendant by marriage of the Souzas and the Coelhos, became Petrolina's major economic influential, and his sons were later to exercise both economic and political control over the community.

The predominance of a few families was paralleled in the economic sector. In its early years as a municipality, Petrolina was reportedly "backward," "resistant" to progress, and lacking "initiative . . . promoting a material and social change that would bring about a relatively civilized human nucleus"; this backwardness was seen as a consequence of "our bourgeoisie" and its limited enterprise, its crude cattle raising, and its failure to establish even a single industry: "there did not exist anything resembling the idea of work."[6] By 1920, however, the development of a rubber industry in the region had brought changes: The volume of commerce had doubled, cotton was being produced, and cattle raising had been intensified. There were three tobacco factories, a cotton mill, a

4 Scattered references of this kind appear in *Correio de São Francisco* 6 (September 11, 1907): 1, and in the first eight issues of *O Farol*. In 1923, for example, he was the second largest merchant and farmer in Petrolina, according to a list of taxpayers published in *O Farol* 8 (February 10, 1923): 2, and (February 22, 1923): 2. In May 1924, he refused payment of alleged discriminatory taxes levied by the Juazeiro municipal government of Tito Nunes Sento Sé and undoubtedly was influential in overturning that government, thereby ending the twelve-year dominance of Colonel Aprígio Duarte Filho (*O Farol* 9 [May 15, 1924]: 1–2 and 9 [May 25, 1924]: 1–2).

5 For a review of the accomplishments of Alcides Padilha during his first year in office, see *O Farol* 9 (November 15, 1923): 1.

6 Avila, "Petrolina de hontem," p. 1.

Table 4.1. *Business income and taxes of political leaders in Petrolina, 1923 (in Reis)*

Leader	Income	Tax
Clementino de Souza Coelho	120,000	700
Octacilio Nunes de Souza	120,000	500
Antônio Gomes da Sá	72,000	460
Juvêncio Rodrigues Coelho Pombo	56,000	380
Alfredo Amorim	20,000	100
João Francisco de Souza Filho	18,000	120[a]
Febrônio Martins de Souza Filho	18,000	120[a]

[a]Higher tax based on type of commercial product.
Source: "Indústria e profissão no exército de 1923," *O Farol* 8 (February 10, 1923): 2, and (February 22, 1923): 2. The source is unclear whether an income or excise tax was applied; the latter is more likely.

vinegar factory, and three soap factories.[7] Table 4.1 reveals the business income and taxes of some of the major political personalities and ruling families in this period. Clementino de Souza Coelho and Octacilio Nunes de Souza head the list, and an Amorim and other Souzas also appear.

Octacilio Nunes de Souza's election as mayor in 1916 signified a shift in local politics. For the next fifteen years, political power alternated between two major tendencies: the faction led by Nunes de Souza, which elected Pacífico Rodrigues da Luz mayor and Francisco Febrônio de Souza vice mayor in 1919 and Alcides Padilha mayor and João Dias Gomes vice mayor in 1922, and the forces of Colonel Clementino de Souza Coelho, in league with Manoel Francisco de Souza Filho, who as a federal deputy coordinated local with state and national politics. The latter faction assumed municipal power in the late 1920s, but not without a struggle. Its rise began with the appeal of Colonel Clementino and João Francisco de Souza Coelho to annul the municipal elections of May 1925. Colonel Clementino had lost the mayoral election (632 to 227 votes) to Dr. Cardoso da Sá, and the colonel's running mate, Colonel Francisco Correia de Figueiredo, had lost the election for vice mayor (636 to 227) to Alfredo Amorim (born a Coelho but adopted and brought up by Colonel Amorim).[8] The Cardoso da Sá–Amorim slate had been supported by

7 Ibid. The region's rubber industry was based on the extraction of the gummed material of the root of the maniçoba plant, which was cultivated from seeds planted in Pernambuco and Piauí. The impact of this industry led Juazeiro's *Correio de São Francisco* (11 [May 11, 1912]: 1) to proclaim Petrolina the future California.

8 *O Farol* 10 (July 16, 1925): 1.

Octacilio Nunes de Souza, Dr. Pacífico Rodrigues da Luz, Manoel Netto (brother of Francisco Febrônio de Souza and cousin of Deputy Souza Filho), and Alcides Padilha. That Colonel Clementino's brother, João Clementino de Souza Barros, also supported this slate signified the instability of the ill-defined factions.[9] Colonel Clementino's initial appeal to the municipal electoral court was denied,[10] but a decision at the state level (undoubtedly influenced by Deputy Souza Filho) annulled the elections and extended the term of Alcides Padilha.[11] Possídio de Nascimento (related to the Coelho family) and Colonel Clementino ran unopposed in the April 1927 elections for mayor and vice mayor.[12] Colonel Clementino's faction was bolstered by the support of João Francisco de Souza Filho, who as president of the municipal council served briefly as mayor in 1928; Souza Barros, who fell into line as mayor from 1928 to 1930; and José Fernandes Coelho, who later as a Coelho-endorsed candidate lost a close contest for mayor in October 1947.

Two points can be made about these differences within the ruling patriarchy. First, families were not always cohesive: For example, Alfredo Amorim, himself a Coelho, opposed his adopted father's ally Colonel Clementino, and Clementino's brother, João Clementino, also aligned with the opposing faction; while some Souzas such as Manoel Netto and Francisco Febrônio moved with the opposition, Deputy Manoel Francisco de Souza Filho and João Francisco de Souza Filho supported the Coelho faction. Despite Nunes de Souza's dependence on the support of Dantas Barreto for his rise to power, Barreto received only 16 of 365 votes cast by the municipality's electors in the 1918 elections for senator,[13] and there was total municipal support (604 votes) for Senator Rosa e Silva in the 1924 elections.[14] Second, Deputy Souza Filho's influence at the state and national levels contributed to some healing of the differences between factions. Thus, during the late 1920s the apparent cleavages were obscured or at least mitigated by the municipality's links to politics elsewhere.

The assassination of Souza Filho in the state Chamber of Deputies in late 1929[15] exacerbated old differences at the local level. In November Mayor João Clementino de Souza Barros had been severely criticized by the leaders who had supported his opposition to his brother in 1925. Octacilio Nunes de Souza, Alcides Padilha, Pacífico Rodrigues da Luz, and others

9 *O Farol* 10 (May 28, 1925): 1.

10 *O Farol* 10 (July 30, 1925): supplement, 3.

11 Interview with Antônio de Santana Padilha, June 16, 1971.

12 *O Farol* 15 (November 7, 1929): 1.

13 *O Farol* 3 (March 10, 1918): 1.

14 *O Farol* 9 (February 28, 1924): 1.

15 *O Farol* 15 (December 28, 1929): 1, and (January 9, 1930): 1, 4.

protested his failure to publish his budget.[16] In January 1930 an editorial entitled "Awaken, People of Petrolina!" appeared in *O Farol,* reiterating the demand that the municipal budget be made public; that salaries of municipal employees, including teachers, be paid; and that the problem of a large public deficit be resolved.[17] In February, twenty-two prominent members of the Nunes de Souza faction protested to the state governor over the closing of schools by the municipal government.[18] In March, Cardoso da Sá recalled the earlier complaint against the government's failure to publish a budget as "the call for a regional political fight in defense of civil rights" and against governmental indifference and abuse.[19] During the same month the Juazeiro newspaper, *O Echo,* praised the government of João Clementino, and this provoked a critical editorial in *O Farol:* "He was a failure . . . incompetent in public administration . . . a man who did nothing."[20]

About the same time, Colonel Clementino took offense over two critical articles published in *O Farol* by Father Mariano de Moura Cavalcanti.[21] He also alleged that members of the diocese had distributed posters on behalf of the Aliança Liberal, whose candidate in the forthcoming presidential elections was Getúlio Vargas (Colonel Clementino was affiliated with the Partido Republicano de Pernambuco, which favored Júlio Prestes). Convinced that Bishop Dom Antônio Maria Malán was active in municipal politics, he openly broke with the diocese's first bishop. According to *O Farol,* "all this represented treason for one who was a close friend of our bishop in this land and who gave him the greatest support."[22] With the temporary withdrawal of Colonel Clementino from Petrolina politics, a slate of candidates supported by Cardoso da Sá, José Fernandes Coelho, and Alcides Padilha was elected. Antônio Coelho and Antônio de Santana Padilha became mayor and vice mayor.[23] The balance of forces had been restored if not in fact tipped in favor of the Nunes de Souza faction now led by Cardoso da Sá and Pacífico Rodrigues da Luz.

16 *O Farol* 15 (November 7, 1929): 1.
17 *O Farol* 15 (January 23, 1930): 1.
18 *O Farol* 15 (February 7, 1930): 4.
19 João Cardoso de Sá, "A postos," *O Farol* 15 (March 8, 1930): 4.
20 *O Farol* 15 (March 18, 1930): 1.
21 Padre Mariano de Moura Cavalcanti, "Coices ao vento," and Miquelino de Souza [pseud.], "Cartas sem sel-o," *O Farol* 15 (March 8, 1930): 1.
22 *O Farol* 15 (March 15, 1930): 1. Colonel Clementino's break with Dom Malán and the church resulted in his moving to Juazeiro. The differences were not resolved until after Dom Malán's death and the arrival of Petrolina's second bishop, Dom Idílio Soares. About the time the new bishop reached Petrolina, the body of one of Clementino's sons was found in the São Francisco River, where he had drowned; the death brought the family close to the church and differences were resolved (interview with João Ferreira Gomes, June 14, 1971).
23 *O Farol* 15 (April 17, 1930): 1, and (April 26, 1930): 1.

The growth of the economy in the 1920s was accompanied by new developments in the cultural sector. In 1920, there were eight primary schools (three private, two state, and three municipal) as well as one, the Colegio Frei Caneca, at the secondary level. Within six years the local diocese (under Bishop Malán) established several new religious schools, including Nossa Senhora Maria Auxiliadora and the Seminário Diocesano; in 1927 the Colegio Dom Bosco was founded. This educational base was strengthened in subsequent years, establishing Petrolina as "the intellectual capital of the São Francisco."[24] Although published reports in the 1920s bitterly protested Petrolina's economic dependence on Juazeiro,[25] there was no doubt that by the 1930s Petrolina dominated in the educational field. That Petrolina manifested pride in its educational system as a means of offsetting its dependence on Juazeiro was sometimes reflected in the importance given to Petrolina as the center of intellectual life.[26]

During these latter years of the Old Republic, there was a proliferation of civic and social organizations. Among the organizations were the Sociedade Filarmônica 21 de Setembro, established in 1910, and its affiliate, the Clube Filhas de Mozart, founded in 1917. On the executive committee of the former were Colonel João Clementino de Souza Barros, Alcides Padilha, Juvencio Rodrigues Coelho Pombo, Colonel João Francisco de Souza Filho, Alfredo Amorim, and Dr. Pacífico da Luz among others; their names repeatedly appear in the lists of officers of these organizations during the period 1915 to 1920.[27] Likewise, on the executive committee of the Clube Filhas de Mozart, the names of the wives, sisters, and daughters of the Souzas, Padilhas, and Coelhos appear regularly.[28] The same families appear among the founders of the Jockey Clube de

24 Although the number of students completing primary and secondary school was small, statistics relative to other cities of the Northeast, especially those in the interior, reveal that Petrolina produced a large number of graduates.

25 See, for example, Felix de Valois, "Pró Petrolina," *O Farol* 9 (November 22, 1923): 1, who called for a rail link between Petrolina and Recife as a means of eliminating Petrolina's dependency on Juazeiro's commerce, its control over river transport, and the resultant large taxes. Valois correctly predicted that Petrolina's dependent status would persist for many years. The opening of a bridge between the two cities in June 1954 and the completion of a paved road to Recife in April 1970 represented Petrolina's definitive break with its past dependency on the neighboring city.

26 Lacking space in their municipality's schools, students from Juazeiro have long sought schooling in Petrolina (or in Salvador, if they could afford it). Because of its poor state of educational affairs, Juazeiro was frequently the butt of Petrolina jokes about the quality of the students who crossed the river, according to an interview with a member of a prominent Petrolina family, June 9, 1971. References to Petrolina as the intellectual capital of the São Francisco were frequent (see, e.g., *O Farol* 26 [February 3, 1941]: 4).

27 See, for example, *O Farol* 1 (September 25, 1915): 3; 2 (September 28, 1916): 1; 3 (September 7, 1917): 1; and 4 (September 17, 1918): 2.

28 *O Farol* 2 (February 26, 1917): 1.

Petrolina, established in 1924.[29] Members of the Souza, Padilha, and Santana families represented the Centro Parochial, established in 1916,[30] as well as the Associação das Damas de Caridade, formed in 1923.[31] As would be expected, their names also appear on the board of directors of the local hospital.[32]

A review of the editorials and major news stories published between 1915 and the 1930 Revolution reveals the major concerns of the community during this period (Table 4.2). Matters related to government and politics comprise half of these. Although *O Farol* was very parochial in its orientation, it devoted major attention to national affairs, followed by municipal politics, then state politics, and finally regional affairs. Less than 1 percent of the issues and problems identified related to intercommunity affairs between Petrolina and Juazeiro. In terms of coverage and in-depth reporting, however, this newspaper was clearly oriented to state and local politics. Attention to national matters tended to be brief, with emphasis upon activities of the president and sometimes the congress; concern with state politics was directed to the activities of the governor, state-funded projects destined for Petrolina, and interaction between local and state authorities; and the major regional issue was the old question of the territory lost by Pernambuco under the empire (on this issue the Liga de Propaganda pró Reivindicação da Camarca do São Francisco waged a vociferous but uneventful campaign at the local and state levels under the leadership of the physician João Cardoso da Sá). International affairs, usually brief news releases on the status of World War I, received about the same attention.

Frequent reference was made to the activities of local civic and social organizations, including lists of executive committees dominated by the elites of the municipality. Local problems and efforts to stimulate development received scant attention, however. Roughly 5 percent of the issues and problems identified fell into the area of local infrastructure. Such matters as urban power and light,[33] street construction and maintenance, and agricultural development were occasionally brought to the public's attention; industrialization and credits and loans were hardly mentioned, and there was no reference to such problems as electricity for rural areas and developmental planning. A bit more than 4 percent of the issues and problems were classified as social services, among which the local police and public security in general received most attention. Often this atten-

29 *O Farol* 9 (January 17, 1924): 1.

30 *O Farol* 1 (February 10, 1916): 1–2.

31 *O Farol* 9 (September 7, 1923): 3.

32 *O Farol* 9 (December 21, 1923): 1.

33 The Empresa Melhoramentos de Petrolina was founded on July 20, 1925, to provide electricity for the city (*O Farol* 10 [July 25, 1925]: 2).

tion was in response to the activities of the Prestes Column, which on one occasion penetrated Juazeiro, and of the bandit Lampião, who also was active in the municipality. Optato Gueiros, Petrolina's police chief in 1924, was later to play a major role in the containment and defeat of Lampião.[34] The widespread concern with Lampião and Prestes, coupled with frequent acts of violence which seemed to be the consequence of the difficult life of the backlands, accounted for the large number (nearly 8 percent of the total) of issues and problems classified as conflict and violence.

Another infrequent local concern was the area of medical services, sewage, and treatment and supply of water. Such problems as the colonization of the São Francisco region or the emigration of people from Petrolina to São Paulo and other points, social morality, juvenile delinquency, and local taxes barely surfaced, although concern for press and other freedoms was sometimes expressed.[35]

Educational affairs received considerable attention (more than 7 percent of all issues and problems identified), and this emphasis was largely attributable to Dom Malán. The activity of the local diocese was elaborately covered in *O Farol,* accounting for 15 percent of all issues and problems identified during the period. Additionally, education was enhanced by sporadic efforts to establish a variety of newspapers.[36]

Other matters receiving considerable attention were river problems and development – sometimes related to Petrolina's concern for Juazeiro's monopoly position over river transport and commerce – and the construction

34 See *O Farol* 10 (September 20, 1924): 1; see also Optato Gueiros, *Lampião: memórias de um oficial ex-comandante de forças volantes*. 2d ed. (São Paulo: Linográfica Editora, 1952). *O Farol* 15 (March 25, 1930): 4, reported Lampião at the farm of Adolfo Vianna, a major political figure at the time. Prestes and his column reached Juazeiro in March 1926, according to *O Farol* 11 (March 20, 1926): 1. Although *O Farol* persistently condemned state and federal governments for ignoring the bandits of the interior, whose presence caused considerable anxiety for the local population, on at least one occasion it offered a sympathetic portrait of Lampião ("Sacco-Vanzetti-Lampião," *O Farol* 13 [September 7, 1927]: 4).

35 Concern for the problem of juvenile delinquency appeared in a lengthy unsigned article in *O Farol* 8 (March 15, 1923): 1, which condemned many parents in Petrolina for ignoring their children and allowing them to roam freely in the streets (as "exhibitionists," "drunks," and "with knives"). Nearly a half-century later, a young, ambitious judge, José Maria Carvalho, criticized parents for the same behavior and initiated efforts to alleviate the problem. His views were elaborated at a Caritas Conference on May 30, 1971, in Petrolina and in an interview on local radio.

36 For example, *O Trabalhador*, founded November 15, 1912, by Colonel João Clementino de Souza Barros; *O Commercio*, organ of "the opposition," edited by João Batista de Aragão; *O Popular*, founded in 1916 and edited by José Fernandes, Jeso Santana, and Nestor de Souza; *A Palavra*, edited briefly in 1918 by Raul Santana; *Revista do Sertão*, founded in March 1918; *Alicate*, a satirical newspaper founded on October 15, 1923, by J. Fernandes and Antônio de Santana Padilha; and *A Tribuna*, established in 1926 by Barros e Cia (*O Farol* 1 [October 10, 1915]: 3; 1 [August 10, 1916]: 1; 9 [October 25, 1923]: 1; and 11 [May 21, 1926]: 2).

Table 4.2. *Major concerns in Petrolina, 1915–70 (%)*

Concern	1915–30 (N = 1,081)	1930–45 (N = 2,564)	1945–60 (N = 2,340)	1960–70 (N = 1,932)	% Satisfied with resolution of problem (N = 118)
Politics and government					
Local government and politics	6.7	6.0	8.3	6.3	32
Local civic and social organizations	4.4	7.3	5.3	7.2	64
Local problems and development	2.5	4.0	7.6	15.2	
State politics	6.2	3.8	8.0	7.2	34
Regional affairs	3.4	4.3	2.2	2.9	
National politics	10.6	12.0	9.4	6.4	31
Electoral participation	3.3	1.0	4.2	1.2	58
International affairs	3.4	11.4	10.4	4.8	
Foreign influence	0.7	1.1	0.9	1.4	18
Violence and conflict	7.9	2.8	0.6	0.8	87
Intercommunity affairs	0.7	0.5	0.0	0.4	30
Infrastructure					
Urban electric power and light	2.2	1.0	1.8	1.7	66
Rural electricity	0.0	0.0	0.1	0.8	46
Street construction and maintenance	2.6	1.4	0.8	1.9	52
Developmental planning	0.0	0.0	0.0	0.2	50
Industry	0.4	1.0	0.5	1.6	41
Agricultural development	1.4	1.3	2.5	3.1	34
Credits and loans	0.3	0.2	0.1	2.0	74

Social services					
Unemployment	0.0	0.0	0.0	0.0	18
Poverty and hunger	0.4	1.1	0.4	0.1	21
Police and public security	3.8	3.8	1.6	2.2	63
Housing	0.0	0.0	0.1	0.9	64
Recreation and parks	0.2	0.0	0.0	0.0	58
Health services					
Medical	2.6	4.3	3.7	4.1	79
Sewage	0.1	0.0	0.1	0.5	28
Treatment and supply of water	0.3	0.3	0.6	0.7	97
Education and culture	7.4	8.4	8.3	10.7	82
Other problems					
Immigration to city	0.0	0.0	0.0	0.0	17
Emigration (to Recife, São Paulo)	0.6	0.4	0.3	0.0	18
Social morality	0.3	0.2	0.0	0.0	
Youth/delinquency	0.4	0.7	0.8	0.5	
Press and freedom	1.2	2.1	1.0	0.8	32
Taxes	0.5	0.7	1.2	0.8	
Drought or floods	1.3	1.3	2.8	0.8	
Colonization	0.2	0.0	0.9	0.2	
River transportation and development	3.3	3.4	1.8	4.0	
Railroad, bridge developments	5.7	3.0	1.6	1.0	
Religion and church	15.0	11.2	12.1	7.5	36

Note: As indicated by reports in the weekly (and sometimes biweekly) *O Farol*. A total of 596 numbers of this newspaper were examined for the period 1915 to the Revolution of 1930, 494 for the period of the Vargas government, 1930–45, 253 for the period 1945–60, and 182 for the period 1960 to August 1971.

of a railroad into Piauí as well as a local railroad station. There was even one reference in 1920 to the possible construction of a bridge over the São Francisco River to link the two cities.

The accession to power of Getúlio Vargas in late 1930 symbolized a break with traditional politics. Pacífico Rodrigues da Luz was promptly named mayor, a post he held until the elections of October 8, 1935, when his colleague and fellow member of the Partido Democrático (PD), Cardoso da Sá, was elected to that post. Cardoso da Sá was the candidate of the coalition Legenda Petrolina Unida, receiving 489 votes.[37] The Legenda was in fact dominated by the PD and closely linked to Carlos Lima Cavalcanti, the intervenor (governor or administrator) appointed by Vargas in 1930 to head Pernambucan affairs.[38] Pacífico Rodrigues da Luz led a group of six PD councilmen who were joined on the Legenda by three councilmen of the Partido Social Republicano (PSR): Crispim de Amorim Coelho, José Fernandes Coelho, and Raymundo Santana. This PD–PSR coalition represented the modus vivendi of the patriarchal forces that continued to characterize local politics. The appearance of the Silva family in these elections presaged its rise to power after World War II. João Ferreira da Silva ("Barracão") joined Alcides Padilha, Antônio de Santana Padilha, Manoel Netto, and Anísio Moura Leal in support of the PD, and his brother, José Ferreira da Silva, was elected a councilman on that ticket. Another relative, José Almeida da Silva (who later became mayor from 1952 to 1955) ran unsuccessfully for councilman on the neofascist Integralista ticket. With the abrupt end of democratic politics at the national level and the establishment of Vargas's New State in November 1937, Cardoso da Sá was replaced by Pacífico Rodrigues da Luz, who remained in office until 1945. Since the 1930 Revolution, municipal governments had accumulated a substantial public deficit, a share of it actually being inherited from the prerevolutionary administrations. Therefore, in 1938 Cardoso da Sá and Pacífico Rodrigues da Luz quarreled over the budgets and deficits of their respective regimes.[39] While the Luz administration maintained a tight rein, general discontent surfaced during the early 1940s. One newspaper editorial complained about the municipal light service and argued that "to govern is not only to collect taxes, but to pay

37 Unofficial tallies gave Cardoso da Sá 1,136 votes (see *O Farol* 21 [October 12, 1938]: 1) in October 1935, but an investigation disclosed voting irregularities which prevented him from taking office until August 15, 1936, with an official vote of 489 votes (see *O Farol* 21 [February 8, 1936]: 3; [August 8, 1936]: 1, and [August 15, 1936]: 1).

38 The PSD was founded in Petrolina in January 1933 with the following executive board: Alcides Padilha, Anísio Moura Leal, Manoel Netto, Antônio de Santana Padilha, and João Ferreira Gomes.

39 Pacífico Rodrigues da Luz, "Desfazendo enganos do Dr. João Cardoso," *O Farol* 21 (February 3, 1938): 4.

attention to local needs."[40] When *O Farol* attacked the mayor for arbitrarily raising meat prices, the mayor countered with a court suit, but the court supported the newspaper's position; *O Farol* promptly announced its victory "on behalf of the people's interests."[41]

More than 54 percent of the issues and problems identified from 1930 to 1945 (see Table 4.2) fell into the general classification of government and politics, slightly more than those identified in the 1915–30 period. Local affairs in general received major attention, as did national politics and international affairs; there was considerably less interest in state politics and regional and intercommunity affairs. International affairs often focused on the rise of communism and fascism, the world financial crisis, and occasionally the influence of the United States in Brazil. National politics focused on developments under the Vargas regime, including the evolution of a new constitution in 1934, elections thereafter, and the establishment of the New State. Compared with the 1915–30 period, there was less concern for electoral participation (which was generally suspended except during 1935–37) and for conflict and violence – the consequences not only of Vargas's dominance but of the failure of the 1935 revolt, the containment of Lampião in 1938, the death of the messianic Padre Cícero, and the police suppression of Cícero's followers not far from Petrolina.[42]

An increase in interest in local civic and social affairs during this period was partially related to the labor legislation of the Vargas government, which spurred the formation of a small labor movement in Petrolina under the direction of Cid de Almeida Carvalho, founder of the União dos Artifices Petrolinenses. On October 14, 1934, the Ministry of Labor officially recognized the formation of the metalworkers' Sindicato dos Empregados no Commercio.[43] As president of the union, Carvalho defined the movement's objectives in terms of the working class, insisting at the same time that workers in Petrolina rejected "communist ideas." The labor movement in Petrolina supported the candidacy of Cardoso da Sá for mayor.[44] This support for the local PD contrasted with the alignment of

40 V. Tudo, "De binoculo," *O Farol* 26 (February 3, 1941): 4.

41 *O Farol* 29 (October 23, 1943): 1.

42 Padre Cícero Romão Batista, who was once assisted by Lampião in defense of Juazeiro do Norte against federal troops, contributed the tower clock to Bishop Malán's cathedral (*O Farol* 17 [September 7, 1931]: 1, 2). The 1935 revolts in Natal, Recife, and Rio de Janeiro were covered in *O Farol* 21 (November 25, 1935): 1; (November 30, 1935): 1; (December 7, 1935): 1; and (December 14, 1935): 1. Lampião's death was extensively reported in *O Farol* 23 (July 30, 1938): 1, and (August 6, 1938): 1. On Pau de Colher, see *O Farol* 22 ([February 3, 1930]: 1; [February 10, 1930]: 1; [February 24, 1938]: 1; [March 3, 1938]: 1; [March 12, 1938]: 1; June 18, 1938]: 1; and [June 25, 1938]: 1).

43 *O Farol* 20 (October 20, 1934): 1, and (October 25, 1934): 4.

44 *O Farol* 21 (February 8, 1936): 1.

the labor movement in neighboring Juazeiro, which in 1935 had formed an autonomous opposition worker's party, the União Trabalhista Juazeirense.[45]

The link between the labor movement and the governing political forces in Petrolina was also attributable to the placement of prominent political personalities, including a Pombo, a Souza, a Gomes da Sá, and a Santana on the executive committees of the local unions. These union–party ties made it difficult to establish an independent union movement. Another obstacle was that labor legislation was not effectively implemented in the interior.[46] Carvalho's efforts in 1938 to organize a Comité de Propaganda e Organização Sindical no Alto Sertão de Pernambuco as a means of attracting attention to the local movement were of little avail, for in October 1938 the Vargas government dissolved the railroad worker's Sindicato dos Ferroviários da E. F. Petrolina-Terezina. For Carvalho it was apparent that the labor movement in Petrolina had come to an end.[47] Four years later he bitterly denounced the local government of Pacífico Rodrigues da Luz for ignoring labor's problems and tolerating exploitation of the labor movement.[48]

Interest in matters related to infrastructure was roughly similar to that of the preceding period, and so was interest in social and health services, except for police and public security affairs. Attention to education increased slightly. Freedom of the press and other forms of expression were frequently discussed, especially in the later years of the Vargas regime. The recurring droughts, river transportation, and the rail links to the north all received attention as in the earlier period, while religious affairs were of slightly less interest.

The Vargas impact on Petrolina politics did not cease with the end of his New State in 1945. Local political forces backing the Luz government switched their support to João Ferreira da Silva (Barracão) and Joaquim André Cavalcanti, and on October 28, 1947, they were elected mayor and vice mayor respectively. Running on the Partido Democrata Cristão (PDC) ticket, Barracão defeated José Fernandes Coelho, the Partido Social Democrático (PSD) candidate, and the PDC captured five of the nine municipal council seats (Table 4.3). Barracão's victory was due partly to a split in the PSD after Pacífico Rodriques da Luz opposed the naming of Raimundo Santana as mayor of Petrolina for the period July 26 to November 14,

45 *O Farol* 21 (October 12, 1935): 1.

46 Cid de Almeida Carvalho, "As leis sociais, sua falta de execução no interior – males que disso se originam," *O Farol* 20 (March 9, 1935): 1.

47 Cid de Almeida Carvalho, "Porque caiu a nossa organização sindical às classes trabalhistas e ao povo de Petrolina," *O Farol* 24 (October 22, 1938): 3.

48 Cid de Almeida Carvalho, "Vida proletária à mercê dos exploradores gananciosos, o proletariado sertanejo vive horas amargas," *O Farol* 27 (March 12, 1942): 1.

Table 4.3. *Party representation on the municipal council in Petrolina, 1947–72*

	Election							
Party	October 28, 1947	July 1, 1951	October 3, 1955	August 2, 1957	August 21, 1959	August 18, 1963	November 15, 1968	November 1972
PDC	5[a]							
PSD	4	3[a]		3[a]	3[a]	6[a]		
UDN		5	1	4	4			
PTB		1				3		
PR			8[a]					
PRT				2	2			
ARENA							9[a]	9[a]

[a]Mayor's party.

1947, a move initiated by his daughter, Cira Padilha da Luz, at the request of Colonel Quelé through Governor Barbosa Lima Sobrinho, to show Coelho strength in the municipality. Pacífico resigned from the PSD, taking with him most of his electors, and sided with Barracão.[49]

Dominated by the Coelho family, the PSD was able to win four seats on the council and place in office José de Souza Coelho and Ulisses Lustoso de Carvalho Pires (who in 1951 emerged briefly as mayor under an agreement between the two groups). Additionally, Nilo de Souza Coelho and Gercino de Souza Coelho were elected state deputies, respectively representing Pernambuco and Bahia.[50]

Despite the dominance of the PDC and the PSD, other parties also surfaced. The Partido Republicano (PR) was headed by Crispim de Amorim Coelho and Nestor de Souza, a bright and controversial lawyer who in 1950 was elected state deputy under an alliance of parties, the Coligação Democrática de Pernambuco, thus in effect filling a slot left vacant by Nilo de Souza Coelho when he became a federal deputy.[51] The PR also attracted José Padilha de Souza, later elected mayor of Juazeiro (1955–59). President of the local Partido Trabalhista Brasileiro (PTB) and unsuccessful candidate for state senator was labor leader Cid de Almeida Carvalho. Under the leadership of Cícero Rodrigues da Luz, the União Democrática Nacional (UDN) achieved importance at the time; later it

49 João Ferreira da Silva explained that he acquired his nickname as a boy working with his brother in a *barracão* or shack alongside the rail line in Piauí; see interview in 1° Congresso Eucarístico de Petrolina, 1 (October 1948): 41. Caio Prado Júnior in *A revolução brasileira* (São Paulo: Editora Brasiliense, 1966) describes the institution of "barracão," arguing that employers furnished goods to workers at extortionist prices but that the relationship was fundamentally commercial and not feudal or semifeudal as often characterized in the literature. In an interview in *Jornal Pequeno* of Recife on October 14, 1947, State Deputy Nestor de Souza complained that "Quelé and his political allies were subject to severe penalities because they were buying votes at 200 cruzeiros each." It was also well known that Barracão had purchased votes through his pharmacy and the fabric shop of his brother-in-law, Anísio de Moura.

50 Nilo Coelho was elected January 1947, when there was clear evidence of the Coelho and PSD strength at the state level. Gercino died in a plane crash on September 11, 1950 (J. Lustoso Cantareli, "A nota de Petrolina," *O Farol* 36 [September 30, 1950]: 3). PSD candidates Nilo Coelho and head of the party Nestor Cavalcanti de Figueiredo received 1,228 and 705 votes respectively, while the coalition candidate of the UDN and PDC received only 232 votes and Nestor de Souza of the PR 219 votes (data from Cartório Eleitoral de Petrolina, "Livro dos atos eleitorais"; subsequent electoral data are also from this source).

51 Nestor de Souza was endorsed by elements opposed to the Coelhos, including *O Farol*, which published his speeches in the state legislature (see 36 [July 31, 1951]: 1; 37 [November 24, 1951]: 1; and 36 [June 30, 1951]: 1). The latter speech was an attack on Communist deputy Pinto Cavalcanti, which received much attention. Souza's split from the UDN (see *O Farol* 26 [August 11, 1951]: 1), along with his earlier break with the Coelho family (before the political success of his sons, Colonel Clementino may have promised support to Nestor de Souza), put an end to his political career.

would include the forces of Barracão. The Partido de Representação Popular (PRP), also established in this period, had little influence.[52]

The intense local political rivalry and Coelho influence in Recife resulted in an intervention by Pernambucan governor Agamenon Magalhães and an agreement between the Coelho forces and those of Barracão: Colonel Ulisses Lustoso de Carvalho Pires, president of the municipal council, was to be the single, agreed-upon candidate for mayor. Municipal council seats would be divided: three for the PSD, one for the PTB, and five for the UDN.[53] For reasons never explained either publicly or, apparently, privately,[54] the new mayor resigned in 1952. A meeting of rival groups resulted in the choice for mayor of a nephew of Barracão, José Almeida da Silva, who was elected unopposed (1,096 votes) along with Francisco Raimundo de Souza as vice mayor.[55]

Various factors accounted for the consolidation of power in the Coelho family in 1955. Nilo Coelho had nurtured the family's influence statewide, having served Governor Etelvino Lins de Albuquerque in the key post of state secretary of finance, and his reelection as federal deputy, along with Osvaldo de Souza Coelho's election as state deputy (with 3,174 votes, winning him the seat held since 1951 by Nestor de Souza, who received a scant 42 votes), ensured the protection of Coelho interests.[56] Locally José de Souza Coelho and Raimundo Santana ran uncontested for mayor and vice mayor in October 1955, temporarily adopting the PR as their party and in the process also incorporating former Coelho political opponents such as Cid de Almeida Carvalho (whose newspaper *O Sertão* had been founded by the Coelhos to represent their interests as opposed to *O Farol*[57]), small merchant Natam Marques dos Reis, and rancher Plínio José de Amorim, whose votes came from the interior of the municipality (both Reis and Amorim had been elected councilmen under the PDC in 1947). Adalberto de Souza Coelho received most votes for councilman. In his inaugural speech José Coelho attributed his victory to

52 For lists of the members of party executive committees, see, for the PDC, PSD, and PTB, *O Farol* 33 (October 4, 1947): 1; for the UDN and PRP, *O Farol* 33 (October 11, 1947): 4, and (October 25, 1947): 1.

53 Agreement signed by Nilo de Souza Coelho, João Ferreira Silva, Cid Almeida Carvalho, José Fernandes Coelho, José de Souza Coelho, and Antônio de Santana Padilha (*O Farol* 30 [May 12, 1951]: 1, and [May 19, 1951]: 1).

54 Interview with Antônio de Santana Padilha, August 25, 1971.

55 In an interview on July 20, 1971, José Almeida da Silva indicated that he had been a conciliation candidate. A note in *O Farol* 37 (July 29, 1952): 1, refers to a meeting of eight representatives of the PSD and eight of the Barracão forces (UDN) and without explanation concludes: "The future mayor will be José Almeida da Silva." Almeida represented the UDN, his running mate the PSD.

56 *O Farol* 40 (October 9, 1954): 1.

57 The publisher of *O Sertão* in 1971 was Geraldo de Souza Coelho.

Colonel Clementino (died June 8, 1952) and José Fernandes Coelho (died January 1955), who had been the family's (unsuccessful) candidate in 1947. He promised to improve the city's lighting system, build a market and a slaughterhouse, and pave streets, promises that were fulfilled, although the opposition frequently protested political preferences which, for example, conspicuously left unpaved those streets that ran in front of a political opponent's home.[58]

Of the UDN candidates, only Tarcísio Araújo had won a council seat. Barracão's forces regrouped under two of his sons. One son, João Ferreira da Silva Filho, picked up 1,319 Petrolina votes in an unsuccessful bid for a state deputy seat in October 1958 (Osvaldo Coelho was reelected with 4,026 votes from Petrolina, while Nilo was reelected federal deputy).[59] In the August 2, 1957, elections Ferreira Filho lost in the race for mayor along with the popular local merchant João Batista Cavalcanti. Running under the UDN, they were easily defeated by the formidable PSD candidates for mayor, Luiz Augusto Fernandes (4,026 votes to 2,569 votes), an engineer from Rio de Janeiro who had married into the Coelho family,[60] and for vice mayor, Diniz de Sá Cavalcanti, a businessman with popular appeal.[61] The other son, Antônio Fausto de Sá e Silva, won a seat on the 1957 municipal council along with Tarcísio Araújo and two other UDN candidates. The PSD, led by José de Souza Coelho, captured only three seats and the Partido Republicano Trabalhista (PRT) two.

The period from the end of World War II to 1960 was one of increasing attention to the affairs of local and state government. As in the earlier periods, more than half of the concerns reported in the press[62] (Table 4.2)

58 See José de Souza Coelho's speech in *O Farol* 41 (November 30, 1955): 1, 4. A list of his accomplishments was published in a Coelho campaign statement (*O Farol* 44 [June 18, 1959]: 4). An interesting eulogy that gives substance to José Coelho's reference to his father is Ermí Ferrari, "Lendas e coronéis," read on the Emissora Rural, May 29, 1970, and printed in *O Farol* 55 (June 30, 1970): 1, 4: " . . . the only colonel to give continuity to his hope, through his sons, preparing them for the future of the great river . . . transforming his dream into reality."

59 The campaign statement of João Ferreira da Silva Filho is in *O Farol* 43 (August 23, 1958): 1.

60 Luiz Augusto Fernandes's accomplishments had previously been in the area of education and culture; he had built a public library and established the Fundação Educação. For an interview in which he discusses these interests, see *O Farol* 45 (September 7, 1959): 1.

61 In 1950 Cavalcanti ran under the PSD for state deputy, attracting few votes. During his campaign, he wrote a brief critique on the exodus of population from the *sertão* (see Diniz de Sá Cavalcanti, "Êxodo Rural," *O Farol* 36 [September 30, 1950]: 2). He served as vice mayor until 1968 and was considered a potential opposition candidate.

62 *O Farol* opposed the Coelhos during most of this period, prompting the family in 1948 to establish *O Sertão* in support of its interests. While I examined *O Sertão* and cite it in the text, I have made no attempt to include it in this historical analysis. Toward the late 1950s the two newspapers tended to reflect similar themes and to support Coelho policies in Petrolina. This was a consequence of the dominance of the family over the municipality's political economy (reflected in the substantial Coelho advertising in the two newspapers) and its many projects on behalf of the city.

related to politics and government. The focus on local and state government and on elections was a reflection of heated politics after the war as well as the now impressive representation of Petrolina in Recife. The larger number of issues on local development was undoubtedly related to the awakening of the community to problems that had long been ignored. Concern for infrastructure was similar to that of earlier periods, although there was more attention to agricultural development. The number of issues related to health, education, and social services in general was similar to that of past periods as well. No particular emphasis was given any other problem except a severe drought in the 1950s.

During the 1960s there was a reemergence of forces under Barracão in response to the desire of the electorate to support an opposition and the rise of populist politics throughout Brazil. Only a third of Petrolina's electorate had given its support in 1955 to President Juscelino Kubitschek and Vice President João Goulart. In 1960, however, most Petrolina votes went to Kubitschek's heirs, losing presidential and vice-presidential candidates Marshal Henrique Teixeira Lott and João Goulart. In 1962 Nilo and Osvaldo Coelho were again reelected federal and state deputy, respectively, with Ferreira Filho receiving 1,622 votes in Petrolina – insufficient for election to state deputy. The major test for Barracão's forces was the election of August 18, 1963. Now running under the PTB, Antônio Fausto opposed José Coelho and lost (4,498 to 1,746 votes, but three other PTB candidates won council seats, including José Borges Viana and Valdomiro José Ferreira who constituted a vocal opposition.[63]

With the 1963 elections, Geraldo de Souza Coelho emerged as a leader in Petrolina politics. Having received the most votes among candidates for the municipal council, he was almost immediately elected president of the council, a post he held throughout the 1960s;[64] unopposed in the November 1972 elections, he became mayor. Meanwhile, Osvaldo Coelho was unanimously elected leader of the PSD bench in the state legislature,[65] and Nilo Coelho maintained his influence in Brasília, where he was named first secretary of the Chamber of Deputies.[66] In 1966 Nilo was elected (indirectly, by the state legislature) governor of Pernambuco, and Osvaldo, who had run successfully to fill Nilo's seat in the federal chamber in December, remained in Recife as secretary of finance.[67]

The success of Geraldo, Osvaldo, and Nilo Coelho clearly marked the

63 Under Olimpio Filho, the short-lived *Fôlha de Petrolina* was published.

64 Geraldo Coelho was at that time a young engineer who had worked at Paulo Afonso (see his piece in *O Farol* 47 [December 30, 1961]: 1) and returned to Petrolina to head the family's construction firm.

65 *O Farol* 48 (May 15, 1963): 1.

66 *O Farol* 50 (February 27, 1965): 1.

67 *O Farol* 52 (December 10, 1966): 4, and (February 16, 1967): 4.

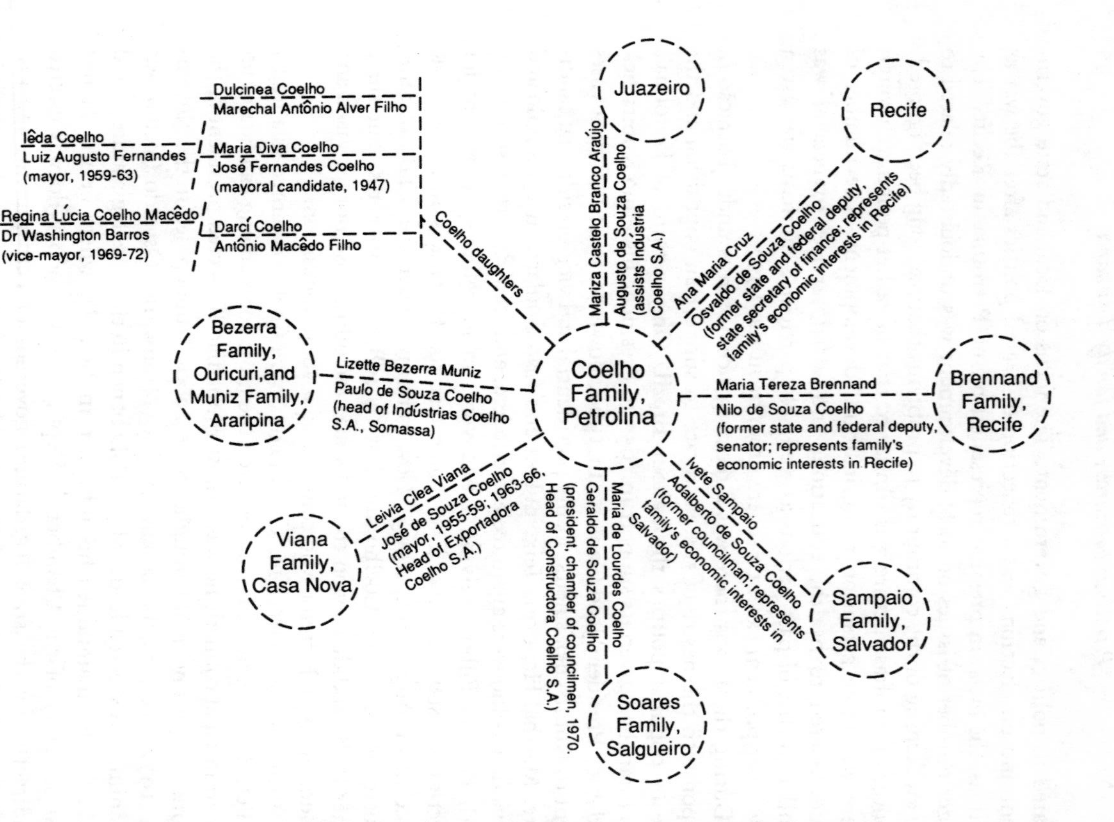

Figure 4.3. Regional influence through family ties: the Coelho family (1970).

culmination of their family's rise to power. Nilo's immediate objective was the construction of a paved road from Petrolina to Recife, and this was completed before the end of his term, partially alleviating the municipality's traditional dependence on Juazeiro and Salvador. In accepting his party's nomination, Nilo announced that his government would be oriented toward "development,"[68] and in fact some development did take place in Petrolina,[69] as a consequence of coordination between the governor and his brother, José, mayor of Petrolina, with such coordination based on family interests. In a speech ending his mayoral term in 1969, José Coelho candidly stated: "We see Petrolina as one family . . . an exemplary family whose members work constructively." Then he listed the accomplishments of the Coelhos during his six years as mayor.[70]

The impact of the Coelho influence and activity was clearly evident in the concerns expressed in the press during the period 1960–70 (Table 4.2).[71] Interest in national and international affairs declined, while emphasis turned to local problems and development (15.2 percent of all issues identified), local civic and social organizations (7.2 percent), and local government and politics (6.3 percent). Interest in industrialization and agricultural development increased, and this interest was accompanied by news of available credit and loans for the financing of new community projects. News on housing was more frequent than in earlier periods, the consequence of the construction of hundreds of *casas populares* or small homes with federal funds under the government of José Coelho. Expanded health and educational facilities and services were also reflected in the press of the period. Matters related to religion and the Church were paid less attention than in previous periods, probably less because of any diminishing prestige of the Church than because of the changing image of clerics in the Northeast with Dom Helder Câmara's emphasis on the need to confront social and economic as well as spiritual problems.

There was considerable attention to problems of the river, including usage of its water for irrigation, construction of dams to control uneven water flows, and solutions to the region's recurrent drought problem. By 1971 the future of the São Francisco River had become an issue of great importance, as a result of the warning given by ecologists that it was drying up. In fact, by the middle of the year river transportation had halted because the low water level made travel precarious. Because the interior was dependent on hydroelectric power generated at Paulo Afonso

68 Acceptance speech after his nomination by the ARENA party; *O Farol* 52 (September 7, 1966): 1.

69 J. Antônio Avila, "798 desafios ao Governador Nilo Coelho," *O Farol* 52 (February 28, 1967): 1, had identified the road to Recife as the key to Petrolina's future and also called for improvements in education, health, agriculture, housing, and the construction of a military barracks.

70 *O Farol* 54 (February 22, 1969): 1.

71 Actually to August 1971, when this study terminated.

and the key to agricultural development was irrigation with water from the river, the nation's press, technicians, and politicians devoted considerable attention to the issue.[72]

Styles of politics

The structure of family rule in Petrolina is delineated in Figure 4.1. Three families dominated the ruling class at the turn of the century and for years thereafter. The Padilha family, originally from Portugal, had settled in Recife, the state capital. Colonel José Rabelo Padilha's political influence indirectly permeated the patriarchy through the marriages of his children (two with the Souza family, three with the Luz family, and one with the Pombo Coelho family). Only two members of the family, Alcides Padilha (1922–27) and Antônio de Santana Padilha (1930), became mayors, but Colonel Padilha was well represented by sons-in-law Octacilio Nunes de Souza (1916–19) and Pacífico Rodrigues da Luz (1919–22, 1930–36, 1937–45). (See Table 4.4 for the political positions held by the various members of these ruling families.) Another son-in-law, Manoel Francisco de Souza Filho, distinguished himself as a federal deputy. The Padilha family was also closely linked through marriage to the Santana family, whose origins were Spanish. The Santanas' involvement in Petrolina politics was represented by Antônio de Santana Filho (mayor 1912–13, vice mayor 1916–18), Marcelino José de Santana (mayor 1913–16), and Raimundo Santana (mayor 1947, vice mayor 1955–59).

The Souza family gave Petrolina its first mayor, Manoel Francisco de Souza Júnior (1893–95), and a brother, Febrônio Martins de Souza, served as vice mayor during the same period. Octacilio Nunes de Souza broke the dominance of Senator Rosa e Silva in Petrolina politics to emerge as mayor in the period 1916–19. Souza Júnior's son, Souza Filho, was Petrolina's most renowned politician of the Old Republic.[73] Two of Octacilio's brothers, Francisco Febrônio de Souza and João Francisco de Souza Filho, were elected vice mayor (1919–22) and mayor (1928) respectively. Another of Souza Júnior's sons, Nestor, was elected state deputy in 1950. João Ferreira Gomes, whose sister was married to a Souza, was mayor briefly in 1952, and Francisco Raimundo de Souza served as vice mayor from 1952 to 1955. José Padilha de Souza, a son of Octacilio, was elected mayor of Juazeiro (1955–59).

72 The July visit of a commission of Pernambucan state deputies produced a brief report on the situation, which was published in Recife newspapers. A check of major agencies in Petrolina failed to uncover a copy of this report. Few town authorities had read it. Thereafter, little news appeared, the matter apparently having been believed resolved on the state level. Locally, the river continued to drop, and the economy suffered from lack of transportation.

73 Two of the city's major streets are named in their honor.

	Ferreira de Silva family	Amorim family	Coelho family	Souza family	Padilha family	Santana family	Pacífico da Luz family	Cavalcanti family
1893–1930		Colonel Antônio Correia de Amorim C Alfredo Amorim VM (1925 election annulled)	Carolino Rodrigues Coelho VM (1895–98) Lucindo Benício Rodrigues Coelho M (1898–1901) Ulysses Amâncio Rodrigues Coelho VM (1898–1901) Col. Clementino de Souza Coelho VM (1913–16, 1927) Crispaniano Crispim Coelho M (1910–12) Possídio do Nascimento M (1927) João Clementino de Souza Barros VM, M (1928–29) Antônio Coelho (1930)	Manoel Francisco de Souza Júnior M (1893–95) Febrônio Martins de Souza VM (1893–95) Octacilio Nunes de Souza M (1916–19) Francisco Febrônio de Souza VM (1919–22) João Francisco de Souza Filho M (1927–28) Manoel Francisco de Souza Filho FD (1922?–29)	Colonel José Rabelo Padilha (C) Alcides Padilha M (1922–27) Antônio de Santana Padilha M (1930)	Antônio de Santana Filho M (1912–13), VM (1916–19) Marcelino José de Santana M (1913–16) Honório Ferreira (married a Santana) M (1930)	Pacífico Rodrigues da Luz M (1919–22)	Agostinho Albuquerque Cavalcanti M (1895–98) José Francisco de Albuquerque Cavalcanti M (1904–7) Colonel José Filgueiras Cavalcanti M (1907–10)
1930–45					João Cardoso da Sá M (1936–37)		Pacífico Rodrigues da Luz M (1930–36; 1937–45)	

	Ferreira de Silva family	Amorim family	Coelho family	Souza family	Padilha family	Santana family	Pacífico da Luz family	Cavalcanti family
1945–60	João Ferreira da Silva M (1947–51) José Almeida da Silva M (1952–55)		José de Souza Coelho M (1955–59) Luiz Augusto Fernandes M (1959–63)	João Ferreira (sister married a Souza) Gomes M (1952) Francisco Raimundo de Souza VM (1952–55) José Padilha de Souza M (Juazeiro, 1955–59)		Raimundo Santana M (1947), VM (1955–59)		Dr. Nestor Cavalcanti M (1945–46) Joaquim André Cavalcanti M (1947); VM (1947–51)
1961–70			José de Souza Coelho M (1963–69) Washington Barros VM (1969–72)					Diniz de Sá Cavalcanti VM (1959–69)
Interviews	João Ferreira da Silva Antônio Fausto de Sá e Silva João Ferreira da Silva Filho José Almeida da Silva Nilberto Moura Leal Paulo Moura Leal	Plínio José Amorim Ivan Araújo Amorim Manuel Amorim	Josefa de Souza Coelho Augusto de Souza Coelho Adalberto de Souza Coelho Osvaldo de Souza Coelho Nilo de Souza Coelho Paulo de Souza Coelho	José Mário de Souza Nestor de Souza João Ferreira Gomes José Padilha de Souza	Antônio de Santana Padilha	Raimundo Santana Juvenal Santana	Cira Padilha da Luz Guy Padilha da Luz	Diniz de Sá Cavalcanti João Batista Cavalcanti

Geraldo de Souza Coelho
José de Souza Coelho
Luiz Augusto Fernandes
Washington Barros
Maria Wilza Barros
Mary Belgium Barros
Lusinete Pombo Coelho
Antônio Macêdo Filho
Alexandre Macêdo
José Muniz Ramos

Note: C = colonel; M = mayor; VM = vice mayor; SD = state deputy; FD = federal deputy.

The Coelho family had migrated to Petrolina from the interior of Piauí state in the late nineteenth century. Carolino Rodrigues Coelho was vice mayor in 1895–98 and Lucindo Benício Rodrigues Coelho and Ulysses Amâncio Rodrigues Coelho were mayor and vice mayor in 1898–1901. Colonel Clementino de Souza Coelho, as rancher and merchant, was omnipresent in the municipality's politics. Although he was apparently not much interested in public office, he was vice mayor from 1913 to 1916 and vice mayor and mayor briefly in 1927. Relatives who also involved themselves in municipal politics were a brother, João Clementino de Souza Barros (mayor from 1928 to 1930), and Antônio Coelho (mayor in 1930). Also linked to the family were Crispiniano Crispim Coelho (mayor 1910 to 1912) and Possídio de Nascimento (Coelho), a distant relative (mayor 1927).[74]

With Getúlio Vargas in power from 1930 to 1945, Petrolina, like political entities elsewhere in Brazil, became largely dependent on decisions at the national level. Much of the autonomy vested in the municipality by the 1891 constitution was eliminated by Vargas's New State.[75] The municipality continued to be more or less neglected by state and national government alike. Economic development was generated locally and through the local patriarchy's connections with Recife, especially Salvador. During this period local politics were dominated by Pacífico Rodrigues da Luz, who was appointed mayor for the periods 1930–35 and 1937–45. An effort to democratize politics resulted in elections in 1935, and Cardoso da Sá was elected mayor, serving briefly from 1936 to 1937.

With the end of the Vargas government in 1945, there began a long struggle to consolidate political power in Petrolina. This challenge was taken up by the sons of Colonel Clementino Coelho. One son, Nilo, was elected a Pernambucan state deputy in January 1947 and a federal deputy in October 1950. Another son, Gercino, was elected Bahian state deputy. A third son, José, won a seat on the municipal council in October 1947. Generally, however, municipal politics in the late 1940s and early 1950s was dominated by a rival clique headed by João Ferreira da Silva ("Barracão"), who was mayor from 1947 to 1951. José Almeida da Silva, his nephew, followed as mayor from 1952 to 1955. A son, Antônio Fausto de Sá e Silva (whose wife, Nilza, was the daughter of Juazeiro's influential Colonel Alfredo Vianna) was elected an alternate deputy in the state assembly in 1954 and in August 1955 took the seat vacated by PTB

74 Possídio de Nascimento was married to Carlota Coelho, whose father, Raul Coelho, was the son of Colonel José Crispiano Rodrigues Coelho Brandão (see *O Farol* 41 [October 29, 1955]: 4). During the formative period of Petrolina's history, the latter had been responsible for a political split, which resulted in the separation of the frequesia of Petrolina from Santa Maria de Boa Vista (see Cavalcanti, "Frequesia").

75 Interview with Antônio Pessoa Leite, municipal judge, on June 1, 1971.

deputy Clodomir Morais.[76] Antônio Fausto de Sá e Silva won a seat on the municipal council in 1959 but lost the race for mayor by a wide margin in 1963. His brother, João Ferreira da Silva Filho, was an unsuccessful candidate for state deputy in 1958 and 1962. These defeats signified the end of the temporary rule of the Silva family.

The complete dominance of the Coelhos over Petrolina politics was represented by José de Souza Coelho's terms as mayor from 1955 to 1959 and from 1963 to 1969. During the interim, Luiz Augusto Fernandes, a young engineer from Rio who had married into the Coelho family, served as mayor, and in 1969 the Coelhos won the mayoralty and the vice mayoralty with the election of Simão Amorim Durando, a manager of their local Mercedes-Benz agency, and Dr. Washington A. F. Barros, who had married into the family. Another son of Colonel Clementino, Adalberto, won a seat on the municipal council (in October 1955) and so did brothers José (in August 1959) and Geraldo (in August 1963 and November 1968). In November 1972 Geraldo was elected mayor, while Augusto Coelho received the highest vote total in winning a seat on the city council. Outside the municipality, the family was represented by Nilo de Souza Coelho as state and federal deputy and, between 1967 and 1971, as governor of Pernambuco. A brother, Osvaldo, was elected state deputy in 1958 and federal deputy in 1967 (although he chose instead to remain with Nilo as state secretary of finance). Luiz Augusto Fernandes joined the government in the key position of coordinating secretary. Their four years in control of state politics brought innumerable benefits to Petrolina and especially to Coelho economic interests, which represented a near monopoly over the municipality. A paved road from Recife to Petrolina was opened, and a new port, bus depot, educational center, and luxury hotel were constructed. Credits for agricultural commerce and industry became readily available to those with money (principally the Coelhos and their allies, along with a few former rivals who now chose to compromise their politics and reap the benefits of their financial interests).

The Coelhos had consolidated their power in a variety of ways. First, after Colonel Clementino died (in an automobile accident in June 1952), his sons decided not to divide but to consolidate the family wealth and to use it as a springboard to gain control over local commerce and to expand their interests in agriculture and industry. Second, they moved quickly to take advantage of the specialized education their father had provided them.[77] With a university degree in economics, Paulo took charge of the family's industrial complex and was joined later by Augusto, who chose

76 *O Farol* 40 (August 20, 1955): 1. Antônio Fausto's activity in the state legislature was covered by *O Farol* 41 (September 30, 1955): 4.

77 That education, however, had been undertaken at the insistence of their mother (interview with Josefa de Souza Coelho, September 7, 1971).

not to practice his profession as a physician (that task was left for Washington Barros, who became head of the local hospital and later regional director of state health services) but to dedicate much of his time to civic and voluntary organizations, such as the Associação Petrolinense de Amparo à Maternidade e Infância (APAMI) and the Casa de Criança. Trained as an engineer, Geraldo, with the assistance of Luiz Augusto Fernandes, directed the family's construction firm, while José managed the commercial segment of the family empire. Adalberto, with a university degree in economics, managed the family's affairs in Salvador, while Osvaldo, with a degree in law, and Nilo, another nonpracticing physician, remained in Recife to protect the family's political and economic interests. Third, the Coelhos expanded their regional influence through marriages into families of political and economic importance. Figure 4.2 reveals these important family ties. Thus, political support might be forthcoming from the Bezerra family in Ouricuri, the Muniz family of Araripina and Alagôas (José Muniz Ramos, a former lawyer and manager of the Coelho industries, was elected a state deputy in 1970), the Viana family in Casa Nova (related to former [1967–71] governor of Bahia, Luiz Viana Filho), and the Soares family, long prominent in Salgueiro. Nilo and Osvaldo married into influential Recife families, while Adalberto's ties were to a Salvadorian family. Augusto symbolically linked Juazeiro to Coelho interests with his marriage into the Castelo Branco and Araújo families of Juazeiro and Casa Nova.[78]

Having consolidated their dominance over the municipality and through marriage extended their regional influence, the Coelhos ultimately assumed executive leadership over Pernambuco government. For the first time in its history, Petrolina emerged as a major center of state politics. How Nilo de Souza Coelho actually became governor is subject to speculation. Although he was a well-known politician in Recife circles, he

78 Details on these marriages are in *O Farol:* for Augusto Coelho, see 50 (January 23, 1965): 1; for Adalberto, see 50 (April 30, 1965): 1; for Osvaldo Coelho, see 45 (January 30, 1960): 1. In 1968, Governor Nilo Coelho awarded a medal of merit to Colonel Veremundo Soares, political chief and industrialist of Salgueiro and head of the family into which Geraldo Coelho had married (*O Farol* 54 [September 7, 1968]: 2). In 1962 there was an attempt to assassinate the father of Paulo Coelho's wife – Fernando Bezerra, political chief of Ouricuri, leader of the local PSD and mayor (1933, 1935–37, and 1945) (*O Farol* 47 [March 24, 1962]: 1). Tereza Christina Leal de Serejo refers to the "new oligarchy" as representing a "modern colonelism" and suggests they had achieved "collegial domination," a term derived from Jean Blondel, *As condições da vida política no estado da Paraíba* (Rio de Janeiro: Fundação Getúlio Vargas, 1957); cited in Serejo, "Coronéis sem patente: a modernização conservadora no sertão pernambucano" (Niterói: Master's Thesis, Instituto de Ciências Humanas e Filosofia, Centro de Estudos Gerais, Universidade Federal Fluminense, 1979), p. 88. See for family influence in recent years, Ricardo Maia, "Sucessão em família: os Maia da Paraíba, querem eleger seu terceiro governador no estado," *Veja* (September 1, 1982): 28–29.

was at the same time suspect for his *sertanejo* allegiances. His rise to power was probably due to the influence of then president Humberto de Alencar Castelo Branco, who had served as commander of the Fourth Army, located in the Northeast. As president after the 1964 intervention, Castelo Branco had tolerated direct elections for some governorships in 1965, but opposition victories, especially in the state of Guanabara, had embarrassed the regime and prompted an abrupt and arbitrary change in legislation. Thus governors in 1967 were indirectly elected by state legislatures, usually with the endorsement of Castelo Branco and the military-dominated federal government. According to one version, Castelo Branco first met Nilo in the workshop of the well-known Pernambuco painter and ceramicist, Francisco Brennand (Nilo was married to a Brennand). Thereafter, Nilo, then a federal deputy in Brasília, lunched weekly with Castelo Branco, and at election time the president "had a decisive role in the selection of Nilo."[79]

As governor, Nilo de Souza Coelho was able to cement his political ties, especially in the interior. After his four years in office, the post reverted to an unknown, Eraldo Gueiros, who also had been hand-picked by the military and who promised to redirect the state's attention to Recife and to the problems of sugar plantation owners. Evidence of Nilo's political strength and that of his allies in the interior was evident soon after Gueiros's assumption of office and his selection of two leaders to rule over the state legislature on behalf of the Aliança Renovadora Nacional (ARENA) party. One of those leaders was Felipe Coelho, who, despite his allegiance to the ARENA party and his marriage to the sister of the wife of Paulo de Souza Coelho of Petrolina, vigorously campaigned against the family during several visits to the city in 1970. The Petrolina opposition to the Coelho family distributed leaflets manifesting "the demands of a free Petrolina" on behalf of "a different Coelho." Among these demands were "the elimination of dominant feudalism," "the extinguishing of an exclusive dominant group," and "the liberation of Petrolina."[80]

Opposition to Gueiros's selection of leaders was manifested by a majority of ARENA state deputies, who signed a statement in late April urging the governor to name two additional ones, one of whom was José Muniz

79 Paulo Fernando Craveiro, "Ponto de encontro," *Jornal do Commercio* (July 23, 1970). Craveiro was secretary of Casa Civil in the Coelho government. There were several other indications of Nilo's relationship with Castelo Branco. The president was unable to attend Nilo's tenth wedding anniversary celebration in Brasília during May 1964 but sent flowers to Maria Tereza, Nilo's wife (*O Farol* 49 [May 31, 1964]: 1); he did not attend a dinner offered by Nilo Coelho in his honor on July 2 (*O Farol* 49 [July 25, 1964]: 1), but his presence was noted at another dinner in Nilo's home during June 1965 (*O Farol* 50 [June 30, 1965]: 1, 4).

80 See "Mandamentos do Petrolinense livre," distributed by "friends of Felipe Coelho in Petrolina," 1970.

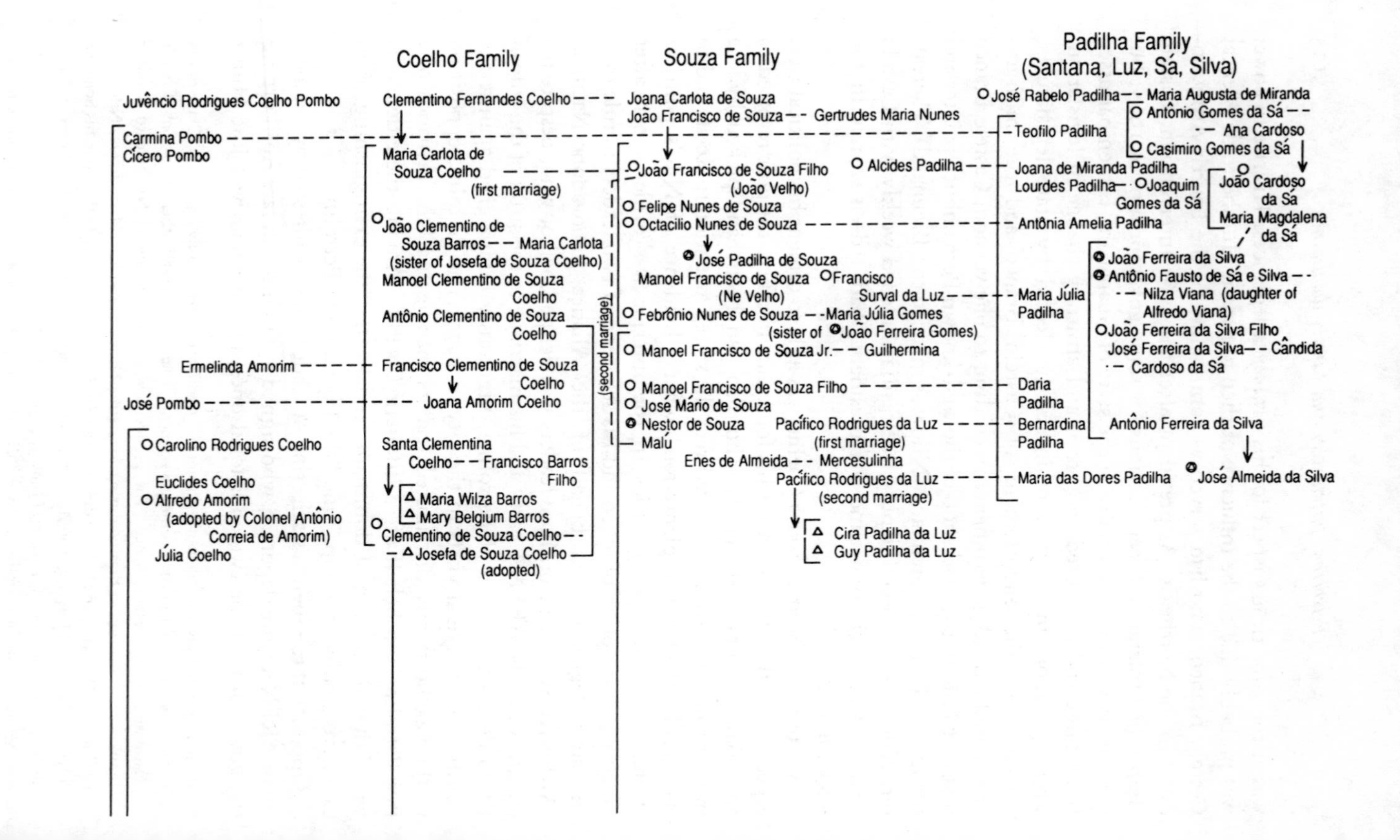

Coelho Family
Souza Family
Padilha Family
(Santana, Luz, Sá, Silva)
Juvêncio Rodrigues Coelho Pombo
Clementino Fernandes Coelho
Joana Carlota de Souza
João Francisco de Souza
Gertrudes Maria Nunes
José Rabelo Padilha
Maria Augusta de Miranda
Antônio Gomes da Sá
Ana Cardoso
Casimiro Gomes da Sá
Carmina Pombo
Cícero Pombo
Teofilo Padilha
Maria Carlota de Souza Coelho
(first marriage)
João Francisco de Souza Filho
(João Velho)
Alcides Padilha
Joana de Miranda Padilha
Lourdes Padilha
Joaquim Gomes da Sá
João Cardoso da Sá
Maria Magdalena da Sá
Felipe Nunes de Souza
Octacilio Nunes de Souza
Antônia Amelia Padilha
João Clementino de Souza Barros
Maria Carlota
(sister of Josefa de Souza Coelho)
José Padilha de Souza
João Ferreira da Silva
Antônio Fausto de Sá e Silva
Nilza Viana (daughter of Alfredo Viana)
Manoel Clementino de Souza Coelho
Manoel Francisco de Souza
(Ne Velho)
Francisco Surval da Luz
Maria Júlia Padilha
Antônio Clementino de Souza Coelho
(second marriage)
Febrônio Nunes de Souza
Maria Júlia Gomes
(sister of João Ferreira Gomes)
João Ferreira da Silva Filho
José Ferreira da Silva
Cândida Cardoso da Sá
Manoel Francisco de Souza Jr.
Guilhermina
Ermelinda Amorim
Francisco Clementino de Souza Coelho
Manoel Francisco de Souza Filho
Daria Padilha
José Pombo
Joana Amorim Coelho
José Mário de Souza
Nestor de Souza
Pacífico Rodrigues da Luz
(first marriage)
Bernardina Padilha
Antônio Ferreira da Silva
Carolino Rodrigues Coelho
Santa Clementina Coelho
Francisco Barros Filho
Malú
Enes de Almeida
Mercesulinha
Euclides Coelho
Pacífico Rodrigues da Luz
(second marriage)
Maria das Dores Padilha
José Almeida da Silva
Alfredo Amorim
(adopted by Colonel Antônio Correia de Amorim)
Maria Wilza Barros
Mary Belgium Barros
Clementino de Souza Coelho
Cira Padilha da Luz
Guy Padilha da Luz
Júlia Coelho
Josefa de Souza Coelho
(adopted)

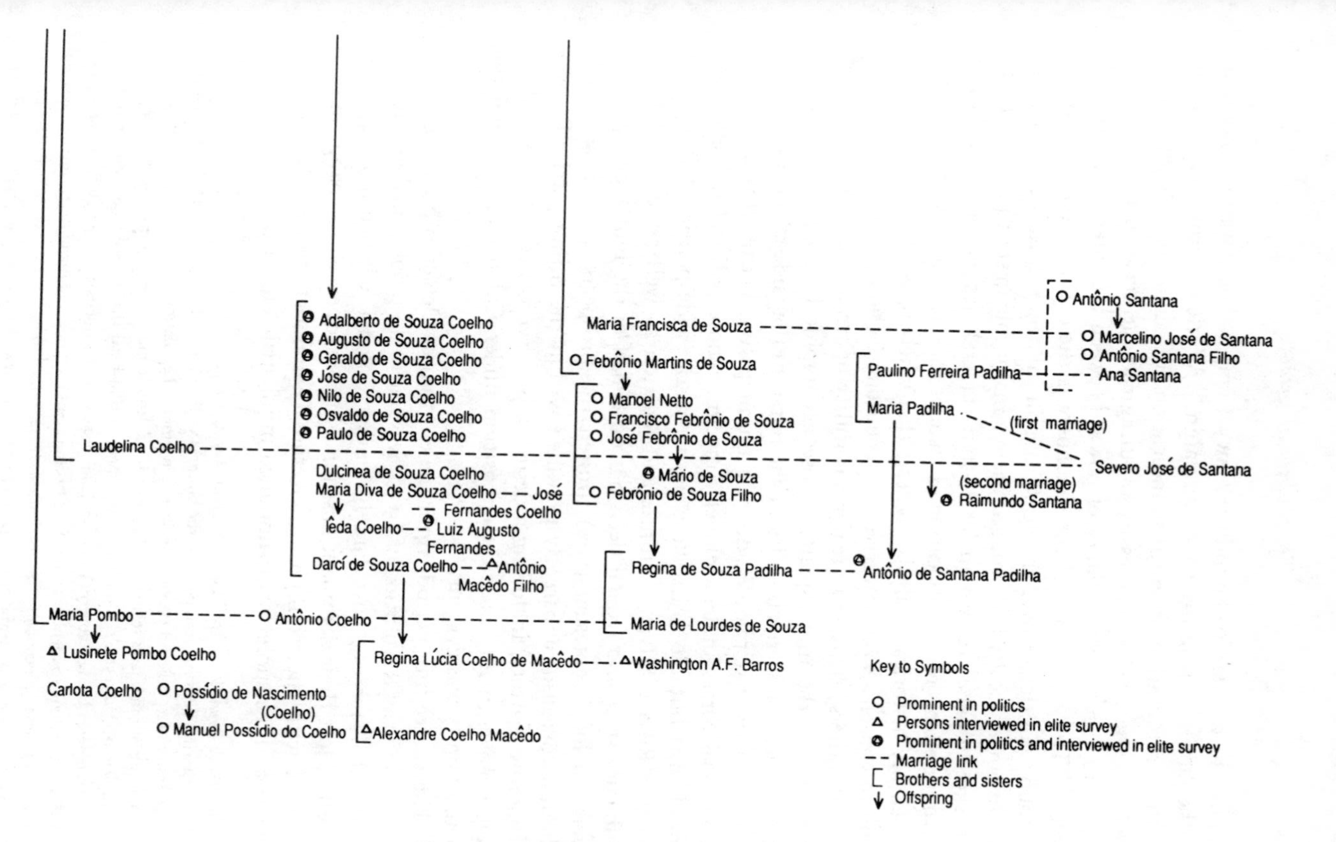

Figure 4.4. Family ties of power holders, Petrolina.

Ramos, the former Coelho industry lawyer who had been warmly endorsed by the family during his 1970 campaign.[81] While Gueiros refused to do so, the confrontation provided an indication of Coelho strength at the state level and the probable necessity of an agreement between the two state groups to ensure some balance of power between the interior and coastal forces.[82] The ascendancy of the Coelhos was the culmination of efforts of Petrolina politicians over the years to gain influence in Recife; consolidation of power locally had brought them a major role in state politics. Table 4.5 sketches the changes in local–state–federal ties over time and their apparent effects on the allocation of state or federal resources to meet local needs. My historical analysis suggests that where opposing political forces achieve consensus on objectives or when one faction achieves dominance over all others, there is a greater possibility of attracting state and federal attention to the municipality whose geographical isolation and lack of communication were obstacles in the pursuit of outside resources.

During its first two decades as a municipality, Petrolina was ruled by traditional forces under Colonel Amorim, whose political influence was largely attributable to his close ties with statewide political forces under Senator Rosa e Silva. Its hinterland location as well as its inability to influence state and federal decisions on behalf of the municipality (there were no local representatives) limited the prospects for assistance. Although consensus apparently prevailed within the ruling patriarchy over economic matters, including a desire to preserve vested interests under a stable government, political opposition under Colonel Padilha and the Souza family was evident.

The succeeding period, from the election of Octacilio Nunes de Souza in 1916 to the Revolution of 1930, was one of deep political division. The traditional forces, now largely under Colonel Clementino de Souza Coelho, lost their dominant position as a consequence of a change in state politics with the triumph of Governor Dantas Barreto. While Nunes de Souza and his successors maintained municipal control for a decade or so,

81 *Diário de Pernambuco*, April 29, 1971, and May 2, 1971.

82 In assessing Pernambucan politics, the business weekly *Visão* (March 29, 1971): 39–40, noted the necessity of a "peaceful coexistence" between groups. Legislation of the late 1960s prevented the running of candidates related to the governor, a definite hindrance to immediate Coelho political ambitions. However, the military government also insisted that there be no criticism of former governments by new governments – a definite asset for the Coelhos. Although Recife newspapers did not hesitate to identify faults of the Coelho administration and many Recife intellectuals with whom I came into contact were also critical, there seemed to be some consensus (partially based on an extensive governmental campaign to promote the "new" Northeast) that progress and development had indeed become realities. The influential weekly *Manchete* credited Nilo with "the miracle of Pernambuco" – the consequence of new industry, road building, educational improvements, and reforms in the secretariat of finance (under the direction of Osvaldo de Souza Coelho) ("O milagre de Pernambuco," *Manchete* 992 [April 24, 1971]: 109–113). These changes were outlined by Osvaldo Coelho in a speech reprinted in *O Farol* 54 (April 15, 1969): 1.

	Municipal consensus–conflict	Position of "traditional" tendency	Position of "popular" tendency	Prospects for state or federal assistance for municipal projects
1893–1916	Traditional faction dominant, dependent on and aligned with statewide politics under Senator Rosa e Silva	Dominant under Colonel Amorim	Harboring latent political dissent but collaborative in defense of economic interests under Colonel Padilha and elements of the Souza family	Fair: municipality weak at state and federal levels
1916–30	Deep conflict with popular faction dominant	Politically effective 1927–30, under Clementino de Souza Coelho and Deputy Souza Filho	Politically dominant 1916–27 under Octacilio Nunes de Souza in alliance with statewide forces under Governor Dantas Barreto	Fair: little assistance obtained
1930–45	Popular tendency in political control with persistent political divisions based on dissident economic interests	Politically ineffective, with continuing substantial economic influence under Colonel Clementino de Souza Coelho and other economic interests	Politically dominant under Luz and Sá governments	Potentially good: popular faction aligned with Vargas Revolution, but municipality largely ignored for lack of effective influence at state and federal levels
1945–55	Deep political conflict with popular faction nominally in control	In the minority, but powerful economically with state and federal influence through Coelho family	Politically in control under João Ferreira da Silva, supported by small commercial and professional interests, but unsuccessful in efforts to achieve state influence	Poor: popular tendency unable to mobilize large-scale assistance at state and federal levels
1955–70	Traditional faction dominant and fully in control	Exercising monopoly of municipal political economy and influence at state and federal levels	Extremely weak but presenting latent opposition	Good to excellent: increase of state and federal resources for municipal projects

Petrolina continued to favor the Rosistas at the state level. This ambivalence seemed to cripple the municipality's chances for gaining favor from state and even federal governments, and the resulting impasse may have provoked Deputy Souza Filho to side with the traditional forces under Colonel Clementino. This alliance signified a realignment of local and state traditional forces, and Souza Filho's state and federal prominence served the municipality's interests. After Colonel Clementino joined with João Francisco de Souza Filho to challenge the 1925 election of Cardoso da Sá and Alfredo Amorim, the local traditional forces under the guidance of Deputy Souza Filho took over the political reins. Under such conditions, prospects for state and federal assistance were improved, although there is little evidence that Petrolina benefited in any material way.

The split within the Souza family was obviously significant for the future fortunes of the Coelho family. Nunes de Souza's faction was favored by the revolutionary regime of Vargas from 1930 to 1945. Again the shift and realignment of municipal with state and federal governments under this "popular" tendency offered improved prospects for assistance. Although Mayor Luz also had had political experience as a state deputy during the 1920s, Petrolina seems to have profited little from the tie. In fact, dependency on state and federal governments was ensured not only by the centralization of politics at the national level, but also by the continuing, now somewhat latent political economic differences at the local level.

These deep-rooted divisions became fully manifest with the liberalization of politics after 1945. Dissent from the Luz government had become apparent in the early 1940s, but new leadership emerged to lead the "popular" tendency under João Ferreira da Silva. His narrow victory for mayor (over a Coelho) signified limited power. Further, his forces held only a slim majority (five of nine seats) in the municipal council and were able to win only an alternate seat in the state legislature. After intervention by the state governor, another Silva emerged as the conciliation choice of the Silva and Coelho forces.[83] At the same time, a slate of compromise unity candidates was elected to the municipal council.

The Coelho dominance at the local level was assured in the family's near sweep (eight of nine council seats and the mayorship) of elections in 1955. Statewide, the family achieved prominence through the PSD, an important party nationally as well. Nilo de Souza Coelho, who was to be the family's first representative in a state office, had attempted as early as July 1946 to direct the attention of Pernambucan officials to Petrolina's problems. In a press interview he had lamented that for years the municipality "had existed in obscurity, unknown to the people and governments of

83 Interview with José Almeida da Silva, July 20, 1971. He served as mayor from 1952 to 1955.

Pernambuco." He denounced the unfilled promises of the Vargas government and called upon Pernambuco to awaken to the reality that Petrolina's "greatest social and economic influence is still Bahian."[84] Nilo's term as a state deputy from 1947 to 1951, his emergence thereafter as a federal deputy, and his acceptance of a post as secretary of finance in the Etelvino Lins government (Petrolina gave Etelvino and the PSD 3,270 votes in contrast to the opposition UDN's 9), gave the Coelho family and the traditional tendency substantial influence outside the municipality. Their subsequent success, however, was also assured by complete control over the political economy of the municipality.

Interestingly, when in July 1971 a delegation of more than twenty state deputies, a federal deputy, and a senator visited Petrolina to study the problems of the São Francisco River,[85] no major Juazeiro political official attended to discuss the very serious problems of drought, river transportation and control, and irrigation. While Petrolina's representative, Honório Rocha, was delivering major speeches on these problems in the state legislature, his Bahian counterpart was publicly silent. A week earlier, in an interview with the Bahian press, Juazeiro's mayor had emphasized tourism as the major regional problem and expressed little concern for the river that for years had been the basis for his city's prosperity. This conspicuous failure to manifest concern over a local problem that had captured national attention may have been related to political differences between his majority municipal faction and an antagonistic state governor.

These contrasting reactions to a regional problem suggest a corollary to the proposition just discussed – that political feuding within the ruling class or a serious split between ruling political and economic sectors will undermine efforts to win state or federal influence. This counterproposition would seem to have applied not only to contemporary Juazeiro but also, as we have just seen, to Petrolina during most of the past half-century. Until the rise of the Coelhos, Petrolina generally remained isolated, lacking resources to resolve problems locally, and this situation was not necessarily always the consequence of geographical location and lack of roads and communications. The attention of local politicians was more often directed to healing divisions or maintaining support on the home front than to mobilizing state and federal governments to the problems of the backlands.

84 Interview with Nilo de Souza Coelho, reported in *O Farol* 31 (July 9, 1946): 1, 7.

85 Within a week, some $200 million had been promised for the construction of dams and other facilities (*Jornal do Commercio* [July 21, 1971]).

Figure 5.1. João Ferreira Gomes, editor of the weekly *O Farol* since 1915. Photo 1984.

Figure 5.2. Governor Nilo Coelho during visit to Petrolina celebration, 1971.

5

The ruling class and the polity

Two strains of rule predominate in the history of Brazilian politics. A centralist tendency prevailed in the colonial and imperial periods: first under the control of governors who reported to the Portuguese monarchy; then directly under the Portuguese queen, who in 1807 had fled in the face of Napoleon's invading army to Rio de Janeiro; and later under the empire from 1822 to 1889. The other tendency was toward a dispersion of power and autonomy at the regional and local levels. During the colonial and imperial periods this decentralizing tendency was the consequence of local loyalties and the difficulty of long-distance communication. According to one interpretation, although the empire was defined strictly as a unitary state, "control over local power structure by the central government, as expressed through the administrative system, was negligible."[1]

The constitution of 1891 promulgated a federal system and the delegation of some power to the states. While the economy retained its agrarian orientation (and its dependence on foreign markets), politics revolved around the regional and local political bosses known as colonels. A system of personal alliances between these local leaders and the state governors reinforced the autonomy of the states in the face of presidential authority at the national level. Alliances between the governors of the states of São Paulo and Minas Gerais determined presidential rule during much of the Old Republic period. The central government was weak, and state administrators, "at the service of rural patriarchs," took "priority over an only partially effective federal administration."[2]

From 1930, when Getúlio Vargas came to power, until his resignation in 1945, the government functioned as a centralized system. The constitution of 1934 restored the federal republic in name only, and absolute power was formally imposed in 1937 under the New State.[3] Under Vargas,

1 Lawrence S. Graham, *Civil Service Reform in Brazil: Principles versus Practice* (Austin: University of Texas Press, 1968), p. 18.

2 Ibid., p. 21.

3 Details of this period are in Karl Loewenstein, *Brazil under Vargas* (New York: Macmillan, 1942). For this period and general background of administrative aspects of Brazilian government, see Graham, *Civil Service Reform;* Frank P. Sherwood, *Institutionalizing the Grass Roots in Brazil: A Study*

Figure 5.3. Vaqueiros or cowboys of the sertão. Festivities in Petrolina, 1971.

a series of administrative reforms was instituted to ensure control and efficient government. The attempt to improve the civil service was largely unsuccessful, however, and patronage, overstaffing, and other traditional problems continued to prevail.[4]

The constitution of 1946 signified a return to federalism and ensured the evolution of a variety of political parties whose activities embraced clan and oligarchical politics at the local and state levels and populism and personalism at the national level. Patronage characterized relations between the president and the party system. In the administrative system, jobs were distributed along traditional lines to persons and groups in the dominant classes who contributed electoral support and along new populist-oriented lines to benefit urban labor and the lower middle class, whose support was institutionalized in political machines.

After 1964 the military regime gradually abandoned the formalities of the 1946 constitution through intervention in the affairs of the states and municipalities with the intention of undermining their autonomy. The

in Comparative Local Government (San Francisco: Chandler, 1967); and Robert T. Daland, *Brazilian Planning: Development Politics and Administration* (Chapel Hill: University of North Carolina Press, 1967).

4 Loewenstein, *Brazil under Vargas*, pp. 102–105.

actions of the military were directed also to opening the new lines of communication from president and party to supportive segments of the masses.

While executive rule has tended to predominate in Brazilian politics, governmental structure theoretically provides for a separation of powers among executive, legislative, and judicial branches. This principle has been applied to national, state, and municipal levels of government. Thus in Juazeiro and Petrolina executive and legislative officers are elected independently and function separately, and the judiciary, in which appointments to office are the rule, maintains some degree of autonomy. In this examination of the role of the ruling classes in the polities of the two communities, we shall look first at the mayor's office and the local, state, and national agencies that provide services to the citizens of Juazeiro and Petrolina, then at legislative offices and activities, and finally at the judiciary and the military police.

The mayor's office

Modifications of the procedures for the election of the president and state governors followed the military intervention of 1964. The regime resorted to indirect elections through Congress or state legislatures, where candidates generally were assured victory by belonging to the government's majority party. As we have seen, indirect elections made Luiz Viana Filho and Nilo Coelho governors, respectively, of Bahia and Pernambuco. Both men were sons of families that had ruled in Juazeiro and Petrolina. Long neglected by state and federal administrations, the two municipalities from 1967 to 1971 became more dependent on policies at the state and federal levels. One political writer in Brazil has noted, however, that the indirect election of governors makes the mayors the most visible elected officials.[5] Although there is little evidence that mayors had in fact become highly visible in state politics (those in the large cities were appointed by state governors), the role of mayor was conspicuous in Juazeiro and Petrolina. In my interviews with members of the ruling classes, 44 percent ranked the mayoralty as the most important of the community political and economic institutions (Table 5.1). Of those interviewed, 82 percent considered the office of mayor as very important. This recognition may be due to the patriarchal heritage that personalizes leadership in these communities.

I interviewed every mayor and vice mayor (Juazeiro did not have such an office) since 1960 and most since 1945, as well as a few from before World War II (Table 5.2). Two of the mayors in Juazeiro and 5 mayors and 2 vice mayors in Petrolina were members of the top echelon of the ruling

5 Riordan Roett, *Brazil: Politics in a Patrimonial Society* (Boston: Allyn and Bacon, 1972), p. 11.

Table 5.1. *Ruling-class views (N = 118) on the importance of institutional groups in Juazeiro and Petrolina (%)*

	Degree of importance				
Institution or group	Most important	Very important	Not so important	Unimportant	No opinion
Mayoralty	44.1	82.2	13.6	3.4	0.8
Banks	13.6	86.4	11.9	1.7	
Businessmen	11.0	80.5	16.1	1.7	1.7
Largest firms	9.3	80.5	14.4	3.4	1.7
Out-of-town firms		33.1	9.3	48.3	9.3
Civic organizations	9.3	72.0	20.3	5.9	1.8
Voters	5.9	66.1	18.6	14.5	0.8
Municipal council	4.2	64.4	26.3	9.3	
Labor leaders	1.7	48.3	23.7	25.4	2.6
None	0.9				

classes – that is, they were among the 39 power holders identified by the panels of community members in the first phase of my study. The 16 mayors and vice mayors I interviewed constituted about one-seventh of the 118 persons interviewed in the second phase, although more than a fifth of Petrolina respondents had served in the office. Most of the mayors and vice mayors were businessmen, although 2 were ranchers, 2 professionals, 1 a newspaper editor, and 1 the director of a radio station. Five of the mayors and vice mayors and the former governor from Petrolina were associated with Coelho business interests.

Half the mayors had had only a primary school education; more than half of them were merchants, nearly a third professional people (Table 5.3).[6] All the mayors were affiliated with the Aliança Renovadora Nacional (ARENA), a sign of the control the military government exercised over local politics; prior to 1964, most mayors had been members of the Partido Social Democrático (PSD).

The attitudes of these and other leaders toward their communities are shown in Table 5.4. The mayors were less enthusiastic than others about schools and housing and were hesitant to praise municipal government's responsiveness to the people. Like the others, they expressed favorable impressions of community pride and spirit, citizen involvement, the spirit

6 Sherwood, *Institutionalizing the Grass Roots*, pp. 100–101, reports of mayors surveyed throughout Brazil in 1958 that nearly a third were farmers. Many of the mayors of Juazeiro and Petrolina also were farmers, but generally this was a secondary occupation. About a fifth of the mayors in the 1958 survey were retail merchants, whereas in Juazeiro and Petrolina most mayors were merchants but usually associated with large industry.

Table 5.2. *Political position in executive, legislative, and judicial branches of polity and occupation*

	Juazeiro[a]	Petrolina[b]
Executive	Mayor, ex-councilman (businessman)[cd]	Mayor (manager, Coelho firm)[c]
	Ex-mayor, (director, Radio Juazeiro)[cd]	Vice mayor (director, regional health service)[c]
	Ex-mayor (businessman)	Ex-mayor, ex-councilman (businessman, rancher)[c]
	Ex-mayor (businessman)	Ex-mayor, ex-councilman (accountant, Coelho firm)[c]
	Ex-mayor, ex-councilman (rancher, chief of police)[d]	Ex-mayor (engineer, Coelho firm)[c]
	Tax collector[d]	Ex-mayor, ex-councilman (manager, Coelho firm)[c]
	Director, state schools (educator)[c]	Ex-mayor, ex-councilman (editor, newspaper)
	Director, municipal schools (educator)[c]	Ex-mayor (civil service)
	Director, agrarian university (educator)	Ex-vice mayor (businessman)[cd]
	Director, high school (educator)	Ex-vice mayor (rancher)
	Director, SUVALE (engineer)[c]	Ex-governor (businessman, Coelho firm) (ex-federal deputy, state deputy)
	Director, health service	Director, state schools (educator)
		Director, university (educator)
		Director, high school (educator)
		Director, SUDENE (agronomist)
Legislative	State deputy (military policy)[c]	Federal deputy (businessman, Coelho firm, ex-state deputy)[c]
	State deputy, ex-councilwoman (politician)[c]	State deputy (educator)[c]
	Councilman (small businessman)[cd]	State deputy (lawyer, Coelho firm)
	Councilman (director, postal service)[d]	Councilman (engineer, Coelho firm)[cd]
	Councilman (lawyer)	Councilman (dentist)[d]
	Councilman (official, Companhia de Navegação)[cd]	Councilman (dentist)[d]
	Councilman (official, Companhia de Navegação)[cd]	Councilwoman (municipal civil servant)[d]
	Councilman (municipal civil servant)[d]	Councilman (state tax collector)
	Councilman (farmer)	Councilman (small businessman)[d]
	Councilman (school director, lawyer)[c]	Councilman (farmer)[d]
	Councilman (small businessman)	Councilman (rancher)

Table 5.2. *(cont.)*

	Juazeiro[a]	Petrolina[b]
Legislative (cont.)	Councilman (farmer)[c]	Councilman (rancher)
	Councilman (small businessman)	Ex-councilman (businessman)
	Councilman (municipal civil servant)	Ex-councilman (small businessman)
	Ex-councilman (agronomist)[c]	Ex-councilman (editor, newspaper)[d]
	Ex-councilman (director, sports association)[e]	Ex-councilman (businessman, Coelho firm)
	Ex-councilman (state civil servant)[c]	Ex-councilman (small businessman)[d]
	Ex-councilman (farmer)[d]	Ex-councilman (tax collector)[d]
	Ex-councilman (artisan)[e]	Ex-councilman (businessman, rancher)[d]
	Ex-councilman (civil servant)[e]	Future councilman (businessman, Coelho firm)[c]
	Ex-councilman (furniture mfg.)	Party executive (physician)[e]
	Ex-councilman (businessman)	Party executive (tax collector)[d]
	Ex-councilman (physician)	Party executive (businessman)[d]
	Party executive (small businessman)[e]	Party executive (civil service)[d]
	Party executive (small businessman)[d]	
	Party executive (small businessman)[d]	
	Party executive (lawyer)[d]	
	Party executive (small businessman)[d]	
	Party executive (small businessman)[d]	
	Party executive (small businessman)[cd]	
	Party executive (engineer)[d]	
	Party executive (farmer)[d]	
	Party executive (physician)[cd]	
Judicial		Judge (lawyer)
		Judge (lawyer)

[a] Total, 46 (executive, 12; legislative, 34) (46 of 66 identified and interviewed; 13 of 23 in upper echelon of ruling class).

[b] Total, 41 (executive, 15; legislative, 24; judicial, 2) (41 of 52 identified and interviewed; 12 of 16 in upper echelon of ruling class).

[c] Top echelon of ruling class.

[d] Member, ARENA Executive Committee.

[e] Member, MDB Executive Committee.

Table 5.3. *Biographical profiles of political leaders in Juazeiro and Petrolina (%)*

	Mayors (N = 14)	Municipal council members (N = 47)	Party executive committee members (N = 40)
Education			
None	0	4	5
Primary, 1–4 years	0	36	40
Primary, 5–6 years	50	13	8
9 years	0	6	10
High school – complete	7	6	8
University – some	7	2	3
University – complete	22	17	15
Vocational	14	13	10
Other	0	3	1
Occupation			
Professional	29	15	15
Merchant	57	38	38
Industrialist	0	0	2
Farmer	14	13	10
Bureaucrat	0	33	35
Other	0	1	0
Party affiliation after 1964			
ARENA	100	89	85
MDB	0	11	15
Party affiliation before 1964			
UDN	29	11	23
PSD	64	45	35
PTB	0	6	3
PR	0	6	8
PL	0	11	5
PDC	0	6	3
Other	7	5	23

of the big companies, and opportunity for economic advance. Their general feelings about their communities were very good or excellent.

The two incumbent mayors were quite different from each other in character. Born in Juazeiro in 1913 of Arab immigrants, Américo Tanuri had followed in his father's footsteps as a retail merchant. His father had apparently established himself in prominent social circles.[7] His possession

7 In his memoir, Pedro Diamantino, *Juazeiro de minha infância: memórias* (Rio de Janeiro: Imprensa Nacional, 1959), pp. 16–17, refers to a group of prominent persons who frequently gathered together in the "Câmara Alta" (Upper Chamber). These included members of the Vianna, Tôrres, and Melo families as well as Antônio Tanuri. A "Câmara Baixa" (Lower Chamber) also existed, made up of sons of the upper chamber, and included Américo.

Table 5.4. *Attitudes of political leaders toward their communities (%)*

	Mayors (N = 14)			Municipal council members (N = 47)			Party executive committee (N = 40)		
	Excellent	Very Good	Poor	Excellent	Very Good	Poor	Excellent	Very Good	Poor
General feeling about community	36	50	14	36	19	25	28	43	30
Opportunity for economic advancement	43	50	7	60	36	4	60	28	22
Schools	36	36	28	51	43	6	45	48	8
Housing	0	43	57	11	53	36	8	43	49
Community pride and spirit	36	29	35	36	40	24	23	40	37
Citizen involvement	36	36	28	36	49	15	28	43	29
Responsiveness of municipal government	21	29	50	21	40	39	23	30	47
Spirit of big companies	21	50	29	15	62	23	18	48	34

of only an elementary education did not interfere with Américo's recognition in the community, for he became an active leader in the social clubs, the Rotary, and the commercial association. As a politician he headed the Integralist movement of the 1930s and then joined the PSD, which he served faithfully until the 1964 military intervention in Brazilian politics. As a member of the government party, ARENA, he worked closely with local unions and worker's organizations, and apparently these groups contributed to his "popular" victory as mayor in 1962. At the end of his first term in office (1963–67), he described his regime as one that placed the municipality in a position "to move forward with order, efficient and honest work, and above all reaching for social–economic progress which signified nothing more than the satisfaction of the people."[8] Certainly popular aspirations were aroused by Tanuri's rise to power, for he had turned against the Vianna family. Near the end of his term, however, the tide had begun to turn against him. Luiz Viana Filho became governor, and since Américo had supported the previous governor, Antônio Lomanto Júnior, he found himself in opposition to the military-supported forces that controlled Bahian politics.

Simão Amorim Durando was born in 1936 in the nearby city of Afrânio, where he carried on the business interests of his father. During the mid-1950s he established a small business in Petrolina and shortly thereafter was named manager of the Coelho-owned Mercedes-Benz agency. He associated with the Coelhos through the PSD and later the ARENA. He was active in all the city's social clubs, having served them in some executive capacity. Friendly and gregarious, he became the choice of the Coelhos when military legislation prevented family succession in office (José Coelho having served as mayor since 1963). Viewed generally as a puppet of the family, he nevertheless exercised independent judgment in small matters, and in 1972 he was named "Northeast Personality" as the mayor who had most distinguished himself administratively in Pernambuco.[9]

Considerable power was concentrated in the position of mayor. He was expected to employ patronage to ensure the strength of his position and party. He served as a community representative, frequently visiting the state capital, making personal appearances, awarding contracts, and granting favors. Even the relatively few rewards that were granted by the municipal council often depended on the goodwill and interests of the mayor. Two examples will perhaps suffice to illustrate the mayor's importance. In Juazeiro, persons interviewed made it clear that candidates nor-

8 Américo Tanuri, "Mensagem à Câmara de Vereadores: administração Américo Tanuri, 1963–1964" (Juazeiro: Prefeitura Municipal de Juazeiro, 1967), p. 1.

9 *O Farol* 58 (October 20, 1972): 1.

mally bought a large share of their votes, a practice underwritten by wealthy businessmen who wished to ensure stable relations with municipal authorities. The cost of each vote for mayor was five times that for councilman and twice that for state and federal deputies.[10] In Petrolina a slush fund existed in city hall to permit payments to needy persons who could produce a prescription or request from a physician in the local hospital; thus the mayor was viewed as a benefactor and an authority.[11] Although this practice also existed in Juazeiro, fulfillment of the demands of needy people there was complicated by political divisions and rivalries, and it was more common for the needy to beg in the streets.

The mayor thus serves the ruling classes in overseeing a traditional order that pervades all levels of administration in the municipality. The notion of "patrimony" evolves in the literature of Brazilian national politics, being seen first and foremost in the establishment of a centralized bureaucracy during the colonial period and after independence in the maintenance of this bureaucracy.[12] As described by one observer, the term refers to "the creation and maintenance of a highly flexible and paternalistic public order dedicated to its own preservation and the preservation of the unity of the nation-state, whether under imperial, republican, or military tutelage."[13] Another writer attributes the weakness of civic and social organizations to "patrimonialism," which makes "the government the supreme patron of society."[14] This "patrimonialism" is a natural outgrowth of the rural society that historically has profoundly influenced the Brazilian political economy, and it provides stability and support for the nation's ruling class – "the plantation owners and cattle ranchers of the Northeast, the coffee entrepreneurs of São Paulo, and the cattle ranchers of

10 See details in Chapter 3, n. 47.

11 I participated in a survey conducted by the Centro de Estudos dos Menores in two poor districts of Petrolina, which included the question, How would you resolve the problems of Petrolina? In response about half of those interviewed suggested specific projects such as the construction of schools or parks. Of 278 interviewed, however, 123 could only answer that they would "speak with authorities." Probing of this response revealed that the "authorities" were sometimes members of the Coelho family or another employer but more often the mayor (Rosália de Araújo Oliveira, Ronald H. Chilcote, and Padre Pedro Mansueto de Lavor, "Estudo sôbre a juventude em dois bairos de Petrolina," Petrolina: CEMIC, 1971).

12 The best analysis of the establishment and evolution of the Brazilian patrimony is Raymundo Faoro, *Os donos do poder: formação do patronato político brasileiro* (Rio de Janeiro: Editora Globo, 1958).

13 Roett, *Brazil,* p. 29; see pp. 26–32 and 48–56 for a useful synthesis of literature and discussion on the Brazilian patrimony.

14 Philippe C. Schmitter, *Interest Conlflict and Political Change in Brazil* (Stanford: Stanford University Press, 1971), p. 362.

Minas Gerais and Rio Grande do Sul."[15] It has also been seen as underlying a centrist tendency in national politics.[16]

In Juazeiro and Petrolina, the public order functions through a relationship between the local ruling classes and outside state and federal authorities that involves both manipulation by the ruling classes and cooperation by those classes of administrative agencies that are subject to decisions and controls coming from outside the communities.

The 1946 constitution provided for decentralization of administration and allowed for some flexibility and autonomy in adopting an organizational pattern congruent with local needs. Accordingly, "the average municipality in Brazil has a range of functions that are as broad as that of the state with the exception of the police and judiciary."[17] State and federal governments were reluctant to provide the municipalities with sufficient resources to meet local needs, however, and this problem could only be resolved through aggressive lobbying and the exercise of influence outside the community. For this purpose, the Coelho family carefully placed its sons in important positions in Recife and Brasília.

The 1967 constitution reduced the autonomy of municipalities. They were permitted to elect their mayors and councilmen, to collect some taxes, and to organize local affairs according to their needs, but these activities were frequently subject to the close scrutiny of resident military officers as well as officials in the state and federal capitals. Failure to meet financial obligations brought outside intervention. In addition, there were regulations about the scheduling of elections and controls on municipal budgets. While local tax revenues were reduced, in the past many funds had not been allocated and, now, under military rule there were greater possibilities of receiving such funds. However, the agencies established to distribute the state and federal tax revenues carefully audited municipal expenditures, thereby eliminating some of the fiscal malfeasance of local officials that had characterized past administrations.[18] These sorts of controls made it mandatory that local ruling classes consolidate their control

15 Roett, *Brazil*, p. 53.

16 Roett, *Brazil*, pp. 48–49, views "the power of the state" as "more realistic and relevant for contemporary Brazil" than "the power of the local, rural aristocracy"; both seem relevant to an interpretation of contemporary politics in Juazeiro and Petrolina.

17 Diogo Lordello de Mello, *Problemas institucionais do município* (Rio de Janeiro: Instituto Brasileiro de Administração Municipal, 1965), p. 16, cited in Sherwood, *Institutionalizing the Grass Roots*, p. 39, n. 13.

18 For a detailed discussion of changes in municipal government after 1964, see Ivan L. Richardson, "Municipal Government in Brazil: The Financial Dimension," *Journal of Comparative Administration* 1 (1969): 321–343. According to Richardson, the basic change was "from almost total local autonomy in expenditures to detailed central controls."

over municipal politics and seek some input into the selection of personnel appointed to state and federal agencies in the municipalities.

Ruling-class control over administrative agencies within the communities was significant in a number of respects. Control made possible the distribution of jobs, contracts, and privileges as immediate rewards for political support. The establishment of a local political machine provided the means for the promotion of chosen members of the ruling classes toward the higher echelons of politics at the state and national levels. Control also ensured access to federal subsidies, usually in the form of small payments to agencies, for special projects, of which an infinite number are proposed and considered each year. Finally, decisions on the location of government field offices affected the number of jobs available and, consequently, "the more government jobs there are in a municipality, the greater the likelihood of economic well-being."[19]

The major administrative units established in Juazeiro and Petrolina are shown in Table 5.5. A first impression is that the two communities have similar arrays of agencies serving their needs. Upon reflection, however, one recalls that Juazeiro had traditionally been known as the "city of bureaucrats" for the attention it has received from state and federal governments. With Salvador being the nearest coastal outlet for the region, federal agencies tended to locate in Juazeiro. Data on numbers of employees in some of these agencies confirm the suspicion that Juazeiro is very much dependent on federal jobs and resources. In 1969 there were, for example, large numbers of persons employed by the ministries of agriculture (110), health (135), communications (57), and finance (51), and smaller numbers in welfare (33) and mines and energy (18). The Superintendência do Vale do São Francisco (SUVALE) had 157 employees and the Companhia de Navegação do São Francisco, which coordinates river transportation with the assistance of federal subsidies, 436.[20] Corresponding federal agencies, where they existed in Petrolina, were more or less appendages of those in Juazeiro. Although I was unable to obtain data, the numbers employed were clearly only a small fraction of those in the neighboring city. Most important were the internal revenue service, health services, and the Superintendência do Desenvolvimento do Nordeste (SUDENE), and the growth of these agencies had accompanied the rise to power of the Coelho family.

An outside agency of considerable importance for Juazeiro and Petrolina was the revenue service. State and federal agencies existed in each community and, according to one source, "exercised considerable political influ-

19 Sherwood, *Institutionalizing the Grass Roots*, p. 74. Sherwood also discusses the tradition of federal subsidies in Brazil and mentions that in 1964 there were 80,000 amendments to the budget bill, most of them proposals for subsidies.

20 Data obtained from files of CODESF, July 8, 1969.

Table 5.5. *Administrative agencies*

	Juazeiro	Petrolina
Agriculture	IBRA (reform) (F)	COMAPE (mechanization) (S)
	Veterinary post	DPV (vegetables) (S)
		DPA (animals) (S)
		IPEANE (research)
Army, air, and other military	Military police[a] (S)	Military police[a] (S)
		Airport (F)
Communication and transport	DNEF (railroads)[b] (F)	DNEF (railroad)[b] (F)
	DCT (post and telegraph)[b] (S)	EMPETUR (tourism) (S)
	Companhia de Navegação do S. Francisco[a] (F, S, P)	DCT (post and telegraph)[b] (S, F)
	Port Authority[a] (F)	DER (roads) (S)
	Companhia Telefônica do S. Francisco (M, P)	DETRAN (transit)
		Port Authority (F)
		Bus depot
		Companhia Telefónica do S. Francisco (M, P)
Education and culture	Núcleo (elementary)[a] (S)	Núcleo (elementary)[a] (S)
	Colegios (secondary)[a] (S)	Colegios (secondary)[a] (S)
	Dept. of Education and Culture (M)	Municipal library (M)
	Agronomy school[b] (F)	Fundação Educacional (S, M, P)
	MOBRAL (literacy) (F)	CEMIC (youth) (F)
		Teachers' college (S)
		MOBRAL (literacy) (F)
Finance	Internal Revenue Services[a] (F, S)	Internal Revenue Services[a] (F, S)
	Banco do Brasil[a] (F)	Banco do Nordeste do Brasil[a] (F)
	Banco do Estado da Bahia[a] (S)	Banco do Desenvolvimento Econômico do Estado de Pernamburo (S)
		ANCARPE (rural credit)[b] (S)
Industry and commerce		Secretariat of Business, Finance, Production (S)

Table 5.5. *(cont.)*

	Juazeiro	Petrolina
Health	Hospital[b] (S)	Hospital[b] (S)
	INPS[a] (F)	Maternity N.S. das Graças[b] (S, M)
	Maternities (S, M, P)	First aid (S, M)
	DNERU (disease) (F)	FSESP (medical)[b] (F)
	FSESP (medical)[b] (F)	DELPA (wells and water) (S)
	SAAE (water)[b] (S)	Casa da Criança (orphans) (M)
		APAMI (maternity) (M)
		SAAE (water)[b] (S)
		SANEPE (sanitary)[b] (S)
Justice and interior	Courts[a] (F, S)	Courts[b] (F, S)
	Secretariat of Police Security[a] (S)	Secretariat of Police Security[a] (S)
	Transit inspection (S)	
Labor and welfare	IAPM (maritime pensions (F)	IPSEPE (pensions) (S)
	IAPC (business pensions) (S)	IAPC (business pensions) (S)
Mines and energy	CHESF (hydroelectricity)[b] (F)	CERPEL (rural electricity) (M, P)
	Division of Water (F)	CELPE (electricity) (S)
	Irrigation Service (F)	
Planning and development	Centro Regional (M)	CODESF (M)
Special agencies	SUVALE[a] (F)	SUDENE[a] (F)
	IBGE (statistics) (F)	IBGE (F)

Note: P = private, M = municipal, S = state, F = federal
[a]Community dependence very significant.
[b]Community dependence moderately significant.

ence as a sort of economic police." Juazeiro, for instance, during the mid-1960s was second in tax revenue for the state of Bahia. Because the state secretary of finance was directly controlled by Governor Luiz Viana Filho, his liaison to Juazeiro, state deputy Ana Oliveira, could exercise influence among the major businessmen; retail merchant Flávio Silva and industrialist Paulo Campelo, in particular, though not politically conspicuous, quite naturally channeled financial support along the dominant lines of state politics. Early in his term as governor of Pernambuco, it is reported that Nilo Coelho called a local tax inspector to Recife in order to make certain that pressure be exerted on those who opposed the family's interests.[21]

The influence of the Coelhos was significant in correcting the imbalance between the two cities in the distribution of outside resources. At the very least, they were effective in attracting new agencies to Petrolina. As part of a federal program, Petrolina was one of three Pernambuco cities to receive funds for the construction (by the Coelho firm) of 440 homes for the needy.[22] In addition, a sewage system was built to serve the city center, and the riverfront, where the prominent members of the ruling class had their homes. Improvements in municipal services tended not to benefit the poor and working classes of the community, however. Several of the outlying districts had no water, no sewage, no electricity, and no paved roads, and many residents lived in run-down shacks and suffered from hunger and malnutrition.[23] Several persons I talked with believed that Petrolina in contrast to Juazeiro had no national health service agency because of the Coelhos' opposition.[24] However, probably as a result of Coelho influence in Recife, a local SUDENE agency was established in Petrolina. At the outset its major task was to administer the nearby Bebedouro experimental farm. As the military government in Brasília began to consider expropriation and irrigation of large expanses of land around Petrolina, it became increasingly important that the Coelhos maintain good rapport with the local SUDENE director, agronomist Antônio Roberto de Araújo, another influential member of the ruling class. About 1970, responsibility for the Bebedouro project was shifted to SUVALE, whose headquarters was in Juazeiro. Although its director, João Nelly de Menezes Régis, resided in Petrolina and associated with the Coelhos, he was subject to outside pressure and decisions. As population and services at all levels expanded in the community, it became increasingly apparent that the dominance of the Coelhos might be undermined by outside authority, and it thus became essential for them to collaborate with state and federal officials as well as potential outside investors to ensure and enhance their own economic and political interests.

Both communties were very much dependent on state support for their

21 Interview, July 5, 1969, with a reliable source who asked for anonymity.

22 *O Farol* 51 (July 21, 1966): 1, and 52 (May 31, 1967): 1.

23 Some of these conditions were reported by the Fundação Serviço Especial de Saúde Pública, "Resultados do inquérito de saneamento realizado em Petrolina no período de 23 de Julho a 14 de Agôsto de 1964," Petrolina, August 26, 1964. Among the report's conclusions: Only 40 percent of the buildings had water service and 22 percent used water filters, garbage collection was not available, and conditions in the local hotels were not hygienic.

24 A health service agency was to be established in Petrolina according to *O Farol* 53 (July 7, 1973): 1. This was probably an external decision over which the Coelhos had little control.

Table 5.6. *Municipal budgets, services, and personnel in Juazeiro and Petrolina, 1971*

	Juazeiro (% of total)	Petrolina (% of total)	Number of personnel[a]
Executive			
Mayoralty	2.0	2.2	3
Administration	3.6	3.7	15
Finance	14.2	11.9	33
Agriculture, industry, and commerce	3.9	25.4	12
Education and culture	11.0	15.7	106
Welfare	1.6	4.8	4
Health	3.0	4.2	6
Urbanism and public works	56.1	31.3	37
Sports stadium	3.5		
Legislative			
Municipal council	1.1	0.8	3
Total	100.0	100.0	219

[a]Personnel totals not available for Juazeiro.

educational programs, and Petrolina, in particular, did well in attracting resources to bolster one of the best school systems in the backlands of Northeast Brazil. As I have pointed out, Petrolina had always been known for its good schools, and the contrast with schools in Juazeiro was startling. Most children, even those from poor families, in Petrolina attended elementary schools, and many of them advanced to one of the five high schools, two of which were public and the others privately operated with state assistance (two by the Catholic church, and the other by the Baptist church). The Faculdade de Formação dos Professores offered a three-year teachers' training program. By 1970 Juazeiro had its school of agronomy and a nearly defunct school of philosophy; it had only two high schools, both overcrowded, and many small single-room elementary schools scattered throughout the city.

A glance at Table 5.5 reveals the importance of some state and federal agencies for the two communities. As noted, Juazeiro was dependent on many of the activities, Petrolina less so. In recent years the police and military had become increasingly important, and the state and federal banks in each community were often decisive in making judgments as to whether a public or private project should be carried forward.

The general orientation of public services is indicated in the breakdown of budget allocations in Table 5.6. The budget of each municipality for 1971 was close to a half-million dollars. One notes similar allocations in the areas of administration, finance, and health as well as in the lesser amounts for the mayors' offices and the municipal councils. In both towns most of the money for the mayor's office was for his salary, which probably amounted to several hundred dollars a month (a large sum compared with the salaries of mayors of other small towns).[25] As one would expect, there was a considerable difference in amounts allocated to education, Petrolina offering more extensive services in that area. Likewise, greater attention to the economy could be anticipated in Petrolina, where many new industries have been established in recent years.

A detailed examination of municipal budgets reveals the structure of municipal administration. Coordinating the affairs of the mayor in Juazeiro was a secretary, usually a politician or person of some influence. Américo Tanuri's first secretary, for instance, was military police captain, and later state deputy, Raulino Queiroz. In addition, there was a secretary for development and coordination of municipal affairs and an executive committee for the administration of the town's sports stadium. Municipal departments were organized along the following lines: finance and budget, tax service, personnel, accounting, treasury, education and culture, agriculture, health, social assistance, electric power, public works, and roads. Over half the budget, much of it in salaries, was expended by these last-named departments, along with the personnel department.[26] Considerable patronage could be found in these areas, although Tanuri insisted that the administrative expansion that occurred under his government was the consequence of developmental policies. Among the accomplishments he reviewed at the end of his first term was the increase in salary for rural teachers, from a half-dollar monthly in 1963 to five dollars in 1967. Perhaps a third of all municipal employees were rural schoolteachers. Their schools consisted of a single room in the house of a farmer or rancher, and their teaching responsibilities were to the children of the owner and his employees and to neighboring children who could be encouraged to attend. Most of these teachers had had only an elementary education. The prevailing system of patronage not only ensured their employment, room, and board, but extended a service to farmers and ranchers whose support was counted on in municipal elections.[27]

Municipal administration in Petrolina appeared orderly and efficient. Under the office of mayor were divisions of administration, finance (taxes, accounting, and treasury), agriculture, industry, and commerce (water, power, and municipal markets), education and culture (elementary and secondary schools and the public library), social welfare (health), and urbanism and public works (transport, sanitation, parks and recreation,

25 Sherwood, *Institutionalizing the Grass Roots*, pp. 99–100, reported that in a 1968 survey of mayors only 1.3 percent received more than $150 in salary monthly.

26 Prefeitura Municipal de Juazeiro, "Orçamento," Juazeiro, 1970.

27 Tanuri, "Mensagem à Câmara de Vereadores."

public works, and the cemetery). Petrolina's budget included the municipal employees identified in Table 5.6. Of the 219 persons in municipal employment, 90 were rural schoolteachers. Their salaries ranged from $15 to $20 monthly, considerably more than those of their counterparts in Juazeiro but well under the salaries of most other employees. The mayor's secretary, who was not a politician, received $60 monthly. The directors of the finance, social welfare, and urbanism and public works divisions received $120 monthly, the highest salaries offered at the municipal level, excluding the mayor. In fact, all salaries totaled only 20 percent of the municipal budget.[28]

Although salaries offered by Petrolina were high relative to Juazeiro and other municipalities of the interior, low salaries accounted for general lack of interest in municipal administration. Administrators and other personnel would prefer to work for state and federal agencies, where higher salaries prevailed. In a survey conducted in 1959 on attitudes of federal, state, and municipal employees in Pernambuco, the municipal employees reported less satisfaction with their work. More than four-fifths were against their children's someday becoming employees of the municipality. Not one of the municipal employees had obtained his position through competitive examination, whereas about three-fourths of the state and federal employees had done so. Nepotistic appointments tended to be the rule, not the exception, in municipal politics.[29]

The city council

In a recent survey of the São Francisco River basin, one informant stated: "In Petrolina the local dictatorship brings progress. In Juazeiro we have democracy but progress is stagnated."[30] I shall attempt to assess this statement in the light of municipal council politics, first by looking at how council members are elected and whom they represent (within the ruling classes and the masses) and then by reporting my observations of a council meeting in each town.

Elections to the municipal council are based on the principle of proportional representation. Candidates run on a party ticket, and their winning of a seat depends on the number of votes they earn for the party as well as the number of seats allowed the party in accordance with the proportion of total votes polled by that party. Tables 3.3 and 3.5 show a breakdown of

28 Prefeitura Municipal de Petrolina, "Establece o orçamento financeiro para o exercício de 1971," Petrolina, 1970.

29 Vamireh Chacón "Burocracia e desenvolvimento," *Boletim do Instituto Joaquim Nabuco de Pesquisas Sociais* 9 (1960): 45–55.

30 Félix Gerardo Tamayo Peña, "Survey of the San Francisco River Basin," Petrolina, United Nations Development Programme, February 1969, p. 106.

party representation for Juazeiro, where until 1972 two factions of the progovernment ARENA party and a smaller representation from the opposition MDB party had prevailed. After 1972 the Movimento Democrático Brasileiro (MDB) disappeared altogether; in Petrolina, it had never won an election (see Table 4.3). Given this situation, whom does the council represent?

Council members professed to represent the masses of citizens living in the cities and the surrounding countryside. Although recruited and carefully selected by the ruling classes, members were elected to office by a broader segment of the population. Often, participation in the council led to an office of the state or national level. Three of the Coelhos were exceptions to this rule, all having won their first elective offices as state deputy. The customary route was followed by Honório Rocha, who served first as councilman before election to the Pernambucan state assembly. State deputies Ana Oliveira and Raulino Queiroz had both formerly served on the council.

These local and state legislators were prominent members of the ruling classes. My interviews included two former federal deputies, two former state deputies, all council members (thirteen from Juazeiro and nine from Petrolina), and a large number of former council members (see Table 5.2). Five of the present and former council members from Juazeiro were businessmen, most of them small retail merchants active in the commercial life of the city. Three were farmers, four professionals, and six bureaucrats. Juazeiro has very little industry, and the only industrialist represented was a small furniture manufacturer. Of the councilmen from Petrolina, six were associated with the Coelho enterprises, four were professionals, four were farmers or ranchers; one councilman and one councilwoman were municipal employees, while another councilman was also the state tax collector.

Whether or not selection of councilmen was contrived, a general pattern of representation was evident. Not all councilmen and former councilmen were identified as power holders in the first phase of the study. In Juazeiro this upper echelon included only the two state deputies, three of the thirteen council members, and one former council member. In Petrolina it was represented by the federal deputy, a state deputy, and a councilman – Geraldo Coelho, who headed the council as had other Coelhos before him. It was important to the Coelhos that one of the brothers serve the council in the family interest.

Indeed, the ruling classes attached very little significance to the affairs of the municipal council (see Table 5.1); only a handful of persons considered it the most important of political and economic institutions. One reason might be that council members received no compensation for their legislative service, although such compensation was provided to council members of larger cities in the Northeast. Another indicator of the low prestige of the council was the small percentage of the municipal budget allocated to it (see Table 5.6).

Whatever prestige and satisfaction council members enjoyed was most certainly derived from their relationship to the general population. Sometimes this was expressed by vote and sometimes in general popularity involving the nonvoting illiterate. Basically, the relationship of council member to masses was a reflection of the patronage that traditionally had pervaded the local political economy. Through the council, this patronage extended to important segments of the population. In Juazeiro there was no female representation, although Ana Oliveira had once served on the council. Among councilmen representing the ARENA faction that supported Américo Tanuri were João Medrado da Silva, the top vote getter, whose strength was the urban working class; Orlando Pontes, a schoolteacher and small merchant whose attractive wife was active in local affairs as head of the municipal department of education and culture (through her influence, votes could be expected from rural teachers); Alvaro Correia da Silva, a retired official of the Companhia de Navegação, from which several hundred votes might be forthcoming; Raimundo Clementino de Souza, a farmer whose influence brought blocs of votes from some areas; and Aurelio Pereira da Silva, head of the post office, with its fifty employees. Opposed to Tanuri was the ARENA faction that included Ivan de Araújo Amorim, a lawyer with influence among professionals; Raimundo Medrado Primo, director of the public high school and respected lawyer; Manuel de Souza Duarte, a retired municipal accountant and descendant of prominent families; Manoel Gonçalves Bomfim, a farmer influential in rural circles; and José Rodrigues Lima, retired official of the Companhia de Navegação and respected by the working class. The representatives of the MDB were Otoniel Pereira de Queiros, a municipal employee and student leader at the school of agronomy, and José Ivan Araújo Lima, the outspoken owner of a small business.

Petrolina's only female representative on the council was Maria Lourdes Ataíde, who also coordinated affairs in city hall. Besides Maria Lourdes and Geraldo Coelho, other councilmen included Diniz Cavalcanti, the leading vote getter and popular owner of a local bus line, gas stations, and a restaurant, whose influence extended into rural areas; José Rodrigues Damasceno, a rancher who could muster several hundred votes from rural areas; Jeconias José dos Santos, a state tax collector; Plínio José Amorim, a rancher; Elpidio Nunes, a retail merchant; Juvenal de Santana, a taxi driver and farmer; and Nilberto Moura Leal, a dentist with links to the old opposition. The interests of these councilmen seem to spread among distinct constituencies – the Coelhos and their now coopted opposition, small and big business, city hall, the state revenue agency, professionals, and farmers and ranchers in the countryside.

Municipal council members were less well educated than mayors (see Table 5.3); two-fifths of them had had only a rudimentary or no education. A third were bureaucrats and more than a third merchants. A very large number were members of ARENA, and though nearly half had served the PSD many other parties had been represented among them.

I attended several council meetings in Juazeiro and one meeting in Petrolina. The meeting in Petrolina took place in July 1969. Meetings there are held infrequently and not publicized. One day while informally chatting with one of the councilmen, I inquired about the possibility of attending a meeting. He suggested an appearance that evening about 8:00 P.M. I arrived at the appointed time at the shabby meeting place, an old two-story building rented by the city for the use of the council and for an occasional court trial. It was located in the midst of homes of the wealthy families of Petrolina: the Coelhos, Borges, Barros, and others. Nobody was outside, but the door was ajar and I entered and went upstairs to the dimly lighted chamber. To my surprise, all the council members were there and the meeting was about to begin – on time. The eight councilmen were dressed in coats and ties, which was unusual in warm Petrolina (indeed unusual even in the large cities of Brazil). The meeting began promptly. There were no spectators; I was the only visitor, and the first business related to me. Geraldo Coelho asked me to speak briefly about my presence and project in Petrolina. After a brief description of my activities, there were no questions. Then the business turned to three or four items that were resolved in the next twenty minutes. The president quickly introduced each item and a vote, always unanimous, was taken. The meeting adjourned about a half-hour after it had begun.

I was left with several distinct impressions. The meeting had been well organized and run in orderly and efficient fashion. The behavior of the council members had been disciplined and formal; respect for the authority of the president was evident. My presence had been an intrusion upon what appeared to be private business. I was not certain whether the public felt uninvited or merely lacked any interest in such proceedings.

In Juazeiro I attended several meetings of the municipal council, which met twice weekly on Tuesdays and Fridays, from 2:00 to 5:00 P.M. over several two-month periods during the year. Meetings were open to the public, and on April 20, 1971, I attended one in the stately old city hall in downtown Juazeiro. The council chamber occupied half of the second floor, the mayor's office the other half (the municipal court building was nearby, down the street). Orlando Pontes, who was to preside over the session, was in the chamber upon my arrival, and we chatted for a few minutes while other councilmen straggled in. Most were dressed in coats of rumpled linen, but not all wore ties, and a few were in shirtsleeves. The meeting finally got under way about an hour late, with all thirteen councilmen in attendance. They sat at small tables arranged in a half-circle with Pontes at the head alongside the secretary, José Ivan Araújo Lima of the MDB party. Behind them were a Brazilian flag and a crucifix. A wooden railing separated the government from the people. On the gallery side of the railing were six benches, which were half-filled at the outset of the meeting. Other persons could observe from the open side entrance. On one side of Tanuri sat the four councilmen who supported him, and on the other sat those of the opposing ARENA faction. The secretary read the minutes of the last meeting with eloquence and formality, and then the president introduced several communications, one an anonymous letter that lawyer Ivan Amorim denounced as irrelevant. Then the meeting turned to the important business of the day, a first reading of proposed legislation on the restructuring of municipal administration. This had been introduced by military technocrats in Brasília to impose administrative conformity on the Brazilian municipalities. Although the Juazeiro council was being asked to rubber-stamp it, the proposed legislation was submitted to intense scrutiny and debate that afternoon. In fact, as the discussion continued on toward dinnertime, no consensus had emerged.

A couple of weeks later, another debate on the municipal reform took place. This second reading of the military proposal was no more subdued than the first, but now a consensus was emerging. Pontes and other Tanuri supporters endorsed the legislation in principle. They were joined by the ARENA opposition to Tanuri, which was especially vociferous in contending with the verbal attacks of MDB councilman José Ivan, who condemned the legislation point by point. Exchanges were rapid, and tempers flared. That the matter was not resolved that afternoon did not disturb the packed gallery of spectators who had gathered to hear the dialogue.

These meetings were reminiscent in spirit of the give-and-take politics of the pre-1964 period in Brazil. Evident in them were differing political orientations within Juazeiro's ruling classes. The politics of the municipal council reflected to some extent the candid discussion and dialogue, openness, and spirit of independence that characterized life in the town.[31] While the council debated controversial limitations about to be imposed upon them by the military authorities, outside the council chambers soldiers armed with machine guns patrolled the city streets. On the day of the council meeting, urban guerrillas had bombed and robbed the Banco da Bahia in Rio de Janeiro, and the local military had immediately taken

31 The Juazeiro municipal council organized itself into administrative subcommittees, including committees on constitutions, legislation, and justice; finance and budget; public health; and agriculture, commerce, industry, and public works. Committee membership cut across party lines, and most of the councilmen seemed to take their responsibilities seriously. Such subcommittees rarely existed in Petrolina, where there was little business to occupy the attention of councilmen.

precautions against such an occurrence in Juazeiro. Meanwhile, in neighboring Petrolina town life continued as always, subdued and orderly; as in the past, the ruling classes could rest assured that events were under their control.

The political parties

Historically, the three prominent parties in Juazeiro and Petrolina have been Brazil's major parties; the União Democrática Nacional (UDN), the PSD, and the Partido Trabalhista Brasileiro (PTB). In Juazeiro all these parties were important in the 1947 municipal elections, and they continued to produce winning candidates throughout the 1950s and 1960s (see Table 3.3). In Petrolina, only the PSD and the UDN were important (see Table 4.3). Before 1965, the spectrum of political parties extended well beyond the three major groupings, and the political shifts at state and national levels affected local politics. In Juazeiro, for instance, the Partido Liberal, a conservative party in Brazilian politics, did well in the municipal elections of 1950, 1954, and 1962. Occasionally candidates and voters would turn to a pre-Vargas party such as the Partido Republicano (PR), as was the case in the 1954 and 1958 elections. At other times, coalitions would bring several parties together, as in 1962. In Petrolina, the PR won eight seats on the council in 1955, while the Partido Republicano Trabalhista (PRT) won two seats four years later.

After 1964, as was true throughout most of rural Brazil, the ARENA party prevailed. In Juazeiro, although there were two ARENA factions, the military government was assured that local politics was under its control. In Petrolina there never was any question of ARENA's predominance as the repressed opposition passed into oblivion.

Political parties in Brazil traditionally have revolved around personalities and have become active only at election times. They are poorly organized, and their ranks are filled by middle- and upper-class voters. This is particularly true in Juazeiro and Petrolina. When I asked members of the ruling classes about the importance of voters, one of every twenty persons interviewed felt that the voters were the most important institution in their communities (see Table 5.1). Two-thirds believed that the voters were very important, while one-seventh considered them unimportant.

I interviewed all members but one of the predominant parties' executive committees, on the assumption that these were persons in a position to influence and deal with different segments of the urban and rural populations. In this sense, their role was much like that of the councilmen. Those identified in Table 5.2 include for Juazeiro seventeen of eighteen members of the executive committee and four delegates of the ARENA; their orientations according to divisions within the Bahian ARENA are made clear in Table 3.5. The one member of the executive committee I did not interview was from a town in the interior of the municipality, where he could be counted on to provide the party with several hundred votes; he did not often visit the city and did not participate in local affairs, including the meetings of the party executive committee. I also interviewed all four members of the MDB executive committee and an alternate member. In Petrolina I interviewed all eleven members of the ARENA executive committee as well as the two party delegates.

Four of the members of the party executive committees were mayors or former mayors. One was a state tax collector with the internal revenue service. Nineteen of the ARENA executive committee members and three of those of the MDB from Juazeiro were councilmen or former councilmen. Nine of the ARENA executive committee members from Petrolina were councilmen or former councilmen. In Juazeiro members of the executive committees tended to be bureaucrats, retailers, professionals, and farmers. In Petrolina they were businessmen, professionals, and (a few) bureaucrats. Most had not completed high school.

Clearly, then, the ruling classes dominated political parties in Juazeiro and Petrolina. The parties served as institutions through which the patronage of the ruling classes could be extended to city and countryside. In the past such patronage had rested in the hands of colonels, who, as patriarchal heads of the region's dominant families, exercised their influence through a network of election bosses known as *cabo eleitores* who would deliver votes in exchange for money, favors, and usually position within the political system itself. This same style of politics was visible in the composition of the party executive committees and the municipal council, whose members were in a position to aggregate votes and support. This cooptation of leaders and masses tended to consolidate the power of the local ruling classes. Through the parties and other political institutions, these classes used their regional power in negotiating with state and national bosses for assistance and favors.[32]

The judiciary and the military police

Responsible for maintaining public order are the courts and the military police. Identified and interviewed as members of the ruling classes were a

32 During July 1969 I attended an informal meeting of Juazeiro's mayor, a physician who exercised considerable influence on the ARENA executive committee, and a councilman who later became a state deputy. At the time they represented the majority faction of the ARENA. In very brief order these three decided who would be local president of ARENA, which delegates would attend a state party convention, and how they would use their regional power to influence the forthcoming gubernatorial elections. I was left with the impression that the decisions of this inner circle were given pro forma ratification by the executive committee.

military police colonel and state deputy from Juazeiro, Raulino Queiroz, and the two judges from Petrolina, José Maria Carvalho and Antônio Pessoa Leite. Queiroz was one of those identified in the first phase, part of the top echelon of Juazeiro's ruling class. As a politician and as a high state official in the military police, his position was very important in the municipality, especially after 1964, when the Brazilian military extended its control into all areas and institutions of the country. In 1964 a military inquiry was conducted into the conduct of the mayor and his municipal government. According to Mayor Tanuri's own account, the inquiry demonstrated that "honesty, action, and work" characterized his administration.[33] Soon thereafter, however, a military battalion was stationed in Juazeiro. Although the name of its commandant was not once mentioned by my panel of community members in 1969, by 1970 the local military was increasingly involved in local affairs. It reorganized the city transit system, and its presence dominated all public ceremonies. Mayor Tanuri, who had been able to maintain some distance from the military authorities through his aide and confidant Queiroz, became compromised in his everyday affairs. It was probably for this reason that an intelligence officer began to inquire about my investigation. He was a part-time teacher at one of Petrolina's private schools, and his name was inadvertently placed on a list of teachers I interviewed. When asked to fill out a questionnaire, however, he returned to his barracks, questionnaire in hand, and by the following day military headquarters in Recife and Salvador had been informed of my activities.

Within a week a young lieutenant from Salvador arrived to begin an interrogation, and shortly thereafter the police chief of Petrolina, a lieutenant in the military police, initiated inquiries. Although the interviews were nearly complete, several important ones had not been obtained. The investigation came to a standstill as rumors circulated that I had been arrested. At the suggestion of two influential community leaders who were sympathetic to my activities, a meeting of influentials of the two towns was arranged at which I was to review the progress and objectives of the project. The commandant was invited, but he sent in his stead the intelligence officer and another officer. They arrived in jeeps filled with soldiers who stood guard outside the meeting hall. The intelligence officer had brought his son, who turned on a tape recorder as I began to address the gathering. To my surprise, several prominent persons offered praise of my study, and one even suggested that perhaps funds could be found to ensure my return and report of the results. Thereafter, I had no further encounter with the military police, and the investigation continued smoothly to completion.

33 Américo Tanuri, "Mensagem à Câmara de Vereadores no 2 ano de govêrno 1964–1965" (Juazeiro: Prefeitura Municipal de Juazeiro, 1964), p. 9.

In general, while the military in Juazeiro was watchful over the divided ruling classes, in Petrolina there was little cause for alarm. As governor of Pernambuco, however, Nilo Coelho arranged for the transfer of a battalion of soldiers from Salgueiro to Petrolina in a move to bring outside resources and ensure stability in the community.[34] A company of military police arrived in the town in June 1970 under the command of Lt. José Mariano da Silva, who immediately was named police chief.[35] A year later a large building had been constructed to house the battalion. At the time of my study the military was not playing a substantial role in community decision making, and no military authority was identifiable as a member of the ruling class.

Only one of Juazeiro's judges was recognizable as an influential, and he received only a single vote from the panel. He also offered a course at the agronomy school. Eccentric and aloof from town affairs, he rarely mingled socially with members of the town's ruling class. His presence was not decisive in local affairs, and I did not interview him. The other judge was also isolated from town affairs. He had jurisdiction over elections. On about fifteen occasions I sought from him the results of past elections, and after three months of prodding he finally produced the official records, which he kept in his home, not in the archives of the municipal courthouse. (This matter was particularly frustrating, because there was no other tabulation of votes; municipal council records included only the names of winning candidates.)[36]

While it was my impression that Petrolina's judges were honest and dedicated in their duties and profession, several respondents, including a very reputable lawyer from Juazeiro and a responsible sociologist, condemned the legal process in their communities as "corrupt" and "dominated by the Coelhos." A young priest attributed the corruption to the Freemasons. Court trials were rare but widely celebrated. In Juazeiro, trials were open to the public and broadcast through loudspeakers placed throughout the town. Lawyers and judges alike resorted to pompous and often irrelevant rhetoric as the courtroom became a platform for their views and knowledge. It was not unusual for all the region's lawyers to attend an important trial.

One such trial was held in Petrolina during July 1971. The case involved a man accused of murder. He had been involved in a riot of some fifty persons, one of whom had died while five or six had been wounded. He had been arrested a year earlier but freed pending trial. Apparently

34 Police crime statistics reveal no reason for concern on this score. In 1966 Petrolina's police investigated fifty crimes, including eleven homicides, twenty-three assaults, five robberies, and one rape (*O Farol* 52 [February 16, 1967]: 8).

35 *O Farol* 55 (June 13, 1970): 1.

36 However, records of the council dating to 1834 were easily accessible in the council chamber.

Coelho interest in the defendant meant that he would be acquitted or given a light sentence. The proceedings were held in the shabby chamber of the municipal council. The chamber was packed with lawyers, the defendant, witnesses, and spectators, including some of the town's notables. The trial began with the judge's reading of the charges. Two of Petrolina's distinguished lawyers, state deputy Honório Rocha and José Walter Lubarino, offered a defense of their client and produced three witnesses on his behalf. The prosecutor, an older gentleman, offered no cross-examination and brought forward no witnesses. The jury consisted of seven persons selected by the judge in a drawing of lots among eighty persons. Technically the judge could not influence their decision. Although two schoolteachers on the jury had earlier voted not to release the defendant from prison, a majority had granted that freedom until trial date. The trial lasted three days and ended, to the surprise of nobody, in acquittal.[37]

In summary, although there are some important differences between the ruling classes of Juazeiro and Petrolina, several trends, which characterize backland politics in particular and Brazilian politics in general, are clear. Politics are important in the rural municipalities. Mayors are highly visible in the local polity. They serve as intermediaries between the ruling classes and the subservient masses and also are the link between the ruling class and the patrimonial order that includes national, state, and municipal agencies and administrators in the local area. Because the municipalities are very much dependent on outside decisions and resources that affect the activities of these agencies, this relationship is especially significant. The municipal councils and the executive committees of the political parties serve as paternalistic intermediaries between the ruling classes and the masses. They aggregate votes and support, which in turn is used as leverage by the ruling classes in negotiations with state and national government. Thus, it is clear that because of the dominant position of the ruling class and its manipulation of the masses, access to the ruling classes is virtually closed to all but those in a position of power and influence.

In interviews with the thirty-nine persons who represented the upper echelon of the ruling classes in Juazeiro and Petrolina, I probed their attitudes toward the political system and found common perspectives. In a series of open-ended questions, I asked, first, how they felt about politics in their community. Sixteen were strongly positive, seven positive with reservation, one slightly negative, and nine strongly negative, with six offering no opinion. Second, I inquired about their views of political

37 I unexpectedly found myself a participant in the trial. A few minutes after the proceedings had commenced, the judge asked me to sit to one side of his platform as a guest of honor. This was embarrassing to one who had wished to remain inconspicuous in the crowd of observers. Such are the problems of field inquiry.

leadership in the community. Here response was more favorable: Seventeen believed that there was very strong leadership and twelve that there was potentially strong leadership, while five indicated that there was weak leadership and six that there was no leadership whatsoever. Third, I was interested in their perspectives of politics. Fifteen respondents were strongly positive about future politics in their community, eleven were positive with reservation, seven were slightly negative, and six were strongly negative. The negative attitudes were manifested by Juazeiro respondents and by those in Petrolina opposed to the Coelhos.

6

The ruling class and the economy

In his classic analysis of the colonial period, Caio Prado Júnior notes the following characteristics of the Brazilian economy:

> Firstly, its *structure*, as an organ of production set up solely as such and with a few entrepreneurs and administrators who ran everything, and the great mass of the population who served as the labor force; secondly, its *function* as the supplier to international trade of the commodities needed; and finally, its *evolution*, a consequence of the two foregoing features, as an extensive and purely speculative exploitation, unstable in time and space, of the country's natural resources.[1]

He attributes the backwardness of Brazil to the colonial ties to Portugal and Europe. Portuguese administrative practices were oriented to enriching the trade of the mother country while repressing any colonialist effort to start up manufacturing industry or other enterprises. Thus, the colony's economic evolution was subject to a series of cycles resulting in "a successive development and decline of one after another of all the country's areas of concentrated settlement." The economy, he believed, rested on uneasy foundations, and there was no "organized system of production and distribution of resources for the material subsistence of the population." At times there was an illusory impression of wealth and prosperity: "As soon as the particular combination of circumstances changed or the available natural resources were exhausted, production declined and withered away, making it impossible to maintain the life it had sustained."[2]

One of these cycles affected the sugar industry of the Northeast, which prospered in response to the worldwide demand for sugar during the sixteenth and seventeenth centuries and declined thereafter. By the twentieth century the Central-South region had outstripped the Northeast in production. In 1920, for instance, 29.1 percent of industrial workers were

1 Caio Prado Júnior, *The Colonial Background of Modern Brazil*, trans. Suzette Macedo (Berkeley and Los Angeles: University of California Press, 1969), pp. 146–147.

2 Ibid., p. 145. Professor Peter Eisenberg of the Universidade Estadual de Campinas, in a comment on my manuscript, writes that Caio Prado Júnior's economic history is inaccurate in the case of sugar, whose production expanded until the late nineteenth century when exports declined, and that there has been a revival of sugar in the twentieth century.

concentrated in the state of São Paulo while 27 percent were in the Northeast; the latter figure had declined to 17 percent by 1950. While São Paulo's contribution to national production increased from 39.6 to 45.3 percent from 1948 to 1955, that of the Northeast declined from 16.3 to 9.6 percent. At that time São Paulo's population was half that of the Northeast, yet its production and per capita income were respectively 2.3 and 4.7 times greater than in the Northeast.[3]

These regional imbalances were the consequence of the decline in the sugar industry and the perpetuation of a traditional agrarian structure. In 1950 about half the rural labor force was settled on landholdings of 150 acres or less. Owing to the small size of these plots and the lack of investment capital, productivity was low. Because the majority of these workers paid rent and did not own their land, there also was little incentive to invest in better production methods. The extensiveness of large private holdings and reluctance of owners to invest capital apparently were deterrents to investment, so they generally went unused or were used inefficiently. The inequality of landholdings was evident in 1960 census data, showing that those as large as 2,500 acres constituted less than 1 percent of all holdings, 11.5 percent of cultivated area, and about 47 percent of total area.[4] Another problem for the Northeast was the movement of private capital to the coffee-producing and industrial areas of the Center-South. This was accompanied by an imbalance in trade between the Northeast and the Center-South, the direct consequence of governmental industrialization policies (import substitution through industrialization and import restrictions) centered in the South, which resulted in the Northeast's buying in the South instead of abroad at less favorable terms of trade.[5] These imbalances have continued since World War II despite a provision of the 1946 constitution obligating the federal government to spend a minimum of 3 percent of its revenues in the Northeast.

The economic dilemmas of the Northeast were aggravated by its dry spells and droughts. Official attempts to help the region have, as we have seen, included the establishment of a number of agencies oriented toward rectifying economic imbalances and promoting development.[6] Created in 1959 partially in response to the drought of a year earlier, the Superin-

3 Celso Furtado, *Formação econômica do Brasil* (Rio de Janeiro: Editora Fundo de Cultura, 1961), p. 264.

4 Werner Baer, *Industrialization and Economic Development in Brazil* (Homewood, Ill.: Richard D. Irwin, Inc., 1965), pp. 157–159.

5 Ibid., pp. 175–176, esp. tables 7.10 and 7.11, which reveal the surplus of export trade for the Northeast and the deficit of trade with the Center-South.

6 Albert O. Hirschman, *Journeys Toward Progress: Studies of Economic Policy-making in Latin America* (New York: The Twentieth Century Fund, 1963), esp. chap. 1, "Brazil's Northeast," pp. 13–91. A review and update of this study is Hirschman's "Policy Making and Policy Analysis in Latin America – a Return Journey," *Political Sciences* 6 (December 1975): 385–402.

tendência do Desenvolvimento do Nordeste (SUDENE) is the most recent of these institutions, and it has played a role in the development and underdevelopment of Juazeiro and Petrolina. Two federal officials reflected critically on its impact.

In a speech to the Brazilian Senate in August 1971, the Pernambucan federal senator João Cleofas attributed the fact that "the Northeast structure remains today almost identical to that of 1950" to SUDENE's policies of financial and fiscal incentives. In 1950 agriculture contributed 40 percent of economic productivity; industry contributed 12.4 percent of production in 1950 and 6.7 percent in 1970. SUDENE's policies were, he said, related to concentration of industry in Bahia and Pernambuco, causing socioeconomic disequilibrium in the region; excessive delays in the implementation of projects, resulting in increased costs for some and abandonment of other projects; exorbitant commissions and brokers' fees, especially for agricultural projects; approval of dubious projects calling for raw materials from the South for the fabrication of products that would in turn be sold in the South; and lack of support for small and medium-sized industries.[7]

The leader of the opposition in the Chamber of Deputies, Marcos Freire, also outlined grounds for criticizing SUDENE policies. He addressed himself to the financial and fiscal incentives, which permit a deduction of half the income tax of enterprises outside the Northeast providing that the deduction be invested in the Northeast.[8] Some $1 billion had been invested in 830 industrial projects during the 1960s, but this had created serious problems. One was that investments were encouraged for the large economic monopolies, especially international ones, thereby relegating small and medium-sized industries to a marginal existence.[9] The consequence was domination of the regional economy by firms from abroad or the Center-South. SUDENE had been unsuccessful on other fronts, especially in the area of agrarian reform, including the restructuring of the agriculture of the Northeast. Proposals for reform remained in the planning stages while resources for agricultural development diminished. In fact, he asserted, SUDENE's share in public investment had been reduced more than 50 percent between 1965 and 1970.[10]

7 João Cleofas, "Cleofas analisa problemática econômica do Nordeste," *Diário de Pernambuco* (August 29, 1971), first section, pp. 24–28. During 1970, forty of seventy-five projects and more than 60 percent of the funds requested for the states of Bahia and Pernambuco were approved.

8 For discussion of Articles 34 and 18 and of investment in general, see Gileno de Carli, *Política de desenvolvimento do nordeste* (Recife: Universidade Federal de Pernambuco, 1971); also Riordan Roett, *The Politics of Foreign Aid in the Brazilian Northeast* (Nashville: Vanderbilt University Press, 1972).

9 Marcos Freire, *Papel da SUDENE na problemática do nordeste. Discurso proferido na sessão de 5 de maio de 1971* (Brasília: Departamento de Imprensa Nacional, 1971), pp. 6–9. Freire identifies some of the monopolies as General Electric, Ray-O-Vac, Vulcan, Springer, Admiral.

10 Ibid., pp. 16–17, esp. tables 3 and 4.

Some of these problems were alluded to by Petrolina's Nilo Coelho in his gubernatorial inaugural address to the Pernambucan state legislature. Recognizing that the viability of small and medium-sized industry in the state was threatened by monopoly capital, he promised to correct the disequilibrium. In particular, he directed attention to the plight of the rural economy. Farmers and ranchers, he argued, had not benefited from governmental programs. Droughts threatened their crops and livestock, and technical assistance was rarely available. In addition, the prevailing commercial system precluded the possibility of profits and investments. He pledged himself to remedy their desperate situation.[11]

One of Coelho's concerns was to provide Petrolina and the interior of the state with an infrastructure. Thus, an early project was the paving of the road from Recife to Petrolina, providing power to farming areas and towns along the São Francisco River, increasing irrigated acreage, and facilitating credits to rural areas. Within Petrolina a sewage system was built, hospital services amplified, and education expanded. Along with the construction of a new tourist hotel, Coelho promoted other projects, including a new port, a bus depot, the building for a battalion of soldiers, and transmission of television from Recife.[12] These developments, in combination with continued complaints that the backlands were being neglected, attracted state and federal officials to Petrolina. Drawn by the modern hotel and reports of the new developments in the interior, tourists also visited Petrolina, now dubbed "the crossroads of progress."[13] Thus, it is not surprising that early in 1971 SUDENE held a meeting of its executive council in Petrolina, the first time that such a meeting had occurred in the interior of the Northeast.[14]

Coelho apparently desired also to integrate the interior with the coastal economy. The Coelho conglomerate of industrial and agricultural enterprise could be expected to benefit from such integration.[15] Such integration was one objective of the Comissão de Desenvolvimento Econômico de São Francisco (CODESF), which also sought to unite the economies of Petrolina and Juazeiro. This sentiment was reflected in an anonymous memorandum, dated 1964, which characterized the two cities as "inti-

11 Nilo de Souza Coelho, "Toma posse nôvo governador," *Informativo Semanal do Escritório do Estado de Pernambuco* 3, no. 77 (February 6, 1967): 21–24.

12 These projects are described in a propaganda brochure, *A integração do Vale do São Francisco* (Petrolina, 1971?).

13 The slogan "Encruzilhada do Progresso" apparently was part of the Coelho government's promotional campaign and was picked up in the numerous reports on the city. See, for example, *Diário de Pernambuco* (May 2, 1971).

14 Details of the meeting and its impact on Petrolina are in Pedro Francisco da Silva, "Petrolina, dos meus amores," *Jornal do Commercio* (March 2, 1971).

15 See, for instance, "Petrolina acompanha dinâmica do progresso no Nordeste," *Jornal do Commercio* (May 7, 1969): 4, in a special section entitled "Pernambuco e sua integração municipalista."

mately tied to each other." Juazeiro historically had dominated the area's commerce through control of duties and transportation facilities to Salvador, and Petrolina had reacted to this situation by establishing not only its own commerce but also means of moving its products to Salvador and other places. In effect, Petrolina had been able to break its economic dependency on Juazeiro. According to the memo, Petrolina's independence was accompanied by a regeneration of its economy, the creation of improved investment conditions, an influx of capital, and better utilization of resources and labor. The parallel development in the two cities was considered indicative of the growth of the region and as ensuring the development of all sectors of the economy.[16]

While this may indeed have been the situation in 1964, clearly Petrolina had emerged dominant by the end of the decade. In the remainder of this chapter I shall examine the economic foundations of dominance and dependency in the two communities, focusing in particular on five sectors of the economy: banking and finance, mining, agriculture and livestock, commerce, and industry.

Banking and finance

My first encounter with banking and finance in Petrolina was after an eight-day boat trip down the São Francisco. In immediate need of cash upon my arrival, I was inclined to go to the nearest bank. At the Banco da Bahia I consulted the manager, who told me that the only way I could exchange a traveler's check was through "one of the Coelho brothers" and directed me to a building at the end of the main street. After receiving similar advice from the other banks in town, I at last took the advice, and a few minutes later had completed the transaction with one of the Coelho brothers. This experience left me with the impression that the financial life of the area was indeed under the control of the Coelhos. Later, after more careful study, I concluded that this was only partially so.

The banks in the area lack administrative autonomy but exert great control over the economy because of the credits they make available. The bank managers are difficult to talk with and are rotated every few years to ensure that their ties with the community do not result in favoritism for certain persons and unfair advantage to the managers themselves. The small businessman may easily be dissuaded from negotiations with a local bank because of the excess of documentation and red tape and the fact that decisions are made elsewhere and may take several months.[17] It is under-

16 "Diferenças no desenvolvimento de Juazeiro/Petrolina, 1964," Petrolina, 1p. in CODESF files.

17 Even the simple transaction of a foreign check necessitated a two-week period for the check to be sent to and approved in Salvador.

Table 6.1. *Bank capital flows in Juazeiro and Petrolina, 1966 (millions of cruzeiros)*

	Deposits	Loans
Juazeiro		
Banco do Brasil	1,000	4,000
Banco do Fomento	394	357
Banco Econômico da Bahia	451	255
Banco da Bahia	430	317
Banco Comercial do Nordeste	286	140
Banco Brasileiro de Descontos	130	145
Total	2,691	5,214
Petrolina		
Banco do Nordeste do Brasil	308	5,429
Banco da Bahia	553	422
Banco Comercial do Nordeste	226	181
Total	1,087	6,032

Source: CODESF.

standable that the Coelhos and other influentials do their banking in Recife and Salvador.

In ranking the institutions in their communities, 13.6 percent of the members of the ruling classes of Juazeiro and Petrolina interviewed considered banks the most important, and 86.4 percent judged them very important (Table 5.1). Historically a number of banks and financial institutions had established agencies in the two communities. Banking power and influence tended to emanate from Salvador and Rio and to filter through Juazeiro. Apparently the Banco do Brasil was the first to establish an agency in the area, in Juazeiro in November 1924. Other important banks located in Juazeiro were the Banco da Bahia (established August 1970) and the Banco do Estado de Bahia; located in Petrolina were the Banco do Nordeste do Brasil (January 1956), the Banco da Bahia (August 1964), and the Banco do Desenvolvimento do Estado de Pernambuco (BANDEP, June 1967).[18] Of the latter, the Banco do Nordeste was the most important. With its headquarters in Fortaleza, it made available general, industrial, and rural credits and was responsible not only for Juazeiro, but also for Petrolina and several surrounding municipalities. In 1966, at the time of Nilo Coelho's ascension to power in Pernambuco, dominance in banking was shifting to Petrolina. There were three banks in Petrolina, two of them Bahian, and six in Juazeiro (Table 6.1). While

18 Banks that had once had agencies but had recently left the area were the Banco Brasileiro de Descontos and the Banco Econômico da Bahia in Juazeiro.

total deposits in the Juazeiro banks were two and a half times those in the Petrolina banks, credit available to each community was about the same. By 1971, however, several of the Juazeiro banks had terminated operations, and credit to Petrolina had substantially increased.[19]

My interviews with the members of the ruling classes included no bank official. Although the banks were acknowledged as very important to the community and satisfaction was expressed with their functioning, the bank manager was not viewed as a decisive influence in local affairs; he was not socially integrated into ruling-class society or involved in politics, and because he was expected to move rather soon to another branch he was not conspicuously involved in local economic decisions. No bank official was named by the panels of judges I asked to select the most reputable persons in their communities, and no bank official was identifiable as a participant in any community issue of the past decade. Bank officials tended to be new and unfamiliar with community affairs, closed in their dealings with others, and, in general, reluctant to discuss any matter with an outsider.

It was evident that the bank official with the local agency and especially the bankers making decisions in the state capitals and elsewhere exercise increasing influence in community affairs. From the mid-1950s to 1970, the Coelhos dominated the economy of the area, and their activities were encouraged and supported by the bankers, who welcomed the prospect of low-risk and stable investment. The expanding activities of SUDENE and Superintendência do Vale do São Francisco (SUVALE) also stimulated the flow of capital to the region. At the same time, the influx of public capital and the encouragement of outside private capital posed a challenge to the monopoly of capital the Coelhos had maintained for decades. The manager of the Banco do Brasil offered the assessment that "SUDENE and SUVALE are building an infrastructure that will ensure the development of the region."[20] To take advantage of this situation, the Coelhos were astutely entering into arrangements with outside capital.

The availability of bank credit and loans was dominated by a banking system in the Center-South. In 1960, for instance, nearly 91 percent of all loans went to that region, while only 7 percent were allocated to the Northeast.[21] What was available to the Northeast was generally oriented as follows: commerce (40 percent), industry (35 percent), and agriculture

19 From 1960 to 1970 the following increases occurred in two of Petrolina's banks: Banco do Nordeste, employees (from 15 to 42), deposits (from 8,863 to 3 million cruzeiros), loans (from 56,000 to 28.5 million cruzeiros); Banco de Desenvolvimento de Pernambuco, deposits (from 560,000 to 2.1 million cruzeiros), loans (from 392,000 to 1.6 million cruzeiros).

20 Interview with Antônio Sebastião Hughes, *Boletim Informativo* (Juazeiro), (June 1968).

21 Banco do Nordeste do Brasil, Departamento de Estudos Econômicos do Nordeste, *Recursos e necessidades do nordeste* (Recife, 1964). Of loans to the Northeast in 1960, 29.8 percent were to Bahia, 27.2 percent to Pernambuco.

(25 percent). Private banks provided short-term commercial credit, while the official banks extended loans for longer periods. Industrial credits, in contrast, depended largely on decisions of SUDENE and were long-term so as to allow for purchase of equipment and start-up operations. During the 1960–65 period only four industrial projects were approved for the Juazeiro–Petrolina region. During 1966 and 1967 credits were reduced because of a decline in demand for cotton and vegetable oils, but several important projects were financed thereafter. Credits for farming and cattle raising were limited to monies for intermediary agencies and seed, fertilizers, and equipment for farmers. Requests for agricultural credit in the Juazeiro–Petrolina region increased from 110 requests in 1960 to 155 in 1963 to 292 in 1965.[22]

Mining

With the exception of rather sporadic and inefficient efforts to mine semiprecious and precious gems, mining activity was limited to the extraction of copper near Juazeiro and gypsite not far from Petrolina. Local authorities had recently been giving increased attention to these two minerals, and interest was being expressed by private entrepreneurs as far south as São Paulo and by foreign investors from Germany, Japan, and the United States.

Copper deposits have been known to exist near Juazeiro since the late sixteenth century. A visitor to the region in 1587 reported the existence of a large escarpment of copper, and an engineer surveying a railroad along the São Francisco in 1874 remarked that "copper is in extraordinary abundance."[23] Numerous studies reveal that about 90 percent of Brazil's copper deposits are located in northern Bahia, about 90 kilometers from Juazeiro, in the region of Vale do Riacho Curaçá, at a mine site known as Mina Caraíba.[24] With reserves of about 35 million tons, the region was expected to produce enough to allow reduction in the amount of copper Brazil must import annually.

Although the potential of copper production in the region was discounted as late as 1942,[25] recent surveys have been more optimistic.

22 Data on loans to the region are sparse, but 1967 figures show 80 percent of all loans allocated to commerce, 14 percent to industry, and 6 percent to agriculture (data from CODESF files).

23 See series of articles entitled "Polígono," by Calazans Fernandes, published in 1967 (exact date and source not identifiable), in files of CODESF, Petrolina.

24 Superintendência do Desenvolvimento do Nordeste, Departamento de Recursos Naturais, *Projeto Cobre. O que é e o que pretende* (Recife, 1967).

25 W. W. D. Johnson, letter to Avelino I de Oliveira, October 16, 1942, in CODESF files, Petrolina, based on visit of July 18 to 20, 1942. Johnson stated: "I hold little hope that the area is economically important."

SUDENE geologists have studied five areas and eliminated four of them; the fifth, however, an area just to the south of the Caraíba mines but ten to fifteen times larger is considered "exceptional" for copper exploitation.[26] In 1968 a mission of German geologists and technicians under contract with SUDENE reported that other potential reserves lay in the region and announced the discovery of a copper deposit in Petrolina.[27] Under Project Bahia, the U.S. Air Force conducted an aerial survey where the copper deposits were known to exist.[28]

Accompanying these surveys were efforts by national and foreign interests to acquire mining rights and set up operations. The extraction of copper in northern Bahia had been incorporated into the national plan of economic development. The plan itself was to be coordinated by SUDENE, which would provide substantial capital and credit to operators in the area. The Grupo Industrial Pignatari of São Paulo (led by the millionaire and international playboy Francisco "Baby" Pignatari) was in the forefront of early activities. The Grupo had organized the Caraíba-Mineração e Metalurgia and purchased land and mining rights throughout an extensive part of the Caraíba region.[29] By 1967 it was engaged in extensive studies of the region and had outlined its production goals: from the Caraíba mine, 100,000 tons monthly of ore in its first phase, initiated in 1969, and double that amount in its second phase, beginning in 1971; from the Area Norte Mine, the eventual monthly production of another 100,000 tons. This would allow Brazil to meet 70 percent of its demand for copper.[30]

The Pignatari group turned to the Japanese Mitsubishi group for technical assistance and financing. Several other foreign consortiums involved in the area were Plumbum do Brasil, affiliated with English Rothschild interests and with the French group Pena Roya and owner of a mine in Buquira, Bahia; the Anaconda Copper Corporation, a U.S. firm that had had access to the information generated by Project Bahia; the Companhia de Minas da Bahia, under German and Canadian control; Refinação Brasileira de Metais-Nacional of São Paulo; Policarbono or Metas Nordeste,

26 Luiz Augusto Fernandes in interview with geologists of SUDENE, based on CODESF memo, Petrolina, January 30, 1967.

27 *O Farol*. 53 (January 31, 1968): 1.

28 Calazans Fernandes, ibid., was critical of the U.S. project, which eventually permitted SUDENE to have copies of the photographs even though these could only be interpreted by technicians and equipment in the United States.

29 According to Calazans Fernandes, the Pignatari holdings stretched about twenty-four kilometers from north to south and sixteen kilometers from east to west and had been purchased for 1.2 million cruzeiros in 1957 from Manoel Nascimento da Silva Torres.

30 Memorandum to Luiz Augusto Fernandes, president of CODESF, from José Epitácio Passos Guimarães, engineer of Caraíba-Mineração e Metalurgia, São Paulo, December 5, 1967 (copy in CODESF files).

under banking interests in Minas Gerais; and the U.S.-owned Kennecott Copper Corporation.[31]

Both Kennecott and Anaconda were being eased out of their holdings in Chile; Anaconda especially had become interested in Bahian copper and, according to a reliable source, was about to invest $70 million in 1969.[32] However, this investment did not materialize; the Brazilian military government and SUDENE took their cue from Chilean nationalists and turned to the Pignatari group. Initial SUDENE financing was to be $100 million. These developments were followed closely not only by the Coelhos, but also by local authorities, who appealed to the Pignatari group to locate its headquarters in Juazeiro. The appeal was signed by the mayor, members of the municipal council, the commercial association, the Freemasons' lodges, the Lions Club, and the Rotary Club; it listed nineteen advantages, among them air, river, road, and rail transportation, telephone service, markets, banks, schools, and the agencies of SUVALE and SUDENE.[33]

While the Ministry of Mines issued reports that the Pignatari group was fulfilling its objectives,[34] the group was attempting to consolidate its holdings in the copper-producing area. Early in 1972 fifty armed men invaded a large farm with bulldozers, trucks, and dynamite, destroying all the buildings and slaughtering the animals. Apparently frustrated by a year of negotiations with the recalcitrant owners, Pignatari had decided to seize control of the 15,000 acres in dispute. The move reportedly was defended by the head of SUDENE in Bahia on the grounds that the copper exploitation deserved priority over agricultural production.[35]

Gypsite is another mineral that has captured the interest of investors. Used chiefly as a soil amendment, as a retainer in cement, and in the making of plaster, gypsite is found in the municipalities of Araripina and Ouricuri, near Petrolina. High-quality deposits, estimated at 7 billion cubic meters in an area of 320 square kilometers, are estimated to exist in

31 "Grupos atuando na província cuprífera curaçãu," Petrolina: CODESF, Ref 08, September 1971, 2pp., typescript. In July 1977 the Inter-American Development Bank approved a $63.2 million loan to assist Brazil in the development of copper in the Caraíba region. The loan was a part of the total cost of the project, estimated at $734.4 million, to be carried out by Caraíba Metais, S.A., a mixed company whose majority stock was owned by a subsidiary of the Banco Nacional do Desenvolvimento Econômico. The project consisted of an ore concentrate plant with a production capacity of 150,000 tons of refined copper a year and a sulphuric acid plant with a production capacity of 450,000 tons a year. See "Inter-American Bank Lends $63.2 Million to Build Brazil's First Major Copper Complex," News Release (NR-42/77) (Washington, D.C.: Inter-American Development Bank, July 14, 1977).

32 Interview with Luiz Augusto Fernandes, July 29, 1969. At the time he was secretary of coordination of the State of Pernambuco, under Governor Nilo Coelho.

33 "Memorial," Juazeiro, January 4, 1971, 4pp., copy in CODESF files.

34 *Jornal da Bahia* (May 30–31, 1971).

35 *La Prensa* (Santiago de Chile) (February 23, 1972).

the Araripe plateau.[36] Gypsite is mined in open pits and transported by truck and train to Petrolina via Araripina, Salgueiro, and other cities of the *sertão*. With the financial support of SUDENE and technical assistance and capital from São Paulo and Constructora Coelho, a factory was established in Petrolina by Gypsum do Nordeste Indústria e Comércio de Gêsso to process the gypsite into gypsum wallboard for use in the construction industry. The Banco de Bahia provided $1 million in credit for the new installations, which were to process 50 tons daily. Located near modern river port facilities, the firm could ship its products up the São Francisco River to interior towns.[37]

Apparently the capital for the new mining venture had originated outside Petrolina, but there were several indications of Coelho involvement. First, the new plant was built by the Coelho construction firm. Second, the Coelhos' lawyer and later state deputy, José Muniz Ramos, who was also related to Lizette Bezerra Muniz, wife of Paulo Coelho, was a native of Araripina.[38] Third, the family was connected through Geraldo Coelho's marriage to the Soares family of Salgueiro. These political and social ties, as well as decisions under Governor Nilo Coelho to pave roads and build a new port, prompted observers to declare that the mining of gypsite would be "integrated into the development of the region."[39]

Agriculture and livestock

Activity in agriculture and livestock has taken two forms. One is based on traditional land tenure and usage and persists to the present. The other, tied to government plans for land reform and outside public and private investment, has slowly taken shape and threatens to undermine the old structure.

Activity in the sertão has always been oriented to the raising of cattle, with agriculture being limited to oases of small farms scattered about the *caatinga*. The farms were located in the most humid and favorable areas, where soils were fertile, for example, along the bed of the São Francisco and its tributaries such as the Salitre near Juazeiro. Agricultural production generally consisted of manioc, maize, beans, cotton, onions, tomatoes, and sugarcane. These farms generally served the needs of the landowners and the cowboys who tended the livestock, but some produce went

36 Document Ref 01, 2pp., CODESF files, Petrolina.

37 *O Farol* 54 (November 12, 1968): 1.

38 Interview with José Muniz Ramos, July 17, 1971. Apparently he and members of his family were involved in the gypsite exploitation and as state deputy he was able to direct public attention to the mining area he represented.

39 See article, "Gipsita será integrada ao desenvolvimento da região," *Diário de Pernambuco* (August 1, 1971): 25; and "Gipsita vai ser integrada no desenvolvimento do Nordeste," *O Farol* 57 (September 7, 1971): supplement.

to markets outside the São Francisco area. At times during the past few centuries some areas of the backlands have passed through cycles of prosperity and decline. Sugarcane and cotton and their derivatives, for example, have brought occasional prosperity, although most of the backlands have remained poor and reliant upon subsistence farming.[40]

Large *fazendas* or ranches provide extensive pasture for animals and some opportunity for agriculture on small farms on the banks of rivers. The land is divided into small parcels and distributed to the workers, who employ primitive methods in their subsistence farming. Various relationships may exist between worker and owner. In some cases the worker is a sharecropper, giving his labor in exchange for half the production. In other cases, the worker is a renter – that is, he occupies land in exchange for payment. Usually this payment is in the form of crops, which the owner either buys at a set price or accepts as remuneration for supplies and foodstuffs. The worker is more or less isolated from the market in a feudallike situation although historians differ on whether feudalism or some form of capitalism characterizes the prevailing economy. His food crops are not usually marketed, and commodities such as cotton are sold or given directly to the landowner. Where the worker is given a portion of the calves born in the herds of cattle he watches over, he must often sell that portion, which eliminates him from competition with the owner and relegates him to a perpetually inferior status. However, the landowner himself is often in a precarious situation because of credit and marketing limitations and controls placed upon him by intermediaries, banks, and other financial institutions.

Large landowners generally live in the cities of the sertão, where they engage in various other economic activities. This means that they are usually absent from their ranches, but while in the cities they market the products of their land and sometimes serve as intermediaries between small producers and large buyers. In Juazeiro and Petrolina, many members of the ruling classes were merchants dealing in foodstuffs and other products of the land. Some of the products went directly to the rapidly growing chain of supermarkets under the direction of Juazeiro's Francisco Etelvir Dantas. So aggressively had Dantas penetrated the food market that a small Coelho chain of supermarkets had fallen under his control after only a few years. João Batista Cavalcanti, an influential in the affairs of Petrolina and once active in the opposition to the Coelhos, had profited from his appliance and furniture stores in Petrolina and Recife, but he too was tied to agricultural activities as owner of large expanses of land. In the late 1960s he established a small cotton-processing industry, Algodoeira

40 Manoel Correia de Andrade, *A terra e o homem no nordeste* (São Paulo: Editorial Brasiliense, 1963), pp. 182–191.

Petrolina. Although this firm later encountered financial difficulties, in 1969 it paid the second highest industrial tax in Petrolina.[41]

The existence of large ranches and scattered small cities throughout the sertão contributes to the isolation of the family and serves to ensure the landowners' control over commerce and industry and local politics as well and, as a consequence, popular expression is often repressed.[42] The sentiment of repression is captured in a popular verse of the backlands:

> . . . here in the Northeast
> The poor have no freedom
> Living always under the yoke
> Each one working daily
> Only to receive half.[43]

Detailed data on land tenure in Juazeiro and Petrolina were unpublished at the time of my study, but trends are evident in the available figures.[44] One recent study based its findings on records of landholdings comprising only 5.6 percent of the nearly 3.5 million acres in the two municipalities. Of the recorded land, 58.5 percent was under cultivation, including 33 percent for livestock and less than 0.5 percent for farming. A total of 3,847 units were registered, including 3,762 classified as minifundios, 95 as latifundios, and 23 as rural enterprises. At work on this land were 138 sharecroppers, 23 renters, and 1,048 salaried laborers. The breakdown of holdings in Juazeiro and Petrolina is shown in Table 6.2.[45] Although large landholdings are not identifiable here, it is known

41 Information provided by the Coletoria Estadual, Petrolina, July 8, 1969. The Coelho industries paid 80 to 85 percent of all industrial taxes, however.

42 Maria de Nazareth Wanderley, *Mudanças e tensões sociais no meio rural de Pernambuco* (Recife: Secretaria de Coordenação Geral, Conselho de Desenvolvimento de Pernambuco, 1970), p. 47, mentions that of sixty-four unions recognized in Pernambuco, only three were in the sertão; of seventy cooperatives, only fifteen were in the sertão.

43 From Manoel Pacífico da Silva, *Queremos reforma agrária* (Alagôa Grande, May 12, 1971), p. 4.

44 Mapping of the Juazeiro–Petrolina area along with a detailed census of landholdings was being undertaken in 1971 as a consequence of elaborate aerial photography of the Northeast and North of Brazil by the Brazilian military under contract with Aero Service Cooperation of Philadelphia. The photography was done with a secret process made available by the U.S. military to the Brazilian government. According to one American technician with the project, the photography was possible through radar and computers under any conditions, through clouds or at night, from an altitude of 25,000 meters. Used for reconnaisance in Southeast Asia and other parts of the world, the cameras could identify golf balls and clubs at such a height (interview with Dean Hodges, August 17, 1971).

45 Comissão de Desenvolvimento Econômico do São Francisco, *Petrolina–Juazeiro, centro regional do baixo médio São Francisco* (Rio de Janeiro: Etas, Alejandro Solari, Engenheiros Consultores, 1969?), table II-12-1c. This date is different than that available in another source, although the trends are similar: Banco do Nordeste do Brasil, *Petrolina–Juazeiro: aspectos sócioeconômicos e área de influência comercial* (Fortaleza, 1968), pp. 8–11. This report was prepared by the Núcleo Etene of Recife, and a summary of the report is in "Área de influência de Petrolina–Juazeiro," *O Estado de São Paulo*

Table 6.2. *Land tenure in Juazeiro and Petrolina, 1970*

Area (hectares)	Juazeiro Number of holdings	Juazeiro Total hectares	Petrolina Number of holdings	Petrolina Total hectares
<10	830	1,733	2,348	8,243
11–100	132	3,660	480	12,595
101–1,000	25	7,750	26	7,932
1,001–10,000	2	4,700	3	16,200
10,001–100,000	1	10,800	0	0
Total	990	28,643	2,857	44,970

Source: CODESF.

that historically there were 3 large ranches in the area: Cachoeira and Pontal in Petrolina and Mandacarú in Juazeiro. These and others had been broken up as a result of illegal subdivisions, sale and inheritance, and outright seizure by squatters, but in recent years there has been one case of concentration of diverse properties. Generally through purchase, the Coelhos have managed to aggregate their holdings to about 8,000 hectares into a single ranch known as Pastos Bons, used principally for grazing cattle. Another large ranch was owned by Raimundo Santana. Together these contributed about 80 percent of Petrolina's taxes on agriculture and livestock.[46] João Ferreira da Silva, owner of a pharmacy in town, and Paulo Moura and his brothers, who ran a soap factory, were known to have extensive land in the interior of the municipality.[47]

That the ruling classes exercised control over the rural and urban economies was evident. Their dominance in local politics assured them of ties to public officials and agencies outside Juazeiro and Petrolina. Throughout the long history of government projects to combat drought, the ruling classes were able to channel state and federal funds for the construction of

(February 23, 1969). The Etene analysis is based on census data for 1950 and 1960. The problems of these data and the discrepancies between the two studies are discussed in Felix Gerardo Tamayo Peña, "Survey of the San Francisco River Basin" (Petrolina: Food and Agriculture Organization, United Nations, February 1969), pp. 46–47.

46 Peña, "Survey," p. 45, elaborates on the legal complexities relating to ownership of the land. These have posed some problems for government expropriation of land for experimental irrigation. The tax percentages cited previously are based on information in the Coletoria Estadual, Petrolina, July 8, 1969.

47 Life on a large ranch in Petrolina is described by Aroldo de Azevedo, *Regiões e paisagens do Brasil*, 2d ed. (São Paulo: Companhia Editora Nacional, 1954), pp. 116–120. Known as the Fazenda Morrinho, this ranch, according to Azevedo, "gives us an idea of the manner in which one comprehends these isolated places with their primitive and rustic cattle raising. No fence appears to limit the area of this property."

roads, reservoirs, dams, and irrigation systems to their ranches. This favoritism served to isolate a large part of the backlands population. Compounding the problem, these privileged landowners also built fences around their property to restrict access to water and grazing lands.

Despite its many advantages, the area suffers from low numbers of livestock. There were five times more ranches dedicated to the raising of livestock in Juazeiro than in Petrolina, yet each community accounted for less than 1 percent of the grazing area of its state. Juazeiro's total livestock population, including goats (43 percent), cattle (22 percent), and sheep (14 percent), was double that of Petrolina. Petrolina's livestock population included cattle (30 percent), goats (27 percent), and sheep (22 percent). In each of these categories the share of Juazeiro and Petrolina in the total livestock populations of their states was less than 2 percent.[48] From 1950 to 1960, the livestock population dropped substantially, from 204,700 to 148,000 head in Juazeiro and from 135,500 to 44,200 in Petrolina.[49] Traditional livestock production lacks the organization and efficiency of modern enterprise, and ranchers have been reluctant to invest capital in the face of climatic uncertainty and high financial risk, preferring instead to dedicate themselves to commerce or industry. Some attribute the decline to attitude changes in the younger generations who now rule in the communities. Because of lack of services and technology, the climate, and other considerations, they argue, the ruling classes are no longer willing to carry on in the tradition of their ancestors.[50]

Important small holdings along the banks of the São Francisco River and its tributaries are known variously as *sitios, granjas,* or *roças* and are visited on weekends by their owners, members of the ruling classes who reside in the cities near their shops and factories. Usually less than 10 hectares, these holdings are fertile and irrigated with water from the nearby river. They are worked by resident *meeiros* or sharecroppers. The owner provides the capital, seed and equipment, and other necessities, the worker gives his labor, and they divide the receipts of the sale of their harvest.[51]

The pattern of land tenure along the São Francisco is shown in Table

48 Based on population 1960 to 1964, although later data are similar. See "Área de influência de Petrolina-Juazeiro."

49 Banco do Nordeste do Brasil, *Petrolina–Juazeiro*, pp. 14–17.

50 Hilmar Ilton Santana Ferreira, "O papel da pecuária na economia do município de Petrolina (Pe)," Petrolina, 196?, in files of CODESF. Livestock expositions have been held in Petrolina since about 1960, presumably to stimulate interest. In that year of twenty-four prizes, eight first places and four seconds were awarded entries of José Coelho, and first place was awarded to one entry of each Adalberto, Augusto, and Geraldo Coelho (reported in *O Farol*, XLVI [November 22, 1960]. At the fifth exposition in 1971, only an honorable mention was awarded the Coelho entries (*Jornal do Commercio* [July 20, 1971]).

51 Andrade, *A terra e o homem no nordeste*, pp. 202–205.

Table 6.3. *Land tenure along the São Francisco River in Juazeiro and Petrolina, 1967*

Area (hectares)[a]	Number of holdings	
	Juazeiro[b]	Petrolina
<1	2	34
1–10	59	110
11–20	2	26
21–30		8
31–40	2	4
41–50	1	
>50	4	4
Total	70	186

[a]Total area 622 hectares for Juazeiro, 1,300 hectares for Petrolina.
[b]Does not include holdings upstream.
Source: Centro Latinoamericano de Pesquisas em Ciências Sociais, "Juazeiro e Petrolina, um polo de crescimento?" (Rio de Janeiro, 1967), pp. 64–66.

6.3. A few properties comprise much of the land. For example, in Juazeiro, the four holdings of more than 50 hectares along the downstream portion of the river constitute 38 percent of all the land; the holdings of more than 30 hectares account for 58 percent. While data are not available for properties upstream, these are owned by important professionals, businessmen, and merchants in Juazeiro.[52] Members of the Vianna family held at least three of the larger properties, and upstream in the valley of the Salitre was the Granja São Clemente, which had been developed by Colonel Aprígio Duarte Filho. The 70 hectares of the Duarte farm, with federal assistance, permit some one hundred meeiros to produce grapes, citrus, and sugarcane.[53] In Petrolina, the single downstream property of more than 50 hectares occupies a fifth of the total land along that portion of the river, whereas the three upstream properties of more than 50 hectares extend over 68 percent of the land at that point.[54]

Some of the land along the river is suited to the cultivation of onions, and the region has become one of Brazil's largest producers of that vegeta-

52 According to information in the Secretaria de Desenvolvimento in Juazeiro, there were 131 properties comprising 1,151 hectares along the Juazeiro side of the São Francisco River (interview with Orlando Pontes, July 8, 1969).

53 Azevedo, *Regiões*, pp. 102–106.

54 Jean Casimir, "De la sociología regional a la acción política (un ejemplo latino-americano)," unpublished manuscript based on the 1966 study of the Centro Latinoamericano de Pesquisas em Ciências Sociais, 1969, pp. 65–67.

ble. After World War II a Turkish immigrant to Juazeiro brought with him onion seeds from the Canary Islands, which he distributed to farmers along the river, guaranteeing them the purchase of their crop. Onion farming in the São Francisco Valley flourished, with demand and prices peaking in Rio and São Paulo in 1958. The profits of this enterprise brought the Turkish immigrant and his brother and two brothers-in-law a small fortune, which they rapidly invested in Juazeiro enterprise and land. Soon they dominated the town's economy, with interests in a Ford franchise, a furniture factory, a canning factory, and the local cinema. Then, heavily in debt, they confronted a series of disasters. Three fires in 1959 and 1961 destroyed their warehouses; banks foreclosed on their property, and their small empire collapsed.[55] In 1962 a plague destroyed the onion crop. At the same time, onion prices fell drastically as the government permitted imports of onions from abroad. As the industry slowly began to recover thereafter, so too did the ambitious Turkish immigrant. Anticipating a good crop in 1971, he invested his capital into the planting of 200 hectares among five parcels of land along the river. The demand that year was high as was the price, and his crop was expected to yield more than 1,000 tons and about a half a million dollars in revenue.[56] The onion farmers that year did not suffer from the damage of the past, but they were dependent on outside markets and manipulation of prices and imports by the government. Politicians called upon the federal government to enact protective measures.[57]

The pattern of agricultural production in the São Francisco Valley is shown in Table 6.4. Although the information is dated, it allows for comparison of land under cultivation, production, and value of production in Juazeiro and Petrolina. It is important to keep in mind the year-to-year fluctuations in such commodities as cotton and onions, which are subject to international demand and price and occasionally to disease. During the early 1970s, buyers from São Paulo were also encouraging the planting of maize. In general, however, it is apparent that farming is a relatively undeveloped enterprise in the valley. Less than 30,000 hectares were cultivated, and this figure had not increased substantially by 1970. The

55 Because the rise of the Hedajiojhi (known as Khoury) brothers challenged the dominance of the Coelhos, their fall was rumored to be the result of arson and Coelho pressure on banks to foreclose on Hedajiojhi property. This allegation was not confirmed, however, in my interview with Shefif Hedajiojhi in Juazeiro, June 5, 1971, in which he recounted the story of his rise and fall.

56 Calculation based on a brief discussion of onion demand and prices, in *O Farol* 56 (July 31, 1971): 1. The revenue would be divided between Hedajiojhi and his meeiros.

57 For example, federal deputy Marco Antônio Maciel, "Contra a importação da cebola, discurso pronunciado na Câmara pelo Deputado Marco Antônio Maciel, da bancada pernambucana," *O Farol* 57 (September 7, 1971): 1; and state deputy Honório Rocha, "Veemente apelo ao Presidente Médici para evitar a importação do produto prejudicial à economia da região," *O Farol* 57 (May 31, 1972): 1.

Table 6.4. *Agricultural production in Juazeiro and Petrolina, 1964*

	Area under cultivation[a] (% of total)		Quantity (tons)		Value (% of total)	
Product	Juazeiro	Petrolina	Juazeiro	Petrolina	Juazeiro	Petrolina
Bananas	0.7	0.2	2,100	1,200	16.1	2.2
Beans	3.9	6.4	126	360	5.9	1.5
Groundnuts	6.0	20.4	128	4,000	2.3	17.4
Coconuts		0.1		103		0.6
Cotton	26.8	48.7	465	4,655	19.1	34.8
Grapes	0.8		30		1.6	
Onions	3.6	0.4	330	360	9.6	9.0
Maize	5.4	16.1	68	3,660	1.5	7.6
Manioc		3.8		17,000		10.6
Melon	22.8		610		1.7	
Sugarcane	16.2	1.8	22,750	4,250	29.0	1.1
Sweet potatoes	7.8	2.1	790	6,000	7.4	15.0
Tomato	6.0		290	26	5.8	0.2
Total	100.0	100.0	27,687	41,614	100.0	100.0

[a]Total area 28,145 hectares for Juazeiro, 1,670 hectares for Petrolina.
Source: Adapted from Banco do Nordeste do Brasil, *Petrolina–Juazeiro: aspectos sócioeconômicos e área de influência comercial* (Fortaleza, September 1968), pp. 11–13.

value of this production was just over a half-million dollars. The comparative data make clear Juazeiro's underdevelopment in agriculture. Petrolina's area under cultivation was 16.5 times, production was 1.5 times, and value of production was nearly 12.5 times that of Juazeiro. Only in production of bananas, grapes, melon, sugarcane, and tomatoes did Juazeiro surpass Petrolina, while Petrolina produced impressively in groundnuts, cotton, maize, manioc, and sweet potatoes.[58]

Despite the cyclical droughts, the imbalanced structure of land tenure, and the lack of private capital and initiative in developing agriculture and livestock, a sense of optimism emanated from the reports and plans of the many officials and technicians who have visited and lived in the area in recent years. Experimental irrigated farms and a proposed dam, in particular, have attracted the attention of these observers. Perplexed by the contradictions of a region so backward and poverty-stricken yet containing 8 percent of the country's population, 10 percent of its livestock, and 11 percent of its electric power, these observers have speculated on the pros-

58 A helpful discussion of these agricultural products is in Carlos Bastos de Medeiros et al., *Estruturas dos processos produtivo e administrativo do setor agropecuário em Pernambuco* (Recife: Secretaria de Coordenação Geral, Conselho de Desenvolvimento de Pernambuco, 1970), esp. pp. 35–40.

pects for the year 2000. By the turn of the century, they have suggested, modern barges will be transporting goods up and down the São Francisco, no longer subject to fluctuating water levels. Some eight dams will have been constructed along the river and its tributaries. One of the more important dams, the Sobradinho, would be capable of providing the region with 800,000 kilowatts of electricity. Sobradinho was to be located fifty kilometers above Petrolina in the state of Bahia.[59]

During the early 1970s, the Sobradinho dam, a project envisaged for many years and discussed by politicians at all levels but never decisively acted upon, appeared to be becoming a reality. Early in February 1972 President Emílio Garrastazú Médici announced that a preliminary phase of the project would be initiated immediately; from 1972 to 1974 the government would allocate $146 million to expand electrification and irrigation, increase the number of modern barges on the river, and finance agricultural and industrial projects.[60] Shortly thereafter he visited the area to confirm the government's intentions and to inspect the Bebedouro experimental farm.[61] Reactions to the plan were varied but generally enthusiastic. The mayor of Casa Nova, Raul Santos, earlier had praised the president; Sobradinho, he believed, would bring "progress to the region."[62] While the project would inundate his municipality, it was probably his assumption that the ruling classes of the area would benefit as always from the influx of federal funds that not only would compensate them for their lost economic interests, but bring them new wealth as well. A Catholic priest, perhaps more sensitive to the social problems that would ensue, was more critical. Four cities and twelve small towns would disappear, leaving eighty thousand persons homeless: "It is a social problem of great scope."[63]

Médici's announcement coincided with the visit to the area by several potential foreign investors. Expressing interest, Rodman Rockefeller praised the Bebedouro project as "the most tangible and visible result" of progress noted on his tour of Brazil and thanked the Coelhos for their warm hospitality.[64] Most dignitaries and foreign visitors to Petrolina were entertained by the Coelhos, who had every intention of influencing any decisions that might affect the economy of the region. The Coelhos may have been involved in a proposed joint private venture to irrigate and farm 50,000 hectares that involved $90 million and twenty-four projects and

59 "O São Francisco do curral ao Kw (1501–1999)," *Realidade* 6 (March 1972): 102.

60 "Millonário plan de desarrollo brasileño," *El Mercurio* (Santiago de Chile) (February 9, 1972).

61 *O Farol* 57 (May 17, 1972): 1.

62 Raul Santos, "Fala o prefeito de Casa Nova," *O Farol* 57 (November 16, 1971): 1.

63 Personal communication, August 20, 1973.

64 Rodman Rockefeller, letter to João Nelly, January 29, 1972, printed in *O Farol* 57 (March 15, 1972): 1.

was backed by the Ministry of the Interior and Twig do Brazil, an English group; ADELA, "a multinational firm and investment banker"; and the Sociedade Anônima do Desenvolvimento do Vale do São Francisco (SADEVAL), a Recife-based firm involving eighteen ranchers of the region.[65] The government's approval of this proposal signified its intention of encouraging private foreign and domestic investors to penetrate the region. In the face of its own indecision and reluctance to commit substantial public funds to experimental irrigation projects, it seemed to be reaching for a partnership of private and public enterprise.

Experimental projects at Bebedouro and Mandacarú served as the basis for the influx of new capital to the region. Situated in Lagoa Grande, about 40 kilometers from Petrolina, Bebedouro was an experimental farm of 10,000 hectares, of which about 1,500 were irrigated with waters from the adjoining São Francisco. The project was initiated in 1961 under a joint agreement of the Food and Agricultural Organization of the United Nations and SUDENE. Experimental farming on 144 hectares involved twenty-three crops that were believed to satisfy three conditions: supplying food for people in or near the production area, meeting deficiencies in the markets of the major centers of the country, and export. Legal obstacles to the expropriation of Mandacarú prevented extensive experimentation there,[66] but the early findings at Bebedouro enticed an Italian firm in São Paulo to invest capital in the neighboring municipality of Santa Maria de Boa Vista.[67]

Beyond irrigation and crop experimentation, the Bebedouro project was to provide for settlement of small farmers in the region. This phase was begun early in 1968 with construction of houses. Settlers were recruited, a school built, and a cooperative formed. Although there were plans to increase the number of settlers to one hundred, by mid-1971 only sixteen families were living at the Bebedouro project. Official announcements stressed the progress of the project. When surveyed for opinions, the settlers were less enthusiastic. While several respondents expressed hope for the project, they felt that government resources were lacking: "Things are promised and not provided"; "It is doing nothing for me"; "It's so disorganized that I want to leave"; "Everything one does is involved in red tape."

65 *O Farol* 57 (May 17, 1972): 1.

66 Mandacarú was a smaller experimental area to which less attention was given. There, experiments were conducted on crops of wheat, barley, tomatoes, cotton, potatoes, elephant grass, alfalfa, and grapes – all considered important. It was also determined that potentially useful crops were sorghum, maize, beans, citrus, figs, and onions. At Bebedouro essential crops were groundnuts, potatoes, sorghum, elephant grass, forage legumes, pasture grasses, cotton, tomatoes, sunflowers, maize, kenaf, melons, onions, beans, millet, and grapes. Details of the experiments are in R. G. Poultney, "United Nations Development Programme: Survey of the San Francisco River Basin. Final Report" (Bebedouro: Food and Agriculture Organization, United Nations, December 1968).

67 *Diário de Pernambuco* (November 23, 1969).

Asked if their situation had improved, some settlers expressed disenchantment: "Before I owed nothing, now I have debts," "In the past I was free to do anything, now no," "I work all the time but nothing gets better."[68]

Among the goals of the projects were the using of untapped resources – especially land and water – for agricultural production; raising the standard of living of the farmers of the region, establishing a regional scheme of settlement; providing the raw material for local food-processing industry; training teams of technicians; and establishing the basis for future agricultural projects.[69] Clearly, in the minds of the settlers these goals were not being met. As settlers, they were also workers regimented to what some critics believed to be a modification of the old patronage system. They were subject to orders from technicians who went home everyday to Petrolina.[70]

Increased public attention to the problems of Juazeiro and Petrolina was precipitated by a drought that brought river traffic to a standstill in 1971 and prompted politicians to appeal for aid as late as 1972.[71] For years João de Vasconcellos Sobrinho, an ecologist at the Universidade Rural de Pernambuco in Recife, had been predicting disaster in the São Francisco Valley as a result of the deforestation of the region caused by the demand for fuel. Where there once had been abundant vegetation, tall trees, and lakes, now there was semidesert. He advocated a program of reforestation and abandonment of projects to construct dams and irrigation channels, arguing that these would drastically affect the flow of water and end navigation altogether. A different view was manifested by agronomist Eudes de Souza Leão, who argued that an elaborate irrigation system was needed at Sobradinho. In response to these analyses, the Pernambucan state legislature formed a commission to study the problem.[72]

Along with numerous other public officials, the commission visited Petrolina in August 1971. Their findings included a series of recommendations. First, because a majority of the inhabitants of the Northeast were dependent on agriculture, they recommended that emphasis be placed on the development of agriculture and livestock through credits and technical assistance. Second, they urged large investment in infrastructure, especially in control of the rivers and irrigation. Third, they called for regulation of the flow of the river as the best means to combat drought and for reforestation of the area. Fourth, they advocated immediate construction of the Sobradinho dam and its related canal system, subsidies for owners of

68 Responses of sixteen interviews with Bebedouro settlers in Tamayo Peña, "Survey," pp. 144–149.

69 *O Sertão* 22 (February 14, 1971): 1.

70 Various interviews with technicians at Bebedouro, May 19, 1971.

71 For example, Honório Rocha in *O Farol* 58 (November 12, 1972): 1.

72 Monsenhor Ferreira Lima, "Relatório da Comissão da Assembléia Legislativa do Estado de Pernambuco" (Recife, August 1971), p. 1, typescript.

riverboats, removal of rocks and dredging of low spots along the river, prohibition of fishing until a means for increasing stock could be found, and provision of long-term credits for construction of pumps to assist farmers in irrigation.[73]

Commerce

Products of the interior flow into and through Juazeiro and Petrolina in exchange for processed and manufactured goods, and the communities themselves are dependent on their coastal state capitals for some of these goods. Thus, commerce is an important economic activity. The cities of the backlands – indeed, of most of Brazil – have small retailers from whom consumers can purchase small quantities of goods near their homes, frequently on credit. Juazeiro and Petrolina both have weekly open-air street fairs consisting of small private retailers, one on Fridays in Juazeiro and the other on Mondays in Petrolina. Small farmers and others, usually from nearby rural areas, come to the cities to sell their produce, generally food for home consumption but also household goods, trinkets, plastic goods, clothes, furniture, and so on. In Juazeiro there are also fixed fairs, located near the municipal market, where small retailers operate every day. Each community also has its public market, where businessmen sell goods from rented booths and compartments within or along the outside walls of a municipal building. Then there are neighborhood stores, including *barracas* (usually shabby, wood, single-room units that sell cereals, some canned goods, fruit, and soft drinks), *vendas* (larger units that allow the customer access to the shelves), specialty stores for one product such as processed meats, and street vendors who hawk their wares. A relatively new type of retail store is the supermarket, where the customer selects products and carries them to a centralized counter for payment; each of the communities has several of these.

In 1960 there were 620 commercial establishments employing 1,272 persons in Juazeiro and Petrolina. These represented only 1 percent of all such entities in Bahia and Pernambuco but 34 percent of all establishments and 41 percent of all employees in the immediate area dependent on Juazeiro and Petrolina. That these two communities were the major commercial centers was shown by their percentage of business in relation to that of the surrounding region as a whole (18 percent in 1950 and 66 percent in 1960).[74]

73 Ibid.

74 The immediate region is officially delineated by seven municipalities, including Petrolina, known as the Zone of the Sertão of the São Francisco; and by ten municipalities, including Juazeiro, known as the Zone of the Lower Middle São Francisco. The data cited are from Banco do Nordeste do Brasil, *Petrolina–Juazeiro*, pp. 27–28.

It also seems appropriate to include under commercial activity service establishments in the communities. In 1960 there were 276 such establishments, of which 201 were in Juazeiro. These employed some 700 persons, 70 percent of them in Juazeiro. The predominant types of services were those offered by hotels, restaurants, and repair shops.

Historically the commerce of the area has been dominated by merchants of Juazeiro. One writer characterized the relationship of Petrolina to Juazeiro as a "suburb,"[75] another writer as "the twin city, truly an extension of the neighboring Bahian city."[76] Both cities extend their influences into surrounding areas; however, Petrolina's links to neighboring Pernambucan municipalities and to the interior of Piauí are especially important, and Juazeiro exercises control over commercial traffic up the river as far as Pirapora and over rail and truck transport with Bahia.

Petrolina's dominance over the neighboring municipalities of the sertão is illustrated in Table 6.5. Among these other municipalities are Cabrobó, Santa Maria de Boa Vista, Belém de São Francisco, Floresta, Petrolândia, and Tacaratú. Petrolina's control over the retail commerce of the area is illustrated by its dominance of almost half of the establishments, owners and employers, expenses and sales. In wholesale commerce, Petrolina's domination is more pronounced, with sales, for example, constituting almost 97 percent of the area's total. A similar tendency is noticeable in services.

Who are the important merchants? One study interviewed twelve merchants, only three of whom had been born in Juazeiro and Petrolina. Their origins were neither working class nor professional or industrial; six were sons of ranchers and four of merchants. Eight had only elementary education, while one had reached high school and three had undertaken vocational courses. Three had become managers of firms whose headquarters were in Salvador, one had become a partner in the parent firm and had gained control of 15 percent of the firm's capital, two had taken over the businesses of their parents, and two had moved their businesses from nearby Remanso. Asked their views of local commerce, they spoke of the "family system" that imposed limits on their commercial activity and influence and of the necessity for "loyalty" to "persons of experience" and

75 Carlos Lacerda, *Desafio e promessa: O rio São Francisco*. 2d ed. (Rio de Janeiro: Distribuidora Record, 1965), p. 95.

76 Azevedo, *Regiões e paisagens do Brasil*, p. 112. The role of Bahian merchants and their opposition to industrialization in Bahia during the nineteenth century is the focus of Eugene W. Ridings, Jr., "The Merchant Elite and the Development of Brazil: The Case of Bahia during the Empire," *Journal of Inter-American Studies and World Affairs* 15 (August 1973): 335–353. He writes: "The Bahian merchant elite, by using their political influence to deny assistance to industry, helped to stifle its growth. . . . In Bahia the attitude of the merchant elite was largely decisive in determining patterns of economic development" (p. 351). The activities of Juazeiro undoubtedly were shaped by the Bahian merchant class.

Table 6.5. *Commerce and services in Petrolina and neighboring municipalities, 1960 (% of total sertão)*

Zone	Establishments	Capital	Number of owners	Number of employees	Expenses	Salaries	Sales
Retail commerce							
Petrolina	45.4	37.3	47.4	59.9	56.7	78.4	48.9
Other municipalities	54.6	62.7	52.6	41.1	43.3	21.6	51.1
Wholesale commerce							
Petrolina	65.2	95.6	67.7	90.1	94.7	95.5	96.9
Other municipalities	34.8	4.4	32.3	9.9	5.3	4.5	3.1
Services							
Petrolina	47.1	53.5	49.9	50.7	63.0	70.7	81.7
Other municipalities	52.9	46.5	50.1	49.3	37.0	29.3	18.3

Source: Data furnished by economist Carlos Alberto Basilio, CODESF, September 1971.

"competence." The researchers suggest that the merchants of Juazeiro and Petrolina have the potential to be "modern businessmen" but "continue to run things in a traditional manner, without organization and without exact accounting, on a day-to-day basis." The changes in the community – the availability of power from the Paulo Afonso dam and the rapid rise of the Coelho family in Petrolina – seem to them to have spurred the traditional merchants to assume the risk of financial investment and "to dedicate themselves once again to seeking new and quick profits." Thus, while these persons are not efficient and modern, they are not typically traditional either. In general, they are persons looking for "a sure and quick profit who lack confidence in themselves."[77]

Although I did not investigate the practices of these wholesalers and retailers to any depth, some observations are in order. In general, customers were attracted to merchants by location and reputation based on personal acquaintance and mode of service. Although used infrequently, advertising was generally through the local radio stations and newspapers. The latter are filled with advertisements of the Coelho firms. In relation to the capital cities, merchants priced their products very high, often 50 to 100 percent higher. Transportation costs, low demand, and inefficiency presumably accounted for these high prices, although lack of competition in the sale of many products allowed them to manipulate prices at will. Where competition existed, prices were based on a fixed margin rather than any attempt to sell below competitors. This traditional practice was altered in the case of self-service supermarkets, where prices were reduced to capture a larger share of the grocery market.

Headquarters of commercial firms were in the local area, generally in Juazeiro. One firm had its headquarters in Salvador. The most important were specialists in clothing materials; two in Juazeiro and one in Petrolina operated both as wholesalers and retailers. Two of the largest firms, headed by influential businessmen Flávio Silva and Luiz Libório, had originated in the nearby town of Remanso. The two had once been partners but later separated, Silva establishing a branch in Juazeiro and another in Petrolina while Libório remained in Remanso. Silva managed to become one of Juazeiro's most important businessmen through hard work and the reinvesting of his capital in new ventures. Later Libório established his business in Juazeiro. In Petrolina, two brothers, Diniz and Eurico Cavalcanti, built a prosperous business around the sale of petroleum products. They began with a gasoline station and later acquired three old buses to inaugurate a bus line between Juazeiro and Petrolina. Eventually they added another gas station and restaurant and invested their capital in land.

77 Centro Latinoamericano de Pesquisas em Ciências Sociais, "Juazeiro e Petrolina, um polo de crescimento?" (Rio de Janeiro, 1967), pp. 36–41, from files of CODESF.

A third success story is that of Francisco Etelvir Dantas, who organized a chain a supermarkets and even took over failing markets partially owned by the Coelhos. Once an employee of the Pinguim chain, founded in 1949, Dantas became its owner in 1957.

A great deal of the commerce in the communities is related to imports and exports. Exports consisted of products of agricultural origin: hides, sisal, wax. About 1965 there were nine firms exporting these products, six of them with headquarters in Salvador and three with headquarters in Juazeiro and Petrolina. Traditionally the most important exporters operated in Juazeiro, but by the late 1960s all but one of them were in decline. The exception was the Exportadora Coelho, under the direction of José Coelho, which in 1965 was exporting more than all other firms combined. Founded in 1953 and integrally related to the family's other enterprises, Exportadora Coelho had branches in Juazeiro and Jacobina (Bahia) and in Ouricuri (Pernambuco) for the purchase of products. These products in turn were sent to the family sales outlet, run by Adalberto Coelho in Salvador. In 1965 some 65 percent of all exports were controlled by the Coelho firm, and this percentage increased in subsequent years.[78]

Traditionally the flow of commerce was dependent on products moving up and down the São Francisco River and back and forth between the interior of Piauí and Bahia through Juazeiro and Petrolina to Salvador. Figure 6.1 shows this flow as it existed in the 1930s. At that time the interior of Pernambuco and Bahia was tied to the economy of the Center-South. Manufactured goods from Rio, São Paulo, Belo Horizonte, and other points flowed through Pirapora at the headwaters of the São Francisco for shipment down the river to Juazeiro and Petrolina. Cattle and goat hides from the cattle-producing areas along the river and in Minas Gerais also moved northward, passing through Juazeiro and on to Salvador. Today, many of these skins are processed in the tanning factories of Juazeiro. Cattle, too, would move down the river to satisfy demand for beef in the towns on the river and along the coast. In exchange, products from the north moved southward. Especially important were groundnuts, candy made from sugarcane (known as *rapadura),* and salt for cattle, all of which were carried up the river in small sailboats.[79]

78 Ibid., p. 15. This report asserts: "It is Salvador that determines commerce. The offices in Petrolina and Juazeiro only follow orders." Figures are available on the products exported by the Coelho firm in 1965: goat skins (42 percent of all products), sheepskins (24 percent), sisal (19 percent), wax (8 percent), cattle hides (3 percent), coroa fibers (1 percent), and other (3 percent). The Exportadora Coelho was increasing not only its share of exports from the area, but also its share of all commerce. By 1969, for example, the Coelho export and construction firms accounted for 95 percent of the area's commercial taxes."

79 Details on commerce during the 1930s are in Orlando M. Carvalho, *O rio da unidade nacional: o São Francisco* (São Paulo: Companhia Editora Nacional, 1937), pp. 61–67.

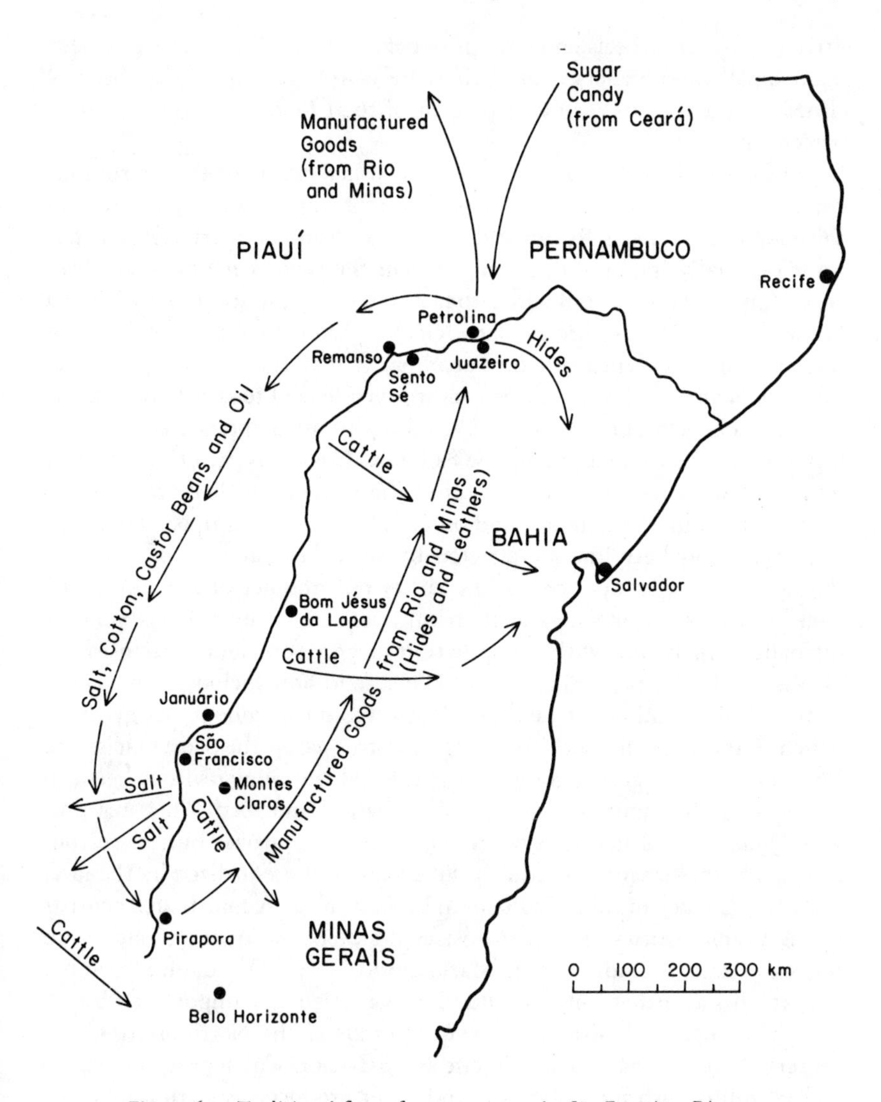

Figure 6.1. Traditional flow of commerce on the São Francisco River.

Today transportation along the river from Pirapora to Juazeiro and Petrolina continues as in the past, interrupted only by the severe droughts and dry seasons. The bulk of commerce up the river generally reaches Januária in Minas Gerais. The commerce and a passenger service are coordinated by the Companhia de Navegação do São Francisco. Although in recent years the line has been turning out propeller-driven barges that are rapid and efficient, many of the boats are wood-burning and steam-driven by paddle wheels and date from before World War I. There are also many small boat owners, but their share of river transportation has declined in recent years, from 54 percent of total tonnage in 1967 to 16.3 percent in 1971.[80]

Commerce, however, is dependent on other means of transportation, chiefly road and rail. Since the paving of roads between Juazeiro and Salvador and between Recife and Petrolina, road transportation has become especially important, cutting in half the travel time between these cities. The paved road to Recife also facilitates communications with Santa Maria de Boa Vista, Cabrobó, and Belém de São Francisco – towns along the river that are dependent on Petrolina. A road also extends from Petrolina to Remanso. From Juazeiro an unpaved federal road runs to Aracarú in the state of Sergipe, and at Canudos this road intersects the main highway from Fortaleza to Feira de Santana. The rail system ties Petrolina with Paulistana in the state of Piauí to the west. From Juazeiro it passes through Bonfim, Alagoinhas, and on to Salvador and Sergipe.

Juazeiro and Petrolina are affected by six territorial areas of influence (Figure 6.2). The first comprises thirty-one municipalities along the banks of the São Francisco and its tributaries, including twenty-two municipalities in Bahia, with a population of 594,000, and nine in Minas Gerais, with 384,000 inhabitants. The second area includes the zone of Araripe in Pernambuco, Ceará, and Piauí. From this zone comes gypsum, which is transported from Juazeiro and Petrolina up the São Francisco to Pirapora. A third area is composed of the Bahian municipalities between Juazeiro and Salvador, which are served by rail and road. This area provides Juazeiro and Petrolina with fruits, manioc, maize, butter, cotton, sisal, and other essential products. Fibers and oils are utilized by the local industry. Copper mining also is found in this area. A fourth area consists of the municipalities on the downstream side of the river and along the road to Recife, including Santa Maria de Boa Vista, Orocó, and Cabrobó. It is in this area that onion production is particularly important. A fifth zone of influence consists of the state capitals of the Northeast, regional centers along the coast such as Recife and Salvador, which provide Juazeiro and Petrolina with fuels, cement, and other products. A sixth zone is the Center-South of Brazil, to which gypsum and copper are transported.[81]

The relationship of Juazeiro and Petrolina with these zones of influence is partially apparent in data on the area's exports and imports. In 1965 exports exceeded imports by five times, with raw materials accounting for

80 Conselho de Desenvolvimento de Pernambuco, Secretaria de Coordenação Geral, "Pôrto de Petrolina–Juazeiro: subsídios para o projeto de viabilidade econômica" (Recife, August 1968), p. 19. This source is a feasibility study of Petrolina's new port and is useful for information on actual and potential commerce between the Juazeiro–Petrolina area and other regions.

81 Ibid., pp. 22–29.

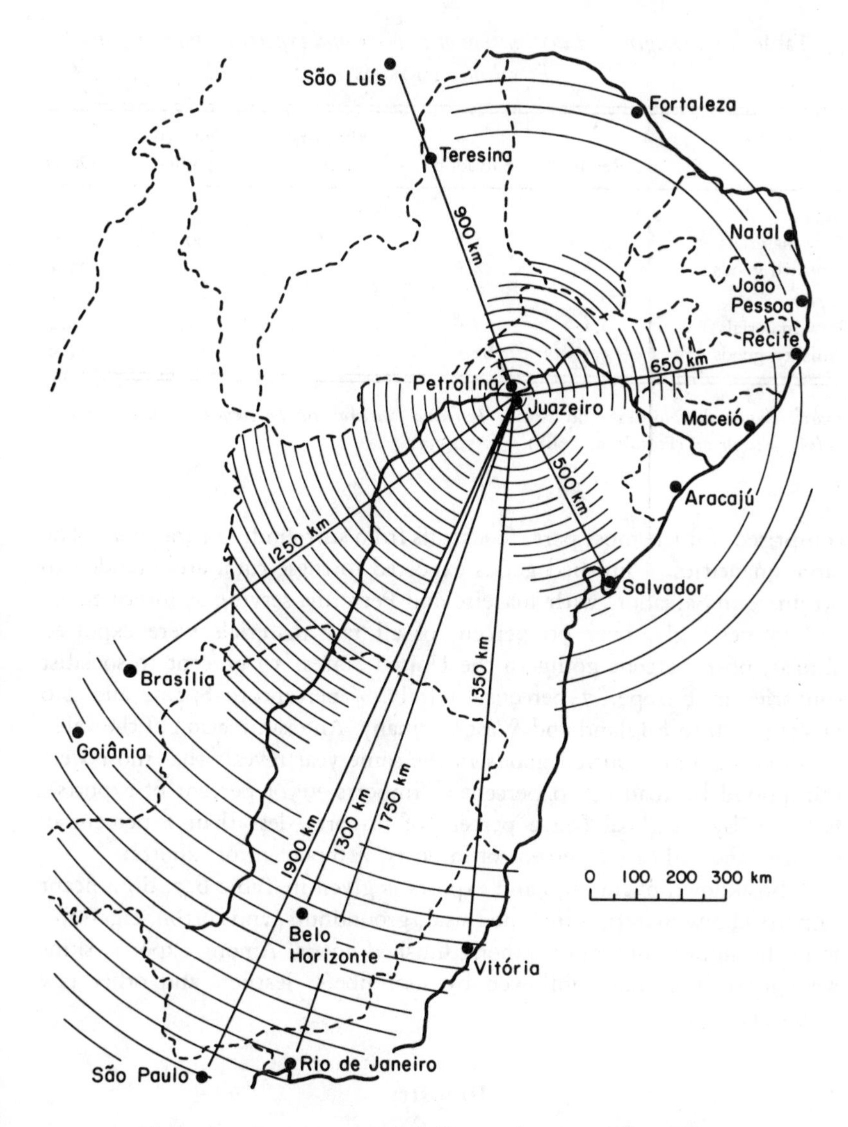

Figure 6.2. Areas of economic influence (Juazeiro and Petrolina).

97 percent of the total and finished goods less than 3 percent. Of the imports in that year, approximately 65 percent were raw materials and 30 percent finished goods. Table 6.6 offers a breakdown of origin and destination of these imports and exports. Of the two regional centers, Salvador exercised more influence than Recife, especially in the provision of finished goods to the area. The large percentage of imported raw materials

Table 6.6. *Origin and destination of imports and exports in Juazeiro and Petrolina, 1965 (%)*

	Recife	Salvador	Other large cities	Foreign points	Other
Exports					
Raw materials	0.1	1.5	5.6	90.2	2.6
Finished goods		4.6			95.4
Imports					
Raw materials	0.1	1.6	0.1		98.2
Finished goods	3.1	81.5	0.5		14.9

Source: Banco do Nordeste do Brasil, *Petrolina-Juazeiro: aspectos sócio-econômicos e área de influência comercial* (Fortaleza, 1968), pp. 50–52.

comprised, for the most part, foodstuffs from surrounding rural areas. The large quantities of finished goods exported to these rural areas tended to originate in Salvador, with Juazeiro and Petrolina serving as intermediaries. Interestingly, over 90 percent of all raw materials were exported abroad, 66.8 percent going to the United States, 17 percent to socialist countries in Europe, 7 percent to Italy, 4 percent to Spain, and 2.6 percent each to England and West Germany. An examination of the value of imported and exported goods in the same year reveals that most were transported by road (47.6 percent of imports, 95.4 percent of exports), followed by riverboat (32.2 percent of imports, less than 1 percent of exports) and rail (20.2 percent of imports, 4.6 percent of exports).[82]

A breakdown of imports and exports is given in Table 6.7. Significant imports of raw materials included sisal, groundnuts, and cotton; cigarettes were the significant import among finished goods. Among exports, skins were most important, followed by sisal fibers, leather, and other raw materials.

Industry

Several types of industry are located in the Juazeiro-Petrolina area. A first type, exemplified by tanning factories, comprises industries located near raw materials but distant from markets. A second includes industries such as those tied to civil construction, which are integrated into the regional market but distant from sources of raw materials. A third type is represented by industries located near both markets and raw materials, such as

82 Banco do Nordeste do Brasil, *Petrolina–Juazeiro*, pp. 50–54.

Table 6.7. *Imports and exports in Juazeiro and Petrolina, 1965 (%)*

Imports		Exports	
Raw materials			
Sisal	20.6	Hides	66.3
Castor beans	16.4	Sisal fibers	12.3
Cotton	10.8	Leather	6.5
Hides	6.3	Castor beans	5.5
Wax	1.4	Castor oil	2.6
Leather	1.1	Wax	2.7
Cotton seed	0.5	Cotton	0.4
Maize	0.3	Gypsum	0.3
Others	4.8	Others	0.8
Finished goods			
Cigarettes	27.0	Cigarettes	0.7
Fruits	1.1	Beverages	0.5
Manioc flour	0.9	Sugar	0.2
Sugar	0.8	Others	1.1
Butter	0.6		
Salt	0.6		
Beverages	0.6		
Soap	0.4		
Others	5.8		
		Cement	0.1

Source: Banco do Nordeste do Brasil, *Petrolina-Juazeiro: aspectos sócio-econômicos e área do influência comercial* (Fortaleza, 1968), pp. 55–56.

furniture factories and rock quarries.[83] Although the tanning factories process a small part of the leather that comes from the South, they have been in decline in recent years. One major factory, headed by Juazeiro influential Paulo Campelo, received credits and assistance from SUDENE in the early 1970s; another, owned by Luiz Libório, had closed down by 1970 pending outside financial assistance. Perhaps the most successful industries have been those extracting plant oils, especially oil from cotton. In the local area these firms, because of their oligopsonist position, have direct control over these raw materials. Also, their large volume of business allows them a privileged position in the productivity of the region. They absorb about three-fifths of the employed labor force and a third of the active working population. In addition, their market potential is considered unlimited.[84]

Industries in Juazeiro and Petrolina were born of commercial enter-

83 Casimir, "Sociología regional," pp. 79–83.

84 Centro Latinoamericano de Pesquisas em Ciências Sociais, "Juazeiro e Petrolina," pp. 56–63.

prises, with the local merchant realizing substantial profits in the short run and thereby gaining access to public credits and assistance. Usually his investment was encouraged and even guaranteed by public agencies seeking to promote economic advance in the region. It is only recently that independent industries have been established. The ties between commerce and industry have been the product of decisions and actions within and among family and business groups whose financial arrangements did not permit sale of public stock, thereby perpetuating their dominance over the local economy. Further, traditional tensions among ruling families and rivalry between Juazeiro and Petrolina have precluded the evolution of interrelated industry in the two cities. The Coelhos once offered financial assistance to Paulo Campelo, but he refused it on these traditional grounds. Historically these conditions have limited prospects for additional investment capital and financing. It is therefore quite natural that these families and groups became dependent on private and public financial resources and sought special favors from public officials. This became especially evident as state and federal governments turned their attention to the development of the backlands region. Usually what capital was available to the business community was destined for the establishment of new industry. Such industry was tied to available raw materials in the local area and to the notion, frequently espoused by the ruling classes, that Juazeiro and Petrolina represented a "pole of development" at the crossroads of backlands economic activity. The acceptance of this proposition by public agencies lessened the risk of new capital investment and also ensured the local families dominance over the economy, both in commerce and in industry. In fact, the alliance of public state and federal capital with local private enterprise brought changes in the pattern of dominance over the local economy. For one thing, the alliance was promoted by the less traditional Coelho brothers, whose aggressive exercise of political influence at the state and federal levels brought them advantage. Often their new firms replaced the old firms of others as new financial arrangements and capital investments were accompanied by innovation and modern technology, and local industry became more monopolistic than oligopolistic.

An "industry" in the area is defined as an industrial enterprise employing ten or more persons. In 1966 there were twenty-three such industries in Juazeiro and eighteen in Petrolina. Twenty heads of these industries were interviewed by a social science team from Rio at that time. All but one had been born in the Northeast, and the fathers of eleven had been born in the same locale. Their average age was forty-three years. Their fathers had been ranchers or farmers (four), merchants (thirteen), professionals (two), and an artisan. Only six of these industrialists had attended university; nine had completed only an elementary education. Asked about the development of the region, they identified the major obstacles to industrial development as the unavailability of credit and lack of a skilled labor force. They generally reported a lack of local competition, although several referred to the problem of lower-priced imports from other parts of Brazil.[85]

Table 6.8 shows the representation of the ruling classes in the economy of Juazeiro and Petrolina. Their role in local industry is particularly important. I have no financial figures for the firms in Juazeiro, but in 1968 the largest consumers of electric energy were the industries of Cortume Campelo, Cortume Libório, INCOMAR, and Aliança Industrial do São Francisco.[86] Cortume Campelo was the largest and most important of the firms in Juazeiro, although these firms were relatively insignificant compared with the Coelho industries.

The Coelho industries accounted for 80 to 85 percent of all taxes collected from industry in Petrolina.[87] Their dominant position is also illustrated in Table 6.9, which includes financial data on Petrolina's three major industries. In 1968 the Coelho group earned a net profit of about 25 percent of their gross income, a total exceeding the gross income of all other industries combined. The second firm, Algodoeira Petrolina, earned a profit of less than 10 percent of total income in 1969, apparently a drop from previous years due to climatic conditions. Whereas the Indústrias Coelho and Algodoeira Petrolina apparently had a decline in income and profit, Irmãos Moura was able to double its income and quadruple its profit.[88]

In every respect the Indústrias Coelho was the dominant industrial firm in the Juazeiro and Petrolina area. It employed nearly 600 workers, 53 percent of the industrial work force. Founded in 1957, it began by processing cotton and went on in 1958 to producing oil from cotton and in 1959 to oil refining and soap making. In 1961 it began to extract oil from other products. Thereafter, it expanded its facilities rapidly so that by 1970 it was processing 11,100 tons of cotton, 8,793 tons of cottonseed, 2,452 tons of Ouricuri palm nuts, 3,107 tons of oil from cottonseed and palm nuts, and 45,141 tons of castor beans. From 1966 to 1970 the firm's sales abroad averaged nearly $5 million annually. Plans for the 1970s included a doubling of storage and productive capacity through SUDENE and other financing.[89]

The Coelho construction firm was the second largest firm in the area, employing 129 persons or about 11 percent of the total industrial work force. Founded in 1953, it doubled its capacity between 1960 and 1965.

85 Ibid., pp. 42–50.

86 Interview with Orlando Pontes, July 4, 1969.

87 Information from Coletoria Estadual, July 8, 1969.

88 As part of a proposal for expansion of its facilities, Indústrias Coelho showed total sales of 36,204,000 cruzeiros in 1968–69 and 39,569,000 cruzeiros in 1969–70, implying that there was no drop in 1969 despite the figures recorded by the Instituto Brasileiro de Geografia e Estatístico (IBGE). See Indústrias Coelho SA, *Projeto de ampliação e integração* (Petrolina, 1971?).

89 Ibid. A SUDENE loan of 20 million cruzeiros was approved early in 1971, according to *O Farol* 56 (April 30, 1971), 1.

Table 6.8. *Representation of the ruling classes in major enterprises in Juazeiro and Petrolina*

	Juazeiro	Petrolina
Banking and finance	Outside interests	Outside interests
Mining	Outside interests	Outside interests Coelho (gypsum)
Agriculture and livestock	Granjas of Viannas Duartes Hedajiojhi Amorim Silva Other families	Pastos Bons (Coelho) Santana Fazenda Fazendas of Silva Moura Amorim Damascena Other families
Commerce	Flávio Silva e Irmãos Supermercados Pinguim (Francisco Etelvir Dantas) Luiz Libório and Cia Gonçalves Irmãos Tecidos (Antônio Carlos de Andrade) Amadeus Damasio Arnoldo Vieira do Nascimento	Exportadora Coelho (José Coelho) Diniz and Eurico Cavalcanti Nordestinho Eléctrico Doméstico (João Batista Cavalcanti) São Luiz Supermercados (Francisco Etelvir Dantas) Farmacia (José Borges)
Industry	Cortume Campelo (Paulo Campelo) Cortume Libório (Luiz Libório) Indústria e Comércio de Marmore (Incomar) (Arnold de Souza Oliveira) Aliança (Flávio Silva) Fábrica de Moveis Brasil (Durval Vicente de Lima) Fábrica de Cataventes (José Fermino dos Santos) Irmãos Khoury Hedajiojhi Torrefação de Café S. Francisco (Américo Tanuri) Cerámica Piranga (Giuseppe Muccini)	Industrial Coelho (Paulo Coelho et al.) Constructor Coelho (Geraldo Coelho) Algodoeira Petrolina Indústria & Comérico (João Batista Cavalcanti) Irmãos Moura (Paulo Moura) Indústrias e Comércio de Moagem Petrolina (João Batista Cavalcanti) Indústria de Ladrilhos São José (Joaquim Gomes da Sá) O Farol (João Ferreira Gomes) Gráfica Petrolina (Cid Carvalho)

Table 6.9. *Financial data for selected major industrial firms in Petrolina, 1968–69*

	Gross income		Net profit	
	1968	1969	1968	1969
Indústrias Coelho (consolidation of several firms – cotton, oil, etc.)	36,346,065	32,444,069	8,955,818	1,288,629
Algodoeira Petrolina		505,835		34,345
Irmãos Moura	417,869	1,005,893	40,479	191,411

Source: Instituto Brasileiro de Geografia e Estatística (IBGE), Petrolina, 1969 and 1970.

Most of its materials came from Recife and Salvador. Its activities were geared to the expansion of the Coelho industrial park and to federal and state projects. For example, it helped in the construction of the roads to Recife and Salvador and in the building of workers' homes on the outskirts of the city.

The Cortume Campelo was probably the third important firm in the area despite a decline in activities during the late 1960s after a rapid growth from 1958 to 1964. It employed about 6 percent of the area's industrial work force. Plans for expansion during the early 1970s were aided by financial assistance from banks and SUDENE.

The attitudes toward the economy of the thirty-nine persons identified as the upper echelon of the ruling classes, sixteen of them from Petrolina and twenty-three from Juazeiro, were generally optimistic, a view partially attributable to the economic "miracle" of the early 1970s. Nineteen were strongly positive about the prospects for economic development, and the same number felt that there was very strong economic leadership in the communities. Ten were positive with reservation, two slightly negative, and eight strongly negative about economic development. While eight believed that there was potentially strong leadership, six said that leadership was weak and three that there was no leadership. These respondents were asked about their views on specific economic activities, and their responses were also positive. As to commerce, fifteen persons were strongly positive, eleven positive with reservations, seven slightly negative, and five strongly negative. Hopes for industry were also high, with fourteen persons being strongly positive and eleven positive with reservations. In agriculture and livestock thirteen expressed strongly positive sentiment, while ten were positive with reservations, eight slightly negative, and six strongly negative.

Another measure of importance of the economy was recorded in Table 5.1. When 118 members of the ruling classes were asked to identify the most important institution in their communities, some 34 percent named the banks, businessmen, and the largest firms as most important, and over 80 percent felt that these were very important.

Clearly the state of the economy was most significant to the ruling classes of the region. Any substantial activity in agriculture is only recent, and the traditional livestock segment of the economy has its limitations. The business life of these communities has depended upon their commerce with the interior and with the coastal capitals. In recent years market limitations and prosperity for a handful of merchants have prompted them to turn to industry. Aided by banks and public agencies oriented to diverting state and federal monies to the development of the region, these merchants were favored in their efforts to maintain dominance over the local economy. However, their alliance with public capital and the determination of the federal government to allow outside private capital, much of it foreign, to penetrate the communities might also undermine the local ruling class hegemony.

This was evident in a government-sponsored study of the region. The conclusions of this study alluded to businessmen who must work "in the mold of a spirit of clientelism," a pattern characterized by exchanges of favors among persons exercising power in the communities and prevailing even with state intervention in the local economy. The researchers suggested that "conscious intervention and planning by SUDENE" would be required for the economic potential of Juazeiro and Petrolina to be realized. Regional development would have to take into account the mentality of "businessmen and the ruling classes," particularly their low level of culture, their allegiance to the family, and the game rules that encourage them to collaborate with public officials in "a spirit of dependency" and with influential persons in "a spirit of bargaining for favors." In the face of these conditions, they advocated that "the lower classes be differentiated into their own autonomous organizations" and that efforts be made to prevent opportunistic businessmen from acting in their own interests rather than in the interest of the community. They argued that otherwise the economy would soon be directed toward monopoly capital. They pointed to the opposition of the ruling classes to the role of the state in the local economy as "revealing the insensitivity of the entrepreneurial class" and saw the traditional dominant classes as opposed to any policy that might threaten "the real interests of an industrial bourgeoisie."[90]

90 Centro Latinoamericano de Pesquisas em Ciências Sociais, "Juazeiro e Petrolina," chap. 5, "Conclusion," from files of CODESF.

7

The ruling class in civic and social life

Statistical data relating to civic and social life today are readily available to the traveler who reaches Juazeiro and Petrolina. In the past an occasional report revealed such information. For example, one could learn that in 1939 in Juazeiro there were 350 people affiliated with labor unions and another 300 with other organizations.[1] A generation later, census data for Petrolina revealed 825 members of sporting clubs, 625 members of social clubs, and 178 members of an artisan union.[2] Military rule of Brazil was characteristic of both periods, and clearly institutional life had become more complex in the interim. Whereas the organization and manipulation of the working classes had been an objective of legislation under Getúlio Vargas during the 1930s, military intervention into unions had resulted in their ineffectiveness or demise by the 1960s and 1970s. It was more appropriate for a worker to belong to a soccer club than to a union, and this was dictated not only by general conditions in Brazil, but by the behavior of the ruling classes in Juazeiro and Petrolina.

When the panels of the initial phase of my study were asked to name the ten most important organizations in their communities, choices for Juazeiro focused on fraternal organizations – the Rotary Club, Lions Club, and the Freemasons' lodges – and then on social clubs and a cooperative of artisans. Respondents in Petrolina favored local coordinating agencies as the Comissão de Desenvolvimento Econômico de São Francisco (CODESF) and the Fundação Educacional; these were followed by the three social clubs, with the Yacht Club at the top of the list, and, finally, the Superintendência do Vale do São Francisco (SUVALE), the federal health service (SESP), and the local hospital. All the organizations so identified were included in a list presented to the 39 members of the upper echelon of the ruling class, who were asked to check all the organizations of which they were members. Juazeiro respondents belonged to an average of 7.7 organizations and Petrolina respondents to an average of

1 Aroldo de Azevedo, *Regiões e paisagens do Brasil*. 2d ed. (São Paulo: Companhia Editora Nacional, 1954), p. 100, n. 17, from *O Observador Econômico e Financeiro* 37 (February 1939).

2 Data for 1970, Instituto Brasileiro de Geografia e Estatística (IBGE), Petrolina.

Table 7.1. *Orientations of the ruling classes to civic and social life*

Orientation	Juazeiro	Petrolina	Total
Religious	3	4	7
Fraternal	6	0	6
Social–recreational	15	25	40
Professional	16	4	20
Civic	5	6	11
Labor	3	2	5
Two or more	16	7	23
None	2	4	6
Total respondents	66	52	118

7.9. Their membership on committees during the previous ten years was on the average of 6.3 committees per Juazeiro respondent and 5.3 committees per Petrolina respondent. Data on membership in committees were based on responses to questions regarding the degree to which each respondent had been involved in decision making in efforts to resolve twelve major issues that had affected the communities during the last decade.

When the same list was presented to the 118 members of the ruling classes identified in the second phase of the study, the total of organizational affiliations averaged 4.0 per respondent in Juazeiro and 3.2 per respondent in Petrolina. Nearly half the Juazeiro respondents were members of five or more organizations, whereas less than a third held that many memberships in Petrolina. In both communities the leading civic and voluntary associations were felt to be important; 72 percent considered them very important (see Table 5.1). Nearly four-fifths of the sample felt that the civic and voluntary organizations were understanding and helpful, while the remaining one-fifth believed that they would only "listen to me but would try to avoid doing anything" or "ignore me or dismiss me as soon as they could." Further evidence of interest in local organizations was evident when 94 percent agreed (30 percent strongly) with the statement: "A good citizen should be willing to assume leadership in a civic improvement organization." Only 6 percent felt that "a citizen should join only those organizations that will promote his own interests."

Table 7.1 reveals the orientations of respondents to organizational life in their communities. In both communities there was a strong inclination to participate in social and recreational clubs, yet in Juazeiro there was also considerable interest in the local commercial association and in fraternal organizations. The orientation of each respondent was determined by a general assessment based on all his or her memberships in organizations.

Thus, although 9 of every 10 persons were Catholic, only a few persons in each community belonged to religious organizations (undoubtedly these persons were the bishops and priests included in the sample).

These respondents were also asked to list their affiliations and to give details on the type of organization, attendance at meetings, financial contributions, and leadership positions. When I assigned values to these organizations reflecting their geographical scope (1 for local, 2 for national, and 3 for international), the results showed 3.2 affiliations per respondent in Petrolina, with an organizational-scope value of 3.8, in comparison with 4.0 affiliations per respondent and an organizational-scope value of 6.5 in Juazeiro. Clearly, civic and social life in Juazeiro is not only more important, but more cosmopolitan than in Petrolina.

In terms of an index of participation based on the assigning of a value of 2 to several important organizations in each community and a value of 1 to the others, multiplying the value by the percentage of meetings of each organization attended by the respondent during the past year, and finally calculating an average percentage of attendance, there were no conclusive differences between the communities. At the lower end of the attendance scale, 24 respondents from Juazeiro and 25 from Petrolina attended less than 30 percent of the meetings; at the upper end, only 2 respondents in Juazeiro but 6 in Petrolina attended meetings more than 90 percent of the time. However, Juazeiro respondents made more financial contributions to their organizations than respondents from Petrolina, an average of 4.2 in contrast to 3.2.

Nearly 40 percent of all respondents had held no position in any organization for the past five years. The 40 Juazeiro respondents who had held offices had had an average of 2.6 positions over that time, whereas the corresponding 31 Petrolina respondents had averaged 3.3 positions.

In summary, among the top echelon, the core of the ruling class, there was considerable involvement in the civic and social life of the communities. In the larger survey, members of this core tend to stand out as leaders, major participants, and major financial contributors. Juazeiro respondents were involved in more organizations and were more cosmopolitan in the types of organizations they supported. Petrolina respondents were involved in fewer organizations but more committed in terms of participation and officeholding.

The great difference between the two communities was that Petrolina respondents joined primarily the social clubs of the community, whereas Juazeiro respondents participated in fraternal and professional associations as well. This pattern was also evident in response to the question "Why are [all] these [voluntary] organizations important?" Nearly a fourth of those from Petrolina felt recreation to be the most important reason, while another fourth believed that involvement in these organizations was benefi-

Table 7.2. *Ruling-class views of the most important civic and social associations in Juazeiro*

	First choice	Second choice	Third choice	Total
Associação Commercial	19	14	11	44
Sociedade de Obras	20	14	8	42
CODESF	11	9	8	28
Freemasons' lodges	5	9	9	23
Rotary Club	5	3	9	17
Lions Club	0	2	4	6
Fundação Educacional	2	1	1	4
APAMI	0	2	1	3
União dos Barqueiros	0	0	2	2
Others	4	12	13	29
Total respondents	66	66	66	198

Table 7.3. *Ruling-class views of the most important civic and social associations in Petrolina*

	First choice	Second choice	Third choice	Total
Fundação Educacional	7	13	9	29
CODESF	19	5	3	27
APAMI	3	9	11	23
Associação Comercial	2	8	2	12
Rotary Club	3	3	3	9
Caritas Diocesanas	1	2	5	8
Sociedade de Obras	2	0	4	6
Fundação Rural	2	1	1	4
Iate Club	1	0	1	2
Others	12	11	13	36
Total respondents	52	52	52	156

cial to the community. Two-fifths of those from Juazeiro cited "social contacts."

When these respondents were given a list of civic and voluntary associations and asked to identify the three most important, they made the choices shown in Tables 7.2 and 7.3. Surprisingly, the organizational orientations of respondents here differ from those of Table 7.1. Whereas those in Juazeiro were inclined to identify professional and fraternal organizations, those in Petrolina, with a list of all organizations before them, cast their votes not for the social clubs, but for the service institutions such as the Fundação Educacional and CODESF. A closer look at the various kinds of organizations may help to explain these choices.

Professional associations

Among what I call professional associations were several commercial clubs and a number of cooperatives. One such club was the Associação Comercial, Industrial e Agrícola de Juazeiro, founded on May 16, 1944. This association grouped together commercial, industrial, and agricultural interests (127 firms as of 1970) and since its founding had been led by the major political and economic personalities of Juazeiro. In one of its publicity brochures the association acknowledged that in the years since its establishment it had remained "obscure," a reference to the fact that its importance was signified more by the prominence of its members than by any political or economic pressure or action it had exerted upon the community.[3] Over the years its leadership had included former mayors Miguel Siqueira, Joca de Souza Oliveira, and Américo Tanuri as well as such dynamic local merchants as Yorgy Khoury Hedajiojhi, Niator Sampaio Dantas, owner of a new hotel and the major furniture store, and Antônio Carlos Andrade e Silva, manager of the largest dry-goods shop. Appropriately, in 1972 the association proclaimed as an honorary member the São Paulo industrialist Francisco Pignatari, to whom the government had awarded concessions over nearby large copper deposits.[4] Juazeiro's Clube Comercial, founded in 1893, was no longer important, although historically it had been a major social and commercial center and even today its premises contain the town's only significant library, including newspaper archives.[5] While Petrolina's Associação Comercial was acknowledged by respondents as significant and its ranks included prominent economic and political personalities, there was little evidence that demands and pressures for changes in the community were manifested under its aegis. Indeed, other channels existed for such purposes.

In addition to these commercial associations, a number of cooperatives had been founded in the communities. In each instance these had been established on behalf of local economic interests and were firmly under the control of the ruling class. Two examples support this assertion. In Juazeiro, the owners of riverboats were organized into the União dos Barqueiros do Médio São Francisco. The local merchant and leader of the

3 *Boletim Informativo* (June 1968), published by the Associação Comercial, Industrial e Agrícola de Juazeiro.

4 *O Farol* 57 (July 31, 1972): 1.

5 The Juazeiro newspapers for the period 1890–1930 that are cited in Chapter 5 were found in these archives; although in poor condition, these newspapers represent one of the very few written sources of information on Juazeiro's early history.

Freemasons Ermi Ferrari Magalhães was prominent in this organization. In Petrolina, ranchers and farmers came together in the Cooperativa Rural de Compras em Comúm de Petrolina; over the years its leadership had included such luminaries as former mayor Pacífico Rodrigues da Luz, João Nelly, head of SUVALE, and Raimundo Santana, one of the largest ranchers in the region.[6]

Fraternal clubs

The Rotary Club included members from both communities, and its leadership occasionally included such prominent personalities as José and Geraldo Coelho of Petrolina, who were presidents respectively in 1960 and 1965, and João Cordeiro Neves, owner of cinemas in both communities, who was president in 1964. Although in my identification of the ruling classes of the communities I paid little attention to the membership of the Rotary Club, the sample turned out to include fourteen of its twenty-nine members.

The Lions Club was founded in Juazeiro in December 1960. While councilman Orlando Pontes and businessman Niator Sampaio Dantas had served as presidents, it was less important than the Rotary. An examination of records of meetings in 1969 revealed that fewer than half of its members attended meetings. One of the Coelho brothers, Adalberto, who resided in Salvador, had served as vice president of the Lions Club in that city, but only seven of the twenty-eight members of its Juazeiro affiliate were included in my sample of the ruling class.[7]

The Freemasons, whose presence in Juazeiro since the 1930s had provoked considerable conflict with the hierarchy of the Catholic church, were represented by two lodges at the time of my study. One was the Grande Oriente, housed in Juazeiro's most majestic building, in the town square near the Catholic church, and consisting of three hundred members led by Niator Sampaio Dantas. The other, with about four hundred members, was called the Grande Loja Unida da Bahia e Brasil and was under the leadership of Antônio Joaquim da Silva, a federal tax collector, and Ermi Ferrari Magalhães. These secret lodges recruited members through an investigative process of three months' duration and an initiation fee of about thirty dollars. Thereafter, monthly dues of about one dollar were paid. Roughly 30 percent of the membership was from Petrolina, including (though they did not acknowledge their affiliation in interviews) members of the Coelho family. The past intense rivalry with the church

6 *O Farol* 49 (Februray 16, 1964): 3.

7 Organizational records of the Lions and also Juazeiro's commercial association were made available by Niator Sampaio Dantas.

had prompted local priests to brand the lodges "houses of the devil," and they had been bitterly attacked by past bishops for usurping the power of the church and that of the local oligarchies. By the time of my study, however, leaders of the Masons argued that their image has changed since the 1960s, when Catholics were first permitted to join. They claimed that Juazeiro's bishop had actually attended one of their meetings and that they now allowed wives and children to participate in special social events. They said that they exercised little influence in local political and economic affairs and that their primary function was in the area of social assistance, generally to needy lodge members. Because membership lists of the lodges were not public and because only a few of the persons interviewed acknowledged their affiliation, it was impossible to determine the involvement of the ruling class in the Masons. Interviews did suggest that their leaders were members of the ruling class. Most of their activities were secret, and it was difficult to determine the extent of their influence in local affairs. My general assessment is that they no longer were very important.[8]

Social clubs

Two levels of social clubs were evident, one elitist and the other oriented to the mass population. Ruling class dominance of both levels was conspicuous.

A glance at the membership lists of the major social clubs gives a reliable indication of the membership of the ruling classes of Juazeiro and Petrolina. In addition, the proliferation of such clubs in each community has symbolized the rivalries and differences between and among segments of the ruling classes. Juazeiro high society has traditionally been affiliated with the music societies, the Filarmônica Apollo Juazeirense and the Filarmônica 28 de Setembro, while the establishment of the Country Clube de Juazeiro represents a recent effort to amalgamate the community's ruling class and to manifest independence in the face of Petrolina's increasing dominance of the region's social life. The Iate (Yacht) Clube Petrolina was Petrolina's equivalent of Juazeiro's country club, but unlike its counterpart it tended to included residents of both communities. A traditional intraclass rivalry was evident, however, between the memberships of two other clubs in Petrolina: the Filarmônica 21 de Setembro and the Petrolina Clube.

According to one account, the Apollo Juazeirense represented populist

8 Interview with Ermí Ferrari Magalhães, September 3, 1971; see also his paper, "A Loja Maçônica e sua influência na vida das cidades do interior" (Juazeiro, January 1968), 13pp., mimeographed copy.

middle-class society in Juazeiro and was dominated by professionals such as the physician Edson Ribeiro. As such it had "no social or racial preconceptions"; white mixed with black and mulatto, and doctors and lawyers mixed with tailors, mechanics, and machinists. In contrast, the Filarmônica 28 de Setembro was a club of the wealthy, including the Viannas, Melos, Bragas, Siqueiras, and others; it incorporated "fine" society, that is, the oligarchs of Juazeiro.[9] What seemed to be an inclination of people in Juazeiro to play down class distinctions probably accounts for the apparent insignificance of these two social clubs, once so important to Juazeiro society, at the time of my study.

Social life in Petrolina was more strongly affected by the rivalry of actions within the ruling class, although social clubs established early in the twentieth century seem to have been unified. One of the very early clubs, for instance, was the Jockey Clube de Petrolina. Lists of directors of this club during the period 1924–26 revealed such prominent personalities as Cardoso da Sá and Alfredo Amorim as well as members of the prominent Coelho, Luz, Padilha, Santana, and Souza families.[10] The women of these same families were conspicuously represented in the leadership of such other civic organizations as the Clube Filhas de Mozart and the Associação das Damas de Caridade (the later a charity organization).[11] The traditional social club of Petrolina was the Filarmônica 21 de Setembro, founded in 1910 by three of the town's prominent figures, Alvaro Moreira da Rocha, Antônio de Santana Padilha, and Joaquim Gomes da Sá.[12] Over the years its leadership has been one and the same as that of the ruling class. Usually conspicuous politicians and businessmen served as its officers and directors, and family names such as Souza, Coelho, Santana, Sá, Luz, Amorim, and Padilha were commonplace.[13] After World War II, with the rise of the Coelhos in the political economy, members of the ruling class divided their attention between the Filarmônica 21 de Setembro and the Petrolina Clube. Because the latter had been established by Coelho interests, the disenchanted opposition to the Coelhos manifested its position through continued affiliation with the

9 These differences are described in the memoir of Pedro Diamantino, *Juazeiro de minha infância: memórias* (Rio de Janeiro: Imprensa Nacional, 1959), pp. 47–50. Lists of officers for the Filarmônica 28 de Setembro were published in *O Farol* 3 (October 26, 1917): 2; 5 (October 19, 1919); and 6 (October 17, 1920), and reflect the dominant families.

10 *O Farol* 9 (January 17, 1924): 1; 10 (June 9, 1924): 1; and 11 (January 28, 1926) and (March 8, 1926).

11 See *O Farol* 2 (February 26, 1917): 1, and 9 (September 7, 1923): 3.

12 Alvaro Moreira da Rocha et al., *Estatutos da Sociedade Filarmônica 21 de Setembro* (Petrolina: O Farol, 1958).

13 A sampling of the lists of officers and directors is in *O Farol* 1 (September 25, 1915): 3; 2 (September 28, 1916): 1; 3 (September 7, 1917): 1; and 4 (September 17, 1918): 2. See September issues of the years thereafter.

Filarmônica 21 de Setembro, while those dependent on or loyal to the Coelhos joined the new club. Presumably to break down this division and consolidate their position, in 1968 the Coelhos constructed the Iate Clube on the bank of the São Francisco River. Its modern buildings, swimming pool, and restaurant and recreational facilities attracted both factions and also incorporated prominent Juazeiro people, although the traditional rivalries continued to be manifested at least symbolically in the festivities and social gatherings of the other two clubs. Among the first officers of the Iate Clube were industrialist Paulo de Souza Coelho; his brother-in-law and director of regional health services, Washington Barros; José Ramos, an attorney to the Coelho industrial complex and later a state deputy; and João Freitas, an engineer in the employ of the Coelhos. Freitas and other officers – Dr. Humberto Carlos Guimarães Pereira, Francisco Etelvir Dantas (the head of a new supermarket chain), and Paulo Campelo (a leading industrialist) – were residents of Juazeiro. An examination of the Iate Clube's membership list for 1969 revealed that of fifty-five male members, thirty-two were identified and interviewed in my ruling-class sample, while another seven were relatives of persons in that sample; of twenty-one female members, six were in my sample and all the others were related to persons in the sample. When the ruling-class participants were interviewed in 1971, most were then associated with the Iate Clube, whose membership by that time had grown to more than two hundred fifty. I concluded that membership in the Iate Clube was an accurate indicator of membership in the ruling classes of Juazeiro and Petrolina.[14]

Another level of social club was represented by the soccer clubs, several of which were sponsored by segments of the Petrolina ruling class. Because Juazeiro's five sporting clubs appeared to have more mass and populist support,[15] I shall focus here on those of Petrolina, whose prospects for success were directly related to financial support and social position and to differences within the ruling class.

As might be expected, the major clubs were financed by the ruling class and the others by constituencies outside that class. The Palmeiras Clube was supported by José Coelho, a former mayor and head of the commercial segment of his family's empire. The Centro Social Caiano was coordinated by Alexandre Macêdo Coelho with financial support from Paulo Coelho, head of the family's industrial complex. The head of the Nautico Clube was long-time councilman Jeconias José dos Santos, who was loyal to

14 Membership lists obtained from the manager of the Iate Clube Petrolina, July 1969; *O Farol* 54 (May 31, 1969): 4.

15 A segment in Diamantino, *Juazeiro*, pp. 53–59, discusses the formation and evolution of soccer teams in Juazeiro, including two teams made up of "youth of the Juazeiro elite." This was in the 1930s when politics were under the control of a few families. Conspicuous ruling-class support of sporting clubs in Juazeiro is less evident today.

Coelho interests. The opposition to the Coelhos supported the América Futebol Clube, headed by merchant Paulo Brito and physician José de Farias Gomes; América's motto was "O Poder Livre," "the independent power," and it had twice as many contributing supporters as rival teams. Support for the remaining two teams was mass-generated, with Flamengo Clube supported by a poor working-class district and Clube Ferroviário by railroad workers.[16]

The promotion of soccer teams in both towns provided a means of diversion for the mass population, especially for the male working classes. An unknown but relatively large proportion of Petrolina's working population, for example, was directly dependent on Coelho enterprises for its income and livelihood. Coelho support was crucial to any effort by the ruling class to maintain stability and passivity among the general population. Clearly, though, this relationship of businessman to worker was not unlike the patronage that in the past had characterized the ruling patriarchy. A survey of the general population in 1966 had revealed very little participation in politics and sports. Of the 500 respondents, about 85 percent had indicated no participation, while only 7.8 percent had been involved in the sporting clubs, 4.2 percent in labor unions, and 1 percent in political parties.[17] Official statistics on membership in organizations in 1970 showed 538 persons affiliated with sporting clubs, 465 with unions or workers' associations, and 625 with the elite social clubs.[18] In Petrolina it was incumbent upon the ruling class to control not only the single political party and the social clubs, but also sporting clubs, and, as I shall show, they were also deeply involved in the manipulation of the community's working-class organizations.

Religious organizations

The Catholic church has always exercised considerable influence in the institutional life of Juazeiro and Petrolina. Juazeiro's U.S.-born and trained bishop, Dom Thomas Murphy, had been active and effective in the town's voluntary organizations since his arrival in 1963. In discussions with leaders of these organizations and in the minutes or published reports of their activities, the bishop's impact was always evident. His intention was to stimulate the involvement and participation of the ruling class in community affairs and, of course, to cement their ties to the church and especially to its efforts to resolve many of the problems of the mass population. He was deeply involved in the Rotary and Lions, in the

16 Interview with Carlos Augusto Gomes, Petrolina, May 17, 1971.

17 Centro Latinoamericano de Pesquisa em Ciências Sociais, "Juazeiro e Petrolina, um polo de crescimento?" (Rio de Janeiro, 1967), p. 111.

18 Data for 1970 from IBGE, Petrolina, September 25, 1971.

commercial association, and in efforts to appeal to state and national authorities to allocate resources to Juazeiro. He was instrumental in mitigating tensions between the church and the local Masons. Further, he was one of the most respected members of Juazeiro society.[19] The social work of the church was carried out through the Sociedade de Obras, considered by respondents one of the most important community organizations (Table 7.2). In fact, a large number of those interviewed had worked closely with this church organization.

Similarly, several of the bishops of Petrolina have taken a deep interest in the affairs of their town. The first bishop, Dom Antônio Malan, built the cathedral, the hospital, and two schools. The second, Dom Idílio José Soares, served Petrolina rather inconspicuously from 1933 to 1943. The third, appointed in 1946, Dom Avelar Brandão Vilela, founded the Centro Social Pio XI; after leaving Petrolina, his distinguished career culminated in his being named a cardinal in 1973. The fourth bishop (since 1957), Dom Antônio Campelo de Aragão, remained generally isolated from community affairs with the exception of church and national commemorations that necessitated his official presence. Intellectually inclined and desirous of being remembered for the construction of a trade school, a nursery school, and a training center, Dom Campelo either remained in the bishop's palace or occasionally ventured into the countryside of his expansive diocese. While philosophically opposed to the activities and beliefs of many of the priests with whom he was associated, he tolerated their liberal and social-reformist inclinations. The activity of these priests in the community accounts for the recognition of Caritas and Sociedade de Obras as associations of some importance (Table 7.3). Before the military coup of 1964 they had been active in the church's controversial literacy program, eventually labeled subversive by the military. After the coup, they continued to manifest their ideals – to the masses through parish preachings and to the elites through the private schools they maintained for the sons and daughters of the ruling class. Additionally, they had the advantage of controlling the region's major radio station.

What was the extent and importance of the church's influence upon the ruling classes of the communities? I probed for an answer through several questions, and the results show recognition of and support for the church role in local affairs. For example, 87 percent of respondents agreed (30 percent strongly) that there should be religious education in the schools. There was some interesting ambivalence over the church's influence, however. Some 39 percent agreed with the statement "The spiritual needs of the citizens are not adequately met by the churches," and 55 percent disagreed with the notion that "in general, church members are better citizens."

19 Biographical details on Bishop Murphy are in *O Farol* 48 (January 31, 1963): 1.

In general, dissatisfaction with or criticism of the church was more evident in Petrolina than in Juazeiro. One can speculate as to some reasons for this. First, the church in Petrolina has long been recognized in the community as a pillar of ruling-class strength. While one church leader told me that the diocese's holdings were insignificant, their material impact upon the community was substantial.[20] Church property included the leading schools, the bishop's palace and cathedral, and the local radio station and new cinema as well as a number of lesser buildings for workers, small farmers, and peasants. Significantly, the church owned the building in which municipal council meetings were traditionally held. It had divested itself of some lands, having donated a tract (originally intended for a seminary) for the campus of the new teachers' training center; it had also sold some land to the Coelho family. The desire of many priests was to rid the diocese of its holdings and to devote its resources to the social needs of the community. Certainly the Petrolina diocese was economically more significant than its more recently established counterpart in Juazeiro, whose holdings were limited to a few buildings and an island in the São Francisco River; each year the bishop would return to the United States to raise funds for his impoverished diocese.

Another reason for negative feelings about the church in Petrolina was the potential threat it posed to the ruling class. Whereas the ruling patriarchy had once been assured a conspicuous place in church affairs, generally the priests now operated independently in the institutional life of the community. Well before the appointment of its first bishop, for instance, there had existed a Centro Paroquial, a social center under the aegis of the church whose directors included Colonels João Clementino de Souza Barros and José Rabelo Padilha.[21] The efforts of the Coelhos to manipulate the affairs of the church had not always been successful, although the family had been a major financial contributor to many church projects. I have referred elsewhere to the break during 1930 between Colonel Clementino de Souza Coelho and Dom Malán, when the colonel had taken offense to newspaper articles published under the pseudonym of a young priest who had supported the political opposition.[22] More than a generation later, the director of the radio station, Father Mansueto, in his weekly program frequently urged the workers and farmers of the region to organize in the face of the oligarchy that exploited them. The vicar-general of Petrolina, a radical young priest named Father Reginaldo, was criticized in the Recife press "for his long hair and advanced clothes."[23] Fathers Mansueto and Reginaldo were supported by an older and respected

20 Interview with Father Pedro Mansueto de Lavor, April 30, 1971.

21 *O Farol* 1 (February 1916): 1–2.

22 See Chapter 4, n. 22.

23 *Jornal do Commercio* (September 10, 1968).

liberal priest, Father Manuel de Paiva Neto. All three had been moved by the radical changes within the church throughout the Northeast of Brazil.

With such divisions within the ruling class, it is understandable that other religious influences would penetrate the community. I have mentioned the activities of the Masons. Evangelical movements also reached the backlands. More than a half-century ago, a warning was published in the local press against Protestant sects that were "perverting the Brazilian people and their Catholic beliefs with Protestant heresy."[24] At the time of my study, Petrolina had a thriving Baptist church and school, directed by an American missionary. Baptist influence in neighboring Juazeiro was also evident, and in November 1970 an evangelical crusade was held in the two communities.[25] A reactionary Catholic organization also made known its presence in the early 1970s. Known as Tradição, Família e a Propriedade (Tradition, Family, and Property), it called itself "a civic society" dedicated "to countering leftist infiltration in Catholic circles."[26] One day several of its militants appeared in the streets of Petrolina and Juazeiro knocking on doors and enlisting support. That evening Father Mansueto warned the community against this "reactionary" movement of "fascist inspiration."[27]

Cultural institutions

Historically the cultural center of the region was Juazeiro, which had a flourishing press at the turn of the present century. There were such organs as *Cidade do Joazeiro, Fôlha de São Francisco, Fôlha do Povo,* and the *Correio do São Francisco,* the latter owned by the Duarte family and edited by Jesuino Ignácio da Silva. Other papers included *Diário de Juazeiro* and *O Direito; O Trabalho* was published by Edson Ribeiro in 1932; *O Echo* was founded by the Araújo family about 1925 and *O Momento* by the Vianna family in 1928. In spite of this prolific tradition, Juazeiro has not had a newspaper since the late 1930s, although an issue of *Tribuna do São Francisco* was published in November 1970. Again, although an academy of letters, Acadêmia Joazeirense de Letras, existed briefly in 1933,[28] today the town's sparse archives and the remnants of its only significant library

24 *O Farol*, 6 (June 28, 1921), 2–3; 6 (July 3, 1921): 1–2, 3.

25 See articles by Waldemir L. dos Santos, Baptist minister in Juazeiro, and Maria Izabel Figueiredo Pontes, director of the Municipal Department of Education and Culture, in *O Evangelizador* (Recife), 28 (October 1970): 5–8.

26 Tradição, Família e a Propriedade, "O que é a TFP?" (two-page leaflet distributed in Petrolina and Juazeiro, September 1971).

27 Speech by Father Mansueto de Lavor, Emissora Rural, A Voz do São Francisco, September 11, 1971.

28 *O Farol* 18 (May 23, 1933): 1. The publisher of *O Echo*, Aprígio Araújo, was a member of its executive committee.

are retained in the inaccessible Clube Comercial, and the only evidence of a cultural tradition is the sponsorship of a folk festival by a small commercially oriented radio station and the inspiration of its well-known celebrity, the singer and composer, João Gilberto.

Petrolina's less conspicuous cultural advances have been marked by its weekly and biweekly newspaper *O Farol,* edited by João Ferreira Gomes since its founding in 1915. When this newspaper took a stand in opposition to the ambitions of the Coelho family after World War II, the family quickly promoted a paper of its own, *O Sertão,* edited by Cid de Almeida Carvalho. Carvalho had learned his trade in the printshop of Ferreira Gomes, and this move by the Coelhos ensured them not only a voice in the community, but also coopted for them the town's most active organizer of the working class. Eventually, *O Farol* came under indirect control of the Coelhos, who provided financial support through advertising.

The town's other cultural attractions included a public library and two cinemas, one of which adjoined the radio station Emissora Rural, A Voz do São Francisco. This theater (Massangano) was also used for other events, including musical programs and an occasional play (Antônio de Santana Padilha was the town's best-known writer and playwright).[29] Petrolina's first radio station, Difusora Guararapes, had existed since about 1948; Emissora Rural was founded in 1961 and moved into its modern facilities in 1970. The Emissora was commercially oriented and dependent upon local advertising, despite the church's intention to use it as a means of reaching people throughout the São Francisco Valley. While professing its political independence of the ruling class, Emissora Rural was closely tied to the community's economic interests, as an examination of its advertising receipts for 1970 reveals. Enterprises controlled by the Coelhos accounted for 34 percent of all receipts in that year, and another 5 percent related to the local supermarkets, then under the control of the Coelhos. Roughly another 5 percent of the income was derived from advertising of an appliance store under the control of João Batista Cavalcanti and from business interests of Diniz Cavalcanti. Both men at one time had opposed the Coelhos politically; João Batista had run unsuccessfully for mayor, and on his defeat in 1957 he had moved to Recife but maintained his economic interests in Petrolina. Diniz had given up contesting the Coelhos and joined their slate as vice mayor from 1959 to 1969.[30]

The ruling classes of these communities are dependent on newspapers and radio for information about local, national, and international affairs. Effective television transmission from Recife and Salvador had not reached

29 See Chapter 4, n. 1, for his publications.

30 Statement of financial receipts for 1970, Emissora Rural, June 21, 1971.

the communities by the early 1970s. Newspapers from the state capitals usually arrived on a daily basis. My interviews with 118 influentials indicated that 73 percent read newspapers regularly and 24 percent occasionally; 79 percent listened to the radio regularly and 19 percent occasionally; 59 percent read magazines regularly and 35 percent occasionally. Only 7 percent never discussed public affairs, while nearly half did so on a regular basis. This interest in daily information contrasted with data from a survey of the broader population made in 1966. Of the 500 respondents in that survey, 22 percent listened to the radio regularly, 42 percent sometimes, and 33 percent never (two-fifths of the families had no radio). Only 2 percent listened to Radio Juazeiro, while 28 percent tuned in to Emissora Rural and 22 percent to stations in the state capitals. Only 18 percent read a daily newspaper; 57 percent read no paper at all.[31]

Labor unions

Although the unionization of workers in Juazeiro and Petrolina has been deliberately slow and uneventful, the ruling classes have recognized the need to extend their influence to urban workers and small farmers. At times some segments of the ruling classes have supported minimal labor organization in exchange for electoral support; this has been especially evident in Juazeiro. In my interviews with members of the ruling classes I inquired about attitudes toward the working classes. Some 93 percent agreed that unions were necessary for workers, and 72 percent believed that unions were important organizations. Only 9 percent felt that unions were the most important organizations in their communities, yet 48 percent considered labor leaders very important; this figure is considerably lower than that for leaders of other aspects of community life, but 73 percent considered labor leaders understanding and helpful in the solving of problems.

In examining labor organizations, it may be helpful to recall the class differences that prevail in these communities. According to the 1966 survey of the urban population, about three-fourths of the inhabitants were lower class, less than a fourth middle class, and 1.4 percent and 3.2 percent upper class, respectively, in Petrolina and Juazeiro.[32] My own survey of the ruling class included some persons who had been active in the organization of labor but whose origins or current social status were middle or upper class. As I have reported, when asked their social class, of 118 respondents only 1 considered himself lower class, although 28 said they were poor and 57 identified with the proletariat rather than the bourgeoisie.

31 Centro Latinoamericano de Pesquisa em Ciências Sociais, "Juazeiro e Petrolina," pp. 110–111.
32 Ibid., p. 97.

Historically, there have been only two periods in which growth of the labor movement has been significant: during the late 1930s, under legislation promoted by the Vargas government, and during the early 1960s, under the populist Goulart government. I have referred briefly to the activities of Cid de Almeida Carvalho in fomenting the beginnings of labor organization in Petrolina. On February 5, 1933, he founded the artisans União dos Artífices Petrolinenses, which he has headed ever since.[33] The organization attempts to provide for the social and cultural needs of its fewer than two hundred members. Councilman Jeconias José dos Santos was long active in the union. Carvalho also founded the metalworkers' Sindicato dos Operários Metalúrgicos about 1935, and later he organized the Comité de Propaganda e Organização Sindical no Alto Sertão de Pernambuco. Outspoken as a leader at that time, he despaired that labor legislation was not being implemented in the backlands.[34] Obviously a threat to some elements of the ruling class, he was condemned as a communist, a charge he vigorously protested.[35]

During this incipient period of the labor movement, other unions appeared. In Petrolina there was the office workers' Sindicato dos Empregados no Commercio, founded in December 1934, and the construction workers' Sindicato dos Operários em Construção Civil, established in the same year. In Juazeiro similar metalworkers' and construction workers' unions were formed, as well as a union for stevedores and other workers in shipping. The latter went on strike in 1934, and shots were exchanged with company officials.[36] So effective was the labor movement in Juazeiro that a workers' party, União Trabalhista Juazeirense, was organized in 1935. It was tied to the opposition Partido Democrata Juazeirense and was unsuccessful in its bid for political power.[37] Thereafter, the movement in both towns seems to have declined. The railroad workers' Sindicato dos Ferroviários was abolished by decree in 1938, and the metalworkers' and construction workers' unions were also closed down, apparently because of repression from the ruling classes. Carvalho lamented "the lack of support of the public power." Without assistance from political authorities, he argued, the proletariat was condemned to hunger – the consequence of exploitation.[38]

33 A description of the União dos Artífices Petrolinenses is in *Album histórico e ilustrado de Petrolina* (Petrolina: Gráfica Petrolina, September 1948).

34 Cid de Almeida Carvalho, "As leis sociais, sua falta de execuąão no interior – males que disso se originam," *O Farol* 20 (March 9, 1935): 1.

35 *O Farol* 20 (January 10, 1935): 1.

36 *O Farol* 20 (November 30, 1934): 1.

37 *O Farol* 21 (October 12, 1935): 1.

38 See statements by Cid de Almeida Carvalho in *O Farol* 24 (October 22, 1938): 3, and 27 (March 12, 1942): 1.

The election of João Goulart to the presidency in 1961 was accompanied by an awakening of the languishing labor movement. Goulart had once served Vargas as labor minister, and his rise to power was due partly to his ties to labor, even though he was a wealthy Rio Grande do Sul rancher. A resurgence of labor activity was evident in Juazeiro, where populist politicians around Américo Tanuri viewed their ties to the working class as essential to efforts to defeat ruling Vianna interests. At the time, organized labor included the river transport workers' Sindicato dos Trabalhadores em Transportes Fluviais and the Sociedade Beneficente dos Artífices Juazeirenses, the latter headed by the furniture manufacturer and politician Durval Vicente Lima.[39] During July 1961 the First Conference of Workers of the Middle São Francisco was held in Juazeiro. Themes of the conference included salary problems, union autonomy, the right to strike, social welfare, agrarian reform, and dues; other topics were clearly politically and ideologically motivated, including such nationalist concerns as antitrust laws, profit remittance abroad, and Brazilian relations with the world. Thereafter the movement gained some momentum with the establishment of centers in the working-class districts and the founding of the Círculo Operário de Juazeiro and the Associação Assistencial de Juazeiro. With the enactment of new government legislation and on the initiative of the Catholic church, a small farmers' Sindicato Rural was also set up. Despite the electoral success of the Tanuri group in 1963 and its continued ties to the working population, the labor movement again declined after the military intervention in national politics and the fall of Goulart in 1964. The river transport workers' union in Juazeiro did, however, attempt, without success, to establish a branch in Petrolina.[40]

Before 1964, however, the political opposition in Petrolina had maneuvered for labor support against the Coelhos. With the support of the opposition councilman José Borges Viana, the construction workers' Sindicato dos Operários em Construção Civil had been recognized (an important development, because the construction industry was monopolized by a Coelho firm), but it was repressed after 1964. In the rural sector and with the support of progressive priests, the Legiões Agrárias were formed about 1962 and came to include about a thousand small farmers and salaried farm workers. These same priests also encouraged the formation of the Sindicato de Trabalhadores Rurais in Petrolina; created in 1963, its membership was over six hundred by 1970. Fearful of repression

39 *O Farol* 45 (January 16, 1960): 4.

40 According to the report by the Centro Latinoamericano de Pesquisa em Ciências Sociais, "Juazeiro e Petrolina," pp. 54–55: "One has the impression that some businessmen of Petrolina consider unions as politicized groups, controlled by minorities."

and not very powerful in the face of Coelho interests, these rural organizations were generally ineffectual.[41]

With the advantage of financial institutions and credit on their side, the Coelhos moved to consolidate their influence over workers. A Centro Educativo dos Operários de Petrolina was founded about 1965 and inaugurated by Nilo Coelho.[42] With funds from the state and federal government, elaborate recreational facilities were constructed on the outskirts of the city, where workers lived. A Sindicato Rural de Petrolina was organized under the presidency of Geraldo Coelho; it apparently served the needs of all farmers and ranchers in the area.[43] The efforts of the church to organize rural workers were also undermined by the plans of Superintendência do Desenvolvimento do Nordeste (SUDENE) and SUVALE, which had supervised the nearby Bebedouro experimental lands where small farmers were recruited to tend the fields. According to one source, these agencies intended to unionize all rural workers of the region as they expanded irrigation to new lands.[44]

It was not impossible to speculate on the prospects of improved working conditions as a consequence of the efforts by the Coelhos and the federal government to consolidate their hold over the working classes of the region. The majority of workers were unskilled and uneducated; even in the cities, many of the industrial firms brought their skilled labor and technicians from other areas. This problem would not be resolved simply by establishing new training centers; it would also be necessary to implement some of the existing labor legislation.[45]

Service organizations

Organizations that served particular needs or constituencies such as the Fundação Educacional, CODESF, the Associação Petrolinense de Amparo à Maternidade e Infância (APAMI), and the Fundação Rural had been established by the members of the ruling class, generally in Petrolina.

41 Interview with Cornelio Casimiro da Rocha, president of the Sindicato de Trabalhadores, July 7, 1969. The Program of the Legiões Agrárias was outlined in Dom Antônio Campelo de Aragão, "As Legiões Agrárias e o futuro do homem do campo" (Petrolina, February 1962). He states that the organization was inspired by Pope XXIII's encyclical, *Mater et Magistra*. At this time peasants and small farmers were being organized throughout the state of Pernambuco by the peasant leagues of socialist deputy Francisco Julião, by radical Catholic priests, and by Communist party militants.

42 *O Farol* 50 (January 23, 1965): 1.

43 *O Sertão* 21 (December 16, 1969): 4.

44 Interview with Father Mansueto de Lavor, July 5, 1969.

45 The report of the Centro Latinoamericano de Pesquisa em Ciências Sociais, "Juazeiro e Petrolina," pp. 51–55, states that of twenty firms studied, ten resorted to contracting outside technicians, and it stressed the need for training and legislation.

CODESF, for example, was first headed by the bishop of Juazeiro; a former mayor of Petrolina served as president at another time, and its secretary-general since its founding in 1964 had been Giuseppe Muccini, a respected physician. CODESF and the Fundação Educacional brought progressive changes to their communities. Established as private entities, they operated with private and public funds under the control of the local ruling classes. For example, twenty-three of the sixty-two persons who endorsed the charter of CODESF were included in my survey of the ruling classes seven years later, as were sixteen of the twenty-six persons who had affirmed the statutes of the Fundação Educacional in 1961.[46] CODESF was the outgrowth of a movement in the 1950s to bring hydroelectric power to the region,[47] and it was effective in exerting pressure on state governments in Recife and Salvador and on the federal government to pave roads to the interior and allocate funds for community projects. The Fundação Educacional stimulated the growth of new educational facilities in Petrolina, including a public high school and the Faculdade de Formação de Professores.

The APAMI and the Fundação Rural served particular concerns in Petrolina. Both organizations were founded and directed by Coelho interests. APAMI's activities were in the area of maternity and child care, including orphans. As president, Augusto Coelho coordinated its activities. The Fundação was founded in 1959 under the municipal government of José Coelho. Its activities included the study and planning of agricultural and livestock industry, and among its facilities was a hostel in Petrolina for farmers visiting from the countryside.

The close and often direct relationship between the major civic and social organizations and the ruling classes of Juazeiro and Petrolina is clear in Table 7.4. In Juazeiro one senses that the fragmented ruling classes reflect weaknesses in the organizational life of the community, whether the problem be in the lack of leadership, scant resources, or diffusion of energies. When the opposition to the Vianna family gained political control, the more general population began to be more involved in the political process, but all this was dissipated by the abrupt shift in national politics with the coup of 1964. Thereafter, it seems, the activities of civic and social organizations were less meaningful. In Petrolina it was not clear that such organizations had ever had much impact upon the community. In any event, they were almost always under the control of the ruling classes. Generally after 1955 the community perception of these institutions seems to have been subject to the whims of the Coelhos. Many of the

46 See "Estatutos da Fundação Educacional de Petrolina" (Petrolina, 1961), 7pp., mimeographed copy. Also see Comissão de Desenvolvimento Econômico do São Francisco, *Carta de princípios, direitos e reivindicações* (Juazeiro, 1964), p. 6.

47 *O Farol* 42 (November 16, 1957): 1.

Table 7.4. *Members of the ruling class in the civic and social life of Juazeiro and Petrolina, 1965–70*

Type of organization	Juazeiro: Name of organization	Juazeiro: Positions held[a]	Petrolina: Name of organization	Petrolina: Positions held[a]
Professional	Associação Comercial, Industrial e Agricola	President (4) V. President (1) Secretary (1)	Associação Comercial	President (1) V. President (1) Secretary (1)
	Clube Comercial	President (1)		
	União dos Barqueiros	President (1) Secretary (1)		
Fraternal	Lions Club	President (3)	Rotary Club	President (3) Director (3)
	Rotary Club	President (1) Director (1)		
	Freemasons	President (2) V. President (2) Other (4)		
Social	Apollo Juazeirense	President (2)	21 de Setembro	President (4) V. President (2) Secretary (2)
	28 de Setembro	Secretary (1) Director (1)		
	Country Clube	Secretary (1) President (1)	Petrolina Clube	President (1) V. President (2) Secretary (1)
	Soccer clubs	President (1)	Iate Clube	President (1) V. President (1) Secretary (1) Treasurer (1) Director (5)
			Soccer clubs	President (4)

Religious	Sociedade de Obras	President (1)	Sociedade de Obras	President (1)
		V. President (1)		Assistant Director (1)
		Secretary (1)		
			Caritas	Director (1)
Cultural	Rádio Juazeiro	Director (1)	*O Farol*	Editor (1)
			O Sertão	Editor (1)
			Emissora Rural	Director (1)
Labor	Sociedade Beneficente dos Artífices Juazeirenses	President (1)	União dos Artífices	President (1)
		V. President (1)		
				V. President (1)
	Círculo Operário	President (1)	Legiões Agrárias	Advisor (1)
	Sindicato Rural	President (2)	Sindicato de Trabalhadores	Advisor (1)
		V. President (1)		
		Secretary (1)		
			Sindicato Rural	President (1)
Service			APAMI	President (1)
				V. President (1)
				Secretary (1)
			CODESF	President (3)
				V. President (1)
				Secretary (3)
			Fundação Educacional	President (2)
				V. President (2)
				Director (2)
			Fundação Rural	President (1)

[a]Figures in parentheses indicate number of persons surveyed who had held the position during the period 1965 to 1970. Many persons had held more than one position over this period.

organizations were also dependent on people and decisions outside the communities. For example, the commercial associations comprised members whose firms usually distributed products manufactured elsewhere. Fraternal groups such as the Rotary, Lions, or the Masons' lodges were affiliated with an international organizational network. Newspapers and radio stations were dependent on outside information and the activities of the church related to decisions emanating not only from Recife and Salvador, but also from Rome.

8

Ideology

Various usages of the term "ideology" run through the literature of social science. The theorists of the Enlightenment identified ideology with the search for truth and the dispelling of illusions; it was a "science of ideas." Karl Marx offered a different conception, arguing that ideology was "false consciousness," or the illusion created by the experience of a social class in a capitalist society. True consciousness, he believed, would come only through class struggle, in which workers would begin to understand their alienation from the process of capitalist production.[1] Karl Mannheim relied on Marx's interpretation but distinguished between a particular conception of ideology as "more or less conscious disguises of the real situation" and a more inclusive conception of ideology as "a concrete historical-social group, e.g., of a class."[2]

Contemporary social science views ideology as a set of values, beliefs, expectations, or prescriptions. Ideologies often are associated with industrialization and the economic and social problems that may ensue. Sometimes ideologies are defined in an unrealistically optimistic context, whether a free market or classless society. Thus, it is suggested, ideologies are becoming exhausted in the modern world. With technology, there may be stability and consensus so that ideologies reach an end.[3] This view has been challenged by many writers. Joseph La Palombara, for example, argued that many ideologies deserve study,[4] and David Apter considered the study of ideology more important than ever.[5] In my study of the ruling classes in Juazeiro and Petrolina, I adopted the accepted definition of ideology as the values and beliefs of a community or group and investigated the content of these classes' ideologies. My approach to the problem

1 Karl Marx, *The German Ideology*, ed. by C. J. Arthur (New York: International Publishers, 1973).

2 Karl Mannheim, *Ideology and Utopia: An Introduction to the Sociology of Knowledge*, trans. Louis Wirth and Edward Shills (New York: Harcourt, Brace, and World, 1936). pp. 55–56.

3 The best example of this end-of-ideology thesis is in Daniel Bell, *The End of Ideology: On the Exhaustion of Political Ideas in the Fifties* (New York: Collier Books, 1962).

4 Joseph LaPalombara, "Decline of Ideology: A Dissent and an Interpretation," *American Political Science Review* 60 (March 1966): 5–16.

5 David E. Apter, ed., *Ideology and Discontent* (New York: Free Press of Glencoe, 1964), p. 17.

was informed by the work of Robert D. Putnam, who studied ideology in elite political culture, emphasizing the British example;[6] Juan Corradi; who examined the culture and ideology of local elites in relation to dependent capitalist development in Latin America;[7] and Peter McDonough, who studied the ideology of Brazilian elites.[8]

Members of the ruling classes in Juazeiro and Petrolina were asked if they agreed or disagreed with a number of statements about life in their communities. Some statements generalized attitudinal items drawn from the work of others; others were specially constructed to test attitudes relevant to other parts of the present study. The following discussion summarizes and analyzes the findings, focusing on the distinction between traditional and progressive and between local and cosmopolitan, understanding of capitalism, attitudes about community services and education, patriotism and nationalism, and the content and agents of socialization into these values and attitudes. An important part of the discussion is an assessment of the extent to which ideologies reflect an emerging bourgeois society whose economic base is largely agricultural and commercial.

Table 8.1 shows roughly similar orientations toward traditional and progressive perspectives in the two communities.[9] My assumption had been that rulers in Juazeiro and Petrolina would be traditional and conservative, and, indeed, most respondents considered religion essential and emphasized protection of property rights. At the same time, however, they demonstrated a sense of community in their rejection of the idea that social needs and the progress of the community depend more on individual than on collective initiative and responsibility. They also manifested progressive sentiments in supporting the notion that wealth should be taxed and profits distributed in accordance with productive work. Only about a third went so far as to favor the idea of a classless society and a commitment to society over the family. Juazeiro respondents were more inclined than their counterparts in Petrolina to protect property rights, yet they favored the replacement of profits with reimbursements for useful work. It was apparent that the impact of competitive capitalism and its values of

6 Robert D. Putnam, "Studying Elite Political Culture: The Case of 'Ideology,' " *American Political Science Review* 65 (September 1971): 651–681.

7 Juan Corradi, "Cultural Dependence and the Sociology of Knowledge: The Latin American Case," *International Journal of Contemporary Sociology*. 8 (January 1971): 35–55.

8 Peter McDonough, "Policy Misperceptions among Brazilian Elites" (Ann Arbor: University of Michigan, July 1977), mimeographed copy. Also see his *Power and Ideology in Brazil* (Princeton: Princeton University Press, 1981).

9 Many of the questionnaire items were taken from a social-attitudes scale in M. Shaw and J. Wright, *Scales for the Measurement of Attitudes* (New York: McGraw-Hill, 1967), pp. 322–324, and discussed and reprinted in John B. Robinson, Jerrold G. Rusk, and Kendra B. Head, *Measures of Political Attitudes* (Ann Arbor, Mich.: Survey Research Center, Institute for Social Research, 1968), pp. 98–99. The scale originally measured conservatism and liberalism on a number of issues.

Table 8.1. *Traditional versus progressive views among the ruling classes*

	% Agreeing	
	Juazeiro (N = 66)	Petrolina (N = 52)
Traditional		
"If civilization is to survive, there must be a turning back to religion."	88	79
"A first consideration in any society is the protection of property rights."	79	59
"The home and the church should have all the responsibility for preparing young people for marriage and parenthood."	97	92
"The social needs of the citizens are the responsibility of themselves and their families and not of the community."	5	10
"A community would get along better if each one would mind his business and others take care of theirs."	44	21
Progressive		
"Large fortunes should be taxed fairly heavily over and above income taxes."	81	71
"Our present economic system should be reformed so that profits are replaced by reimbursements for useful work."	64	48
"True democracy is limited because of the special privileges enjoyed by business and industry."	36	42
"A classless society should be established."	30	27
"Allegiance to the collective society should replace dependence on the family."	20	29

individuality and greed had not destroyed altogether a traditional ideal and practice in which family, church, and community were respected along with values of togetherness and equality.

Further evidence of this ambivalence is seen in Table 8.2 where strong support for private enterprise is revealed, especially in Juazeiro, where municipal laws and regulations are expected to serve business.[10] Further, the welfare of the community was perceived as largely dependent on industry and business. Yet the individual entrepreneur was not to be permitted free rein to accumulate wealth; relatively few respondents ruled

10 Many of the statements for Tables 8.3, 8.4, and 8.5 are taken from a community-attitude scale in C. Bosworth, "A Study of the Development and the Validation of a Measure of Citizens' Attitudes toward Progress and Game Variables Related Thereto" (Ann Arbor: Ph.D. dissertation, University of Michigan, 1954). The scale is reproduced in Robinson, Rusk, and Head, *Measures of Political Attitudes*, pp. 392–396.

Table 8.2. *Ruling-class views on capitalism*

	% Agreeing	
	Juazeiro (N = 66)	Petrolina (N = 52)
"Municipal laws and regulations should be such as first to ensure the prosperity of business, since the prosperity of all depends on the prosperity of business."	94	54
"The well-being of the community depends mainly on its industry and business."	91	67
"Individuals with the ability and foresight to earn and accumulate wealth should have the right to enjoy that wealth without government interference and regulation."	46	35
"No community improvement program should be carried on that is injurious to a business."	35	31
"The first and major responsibility of each citizen should be to earn dollars for his own pocket."	11	17

out government regulation to ensure some balance in the economy. Likewise, respondents felt that business should not be given preference over community projects, and that citizens should give first consideration to fellow citizens rather than to their own financial gain.

Response to a number of statements about the provision of community services and education also reflects a commitment to community. In each case Juazeiro respondents demonstrated greater agreement with this ideal than those in Petrolina (Tables 8.3 and 8.4). Unemployment insurance was understood as a right, and communities were held responsible for the care of older people. The government was expected to control housing rents and values, to clean up slum areas, and to provide recreation facilities. Respondents said that educational facilities should be expanded and all Brazilians provided access to school, that education at all levels should be at public expense, and that special programs should be made available for adults and other constituencies. At the same time, they overwhelmingly believed that religious instruction should be permitted in public schools (see Table 8.4).

Various measures were used to determine whether members of the ruling classes were oriented toward local or toward cosmopolitan concerns.[11] Given the parochial nature of these two isolated communities, I

11 In their *Local Power and Comparative Politics* (Beverly Hills, Calif.: Sage Professional Papers in Comparative Politics [01–049], 1974), Mark Kesselman and Donald Rosenthal demonstrate the fruitfulness of a strategy that "incorporate(s) concerns about localism, local government, institutions, and localistic political processes into a framework that ties the local dimension to an understanding of national political processes."

Table 8.3. *Ruling-class views on community services*

	% Agreeing	
	Juazeiro (N = 66)	Petrolina (N = 52)
"Unemployment insurance is an inalienable right of the working man."	97	89
"The responsibility for older people should be confined to themselves and their families instead of the communities."	14	29
"The government should control all rents and the value of housing."	76	54
"Improving slum areas is a waste of money."	7	17
"While it grows, a community need not provide additional recreational facilities."	7	13

Table 8.4. *Ruling-class perspectives on education*

	% Agreeing	
	Juazeiro (N = 66)	Petrolina (N = 52)
"Some sort of religious education should be given in public schools."	88	85
"Adult education is not necessary as a part of the local school program."	8	15
"Educational facilities should be expanded so as to allow all Brazilians to attend school freely, from elementary to higher education."	91	87
"Municipal aid for the construction of schools is long overdue and should be instituted as a permanent policy."	100	65
"All individuals who are intellectually capable of benefiting from it should get university education at public expense if necessary."	76	54

had assumed that people would manifest more interest in local events, and would tend to be more aware of governmental affairs at the local than at the state, national, or international level. Further, I supposed that they would have more confidence in local government than in government at other levels. Not all these expectations were fulfilled.

One measure consisted of items designed to learn if respondents were more interested and involved in local than in national and international

Table 8.5. *Local versus cosmopolitan orientations among the ruling classes*

	% Agreeing	
	Juazeiro (N = 66)	Petrolina (N = 52)
"The most rewarding organizations a person can belong to are local clubs and associations rather than large nationwide organizations."	94	88
"National and international happenings rarely seem as interesting as events that occur right in the local community in which one lives."	81	63
"Although newcomers to the community are probably capable people, when it comes to choosing a person for a responsible position in the community, I prefer a person whose family is well established in the community."	57	51
"The local community constitutes the strength of Brazil."	52	67
"I have greater respect for a man who is well established in his local community than a man who is widely known in his field but has no local roots."	57	47

affairs, if they related more to local clubs and associations than to nationwide organizations, and if they respected individuals with local reputations more than individuals with national ones (Table 8.5).[12] In general, Juazeiro respondents tended to express more commitment to local concerns than their counterparts in Petrolina. However, leaders in both communities overwhelmingly agreed that local clubs and associations were more rewarding than nationwide organizations and that happenings in the local community were more interesting than those at the national and international levels. In choosing a responsible person for a position in the community, respondents preferred a person from a well-established local family, and they agreed that the strength of Brazil as a nation rested primarily in the local community.

When asked if they followed what was going on in government, 70 percent of respondents replied that they paid attention to governmental affairs most of the time and 20 percent that they were interested some of the time. Given such interest, they were then asked to rank-order the levels of government that they followed most closely. Their choices are identified in Table 8.6, in which national affairs appear most important,

12 The five Likert-type items were used originally by Thomas R. Dye in a random sample of 340 residents and 105 elected public officials drawn from sixteen suburban municipalities in the Philadelphia metropolitan area. See Dye's "The Local-Cosmopolitan Dimension and the Study of Urban Politics," *Social Forces* 41 (1966): 239–246.

Table 8.6. *Level of governmental affairs followed closely by members of the ruling classes in Juazeiro (N = 66) and Petrolina (N = 52) (%)*

Level of affairs	Rank of how closely followed			
	First	Second	Third	Fourth
International				
Juazeiro	0	5	24	71
Petrolina	10	11	9	67
National				
Juazeiro	68	11	19	7
Petrolina	45	24	30	3
State				
Juazeiro	14	48	27	11
Petrolina	18	29	44	11
Local				
Juazeiro	18	36	30	14
Petrolina	27	36	17	19

Table 8.7. *Awareness of government among the ruling class (%)*

Rank ordering	Confidence in government		Follow government closely	
	Juazeiro (N = 66)	Petrolina (N = 52)	Juazeiro (N = 66)	Petrolina (N = 52)
Municipal–state–national–international	0	2	14	19
State–municipal–national–international	2	6	8	6
State–national–municipal–international	2	13	3	15
State–national–international–municipal	65	40	54	34
National–state–international–municipal	22	31	14	9
National–international–state–municipal	5	8	6	11
International–national–state–municipal	4	0	0	6

followed by state, then local, and finally international ones. Table 8.7 examines a ranking of choices from local to international dimensions. The four levels of government can be ranked in any one of twenty-four ways, yet seven of these orderings characterized the responses of leaders. In Juazeiro especially but also in Petrolina the level of interest and awareness tended toward the state–national–international–municipal order. Similarly, most confidence was expressed in state and national levels of government. This finding probably reflects that historically Juazeiro as a regional administrative center had several state and federal government agencies, whereas Petrolina has close ties with state government as a consequence of

Table 8.8. *Degree of confidence in level of government among the ruling classes in Juazeiro (N = 66) and Petrolina (N = 52) (%)*

Level of affairs	Rank of confidence			
	First	Second	Third	Fourth
International				
Juazeiro	2	5	27	64
Petrolina	5	9	29	58
National				
Juazeiro	88	8	2	2
Petrolina	73	13	11	2
State				
Juazeiro	8	63	23	6
Petrolina	13	39	35	12
Local				
Juazeiro	2	24	48	27
Petrolina	9	39	25	28

Coelho control of the Pernambucan gubernatorial office.[13] However, Table 8.8 reveals that respondents had most confidence in national government, least confidence in international activities.

This interest in national and state government is reflected in a degree of patriotism and nationalism. Patriotism is the conviction among people that society must be preserved or expanded. Patriotism is tied to cultural heritage and ritualistic symbols of nationality such as independence, heroes, and territory. Nationalism involves both recognition of symbols of nationality and acceptance of the nation-state as the supreme arbiter of human activities.[14] Those interviewed were queried as to their agreement with some statements that describe characteristics of national unity. Their responses, in Table 8.9, displayed strong feelings of patriotism with nearly unanimous agreement in Juazeiro and overwhelming support in Petrolina. Obviously such symbols of nationality as the Portuguese language, the flag, consciousness of nation and territory, and the idea of independence or autonomy were intrinsic to the patriotism of local notables in Juazeiro and Petrolina.

Patriotism and nationalism were tested with the nine items shown in Table 8.10. Members of the ruling classes of Juazeiro and Petrolina agreed

13 The ordering in Tables 8.6 and 8.7 is based on a scale developed by M. Kent Jennings, "Pre-adult Orientations to Multiple Systems of Government," paper presented to the Midwest Conference of Political Scientists, April 1966, and summarized in Robinson, Rusk, and Head, *Measures of Political Attitudes*, pp. 400–402.

14 This definition comes from Kalman H. Silvert, ed. in *Expectant Peoples: Nationalism and Development* (New York: Random House, 1963), introduction and p. 440.

Table 8.9. *Ruling-class recognition of symbols of national unity*

Symbols of national unity	% Agreeing Juazeiro (N = 66)	% Agreeing Petrolina (N = 52)
A single language	97	98
A single territory	98	98
The heritage of customs	97	83
Flag, anthem, parades, etc.	98	98
Single government	100	98
Autonomy	100	90
Self-determination	100	94
Consciousness of nation among citizens	100	96
Creed of loyalty	98	90
Justice for all	100	81

Table 8.10. *Patriotism and nationalism among the ruling classes*

	% Agreeing Juazeiro (N = 66)	% Agreeing Petrolina (N = 52)
"No duties are more important than duties toward one's own country."	70	72
"This nation's frontiers should be open to all those who wish to settle here."	87	81
"When a national government is incompetent, the use of force to remove it can be justified."	74	73
"Our nation ought to be willing to give up its independence and submit to the authority of a United States of the World."	8	4
"One should always show greater loyalties to the president and the government than to a national political party."	89	62
"All human beings are equally important. No Brazilian is of more value than any person from any other country."	99	94
"Our nation ought to support the establishment of a world government that could solve international disputes by force."	25	16
"The defense of our nation can never justify the taking of another human life."	56	45
"One should show greater loyalty toward humanity than toward Brazil as a nation."	60	78

that president and government are more important than a national political party and that duty to country is of the highest importance, but at the same time accepted the use of force to remove an incompetent government. Although they were dubious of efforts in the direction of world government and international reconciliation of disputes, they indicated a willingness to open the nation's frontiers to those who wished to settle in Brazil and a belief that all human beings are equally important and that the defense of the nation can never justify the taking of human life.[15]

When respondents were asked to assess the degree of national unity in Brazil, substantial differences between Juazeiro and Petrolina emerged; 80 percent in Juazeiro and only 31 percent in Petrolina said that unity was great. A number of obstacles to national unity were identified, including "regionalism," "administrative bureaucracy," "lack of education," and the "selfishness of people."

Responses to my request for a list of the most notable characteristics of the Brazilian suggested respect and pride: "a good person," "astute," "altruistic," "intelligent," "sentimentalist," "courageous," "cheerful," "pacifist," "tolerant," "obedient," "flexible," "hospitable." The Brazilian was viewed as "patriotic and a defender of the national wealth" and a person with a "spirit of solidarity and patriotism." Imbued with "confidence" and "defense of the nation," the Brazilian would "assure the development of the nation."

While nationalism was associated with various Brazilian movements in search of independence throughout the nineteenth century, the country's regional disparities kept it from being very significant until the 1930s. The Vargas regime introduced restrictions on immigration and the exclusion of non-Brazilians from public office, nationalized the railroads, promoted a government airline, and established a national steel industry. Under President Juscelino Kubitschek, the Instituto Superior de Estudos Brasileiros was founded in 1956 to study and promote nationalism as an ideology for Brazilian development, and although this institute was dissolved by the military in 1964, nationalism continued as a powerful force.[16]

Because nationalism in Brazil tends to be related to political and economic development, I asked members of the ruling classes of Juazeiro and Petrolina about this relationship. Nationalism, it is sometimes argued, provides an impetus and motivation for political development by enhancing people's identification with the nation and thereby both reinforcing

15 The items in Table 8.10 are from a national patriotism scale in B. Christiansen, *Attitudes toward Foreign Affairs as a Function of Personality* (Oslo: Olso University Press, 1959). A brief discussion of this scale is in Robinson, Rusk, and Head, *Measures of Political Attitudes*, pp. 351–352.

16 See Frank Bonilla, "A National Ideology for Development: Brazil," in Silvert, *Expectant Peoples*, pp. 232–264.

Table 8.11. *Ruling-class views on nationalism and development*

	% Agreeing	
	Juazeiro (N = 66)	Petrolina (N = 52)
"The government should build support for its actions by propagating its ideology."	97	73
"Consumption should be limited to the needs of the people, with luxury items eliminated."	62	64
"The government should assume control of all industry."	38	69
"The government should build infrastructure (roads, power, transport, etc.)."	100	100
"The land tenure system should be reformed so as to allocate land to all those who need it."	100	89
"The government should control all natural resources."	91	91
"Protective tariffs should be established."	97	86
"Foreign enterprise should be nationalized."	65	67
"All public utilities should be nationalized."	84	85

governmental legitimacy and authority and opening up the system to greater participation. In Juazeiro, the ruling class showed consensus with this position, agreeing almost unanimously with the view that the government should build support by propagating its own ideology; those in Petrolina offered strong though not unanimous support for this proposition (Table 8.11). Nationalism affects economic development through demands for greater production, egalitarian distribution, defense of natural resources, and reaction against imperialism; this may lead to policies favoring protectionism and the building of an economic infrastructure so as to stimulate industrialization. Nationalism may result in limiting consumption to the basic needs of the people while restricting the importation of luxury goods; a majority of those interviewed in Juazeiro and Petrolina accepted this notion. Nationalism sometimes leads to government control of all industry; this idea was acceptable to Petrolina respondents but not to those in Juazeiro. This may have been a reaction to the dominant Coelho enterprise in Petrolina, whereas Juazeiro respondents believed new private enterprise to be necessary. Nationalism implies land reform and the allocation of land to all those who need it, an idea enthusiastically endorsed in the two communities. Respondents also supported protective tariffs; the building of an infrastructure of roads, power, transport, and so on; defense of natural resources; and nationalization of foreign enterprise and public utilities. When asked if local and regional values should be subordinated to national ones, respondents said no, but they

Table 8.12. *Patterns of decision making in the family in Juazeiro (N = 66) and Petrolina (N = 52) about general issues and about voting (%)*

	Respondent at 16 years		Respondent's family now		Voting of respondent's family	
Decision maker(s)	Juazeiro	Petrolina	Juazeiro	Petrolina	Juazeiro	Petrolina
Father alone	34	33	5	8	20	13
Mother alone	12	12	4	0	0	2
Both parents	46	43	84	80	14	39
Each parent separately	2	0	2	6	54	39
Other	6	12	5	6	12	7

did feel that foreign values should be played down in the face of national ones.

Finally, in an attempt to trace the origins of the attitudes expressed by respondents, I asked a series of questions on the content and agents of political socialization. Socialization is the inculcation of skills, motives, and attitudes that people use in their activity in society. In the social-science literature, socialization has to do with what is learned as this is affected by national history, education, ideology, religious doctrine, and so on. This literature also identifies agents of socialization, such as the family, school, or job, through which learning occurs. Political socialization, as Fred Greenstein has defined it, is in its narrow context "the deliberate inculcation of political information, values, and practices by instructional agents who have been formally charged with this responsibility." Broadly conceived, it encompasses "*all* political learning, formal or informal, deliberate and unplanned, at every stage of the life cycle, including not only explicitly political learning but also nominally non-political learning."[17]

Members of the ruling classes in Juazeiro and Petrolina were asked how decisions had been made in their families when they were about sixteen years old and then asked to compare that situation with the way decisions were made in their present families. Responses showed similar patterns in the two communities (Table 8.12). For nearly half of the respondents both mother and father had made decisions together, but for a third the father had acted alone. In contrast, in four out of five cases today the two spouses reportedly acted together. (I had expected males to prevail, both in the past and in the present.) Decisions on how to vote, in particular, are

17 Fred I. Greenstein, "Political Socialization," in *International Encyclopedia of Social Sciences* (New York: Macmillan and Free Press Publishing Company, 1968), 14: 551.

Table 8.13. *Parental interest in politics during respondent's childhood in Juazeiro (N = 66) and Petrolina (N = 52) (%)*

	Father		Mother	
Degree of interest	Juazeiro	Petrolina	Juazeiro	Petrolina
Very much interested	47	40	11	12
Somewhat interested	15	18	20	22
Didn't pay much attention	32	30	66	64
Other	6	12	3	2

generally made either by both spouses acting together or each spouse acting individually.[18]

Several follow-up questions attempted to delve into the relationship of the respondent to his or her family. For example, 58 percent of those interviewed in Juazeiro and 44 percent in Petrolina indicated they felt their parents understood their needs very well. About a fourth of the interviewees in both towns felt they had had considerable influence in family decisions affecting themselves, and about half believed that they had had some influence. More than three-fourths were satisfied with the amount of influence they had had in decisions as teenagers. The responses to these questions suggest that the close-knit families of the Brazilian hinterland encourage a reasonable amount of involvement by all members, including children, in family decisions.[19]

When respondents were asked how interested their mothers and fathers had been in public affairs and politics, nearly half reported that their fathers had been very much interested, while only one in ten reported such interest on the part of their mothers. Two-thirds said that their mothers had not paid much attention (Table 8.13). Some 43 percent in Juazeiro and 56 percent in Petrolina reported that they sometimes talked about public affairs and politics with their spouses. Only 22 percent in Juazeiro and 39 percent in Petrolina said that they disagreed with their spouses over politics, and local politics was the topic that tended to divide husband and wife. Most respondents in both communities believed that their children should be involved somewhat in family decisions while a smaller

18 Similar questions were asked by Gabriel A. Almond and Sidney Verba in *The Civic Culture: Political Attitudes and Democracy in Five Nations* (Princeton: Princeton University press, 1963). Some of my data on attitudes of adolescents was reported in Ronald H. Chilcote and Roy Goldman, "Status Quo and Reform Attitudes of Backlands High School Students of Dominant Class Parents in Brazil, Chile, and Mexico," *International Journal of Comparative Sociology* 16, nos. 1–2 (1975): 37–50.

19 These questions were also drawn from Almond and Verba's *Civic Culture*.

number felt their children should be involved little or not at all (24 percent in Juazeiro and 19 percent in Petrolina). When queried as to their expectations for their children within the next few years, parents hoped that they would acquire a profession (42 percent in Juazeiro and 83 percent in Petrolina) or attend a university (33 percent in Juazeiro and 6 percent in Petrolina) or simply become cultured and educated (11 percent in both communities).

Clearly, the content of political learning is shaped by experiences in the school as well as family. Thus, respondents were asked to remember how much time they had spent in school studying current events and the government of their country.[20] Their answers suggested that very little attention had been devoted to these matters (only 26 percent in Juazeiro and 35 percent in Petrolina had spent some time). Given a list of things that children might be taught in school, they indicated that love of one's country was most stressed (83 percent in Juazeiro and 69 percent in Petrolina), followed by obedience to the law (13 percent in Juazeiro and 16 percent in Petrolina). When asked what chance children had in their schools to discuss and debate political and social issues and to make up their own minds, nearly half said none (44 percent in Juazeiro and 50 percent in Petrolina), while others indicated some (28 percent in Juazeiro and 34 percent in Petrolina), or a lot (25 percent in Juazeiro and 8 percent in Petrolina). Thus the content of learning about politics seems to emphasize authoritarianism and nationalism, themes reflected in governmental propaganda and direction; schoolchildren are expected to respect authority, obey the law, and love their country, not to be challenged by political issues or to become involved in dialogue and criticism.

Those interviewed indicated that their teachers had shown a lot of interest (56 percent in Juazeiro and 34 percent in Petrolina) or some interest (30 percent in both communities) in them as individuals. The majority (70 percent in Juazeiro and 62 percent in Petrolina) had felt free to talk to their teachers when they felt they had been treated unfairly or disagreed with something the teacher had said.

Asked if they were satisfied with the education received in school, 76 percent in Juazeiro and 85 percent in Petrolina replied affirmatively. In response to inquiry about what should be the principal task of education, quite different orientations were evident (Table 8.14). Generally, Juazeiro leaders felt that education should prepare youth to be good citizens, whereas those in Petrolina preferred that education prepare youth professionally and technically, this possibly reflecting recent developments. A university education was not considered a minimum level that the major-

20 The following questions about learning and the school were used in Almond and Verba's *Civic Culture*.

Table 8.14. *Principal task of education (%)*

	Juazeiro (N = 66)	Petrolina (N = 52)
Create a national spirit in youth	17	14
Prepare youth to be good citizens	52	29
Prepare youth professionally and technically	23	42
Form cultured men	8	12
Other	0	3

ity of youth should achieve; thus, Juazeiro interviewees identified secondary (47 percent) and vocational and technical (33 percent) education as their preference in contrast to those in Petrolina (respectively 21 percent and 58 percent). Support for public or private education was evenly divided among the respondents, although 45 percent in Juazeiro and 71 percent in Petrolina had placed their children in private schools.

Finally, these people were asked which was worse for their children, that their teachers be severe or that they be tolerant. Juazeiro respondents were evenly divided on the question, whereas, their Petrolina counterparts were concerned that teachers were too tolerant or lax (55 percent). These data do not really confirm the observation that authoritarian patterns dictate the style of learning in the schools, but overall a majority respected this direction. Only 29 percent in Juazeiro and 38 percent in Petrolina acknowledged that there were important things over which they disagreed with their children, mostly over their behavior, their education, and family matters. Only 10 percent in Juazeiro and 15 percent in Petrolina felt that their children had ever been taught or told things in school that they did not like; these related to sex education, vices, and the behavior of the teacher. A few mentioned politics as a concern, but almost all agreed that their sons and daughters should study the politics and government of Brazil in school.

In general, these glimpses of political socialization in the two communities conformed with my expectations. While the impact of traditional life was apparent, the absence of any stronger evidence of values, motives, and attitudes that reflected rural life in the backlands may be attributable to Juazeiro and Petrolina's strong school systems relative to those of other backlands communities. Further, the importance of authority and the insistence on rules and respect for those who run the schools conforms with the direction emanating from the national level of the Brazilian educational system. Cohesive families and the norms and values emphasized in family learning also reinforced these tendencies in the school system. These data on socialization are more suggestive than definitive.

In summary, although the ruling classes of Juazeiro and Petrolina are generally traditional and conservative in their views, the tradition they value is more closely linked to patriarchy and paternalism than to competitive capitalism. Equality and collectivity are ideals not to be repressed, and there is general agreement that the welfare of every member of the community should be respected. Thus there is a strong desire both to defend private property rights, family, and religion, and to favor distribution of wealth. Although merchant capital is very much in evidence and industrial capital has begun to establish itself, the behavior of the ruling classes in Juazeiro and Petrolina is not altogether characteristic of fully developed capitalism. Further, the ruling classes do not necessarily orient themselves only toward the local situation; indeed, they express greater confidence in state and national government than in municipal government, undoubtedly because most financial resources are allocated by those entities. Locally oriented and parochial, they are nevertheless often informed, interested, and involved in governmental affairs at the state and national levels. They are patriotic and nationalistic, skeptical about world affairs and international capital and foreign investment. A look at the agents and content of political socialization – family, church, school, and society – sheds some light on the ways these values and attitudes are inculcated and reinforced.

9

Development and underdevelopment

In 1963 the Brazilian economist Celso Furtado noted that the masses of Brazilians who work in the fields had not benefited from the notable economic development of recent years. Their standard of living had declined in comparison to that of people in commerce and other services. Furthermore, the living conditions of industrial workers had not improved. Brazilian development had disproportionately favored higher-income groups, generally in the Center-South urban areas such as Rio de Janeiro and São Paulo. The distortions in Brazilian development were the consequence of policies that permitted a growing concentration of income, both socially and geographically. Furtado saw revolution as one solution and pointed to two aspects of a possible revolutionary process in particular: On the one hand, peasant movements, adopting techniques of Marxism–Leninism, might take the lead in dismantling the archaic agrarian structure; on the other, a Marxist–Leninist revolution might substitute the dictatorship of one class for that of another class. He argued that reforms in the agrarian structure and in government administration would be preferable to these revolutionary alternatives, but he expressed sympathy for the Marxism that permeated Brazilian thought, especially among the youth, because it "affords a diagnosis of the social reality and a guide to action."[1]

The military intervention of 1964 was counter to Furtado's vision of reforming Brazil as an open society. The military undertook to restructure society but in a way that would perpetuate, indeed accentuate, class differences. Some of the economic goals included control of inflation, stimulation of economic growth, and elimination of inefficiencies and corruption in the government bureaucracy. Drastic fiscal and monetary restraints were applied to the economy while the political system was purged of liberal and radical elements.[2] By the early 1970s, observers were

1 Celso Furtado, "Brazil: What Kind of Revolution?" *Foreign Affairs* 41 (April 1963): 526–535.

2 Two important works on the military with emphasis on the period since 1964 are Alfred Stepan, *The Military in Politics: Changing Patterns in Brazil* (Princeton: Princeton University Press, 1971); and Ronald M. Schneider, *The Political System of Brazil: Emergence of a "Modernizing" Authoritarian Regime, 1964–1970* (New York: Columbia University Press, 1971). Kenneth Erickson's *The Brazil-*

proclaiming a "Brazilian miracle."[3] Gross domestic product had risen 9 percent annually for a number of years and overall had doubled since 1964, while exports, a third of them manufactured goods, had nearly tripled over the same period.

The Brazilian generals and many traditional economists believed that backwardness in Northeast Brazil could be overcome through a combination of foreign aid and investment and centralized planning. They favored capitalism within a nationalist framework. Foreign capital was tolerable, given certain constraints. The objective was to encourage capital accumulation, promote industrialization, and spread development so as to diffuse the feudallike structure of the rural areas. Thus, the military dictatorship promised order, allowed the penetration of large amounts of U.S. aid, and through concessions enticed businessmen to invest their capital in the area.

In the 1970s, however, the economy was subject to a number of new international pressures and influences; the foreign debt stood at more than $10 billion by 1973, foreign reserves began to erode in the face of higher petroleum prices worldwide, debt repayment and servicing amounted to nearly $4 billion, and the trade gap was $1.5 billion.[4] Further, the international petroleum crisis of 1973 threatened to erode many of the achievements of the Brazilian economy, resulting in increased inflation and economic difficulties at home. These pressures were to lead by the end of the decade to a "democratic opening" but not necessarily to a resolution of the political and economic problems.[5]

ian Corporate State and Working-Class Politics (Berkeley: University of California Press, 1977), emphasizes the impact of the authoritarian corporate state upon the labor movement.

3 Two examples of the lavish praise for the Brazilian "miracle" are Milton Friedman, "Economic Miracles," *Newsweek* (January 21, 1974): 78; and a comment by U.S. Federal Reserve Board Chairman Arthur F. Burns that Brazil's growth represented "one of the great economic miracles of our time," quoted in Dan Griffin, " 'Miracle Brazil' Grows Dizzily," *Cleveland Plain Dealer* (April 22, 1973): 3-AA.

4 *Latin America* (London), (March 1, 1974): 74; (May 10, 1974): 143; and (May 24, 1974): 154, 156.

5 Ronald H. Chilcote and Timothy F. Harding, "Introduction," *Latin American Perspectives* 6 (Fall 1979): 2–15. Issues 23 (1979) and 24 (1980) of this journal are devoted to an assessment of Brazil during the 1964 to 1980 period. Perspectives among specialists vary from the uncritical, positive assessment of M. S. Marzouk, "The Brazilian Economy: Trends and Prospects," *Orbis* 18 (Spring 1974): 277–291, to the criticism of the Berkeley Development Assistance Program by Donald L. Huddle, "Review Article: Essays on the Economy of Brazil: The Berkeley Group," *Economic Development and Cultural Change* 20 (April 1972): 560–574. A rebuttal to Huddle is Alan Abouchar, "The Performance of the Berkeley Program in Brazil: Comment," *Economic Development and Cultural Change* 20 (April 1974): 503–506. The Berkeley economists assisted the military government in establishing a centralized system of planning. Albert Fishlow was one of the Berkeley economists who offered a rather candid appraisal of the economic "miracle"; see his "Brazil's Economic Miracle," *The World Today* 19 (November 1973): 474–481, and "Some Reflections on Post-1964 Brazilian Economic Policy," in *Authoritarian Brazil*. ed. Alfred Stepan (New Haven: Yale University Press, 1973), pp. 69–113. Gary S. Fields takes issue with Fishlow and others by arguing that the

The contradictions of capitalist development through diffusionist policies (i.e., capital and technology are spread to less-developed areas) were apparent even in the conservative U.S. press, where it was reported that the "miracle" was "being achieved at the expense of the poor," that "tens of millions of Brazilians are not sharing in the new prosperity," that "the gap between rich and poor is growing wider," that "the government has encouraged the accumulation of capital for investment by systematically holding down wages," and that "per capita income in the impoverished Northeast region is less than half that in the country as a whole."[6] Brazilian critics of the "miracle" charged the military with establishing the nation as a bridgehead for U.S. capital interests, a "subimperialist" dependency of the outside world.[7] The political implications of this subimperialism were evident in the pride of the Brazilian leadership in its image of being imperialist, an indication of its success.[8] Brazil preached a policy of friendship and trade but clearly its desire was expansionist – control of markets in Latin America and establishment as a regional superpower. There were reports of Brazilian meddling in the internal affairs of neighboring countries, in particular Argentina, Bolivia, and Chile.[9] During the 1960s Brazil increased its trade with other Latin

poor in Brazil did participate beneficially in the economic miracle; see his "Who Benefits from Economic Development? – A Reexamination of Brazilian Growth in the 1960s," *American Economic Review* 67 (September 1977): 570–582. D. D. Goodman draws on data in the Northeast to demonstrate the regional inequities caused by the miracle: "The problem of poverty and inadequate family income is even more acute in the smaller cities of the Northeast. . . . The downward pressure on earnings exerted by migration flows offers a far more convincing interpretation of the greater degree of absolute poverty." Quoted in his "The Brazilian Economic 'Miracle' and Regional Policy: Some Evidence from the Urban Northeast," *Journal of Latin American Studies* 8 (May 1976): 1–27. Three other studies are relevant to an assessment of the Brazilian development: Stephen S. Kaplan and Norman C. Bonsor, "Did United States Aid Really Help Brazilian Development? The Perspective of a Quarter-Century," *Inter-American Economic Affairs* 27 (Winter 1973): 25–46; Werner Baer and Andrea Maneschi, "Import-Substitution, Stagnation, and Structural Change: An Interpretation of the Brazilian Case," *The Journal of Developing Areas* 5 (January 1971): 177–192; and Samuel A. Morley and Gordon W. Smith, "The Choice of Technology: Multinational Firms in Brazil," *Economic Development and Cultural Change* 25 (January 1977): 239–264. The first of these essays concludes that while aid to Brazil has not resulted in major redistribution of wealth, it has promoted economic growth; the second argues that import-substitutive industrialization as practiced by Brazil during the 1960s leads to stagnation; and the third looks at the major role of foreign-directed investment by multinational firms in Brazil.

6 See the editorials in the *Los Angeles Times:* "Brazil's 'Miracle' Skips the Poor" (May 22, 1973), which bases its position on a warning by fourteen Roman Catholic bishops in northeastern Brazil, and "Fear Amid the Miracle" (February 15, 1974).

7 The concept of "subimperialism" is elaborated by Ruy Mauro Marini in *Subdesarrollo y revolución* (Mexico: Siglo Veintiuno Editores, 1969), esp. pp. 122–129; also in an interview with Luis Angeles, "Dependencia y subimperialismo en América Latina," *Cultura en México*, supplement to *Siempre* 1030 (March 21, 1973): v–vii.

8 Marvine Howe, "Brazil's Policies Vexing Neighbors," *New York Times* (April 9, 1973).

9 Marlise Simons, "The Brazilian Connection," *The Washington Post* (January 6, 1974): B3.

American nations tenfold. Trade policies and expansionism were associated with the granting of large credits to its neighbors.

Subimperialism also involved the penetration of foreign interests into the Brazilian economy. Foreign control grew throughout the economic boom of the decade. Only in petroleum, electricity, and textiles were Brazilian interests dominant; the automobile (100 percent), tobacco (91 percent), rubber (82 percent), and chemical (54 percent) industries were under foreign control. Bethlehem Steel Corporation was involved in exploiting new reserves of iron ore, while the large multinational firms established extensive operations in the country.[10] Thus infusion of capital and technology into Brazil was a reality. So too was the poverty and hunger of the mass of the population, which did not benefit from the apparent prosperity of the "miracle."

This is the essential political and economic background for my study. Beyond this, however, any political–economic study of the Brazilian backlands will necessarily be shaped by the theoretical literature on development in Latin America. In the remainder of this chapter, therefore, I will review this literature and relate it to the historical experience of Juazeiro and Petrolina and to their contemporary situation as their ruling classes see it.

Furtado identifies three schools of development theory: classical, neoclassical, and Marxist. In considering each of these schools he focuses on the "central problems dealt with by the theory of development": "the increase in productivity of labor and its repercussions on the distribution and utilization of the social product."[11] The classical school (represented by Adam Smith, David Ricardo, and others) argued that development is economic progress, occurring naturally in all nations. According to Furtado, this interpretation tends to be restricted to a description of process and ignores analysis of real technical progress and productivity increases. Then too some proponents of the classical school limited themselves "to demonstrating that the prime mover of social progress, profit, is permanently threatened in its operations by the rising costs of manpower."[12] The neoclassical school believed that all economic agents tend to maximize their positions. According to Furtado, "The consuming agent tends to optimize his position by maximizing the marginal utilities in

10 Fred Halliday and Maxine Molyneux, "Brazil: The Underside of the Miracle," *Ramparts* 12 (April 1974): 14–20. They report that this expansion of foreign control was accompanied by a polarization of income: Between 1960 and 1970 "the richest ten percent of the country increased their share of total income from 39.66 percent of 47.79 percent, while the poorest ten percent's share fell from 1.17 to 1.11 percent in the same period" (p. 18).

11 Celso Furtado, *Development and Underdevelopment*, trans. Ricardo W. de Aguiar and Eric Charles Drysdale (Berkeley and Los Angeles: University of California Press, 1964), p. 5.

12 Ibid., p. 11

every direction. . . . This apologetic attitude inherent in neoclassical thinking comes out to the full in the so-called 'economy of welfare.' "[13] The Marxist school relates economic analysis to a philosophical approach to history. According to Furtado, Marx concluded "that the production of mankind's means of sustenance is a social fact from which various necessary relationships of production are derived and that those relationships correspond to the development of productive powers."[14] Marx was interested in identifying the fundamental production relations in a capitalist system. In particular, he was interested in knowing what allows such a system to develop, and he understood development as the creation of the conditions for the displacement of capitalism, these conditions being created by internal contradictions. Capitalist development involves repeated crises and waste of resources.

The reality of crises and waste is especially apparent in the capitalist nations of Latin America. In Furtado's analysis, the expansion of the European industrial economies toward Latin America sometimes was oriented to trade and sometimes to the extraction of raw materials for which demand was rising in the industrial centers. The penetration of capitalism "almost always created hybrid structures, part tending to behave as a capitalistic system, part perpetuating the features of the previously existing system."[15] The result, in his view, was a dual society. Capitalism, he argued, penetrates but does not necessarily become dynamically linked with the archaic economy of a region, "for the mass of profit does not become integrated into the local economy." Only the entrepreneurial class has the dynamism characteristic of the capitalist economy.[16] This class operates in the developed sector of the economy, in which modern technology predominates, and it produces for external or domestic markets. No matter what its rate of capital formation or increase in per capita product, this class does little to promote improvements in the backward sector of the economy as long as the developed sector increases its product without absorbing new labor and population growth.

A critique of this dualist view of development may be found in the writings of André Gunder Frank.[17] His position is as follows: First, underdevelopment is part of the historical product of relations between underdeveloped satellite and developed metropolis. Second, metropolitan–

13 Ibid., pp. 43–44.

14 Ibid., p. 13.

15 Ibid., p. 8.

16 Ibid., p. 131. For another example of the dualist interpretation of Brazilian society, see Jacques Lambert, *Os dois brasis* (São Paulo: Companhia Editora Nacional, 1967).

17 André Gunder Frank, *Capitalism and Underdevelopment in Latin America: Historical Studies of Chile and Brazil* (New York: Monthly Review Press, 1967).

satellite relations are found within countries as well as in the imperialist world order. Third, the development of the satellite is limited by its dependent relationship to the metropolis, and growth is experienced only when its links to the metropolis are weakened, for example, during depression or world war; the most underdeveloped regions are those most closely linked to the metropolis. Fourth, the dualist interpretation must be rejected because capitalism has effectively and completely penetrated the underdeveloped world. The latifundia, for example, originally were capitalist enterprises responsive to the growing demand in the national and international market.[18] Frank emphasizes commercial monopoly rather than feudalism and precapitalist forms as the economic means whereby national and regional metropolises exploit and appropriate the economic surplus of their satellites. It is capitalism that on a world scale produces a developing metropolis and an underdeveloped periphery, for the now so-called advanced nations were never underdeveloped, although they were once undeveloped. This same process is found within nations between a domestic metropolis – a capital city, for example – and the surrounding satellite cities and regions.

Frank rejects the conception of two Brazils, one modern and developed through capitalism and the other backward and underdeveloped, with precapitalist, feudal, or semifeudal forms. Utilizing some analysis from the writings of Furtado and Caio Prado Júnior,[19] he offers a series of historical examples of the capitalist development of underdevelopment in Brazil. One relates to sugar and the Northeast. As demand for sugar increased during the colonial period, Portugal expanded its industry by planting cane in Permambuco and other parts of the Northeast, and black slaves were imported from Africa to work the fields. The industry that developed in Brazil, however, was concentrated in the hands of a few owners of land and sugar mills and of merchants, all of whom were directly tied to and dependent on Portugal. As a consequence, little domestic investment was made in Brazil; wealth for the most part remained in Portugal, and production was for export only. The power of Portugal declined in the seventeenth century after union with Spain, the occupation of the Northeast by Holland, and the granting of economic concessions to England. The Northeast remained viable as a sugar producer until the Dutch, turning to the West Indies, established sugar plantations which caused world supply to increase, prices to decline, and exports from the Northeast to decreased. With the weakening of Portu-

18 For an excellent summary and critique of the Frank theses, see Ernesto Laclau, "Feudalism and Capitalism in Latin America," *New Left Review* 67 (May–June 1971): 19–38.

19 See Celso Furtado, *Economic Growth of Brazil: A Survey from Colonial to Modern Times* (Berkeley and Los Angeles: University of California Press, 1963).

guese ties to the Northeast, "the development of the system as a whole produced the involution of its Northeast Brazilian satellite."[20]

Frank then describes the sugar economy as generating a satellite of its own. This was based on livestock raising: "Livestock was used for meat, for hides, for draft animals to run the sugar mills, for fat to grease their works, for beasts of burden to carry the huge quantities of firewood used in the boilers. . . . The stockmen were exploited by the sugar mills whose satellite they were. Livestock grazing expanded into Bahia and toward the North. Livestock came to be the mainstay of the inland *sertão* region."[21] Frank illustrates the impact of capitalism on modern and backward areas, the interpenetration of capital everywhere. His analysis thus refutes the notion of dual economy and contributes to a theory of dependent relationships in the capitalist world.

A similar concern with underdevelopment led Stanley and Barbara Stein, historians with research experience on Brazil, to the position that an underdeveloped society has little hope of becoming fully independent and autonomous. Even where independence came a century and a half ago, the underdeveloped society does not make its own decisions.[22]

Over the past two decades, this perspective on Latin America has become known as dependency theory. In it, both development and underdevelopment are seen as consequences of outside capitalist influence. More specifically, a given economy is seen as conditioned by its relationship to another economy that is dominant and capable of expanding and developing. The dependent nation may either develop as a reflection of the expansion of the dominant nation or underdevelop as a consequence of its subordinate relationship.[23] Brazilians have contributed many of the important

20 Frank, *Capitalism*, p. 154. Heitor Ferreira Lima in "Problemas do Nordeste," *Revista Brasiliense* 17 (May–June 1958): 13–33, assumes a different position by identifying the persistence of semifeudal conditions as the cause of underdevelopment in the Northeast. He focuses on the problems of underconsumption, low income, land tenure, and emigration, and concludes that existence of rich resources will lead to solutions. In an informative article, Stefan H. Robock, "Recent Economic Trends in Northeast Brazil," *Inter-American Economic Affairs* 16 (Winter 1962): 65–89, rejects three widely accepted evaluations for underdevelopment in the area – droughts, lack of capital investment, and discriminatory federal policies; he concludes that productivity is low because of limitations in natural and human resources and a lack of technological innovations. Jimmye S. Hillman, "Economic Development and the Brazilian Northeast: What Is Economic Development?" *Inter-American Economic Affairs* 10 (Summer 1956): 79–96, analyzed underdevelopment by reference to traditional criteria such as high rate of mortality, poor food, and low per capita income due to labor inefficiency, poor use of resources, inefficiency in capital formation, and low rate of technological change and innovation.

21 Frank, *Capitalism*, p. 154.

22 Stanley J. Stein and Barbara H. Stein, *The Colonial Heritage of Latin America: Essays on Economic Dependence in Perspective* (New York: Oxford University Press, 1970), p. vii.

23 Theotônio dos Santos, "The Structure of Dependence," *American Economic Review* 60 (May 1970): 231–236.

ideas on dependency.[24] The writings of Theotônio dos Santos, Ruy Mauro Marini, and Fernando Henrique Cardoso have been especially significant.

Dos Santos has considered Brazil as representing a "new dependency."[25] In his typology, colonial dependency characterized the relations between Europeans and the colonies, in which a monopoly of trade complemented a monopoly of land, mines, and manpower in the colonized countries. Financial–industrial dependency became consolidated at the end of the nineteenth century with the concentration of capital in hegemonic centers and investment of capital in the periphery for raw materials and agricultural products to be consumed by the centers. The new dependency, based on investments by multinational corporations, emerged after World War II. Dos Santos calls this a technological–industrial dependency and says that it limits the development of Latin American economies. Industrial development in countries like Brazil is dependent on exports, which generate foreign currency to buy imported capital goods. Exports like sugar and cotton in the Northeast, for example, are associated with traditional sectors of the economy controlled by intransigent ruling families and oligarchies. These traditional sectors often are tied to foreign capital and remit their high profits abroad. Thus it is not unusual for foreign capital to control the marketing of exported products even in the face of nationalist measures designed to restrict exchange, to impose taxes on exports, and to gain control over production.

Marini's main contribution to the discussion has been the idea of subimperialism mentioned earlier (see n. 7). Assuming a Marxist–Leninist position, he has suggested the possibility of breaking dependency and eliminating underdevelopment through socialism.[26]

Fernando Henrique Cardoso has shown how capitalist development occurs within dependent situations.[27] Drawing heavily upon his empirical investigation of entrepreneurs in Brazil and elsewhere,[28] he argues that

24 I have synthesized the literature more exhaustively elsewhere. See Ronald H. Chilcote, "Dependency: A Critical Assessment of the Literature," *Latin American Perspectives* 1 (Spring 1974): 4–29; and "Issues of Theory in Dependency and Marxism," *Latin American Perspectives* 8 (Summer–Fall 1981): 3–16.

25 See Theotônio dos Santos's chapter on Brazil in *Latin America: The Struggle with Dependency and Beyond*. ed. Ronald H. Chilcote and Joel C. Edelstein (Cambridge, Mass.: Schenkman Publishing, 1974). Also useful is his discussion on Brazil in *Socialismo o fascismo: dilema latinoamericano*. (Santiago: Colección América Nueva, Editorial Prensa Latinoamericana, 1969).

26 Ruy Mauro Marini, *Dialéctica de la dependencia*. 2d ed. (Mexico City: Ediciones Era, 1974). A prolonged debate ensued between Marini and Cardoso; Marini's response is in "Las razones del neodesarrollismo (respuesta a F. H. Cardoso y J. Serra)," *Revista Mexicana de Sociología*. 40 (1978): 57–106.

27 Fernando Henrique Cardoso, "Associated Dependent Development: Theoretical and Practical Implications," in *Authoritarian Brazil: Origins, Policies, and Future*. ed. Alfred Stepan (New Haven: Yale University Press, 1973), pp. 142–176.

28 Fernando Henrique Cardoso, *Cuestiones de sociología del desarrollo de América Latina* (Santiago: Colección Imagen de América Latina [3], Editorial Universitaria, 1968).

capitalism and imperialism today differ from Lenin's earlier conceptions; that capital accumulation is more the consequence of corporate than of financial control; that investment by multinational corporations in Latin America is moving away from raw materials and agriculture to industry; and that monopoly capitalism and development are not contradictory terms. He believes that dependent capitalist development has become a new form of monopolistic expansion in the Third World. In the case of Brazil international capitalism has gained a disproportional influence in industry, yet new foreign capital is not needed in some areas where there are local savings and reinvestment of profits in local markets. In fact, he argues, during times of monopolistic imperialist expansion dependent economies can export capital to dominant economies.

Dependency theory has been both widely accepted and criticized from a variety of positions – for example, for neglecting internal class struggle, for being overly schematic, for not clearly defining "dependency," for obscuring the reality of imperialism. Further, this theory fails to relate explicitly to a class analysis; it emphasizes relations of exchange and questions of nationalism and underdevelopment. Rarely do its advocates suggest strategies for development through noncapitalist means or perform the case studies and serious analysis required to verify its assumptions.[29]

The deep interest in these questions among Brazilian scholars persuaded me of the importance of testing some of the prevailing ideas in my study of Juazeiro and Petrolina. I have written widely on underdevelopment and dependency, and the notions of capitalist underdevelopment and dependency have helped my students to understand the impact of capitalism in Latin America. Nevertheless, it should be clear that these ideas do not constitute a unified theory. I hoped, therefore, that investigating development in Juazeiro and Petrolina would contribute to an analysis that might eventually lead to solutions for old problems.

Dependency is a recurrent theme in the history of Juazeiro and Petrolina. Some examples, several of them drawn from the historical syntheses of Chapters 3 and 4, are the following:

1895: A demand by a citizen that a new state be established that would tie Juazeiro and Petrolina into a single capital and incorporate the surrounding region.[30]

29 While interest in dependency continued into the decade of the eighties, especially among non-Marxist scholars in the United States, Cardoso and Frank had abandoned interest and shifted attention to other directions. Marini, Dos Santos, and other respected scholars in Latin America, however, continued to combine dependency with Marxism. Assessments of the relationships of dependency and Marxism are found in several issues of *Latin American Perspectives*, specifically issue 1 (1974), issue 11 (1976), and issues 30–31 (1981).

30 Arvonymo de Uzeda, "Estado do São Francisco," *Cidade de Joazeiro* 1 (July 23, 1896): 1.

1907: A critical observation by a local paper on the "superfluous and inept bureaucracy whose existence is known only on the payroll" – a reference to the means whereby Juazeiro's dependency on Bahia and the federal government was cemented.[31]

1920: Concern about Petrolina's "economic dependency . . . living under absolute dependency on Juazeiro which always treated Petrolina as a mere tributary."[32]

1923: A plea in Recife to establish a railroad to Petrolina because "Petrolina depends on Bahia which imposes the heaviest taxes on commercial goods and which still cynically exploits the São Francisco region with its river transport."[33]

1967: An appeal to the Bahian state legislature to assist Juazeiro in the solution of its many problems which had become aggravated because of the dominance of Petrolina over the region.[34]

1968: A declaration by the mayor of Juazeiro "on the danger of Bahia's totally losing Juazeiro and other municipalities along the São Francisco to the state of Pernambuco."[35]

Today these continue to be relevant. To test the recognition of these dependency relationships by members of the ruling classes in Juazeiro and Petrolina, I asked, first, whether respondents felt there were detrimental foreign influences in Brazil. Of 118 respondents, 61 replied in the affirmative, 45 in the negative. A follow-up probe sought to identify two of these detrimental influences; nearly two-thirds mentioned capitalist imperialism, a third foreign ideological and cultural influences, and a sixth foreign exploitation of natural resources. Those who believed that foreign influences were not harmful mentioned financial assistance, industrialization, and technology as beneficial.

These latter tended to be businessmen, who probably benefited from their outside ties. They might be expected to have a vested interest in the world outside, perhaps performing certain functions (e.g., supplying local materials) for interests at the state, national, or international levels and in return being assured of a privileged and increasingly dominant position within their own community. Most of these respondents had some contact with business; 34 acknowledged frequent dealings with businessmen at the state and national levels, and 11 of these (all of them part of the upper echelon of the ruling classes) also dealt with foreign firms.

Because most private enterprise is influenced by foreign interests in Brazil, the bureaucracies might become involved in those interests. The interests, privileges, and actions of local bureaucrats might relate not only to foreign private capital but also to foreign aid distributed through banks

31 "Governo municipal," editorial in *Correio do Sáo Francisco* 6 (September 15, 1907): 1.

32 J. Avila, "Petrolina de hontem, de hoje e de amanhã," *O Farol* 6 (October 24, 1920): 1.

33 Felix de Valois, "Pró Petrolina," *O Farol* 9 (November 22, 1923): 1. Reprinted from *A Tribuna*.

34 Appeal signed by Bishop Dom Tomás Guilhermo Murphy and others, "Memorial," Juazeiro, September 1, 1967.

35 "Bahia poderá perder a região do baixo-médio São Francisco diz Prefeito," *O Farol* 53 (June 8, 1968): 1.

Table 9.1. *Recognition of dependency in Juazeiro and Petrolina*

Problem	% Affirmative Juazeiro (N = 66)	Petrolina (N = 52)
Outside control over community	20	8
Outside control over production	53	14
Outside control over marketing and distribution	53	15
Outside control over patents and licenses	7	10
Competitive advantage of outside firms over local firms	18	19
Outflow of capital, including profits	30	19
Export of local products, thus limiting availability of products locally	8	6
Outside technology causing unemployment	12	14
Increased need to import capital goods	49	27
Outside introduction of managerial class	47	12

and agencies. The respondents were asked about contacts with governmental agencies. Nearly 70 percent had worked with state and federal agencies, including 7 persons who had dealt with foreign agencies. When asked why they supported contacts with business and government, two-fifths of all the respondents replied that these contacts brought improvements and recognition to the communities, while another fourth felt that contacts enhanced their own business.

Respondents were also asked about the existence in their communities of various obstacles to economic development, all of them related to outside control over the community. The degree to which these problems were perceived to exist in the two communities is indicated in Table 9.1. Whereas it is not unusual in Brazil for foreign corporations to buy out national industry, this has not happened in Juazeiro and Petrolina. Nor had there been much intervention by national corporations in the local community. Thus it is not surprising that respondents generally were unaware of or insensitive to issues of outside influence. Petrolina respondents showed less concern than their counterparts in Juazeiro. After all, their community now dominated the region. Then too, many of them had established and were involved in local industry. In many cases their investment had been locally stimulated. Outside investors had only recently become interested in their region. In contrast, respondents in Juazeiro were alarmed. Over half of them were disturbed by outside control over local production and over marketing and distribution. They considered the dependence on imports of capital goods a serious problem, and they were also disturbed by the outside introduction of a managerial class into their community. Others expressed dismay over the competitive advantage outside firms seemed to have locally.

Those acknowledging the impact of outside control over the local economy tended to attribute the problem to a variety of causes. One person stated flatly that the problem was due to "foreign capital unknown to the government." Several felt that it was the consequence of federal pricing and wage policies, while another believed that banking activities had caused inequality. In general, their responses were vague and imprecise. Their understanding of the degree of outside control over local production was somewhat sophisticated, however, and they traced the problem to the dominance of the Center-South. Frequently mentioned were government controls on markets of some agricultural products; onions, for example, were grown in abundance in the São Francisco Valley, yet the government allowed São Paulo distributors to import onions from abroad. Respondents viewed this and other discriminatory practices with alarm: "Control should be internal," "Strangulation," "They don't relate to the people," "It's an indication that we do not control what is ours," "Initiative is taken from us," "What happens here is a reflection of the control over all producing regions." As to the issue of outside control over marketing and distribution, they reasoned that there should be some internal control over the local area: "The monopoly is in the hands of persons outside the community," exclaimed one person. "Beware of foreign interests," warned another. As to outside control of patents and licenses, only a small percentage of respondents were aware of any problem; these were industrialists and others who relied heavily on outside technology. One person mentioned the difficulties of obtaining licenses to export and import products. Another attributed the problem to the "bureaucracy." Others had only "read about the problem."

I inquired about the effect of increasing competitive advantages for outside firms over local firms because such advantages are apparent among large-scale industries, especially foreign enterprise and monopolies in Brazil. Understanding of the roots of the problem was limited. Price, market influences, and devaluation of currency were mentioned. Only one person referred to the large outside firms. In short, there was a problem but nobody could articulate how it affected the communities.

Another concern, identified by one-fourth of those interviewed in Juazeiro and Petrolina was the flow of capital and profits to areas outside their communities. As with previous questions, elaboration on the problem was brief, and understanding of its causes was vague. They simply affirmed that "the money should remain" or "there is no local control." Identifiable causes of the outflow of capital included the sports lottery, which was controlled from the south of the country, "provoking the impoverishment of the population in all its social classes," "investments from the south," and "withdrawals by private banks."

Sometimes a local economy adjusts to outside dominant economies so that specialized exports are also supplied locally at disadvantageous prices. Respondents were asked if this were a problem and, if so, did it limit the market and availability of local products within the communities. One person felt that "they export the best and leave the worst for the city." However, few respondents referred to any specific products.

In many countries domestic markets are restricted by unemployment – the consequence of the introduction of advanced, capital-intensive technology, without regard to size or composition of the local labor market. Brazil is no exception to this practice, and nearly one in eight respondents acknowledged its existence in Juazeiro and Petrolina. Only one respondent seemed to grasp the problem: "Outsiders should be taught to agree with conditions here." Others, while recognizing the problem, said that technology was necessary no matter what the impact on local labor.

In most underdeveloped countries there is a lack of a domestic capital goods industry, resulting in increased dependence on imports. Two-fifths of the persons interviewed in Juazeiro and Petrolina agreed that this was a problem. They tended to condemn industrial areas of São Paulo and Rio as well as foreign countries like the United States for creating and perpetuating this condition: "Our economy has been strangled," "Income has diminished," "Private enterprise lacks freedom," "The possibility of growth has lessened."

When asked about the impact of a managerial class introduced from outside, undercutting local initiative in economic development, a third of the respondents agreed that this was a problem. Those from Juazeiro understood the problem in terms of government selection of outside persons to run local agencies. Some Petrolina respondents, while recognizing this as a problem, also objected to the presence of foreigners in the community.

Those who felt that outside control had limited development of their community were asked to explain how. Was the control caused by one community's ties to the other community? What about the relationship to the state and federal governments? Were outside business interests involved? What about foreign influences? In general, respondents were concerned about the influence of outside capital from other parts of the country. They were asked, for example, about the activity of the São Paulo industrialist Francisco Pignatari, who was exploiting nearby copper deposits; 103 interviewees (87 percent) replied that this activity was detrimental to the local economy, while only 1 found it beneficial. This question was particularly significant because it referred to a concrete case of outside involvement, and the responses reflected widespread local concern that outside capital was either unnecessary for local development or might lead to negative consequences.

The upper echelon of power holders in these communities was more aware of the implications of outside influence than those on lower levels of power. These power holders were able to offer in-depth analyses of the problems and their impact on the communities. Their awareness was clearly attributable to their deep involvement in the political economy on a daily basis. They ran the large industries and the farms and cattle ranches; were the large merchants, exporters and importers; were dependent on the banks and the government for credit; and even sometimes joined with outside investors to promote enterprise. Further, they were the high officials in the communities who came in contact with politicians at the state and federal levels. They also were highly educated and could relate to the problems that modern capitalism creates for the less developed parts of the world. The respondents who could not identify with problems of dependency were unsophisticated about the relationship of their community to the outside world. They tended to attribute their community's problems to local causes. Workers were lazy or administrators inefficient, they argued; local authorities might be able to achieve autonomy for the communities. Many respondents seemed to be saying that the capitalism of the outside world had limited their own advancement, and they advocated autonomy and local control over their political economies as well as safeguards against outside private and public forces. These critics, however, were not calling for an end of capitalism. Indeed, they firmly believed in the premises of capitalism and fully expected that, once rid of outside controls and pressures, they and their communities would prosper under a capitalist system.

Given their views on outside influence, what was the meaning of development for the rulers of Juazeiro and Petrolina? All but two of those interviewed offered a definition around some essential theme – for example, progress and growth (43 percent), participation and equal opportunity (17 percent), culture and education (14 percent), economy (11 percent), and central planning (5 percent).[36] One of the bishops stated that development implied "positive progress in the material and spiritual sense of dealing with needs common to all." A leading educator said that development "signified economic and social progress affecting all aspects

36 Peter McDonough and Amaury de Souza analyzed the development priorities of "elites" in Brazil and found a principal interest in economic development. This result was not surprising because of the emphasis of the military regime. Their findings are similar to the perceptions of our interviewees in Juazeiro and Petrolina. See their "Perceptions of Development Strategies in the Brazilian Elite," paper presented at the American Political Science Association Annual Meeting, September 1–7, 1977, Washington, D.C.

Table 9.2. *Sacrifices considered acceptable to allow Brazilian development*

	Juazeiro (N = 66)			Petrolina (N = 52)			Total (N = 118)		
	Yes	No	Other	Yes	No	Other	Yes	No	Other
No salary increase	44	20	2	13	35	4	57	55	6
Pay higher taxes	54	11	1	17	29	6	71	40	7
Give up automobile or television	48	17	1	20	30	2	68	47	3
Spend less on vacation or luxury goods	61	4	1	43	6	3	104	10	4

of a political people." A former state deputy understood development in terms of "participation by all people." A leading merchant believed it signified "peace, justice, and progress for all." One of the Coelho brothers asserted: "Development is the participation of all."

Thus development was seen in a somewhat idealistic context, as something to be realized in the future and probably not attainable in the present. Some indication of commitment to development, however, was revealed in response to the question of what sacrifice each respondent would be willing to make in order for Brazil to advance economically in the next few years. The results (Table 9.2) show a general willingness to spend less on a vacation or luxury goods, but attitudes of leaders in Juazeiro and Petrolina differed sharply. A large majority of persons in Juazeiro offered to relinquish a salary increase, pay higher taxes, and give up such material possessions as an automobile or television set. Their response was in line with my personal impressions, gleaned from interviews and observation, that the notion of work toward a common goal and sharing in material progress was congenial to this community. In contrast, the overwhelming rejection of sacrifice among respondents in Petrolina reflected the belief, often expressed in the community, in individual endeavor rather than collective effort.

10

Participation, mobilization, and conflict

Concerted efforts to integrate rural and urban life in Brazil began with the Vargas regime in the 1930s and intensified after Word War II, partially through government regulation and partially through the activities of several national parties whose networks reached into the hinterland. Under the military regimes after 1964, greater federal control was imposed upon local areas, and a contrived system of government and opposition parties served as a means whereby the military could control political participation. In form the military had modeled its two-party system after that of the United States, but in practice participatory democracy was subject to severe constraints and limitations. Prior to the military takeover, various political and economic forces had been involved in struggles over popular issues such as extension and expansion of rights and services to all people and mobilization of national sentiment against foreign aggression and imperialism.

Participation and democracy are terms common to the study of politics in the United States and usually refer to the practice of pluralism – that is, competition among groups and individuals for power and influence over decisions and policies. Samuel Huntington limits his definition of "participation" to influence on governmental decision making by private citizens; he excludes the activities of political professionals such as government officials, party officials, political candidates, and professional lobbyists. Further, he focuses on governmental activity, so that a strike that influences government to increase wages for public employees is political participation whereas a strike aimed at management of a private corporation is not.[1] Huntington suggests that political participation takes different

1 Samuel P. Huntington, *Political Participation in Democratic Countries* (Cambridge, Mass.: Harvard University Press, 1976), pp. 4–6. Huntington and others related political participation to modernization in the form of urbanization, industrialization, and high levels of education and communication. Judith Lynch Lamare has argued that such studies have resulted in "a rather confusing set of contradictory claims about the relationship between development (or modernization) and political participation." She attempts to resolve this problem by applying both a quantitative and a contextual approach to the study of local political participation in communities of the state of Minas Gerais, Brazil. See Lamare's "Causal vs. Contextual Analysis: A Case Study of Brazilian Local Political Participation," *Western Political Quarterly* 27 (March 1974): 117–142.

forms – for example, electoral and organizational activity, lobbying, and contracting – and he identifies the bases of political participation as including class, communal group, neighborhood, party, and faction.[2]

This definition of participation approximates my own usage of the term here and is particularly evident in the nature of a series of questions asked people in Juazeiro and Petrolina, although my preference would be to apply the term "participatory democracy" to the intense involvement of all people in shaping decisions at all levels of society. In most societies this notion of participation is but an ideal, for in capitalist societies the ruling bourgeoisie tends to manipulate groups and individuals in the direction of its own interests, while in socialist societies the ruling bureaucracy tends to act in the interests of the state rather than the people.

Huntington goes on to suggest that participation may be mobilized – that is, produced by manipulation or influence – or autonomous. Because most participation involves some degree of pressure and influence, he chooses not to separate mobilized from autonomous participation, and I follow his lead here.[3]

The questions I asked members of the ruling classes in Juazeiro and Petrolina about participation and mobilization in the political economy involved their views on the rights and obligations of citizens and their feelings about governmental affairs; the authority of government to regulate at local, state, and national levels; and how the individual might shape policy. I was also interested in how they became involved in issues

2 Huntington, *Participation*, pp. 7–10.

3 Huntington's thesis is developed in his *Political Order in Changing Societies* (New Haven: Yale University Press, 1968). A useful summary of his assumptions as applied to Latin America is in J. Mark Ruhl, "Social Mobilization and Political Instability in Latin America: A Test of Huntington's Theory," *Inter-American Economic Affairs* 29 (Autumn 1975): 3–21. I disagree with his conclusion that demands not satisfied in the socioeconomic sphere will cause political participation and stress on the political system thereby leading to political instability and decay of institutional life. Whereas Huntington sees the breakdown of institutional life as undermining the progressive evolution of society, I belive that the instability that may ensue offers the possibility of challenging and changing structural conditions in backward societies dominated by traditional ruling classes. This assumption is illustrated in Barrington Moore, Jr., *Social Origins of Dictatorship and Democracy* (Boston: Beacon Press, 1966), who focuses on mobilization and development by examining several countries within a comparative and historical framework. Moore's approach comes close to that of Marxist social science that assumes that through the development of capitalism there will ensue a class struggle in which workers and capitalists will fight it out. David R. Cameron, "Toward a Theory of Political Mobilization," *Journal of Politics* 36 (February 1974): 138–171, warns of social determinism implied in much of the work on political mobilization, whether in studies emphasizing modernization or conflict theory. J. P. Nettle, *Political Mobilization* (New York: Basic Books, 1967), attempts to synthesize contrasting approaches into a new methodology for studying development, especially in underdeveloped countries.

Table 10.1. *Ruling-class views on citizens' rights and obligations (%)*

	Juazeiro (N = 66)				Petrolina (N = 52)			
	First	Second	Third	Fourth	First	Second	Third	Fourth
Rights								
Equality before the law	92	5	3	0	63	19	12	6
Free education for all	3	15	76	6	27	32	28	13
An effective voice in the political process	2	78	11	9	8	34	27	31
Access to social services	3	2	10	85	2	15	33	50
Obligations								
Obey laws, respect authority	61	1	3	35	54	26	14	6
Vote	33	46	6	15	21	32	23	24
Be informed about government	5	50	42	3	12	20	41	27
Participate in public and political activities	1	3	49	47	13	22	22	43

affecting their personal life-styles and how they kept informed about political and governmental affairs.[4]

Participation, it is often argued, entails rights and obligations. During the time of my study the Brazilian military regime was stressing the moral obligations of citizens rather than their rights, a matter of considerable sensitivity in the face of accusations by Amnesty International and other human rights organizations of torture and repression. Thus the Juazeiro and Petrolina ruling classes were asked to rank in order of importance four items pertaining to citizens' rights. Juazeiro respondents almost universally emphasized the statement "equality before the law" as their preference, whereas Petrolina respondents also leaned toward "free education for all." Of less concern were "an effective voice in the political process" and "access to the social services of the nation." These results, as reported in Table 10.1, show that Juazeiro citizens are proud of their community image of equality and justice. They also believed, as did their counterparts

4 Some of the questions used, in particular those relating to rights and obligations, were drawn or adapted from a portion of a questionnaire concerning participation that was used by José Silva Michelena in a study sponsored by the Centro de Estudios del Desarrollo (CENDES) of the Universidad Central de Venezuela and the Center for International Studies of the Massachusetts Institute of Technology. A report of this ambitious study is in *A Strategy for Research on Social Policy*, ed. Frank Bonilla and José A. Silva Michelena (Cambridge, Mass.: MIT Press, 1967). Other questions on participation and mobilization were based on portions of the questionnaire in appendix B of Gabriel A. Almond and Sidney Verba, *The Civic Culture: Political Attitudes and Democracy in Five Nations* (Princeton: Princeton University Press, 1963).

in Petrolina, that the right of equality before the law was guaranteed for all Brazilians (81 percent agreeing). There was also consensus (82 percent agreeing) that all Brazilians had a right to access to social services, while there was less agreement as to free education for all (71 percent) and an effective voice in the political process (69 percent).

When respondents were asked to identify the obligations every person owes his country, about half of them said "to love one's country, to be loyal and respectful, to speak well of it, and to represent it well in other countries," which was followed by "to obey the laws, respect authority" and "to be honest, moral, work to better the nation." When forced to choose among the four participation-oriented statements shown in Table 10.1, they emphasized respect for authority and voting and ranked being informed about government and participating in public and political activities very low.

When asked why people had trouble understanding political and governmental affairs, respondents were almost equally divided as to the reasons. Roughly a third of them felt that the problems were too complex, another third that people did not care and did not try, and the remainder that those in power did not help people to understand. When asked if they agreed or disagreed with the statement that some people or groups have so much influence on the way government is run that the interests of the majority are ignored, only 21 percent in Petrolina agreed, 31 percent partially agreed, and 37 percent disagreed, while Juazeiro the corresponding figures were 52 percent, 8 percent, and 38 percent. Finally, when asked how the ordinary person ought to be involved in the local affairs of his town, 51 percent of all respondents said the citizen should simply take an interest in local affairs, whereas 14 percent believed in taking part in nongovernmental organizations dealing with local affairs such as community groups and charitable activities; 13 percent suggested that one should try to understand and keep informed, and 9 percent advocated participation in local governmental groups, organizations, and committees.

Another series of questions probed for reactions to a situation in which a regulation under consideration by government was considered very unjust or harmful. Respondents were asked how they would react in such a situation, how likely they would be to succeed, and whether they would actually do something about the situation were it to arise. These questions were directed to situations at local, state, and national levels; the responses are shown in Table 10.2. Interestingly, most persons in Juazeiro and Petrolina said they would take action against an unjust regulation. The course most frequently mentioned in Juazeiro was protest, even violent action; in Petrolina the inclination was to make personal contact with an influential councilperson or state or federal legislator. This finding appears

Table 10.2. *Ruling-class views on dealing with an unjust regulation (%)*

	Local level		State level		National level	
	Juazeiro	Petrolina	Juazeiro	Petrolina	Juazeiro	Petrolina
What would you do?						
Nothing	2		4	15	6	25
Work through informal, organized groups	3	10	3	10		10
Work through party	6	12	4	12	5	10
Work through formal, organized group	14	15	15	12	14	6
Talk to councilperson	27	35	17	25	29	23
Consult with lawyer	5	14	2	4	3	4
Vote		4		2		4
Protest, take violent action	42	10	55	17	43	14
Other	1			3		4
Would you succeed?						
Very likely	50	25	46	19	38	14
Moderately likely	17	12	17	10	17	12
Somewhat likely	11	37	23	27	27	19
Impossible	11	2	5	10	8	21
Only if others joined in	8	15	6	19	6	15
Other	3	9	3	15	4	19
Would you really do something?						
Very likely	86	33	85	25	85	25
Moderately likely	2	14	3	12	2	8
Somewhat likely	3	29	3	23		19
Impossible		2		4	3	12
Depends on issue	5	14	5	19	6	17
Other	4	8	4	17	4	19

Table 10.3. *Ruling-class views of various ways of influencing government decisions in Juazeiro (N = 66) and Petrolina (N = 52) (%)*

	Most effective		Least effective	
	Juazeiro	Petrolina	Juazeiro	Petrolina
Working through personal and family connections	5	12	11	14
Getting people interested in forming a group	39	27	2	6
Working through a party	53	40	2	4
Organizing a protest demonstration	2	4	85	56
None		8		12
Other	1	9		8

to be in line with my earlier observation that Juazeiro politics tend to be open and competitive, Petrolina politics closed and manipulative.

Expectations of success in resolving the situation of an unjust regulation were high for both communities. Nearly half of those interviewed in Juazeiro believed that their chances were very good; those in Petrolina were somewhat reserved on this point, considering the prospects at the local level better that those at the state and national levels. A follow-up question revealed that a very large majority in Juazeiro believed they really would do something to correct such an unjust situation at all levels of government. In contrast, those in Petrolina manifested more passive feelings about becoming involved. A further question showed that few persons in either community had ever done anything to influence legislation: 85 percent had never made an effort to affect the outcome of an act of the state assembly, and 90 percent had never tried to influence the national congress.

It seemed useful to probe more deeply into how individuals would work together to influence a government decision. Those interviewed were given a list of things they might do and asked to choose which of the approaches might be the most effective and least effective. Their responses, summarized in Table 10.3, leaned toward working through the political party to influence government, although the thought of forming a group of interested people was very much in their minds. Their idea of least effective means of influencing government was the organization of a protest demonstration. Juazeiro citizens overwhelmingly opposed this means, an obvious indication of their anxiety over repercussions from military authorities should there be any disruptions in town. This partially explains the apparent contradiction between their concern for a demonstration involving many persons and their willingness to protest as

Table 10.4. *Ruling-class views on various ways of understanding issues (%)*

	Juazeiro (N = 66)	Petrolina (N = 52)
Talk to people – friends, neighbors, relatives, fellow workers	3	10
Talk or write to party official or representative of a government agency	5	12
Talk or write to specialist not in government or party – newspaper editor, lawyer, etc.	62	35
Talk or write (no particular person mentioned)	17	4
Read about it – newspapers, magazines	9	33
Read a specific source	2	6
Other	2	

individuals. The political climate simply was not conducive to mass participation along the lines followed in Juazeiro in the past.

Involvement in politics relates closely to assessment of public issues that are often complex and difficult to understand. Interviewees were asked what they would do if an issue arose that might affect their way of life and they did not understand it fully. What would they do to find our more about it? Their responses are given in Table 10.4. In Juazeiro people preferred to seek information directly from a specialist knowledgeable about the particular issue. Only rarely would they read about it, pursue the matter through a party or government representative, or look for assistance to a friend, neighbor, relative, or fellow worker. In Petrolina there was a willingness to read about the issue in a newspaper and magazine, although the counsel of specialists was recognized as an effective means of clarifying complex matters. Though apparently not much accustomed to exploring issues through the press, people in Juazeiro and Petrolina, and especially in the former, indicated that they followed political and governmental affairs regularly, read newspapers and magazines regularly, often listened to the radio, and even discussed public affairs with others (Table 10.5).

Most respondents in both communities believed that decisions should be based on popular acceptance and involvement of the masses, that the party system was an effective means through which people might participate, that the franchise should be extended to all people, and that a vocal opposition should be encouraged and tolerated (Table 10.6). One might assume that these views reflected some concern with the policies of the military regime that had stifled most political participation since 1964 and that this concern was shared by those who supported the regime. Petrolina notables were more skeptical than their counterparts in Juazeiro

Table 10.5. *Ruling-class habits with regard to information on political and governmental affairs (%)*

	Juazeiro (N = 66)			Petrolina (N = 52)		
	Regularly	From time to time	Never	Regularly	From time to time	Never
Follow political and governmental affairs	77	21	2	54	44	2
Read newspapers	76	21	3	69	27	4
Read magazines	61	35	4	58	34	8
Listen to radio	89	11		65	29	6
Talk with other people	54	38	8	31	63	6

Table 10.6. *Ruling-class views on electoral participation (%)*

	Juazeiro (N = 66)	Petrolina (N = 52)
"Decisions should be based on popular acceptance and the will of the people."	89	85
"The party system should involve the masses."	86	81
"A free press and radio should be maintained."	94	88
"The vote should be given to all Brazilians."	80	90
"A vocal opposition should be encouraged and tolerated."	91	69

about tolerating and encouraging a vocal opposition, but this attitude probably was attributable to members of the dominant Coelho faction.

My study of the power structure in Juazeiro and Petrolina began, as I have said, with the identification of the local issues and decisions of the 1960s. Interviews with a panel of representative persons in each community produced the issues listed in Table 10.7 in order of importance;[5]

5 A sense of urgency over these issues was evident in a statement, signed by Orlando Pontes, approved by the Juazeiro city council on August 28, 1967, and published in *O Farol* 53 (September 7, 1967): 4. This statement was addressed to Governor Luiz Viana Filho as a plea for more electric power, extension of rural electricity, construction of housing for the poor, technical assistance so as to develop economic planning, construction of a new hotel, establishment of new industry, paving and maintenance of highways to nearby cities, irrigation for farming, increased funding for secondary and higher education, and elaboration of a health plan for the region. A similar statement, signed by the mayor, Joca de Souza Oliveira, and other community leaders, is "Memorial," September 1, 1967, in files of Comissão de Desenvolvimento Econômico de São Francisco (CODESF), Petrolina.

Table 10.7. *Local issues and decision, 1960–70 (number of nominations)*

Issue or decision	Juazeiro (nominations)	Petrolina (nominations)
Power	7	5
Sanitation, sewer system	5	7
Paved road to state capital	3	7
Education	4	5
Rural electrification	1	5
Health care	2	4
Water supply	1	4
Water treatment	2	2
Housing	3	1
Industrialization	0	3
Urban planning	1	0

power, sanitation, paving of a road to the state capital, education, health care, and water supply, among others, were identified. Clearly, these issues were those that had been controversial; less dramatic ones may have been overlooked. It is also likely that the full range of issues was not represented in the lists.[6] Nevertheless, the list was useful for the construction of questions on the topic for members of the ruling classes of the two communities.

For the purposes of this study, community issues – economic, political, educational, and social – during the 1960s were selected according to the following criteria:[7] The issue had to have been at least partially resolved by a decision. That decision had to be perceived by those interviewed as significant and had to involve the use of resources so as to have impact on the local population, choice among alternatives, and implementation by the local power structure. These criteria, of course, exclude issues that are not discussed or are directly or indirectly suppressed.[8]

The issues selected were classified by members of the ruling classes of Juazeiro and Petrolina in terms of five dimensions first proposed by Ernest A. T. Barth and Stuart D. Johnson: unique–recurrent, salient–nonsalient to leadership, salient–nonsalient to community publics, effective action

6 Peter Russi, "Community Decision Making," *Administrative Science Quarterly* 1 (March 1957): 438–439, has identified these and other problems.

7 These criteria are adapted from those used in a study of Syracuse by Linton C. Freeman, Thomas J. Fararo, Warner Bloomberg Jr., and Morris H. Sunshine, "Locating Leaders in Local Communities: A Comparison of Some Alternative Approaches," *American Sociological Review* 28 (October 1963): 791–798.

8 These problems and remedies for them are discussed by Willis D. Hawley and Frederick M. Wirt, eds., in *The Search for Community Power* (Englewood Cliffs, N. J.: Prentice-Hall, 1968).

possible–impossible, and local–cosmopolitan.[9] All the issues except water supply and treatment and foreign influence were identified as recurrent; all except foreign influence were judged highly salient both to the members of the ruling classes themselves and to the community at large; all were considered resolvable (Table 10.8). A local solution seemed possible for street construction and maintenance and recreation, and planning for development and electoral participation were envisaged essentially as local matters. Issues of power and light, rural electricity, social security, education, and emigration were seen as state concerns, whereas agricultural development, credits, unemployment, housing, medical services, sewage, and water supply and treatment were perceived as federal problems. With the exception of this local–cosmopolitan dimension no significant distinction appeared in responses. Leaders agreed that issues presented them were identifiable in the experience of their community, central to their own interests and those of the community, and resolvable.

Respondents were not particularly impressed by the efforts to solve most problems, however. There was rather a strong dissatisfaction over the issues of rural electrification, industrialization, agricultural development, unemployment, poverty and hunger, sewage, movement of people from countryside to city, and outflow of people to coastal areas. There was general dissatisfaction over street construction and maintenance, as well as planning for development, while concern also was expressed over electoral activity. Considerable satisfaction appeared over such issues as power and light, credits and loans, social security, housing, recreation, medical services, water supply and treatment, and education.

My interest in the violent history of the backlands led me to ask some further questions about conflict. As I have said earlier, a general reading of the literature on Northeast Brazil produces the impression that violence has long been the norm in the behavior of the backlands' elites and masses.[10] Nearly a half-century ago, Petrolina's weekly newspaper cited a series of revolts over several centuries and asserted that "they were not mere isolated events – they were rooted in certain sociological conditions."[11] Indeed, as we have seen, the authoritarian behavior of the backlands' colonels was directly linked to the patriarchal social system, and violence often emanated from family feuds or revenge, such as that involving the Evangelista Pereira e Melo and Miguel Siqueira families in

9 These dimensions are drawn from Ernest A. T. Barth and Stuart D. Johnson, "Community Power and a Typology of Social Issues," *Social Forces* 38 (October 1959): 29–32.

10 See *Protest and Resistance in Angola and Brazil: Comparative Studies*, ed. Ronald H. Chilcote (Berkeley and Los Angeles: University of California Press, 1972), especially the editor's chapter 12, "Protest and Resistance in Brazil and Portuguese Africa: A Synthesis and a Classification," pp. 243–302, which includes an interpretive bibliography.

11 Albano Taveira, "Remember," *O Farol* 10 (December 4, 1924): 1.

Table 10.8. *Dimensions of decision making in Juazeiro and Petrolina (%) (N = 118)*

Issue (ranked, order of importance)	Perception of issue				Resource solution					Assessment of resolution				
	Recurring issue	Salient to leadership	Salient to community	Effective action possible	Local	State	Federal	All three	Other	Very satisfied	Somewhat satisfied	Somewhat dissatisfied	Very dissatisfied	Undecided
1. Industrialization	92	95	99	98	16	11	11	41	21	13	28	18	40	1
2. Elementary education	79	98	98	100	5	23	3	35	34	27	57	11	4	1
3. Planning	91	97	97	99	39	9	2	36	14	13	38	18	28	3
4. Rural electrification	84	95	98	98	9	30	17	26	18	23	24	9	39	5
5. Agricultural development	95	94	98	100	10	6	16	47	21	9	26	23	40	2
6. Credits and loans	87	92	98	100	3	7	28	28	34	26	49	10	7	8
7. Power and light	98	98	98	100	5	32	15	32	16	42	25	7	26	0
8. Sewage	94	100	99	100	6	12	24	33	25	8	21	14	56	1
9. Poverty	88	94	97	94	5	6	12	60	17	4	17	11	61	7
10. Unemployment	89	96	97	98	4	8	11	59	18	8	10	17	57	8
11. Medical services	78	99	98	100	2	12	24	38	24	29	51	15	4	1
12. Water supply treatment	34	99	100	100	18	12	18	34	18	75	22	2	1	0
13. Housing	93	95	99	98	17	4	9	44	26	12	53	21	13	1
14. Secondary education	82	97	98	100	2	26	2	39	31	23	58	14	5	0
15. Electoral participation	75	92	92	97	29	5	5	45	16	21	39	18	15	7
16. Social security	96	97	100	98	6	39	4	35	16	11	52	19	15	3
17. Street maintenance	95	94	98	99	72	3	0	20	5	11	41	25	21	2
18. Recreation	92	92	94	100	50	2	1	30	17	9	50	24	16	1
19. Rural-to-urban migration	78	75	80	89	8	6	16	36	34	3	16	28	39	14
20. Migration to coast	74	77	79	93	8	12	11	38	31	6	14	29	33	18

1928.[12] Sometimes the dispute involved political rivalry, for example, that in 1949 between Adalberto and Osvaldo de Souza Coelho, on the one hand, and Raul Gomes da Sá, a councilman and his brother Alberto, on the other.[13] At other times the population was called upon to choose sides in a local political struggle against state or federal authorities. In early 1920, for instance, Juazeiro was seriously threatened with attack by some 1,500 *jagunços*, or hired gunmen, who had seized nearby Remanso.[14] Political leaders in Juazeiro and Remanso aligned to oppose revolutionary forces in October 1930, and two years later in Remanso armed bands under political chief Francisco Leobas continued to resist.[15] Anxious local authorities and the population of Juazeiro quickly called for state and federal support in March 1926 when Luiz Carlos Prestes occupied two *fazendas* in the interior of the municipality.[16] In early 1968 students protesting intolerable conditions in Petrolina's only movie theater were dispersed by the discharging revolver of the enraged owner.[17] When there remained no alternative, the desperate, drought-stricken, starving *sertanejo* often resorted to violence; occasionally a train or a warehouse would be robbed for food. Desperate drought conditions and unemployment provoked an invasion of Agua Preta in 1971 by nearly 1,500 workers demanding food. Unemployed sugar workers near Recife threatened to invade three cities in May 1971. Usually police attributed the agitation to "subversive movements."[18]

In a separate study, I examined themes of conflict in 683 pamphlets of popular poetry. While 25 of these pamphlets focused on national disasters (such as droughts and floods) and 146 on political issues involving assassination (John Kennedy), suicide (Getúlio Vargas), or execution (Chessman), 171 pamphlets dealt with religious mystics and fanatics who challenged political authority (e.g., Padre Cícero). Half the pamphlets (341) emphasized violence, including social banditry, personal and family feuds, acts of bravery, and so on.[19]

12 Two persons died in an attack by Antônio de Souza, his son, and a group of *capangas* or hired henchmen; see *O Farol* 13 (April 26, 1928): 1.

13 Osvaldo Coelho received a knife wound, and Alberto Gomes da Sá died in a gun battle along with an accomplice of the Coelhos; see *O Farol* 34 (February 28, 1949): 1. Another example of political rivalry occurred in Juazeiro when Colonel Miguel Siqueira, accompanied by two sons and henchmen, accosted Professor João Leal; see *O Farol* 20 (March 16, 1935): 1.

14 See *O Farol* 5 (January 11, 1920): 1; (February 8, 1920): 1; and (February 22, 1920): 3.

15 *O Farol* 17 (November 12, 1932): 1. For the 1930 developments, see *O Echo*. 5 (February 14, 1930): 1.

16 *O Farol* 11 (March 20, 1926): 1.

17 See details in *O Farol* 13 (March 29, 1968): 1, and (April 7, 1968): 1.

18 *Tribuna de Bahia* (May 5, 1971).

19 Ronald H. Chilcote, "The Politics of Conflict in the Popular Poetry of Northeast Brazil," *Journal of Latin American Lore* 5 no. 2 (1979): 208.

I chose five historical instances of conflict for closer study, asking members of the ruling classes of Juazeiro and Petrolina whether they were familiar with them and, if they could provide details, where they would elaborate on the importance of each. I then compared their responses with those of fifteen singers and poets I interviewed, with the assistance of folklorist Sebatião Batista, in 1967 (Table 10.9). Although the singers and poets recognized the cases, about half of those interviewed among members of Juazeiro's and Petrolina's ruling classes did not.

The first case concerns Palmares. In the midst of the internal struggles and general instability that characterized Portuguese rule during the seventeenth century, many slaves escaped from the sugar plantations, especially in Bahia and Pernambuco, and a group of them founded the Republic of Palmares in the interior of Alagôas in 1630. Despite a series of military expeditions whose objectives were the conquest and pacification of the liberated slaves,[20] Palmares resisted until 1695, when it was finally overcome. It was a refuge for some twenty thousand slaves living in fortified villages. The strategy of these rebels was primarily defensive and when attacked they usually moved elsewhere. Thus, it is not surprising that there were *quilombos* along the São Francisco River during the first quarter of the eighteenth century.[21]

Palmares was significant as a movement of black African resistance to slavery. While I had expected to find little recognition of it among the poets and singers because it is ignored in their verse, they were quick to identify it. One poet referred to singers who mentioned Palmers. Another indicated that Palmares represented "a cry against oppression." Respondents from the ruling classes of Juazeiro and Petrolina offered little detail; those who were familiar with it believed it was simply "a prelude" to the abolition of slavery in Brazil, "awakened national attention," and was "a cry for liberty."

A second event of major significance in the backlands was the millenarian movement established by Antônio Conselheiro at Canudos, about 160 kilometers southeast of Juazeiro. As I have pointed out in an earlier chapter, Conselheiro and his followers lived in poverty, alienated from Brazilian society but united in their desire to seek a heaven on earth, and their criticism of government policies during the early 1890s provoked the sending of several expeditions to maintain order. Canudos never surren-

20 Edison Carneiro, *O quilombo dos Palmares, 1630–1695* (São Paulo: Editora Brasiliense Limitada, 1947), identifies two Dutch (in 1644 and 1645) and fourteen Portuguese–Brazilian (between 1667 and 1694) expeditions against Palmares.

21 Nina Rodrigues, *Os africanos no Brasil* (São Paulo: Companhia Editora Nacional, 1932). Quilombo refers to "a house in a forest where fugitive Negroes are sheltered" and is a term of Angolan origin; see Gustavo Barroso, *Segredos e revelações da história do Brasil*, 2d ed. (Rio de Janeiro: Edições O Cruzeiro, 1961), pp. 58–59.

Table 10.9. *Recognition and assessment of historical examples of conflict*

	Poets and singers (N = 15)			Ruling classes (N = 118)		
	Positive impression	Negative Impression	Not recognizable	Familiar	Heard of	Not recognizable
Palmares	9	3	3	16	31	71
Canudos and Conselheiro	9	5	1	19	39	60
Banditry (Lampião)	12	2	1	43	37	38
Padre Cícero	15	0	0	23	42	53
Peasant leagues (Julião)	6	5	4	18	32	68

dered, although its population was annihilated in 1897. Its history signified that illiterate peasants could find a sense of community in the backlands, that religion could be a source of social and political action, and that through unity successful resistance to authority was possible. The happenings at Canudos are of particular interest in that the community was not far from Juazeiro. In fact, late in 1896 Juazeiro was in a state of panic over the impending visit of Antônio Conselheiro, who reportedly had purchased construction materials from one of the city's "distinguished businessmen." The population's alarm was manifested in a telegram from local merchants to Governor Luiz Viana: "Urgent request to send forces . . . in view of probable assault within a week. Panic increasing. Lacking guarantees, families are fleeing."[22]

Despite the importance and proximity of Canudos, members of the ruling classes generally did not consider it significant; for them it was more or less an isolated case, attributable to "lack of culture," "illiteracy," and "fanaticism." In contrast, for the singers and poets Antônio Conselheiro was a "great man" and Canudos "represented the bravery and ignorance of a past time"; they were familiar with the writings of Cunha and recognized the importance of Canudos in Brazilian history, even though it was mentioned only rarely in their verse.

A third instance of conflict involved banditry, a nineteenth-century phenomenon whose influence extended until the middle of the present century.[23] Bandits such as the renowned Antônio Silvino and Lampião had considerable prestige in the backlands, where they were largely ignored by federal and state authorities and easily established links with the local political chiefs. As we have seen, the existence of banditry in the Northeast backlands has been attributable variously to the sociocultural backwardness of the backlands, the lack of communications, and the failure to guarantee justice there; to the excessive heat and recurrent droughts; and to the prevailing institutionalized violence and the patriarchal order.

22 *Cidade de Joazeiro* 1 (November 8, 1896): 2. See also the news of Canudos in 1 (November 1, 1896): 2; and 1 (November 29, 1896): 1.

23 A sort of Mafia-type organization tied closely to local politics had penetrated many of the cities of the Northeast in the 1960s and 1970s. Not dissimilar to organizational alliances of the past between political chieftains and *cangaceiros* or bandits, this contemporary organization was known as the Sindicato de Morte or Death Syndicate. In July 1971, for example, federal police implicated an ex-governor of Alagoas, two former deputies, a former mayor, a police chief, and two ranchers for their syndicate activities in the state of Alagoas; see *A Tarde* (July 24, 1971). The former governor, Muniz Falcão, was from Araripina and a relative of Pernambucan deputy José Muniz Ramos. Further research is necessary to support the sometimes suggested idea that the syndicate operates with social objectives on behalf of depressed peoples outside Brazil. Eric Hobsbawn in *Primitive Rebels: Studies in Archaic Forms of Social Movements in the 19th and 20th Centuries* (Manchester, England: University of Manchester Press, 1959), analyzes the social orientation of the Sicilian Mafia.

Lampião's band of some eighty members was active in the interior of Juazeiro at least on one occasion, and his presence was of considerable concern to the local population.[24] His actions were regularly reported by the local press, which decried the inattention of state and federal governments to the needs of the local constituency.[25] Lampião was finally encircled and killed in 1938, an event that was extensively covered in the Petrolina press.[26] Although banditry effectively ended with his death, his followers carried on until the mid-1940s.[27]

Interestingly, the presence of Lampião had considerable impact on the majority of the respondents, many of whom not only could give substantial detail on his activity and importance but also had had personal contact with him. For the singers and poets, Lampião symbolized a potentially revolutionary threat to legal authority, especially police and army, who might repress a sympathetic rural population: "He was a man of order whose position was respected"; "He was a strong fighter"; "The people admired his exploits"; "He will remain immortalized in the heart of the people." Respondents in Juazeiro and Petrolina offered negative feelings about Lampião describing him as "illiterate," "a disrupter of the rural population," and a "terrorist."

The fourth event concerns Padre Cícero Romão Batista, who emerged as the powerful patriarch and cleric of the Northeast, first through a series of miracles in the period from 1889 to 1891; later as mayor of his city, Juazeiro do Norte in the state of Ceará; and finally, after his victory in 1914 over a battalion of state militia when he became virtual ruler of the state and much of the Northeast. Cícero's impact on Juazeiro and Petrolina was not great, although he may have reached the former city in June or July 1905 en route home from Rio de Janeiro (reportedly he took a train from Salvador into the interior along the line that terminates in Juazeiro). He was best known in Petrolina, however, for his gift of a clock to the local cathedral.[28] Additionally, one of his followers, José Lourenço, founded a communal sect at Caldeirão in the Serra do Araripe near Juazeiro do Norte, and after being dispersed in November 1936 some of these followers moved to Pau de Colher, not far from Petrolina. A police force from Petrolina devastated the

24 See *O Farol* 15 (March 25, 1930): 4; "Virgolino-o sicário!," *O Echo* 5 (March 27, 1930): 1.

25 See, for example, "Lampião com o rifle e o punhal domina o sertão," *O Farol* 11 (June 5, 1926): 1; "A obra do banditismo," *O Farol* 12 (May 3, 1927): 1; "Lampião, ainda e sempre!," *O Farol* 12 (June 2, 1927): 1; and "Porque floresce o banditismo," *O Farol* 14 (August 31, 1934): 1.

26 See *O Farol* 23 (July 30, 1938): 1, and (August 6, 1938): 1. In 1971, Antônio Luís Tavares, an old cangaceiro who had served Lampião, announced to the press that Lampião was still alive in the backlands of Mato Grosso; see *Diário de Pernambuco* (July 19, 1971).

27 For the activities of José Moreno, see *O Farol*. 31 (February 28, 1946): 1.

28 See *O Farol* 14 (April 6, 1929): 1, and 17 (September 7, 1931): 1, 2.

new site in February 1938.[29] Padre Cícero is also remembered by many sertanejos who visit Juazeiro do Norte on annual pilgrimages or who are familiar with the prolific literature on him.[30]

Thus, Padre Cícero was well known to most of our respondents. Singers and poets eulogized him: He was "the best-known figure, most sung about, most admired, and most loved by the people"; "almost equal in importance to Christ"; and "appeals to people everywhere." Juazeiro and Petrolina rulers were equally positive, for Cícero "built many schools and health centers"; "motivated people to work"; and "brought good to the region."

Labor unrest, the fifth instance of conflict, had become prevalent in Brazil by the early 1960s. In the rural sector, hundreds of peasant leagues emerged, especially in Pernambuco and Paraíba states, after the successful defense by lawyer and politician Francisco Julião of a group of peasants who had been expelled illegally from the Galiléia plantation near Vitória de Santo Antão.[31] The organization of the peasant leagues paralleled efforts by the Partido Comunista Brasileiro to organize sugar and coffee workers. Catholic Church-supported rural unions, officially sanctioned by the government, were also founded in this period. In the urban centers, the organization of skilled and unskilled labor was extended into most major sectors of the economy. These developments were not entirely ignored in Juazeiro and Petrolina, where a small labor movement, an offshoot of an organization first founded in the 1930s, reemerged with demands and actions.[32] The response to Julião of the ruling classes in Juazeiro and Petrolina was uniformly unsympathetic.

He was not much respected among the singers and poets, either: "People did not understand him," "They feared him," "He once was important, but in the future he will disappear." For political reasons they were unwilling to discuss him, since the military coup of 1964 had forced him into exile.

29 *O Farol* 22 (February 3, 1938): 1, and (February 10, 1938): 1. The reemergence of the movement was reported in *O Farol* 22 (June 18, 1938): 1, and (June 25, 1938): 1.

30 Ralph della Cava's *Miracle at Joazeiro* (New York: Columbia University Press, 1970), and Otacilio Anselmo, *Padre Cĩcero: mito e realidade* (Rio de Janeiro: Editora Civilização Brasileira, 1968), are especially noteworthy. Interestingly, a movement emerged in mid-1971, led by Padre Helvidio Martins and writer Rachel de Queiroz, whose objective was to "rehabilitate" Padre Cícero (the Vatican had refused to accept the miracles but allowed him to remain in Juazeiro without his priestly rights). See *Jornal do Commercio* (June 1, 1971), and (June 3, 1971).

31 Julião describes these developments in his *Que são as Ligas Camponesas?* (Rio de Janeiro: Cadernos do Povo [1], Editora Civilização Brasileira, 1962).

32 Only fragments of information appeared in *O Farol*. One that condemned Julião's "Methods and Solutions" argued, however, that "the hour has arrived for us to struggle for the redemption of the man of the Northeast, eliminating the shameful exploitation and the tremendous injustice that have been committed against him." See *O Farol* 47 (December 11, 1961): 3.

Only one in ten of the Juazeiro and Petrolina respondents considered these instances of conflict related to the cultural and social conditions of the backlands. Those who agreed offered a number of explanations for the prevalence of conflict: "the dominance of politicians," "the ignorance of the people," "family groups," "the climate," "lack of education, ignorance, and illiteracy," "injustice." Thus members of the ruling classes were obviously less aware of the historical examples of conflict than the singers and poets, and the two groups often assigned opposite values to the personalities involved. This is not unexpected, perhaps, given that the rulers were reasonably well educated and life in the towns, in contrast to the countryside, had been relatively stable and secure, thereby protecting the rulers' vested interests.

In contrast, the peasant singers and poets tended to be less well educated but well informed about matters that affected the rural populations. The sample of fifteen included seven poets, three singers, and five who were both poets and singers; of the twelve poets, nine had published poetry.[33] Nine were over fifty years of age, two under thirty. All but five were born in Paraíba, the heartland of poets and singers. Only eight had attended elementary school, most for only a year or two. Nearly all of them were aware of and expressed positive feelings about the historical examples. Singing and writing about events of conflict appealed to their constituency of peasant farmers and town poor who gathered at local fairs.[34]

Some conclusions can be drawn from this chapter. First, while violence and conflict pervade the historical experience of these backlands communities and are considered normal by contemporary poets and singers, the

33 Since the late nineteenth century the poetry of these troubadors has been published as *popular poetry*. and because pamphlets of poetry used to be hung on a string and displayed in local markets, the poetry also became known as *literatura de cordel*.

34 Constraints on political participation affected all sectors of the population. A survey of youth, aged twelve to twenty-two years, in two working-class districts of Juazeiro and Petrolina, revealed a negative and pessimistic outlook. Most respondents were of poor working-class origin and had come from traditional rural areas to seek opportunities in the city. They envisaged little or no prospect for social mobility even though most had access to education. Even with education, their occupational skills differed little from those of their parents. In fact, the families and schools in these districts seemed to condition the youth to confront the realities of life in their communities, that is, to recognize that their prospects for advancement were indeed poor. Unemployment was extremely high for those not in school. The youth also perceived clearly the problems of their existence and community, but they had no clear perspectives on how resources, human or material, could be mobilized. Lacking organization and effective leadership, they accepted subservience to the authority of community officials. This relationship was coupled with an apparent inability to manifest public concern over their particular needs and problems. Such a situation seemed likely to ensure the maintenance of the status quo in their districts. See Rosália de Araũjo Oliveira, Ronald H. Chilcote, and Padre Pedro Mansueto de Lavor, "Estudo sôbre a juventude em dois bairros de Petrolina" (Petrolina: CEMIC, 1971).

ruling classes in Juazeiro and Petrolina attribute them little importance. Second, political participation in the two communities is constrained largely by the controls of local and national government. Political activity is generally limited by the military regime. In Petrolina this worked to the advantage of the dominant Coelho family, whereas in Juazeiro factionalization of parties and groups characterized local politics.

PART II

The sertão revisited

11

Political challenge to traditional hegemony

The celebrated study of Middletown by Robert and Helen Lynd has been the point of departure for most of the community studies that followed it, and this one is no exception. Middletown – Muncie, Indiana – itself has attracted scores of investigators and has even been portrayed in a public television series. Many studies of Middletown in transition have implied that families there and elsewhere in America are falling apart.[1] My examination of Juazeiro and Petrolina suggests that while their families may be encountering problems in maintaining their hegemony, this does not necessarily imply any undermining of family cohesion in the *sertão*. Change in these communities in recent years is more a matter of response to the rise of merchant capital and the penetration of state and private corporate capital into the traditional local and regional economy. The demands for bourgeois democracy that usually accompany these developments affect the structure of community power, thereby sometimes stimulating capitalism and sometimes impeding it. Like the Lynds, I decided to return to the towns I had studied to note changes and assess my findings ten years later. Thus, this concluding part is based on my investigations during July and August 1982 and July 1983.

Juazeiro revisited

Juazeiro had grown in many ways during the decade of the seventies. Its population had doubled, reaching 120,372 (62,366 in the city and 58,016 in the interior) by 1980. A younger generation of activists, their university education completed in nearby Salvador or other urban centers, was making its impact. They had founded several newspapers in an effort to revive Juazeiro's cultural legacy and to mobilize a broader segment of society for political participation. *Rivale* (for "Renovation and Integration of the Valley"), had first appeared on March 19, 1972. Its publisher was

1 Ellen Goodman reports, however, that thirteen studies of Muncie in the late 1970s concluded that family life there not only continues but in some ways is more cohesive than in the 1920s; see her "Myth of the Perfect Family Conceals Underlying Strength," *Los Angeles Times* (April 30, 1982).

Paganini Nobre Mota, a physician; Flávio Luiz Ribeiro Silva, an economist, was its financial director, and Jorge Khoury Hedage, an agronomist, its secretary. Later Herbet Mouze had become managing editor. All were to become influencial in Juazeiro politics. Paganini had left the group over political differences to reestablish *Tribuna do Povo,* which had circulated between 1957 and 1963 under the editorship of Jorge de Souza Gomes and included as collaborators State Deputy Raulino Queiroz and Walter Dourado, aspiring town historian. *Tribuna do Povo* had reappeared on December 23, 1972, under the banner "A Merry Life, Offering Information, Orientation, Criticism, Collaboration, and Debate." Its editor was Arnold de Souza Oliveira. In April 1973 it had published charges by Mayor Durval Barbosa Lima of financial irregularities in the previous administration, that of Américo Tanuri, and an improper payment by Luiz Viana Filho to a committee of auditors responsible for the review of municipal finances.[2] On December 24, 1972, Paganini had launched *Jornal de Juazeiro,* which had assumed an independent line under editor Moacyr dos Santos despite its publisher's being a municipal councilman. The *Jornal de Juazeiro* and *Rivale* were still publishing a decade later; Ermi Ferrari had become publisher and editor of *Rivale* in 1977. On Jorge Khoury's election as mayor in late 1982, Ermi had joined his administration and the paper's municipal subsidies had necessarily come to an end, forcing the paper to stop publishing in 1983. In addition to these papers, the diocese in the late 1970s had begun publishing an information bulletin, *Caminhar Juntos,* that reported on church activities and the speeches of the bishop.[3] These journalistic endeavors had been accompanied by occasional demands upon the municipal government and the people to preserve and enhance their unique culture. Maria Isabel Figueiredo Pontes, for example, had continued her campaign in this direction.[4] Ermi Ferrari had been aggressive in pushing for projects in the community and had organized and published a petition signed by civic leaders demanding the establishment of a university.[5]

Many of the persons who had constituted the ruling class of Juazeiro a decade earlier remained active in town politics. Flávio Silva, whose business interests had collapsed and whose economic influence had declined, was attempting to build anew. Politically he supported Viana interests and the local candidacy of João de Oliveira. Ana Oliveira no longer represented the area as a state deputy, but the businessman Etelvir Dantas occupied a

2 *Tribuna do Povo* 12 no. 189 (April 23, 1973): 1.

3 Maria Izabel Figeiredo Pontes, "Folclore e tradições juazeirenses," *Rivale* 6 (July 15, 1977): 5.

4 Carta de Juazeiro clamor do seu povo," *Rivale* 8 (May 30, 1980): 1. Dated May 29, the document contained a list of sixty-eight demands.

5 Details of the history of the press in Juazeiro are in Wilson Dias, *História de imprensa Juazeirense* (Juazeiro: Gráfica Santa Inez, [1982]).

seat in the state legislature and in 1982 was elected federal deputy. The school administrator Raimundo Medrado Primo had moved to Salvador, and businessmen Luiz Libório and Paulo Campelo had retired there. Doctor Antônio Carlos de Andrade e Silva had also left the area. Dom Tomás had retired in 1975, and his place as bishop had been taken by activist Dom José Rodrigues de Souza. Two former mayors, Américo Tanuri and Durval Barbosa, had died (in 1975 and 1979, respectively).

In the course of my initial interviews with town leaders, I found Giuseppi Muccini especially optimistic.[6] The newest and most obvious accomplishment he pointed to was the construction of the Sobradinho Dam on the Rio São Francisco, the culmination of a series of studies and recommendations dating to the early years of this century. Muccini recounted how in September 1971 the Comissão de Desenvolvimento Econõmico de São Francisco (CODESF) had organized meetings with state deputies from Bahia and Pernambuco to study the possibility of such a project. Once the government had decided to construct a dam, CODESF had lobbied for the building of a lock so that river commerce and the ports of Juazeiro and Petrolina could be maintained; irrigation of the lands contiguous to the river was also considered a priority. Since the completion of the dam, settlers in the irrigated projects had prospered, and some had been able to move to the city. Overall, Muccini believed that Juazeiro and Petrolina had profited from the dam. The Coelhos, while not directly benefiting from the project, had gained influence, political and economic, and extended their holdings into Bahia with cattle-raising ventures. They maintained close ties with the Vianas of Casa Nova. New family leaders linked to Luiz Viana Filho, now a federal senator, had emerged in politics, and to Muccini they represented "visionary politics throughout the region."

The handsome Grande Hotel de Juazeiro had been inauguarated on March 23, 1972. Juazeiro had celebrated its centenary in 1978. An industrial park established in 1978 had attracted some industry, including a tanning factory run by the sons of Paulo Campelo, a gas-bottling facility, and small factories producing biscuits and macaroni. The Coelho group was planning to open a small plant. In addition, Conservas Alimentícias Cica-Norte was processing tomatoes. In an effort to coordinate and stimulate development, the municipality had just formed a development council.[7]

New industries had been established in the area, including Agrovale, which converted sugarcane into alcohol for fuel and in the process dumped

6 Interview with Giuseppi Muccini, Juazeiro, July 26, 1982.

7 See "Criando Conselho de Desenvolvimento Municipal de Juazeiro 'CODEM' mais um passo da reforma administrative," *Rivale* 10 (April 3, 1982): 4–5; "Demonstração de confiança nas possibilidades agro-indústrias do São Francisco," *O Farol* 62 (March 23, 1977): 1; also, interview with Ermi Ferrari Magalhães, Juazeiro, July 27, 1982.

its waste into the nearby river.[8] Industrialization in the region was limited to food processing and a few other activities. The construction of the dam had offered the hope that someday the area around Juazeiro and Petrolina would be irrigated and productive. In the late 1970s there had been talk of building a $400 million steel mill with a capacity of half a million tons near Juazeiro, one of three Bahian sites under consideration by the Companhia de Projetos Industriais. Availability of water and power from Sobradinho were essential to such an undertaking, but because there were no known iron ore deposits around Juazeiro the area was presumably not given serious consideration.[9]

The reserve of unemployed labor left behind by the construction of the dam might, however, have been useful to the copper mine in nearby Jaguararí.[10] The state had assumed control of the mine, then owned by São Paulo industrialist Baby Pignatari, in 1975. Known as Caraíba Metais, the project comprised the mine in Jaguararí and a mill in Camaçarí, fifty-three kilometers from the state capital. Mill capacity was 150,000 tons annually, enough to meet the demands of the internal market. Mining at Jaguararí was expected to produce 50,000 tons of copper each year, to be supplemented with copper mined at Salobo in Carajás, Pará. Reserves of Jaguararí copper were estimated to last about twenty years. The project was conceived as in the national interest in obviating costly imports of copper. Consequently, the government had invested $1,350 million in the project and expected to spend another $100 million.[11] In 1982, however, the government suspended mining operations at Caraíba, having arranged to transfer the whole project to the Canadian multinational Noranda Mines for $100 million. The Bahian Association of Geologists protested that the copper reserves were Brazilian and denationalization would "compromise the future of the country" in that 47 percent of Brazil's 177 mining firms were already in the hands of foreigners. They argued that the transfer would lead to international manipulation of the domestic market and exploitation of nonrenewable resources.[12] This nationalistic appeal to

8 In March 1984, Dom José led marches involving 5,000 people in Juazeiro and Petrolina protesting the pollution in the river, which was said to have killed 500 tons of fish. See "Vinhote da Agrovale foi jogado na São Francisco," *A Tarde* (March 25, 1984). Agrovale's principal owner was Gustavo Colasso, a Recife sugar refiner.

9 "Juazeiro poderá ter uma siderúrgica," *Rivale* 8 (March 30, 1979): 1.

10 Giuseppi Muccini, "Sobradinho: solução vivável para metalurgia do cobre," *Rivale* 7 (February 25, 1978): 4–5. This view also was expressed by Deputy Manoel Novais in a speech to the Chamber of Deputies See "Deputado Manoel Novais defende metalurgia do cobre da Caraíba em Sobradinho," *Rivale* 7 (May 27, 1978): 3; continued in 7 (June 3, 1978): 3.

11 Paterson Pereira, "Caraíba tem dificuldade em vender cobre," *Folha de São Paulo* (August 21, 1983).

12 "Associação de Geólogos é contra privatizar Caraíba," *A Tarde* (July 22, 1982). Reprinted in *Caminhar Juntos* 71 (September 1982): 15.

the public, along with a decline in copper sales, apparently stalled the transaction, although my interviews in 1983 suggested that it was still under consideration.[13]

What were viewed by some as positive indicators of growth were viewed critically by others. For Bishop Dom José Rodrigues the negative consequences of the Sobradinho Dam weighed heavily on the inhabitants of the four municipalities that had been forced to move. Although electric power from the dam now headed north to Belém, it did not extend to the reconstructed town of Sento Sé. He argued that completion of the dam had left 3,000 families unemployed and 10,000 persons impoverished. Further, the release of water below the dam had flooded the banks of the river, resulting in devastation of farms, loss of boats, and isolation of communities.[14]

Many other problems afflicted the city, according to the bishop. Although the government had established six irrigation projects in Juazeiro, none were benefiting small farmers, who had been forced off their land without adequate compensation. Once acquired, this land had been sold or leased to medium-sized and large enterprises. *Grilagem* (in which land occupied by small farmers is seized, acquired fraudulently, or purchased at unfair prices by outside firms or investors) was widespread. Dom José decried the general misery of the region, the high infant mortality (15 percent die in the early months of life), the high illiteracy (90 percent in some areas of the Northeast), and the lack of schools for the thousands of children in Juazeiro who did not attend classes. Begging and prostitution were rampant. He attributed these problems to the political domination of local oligarchies. Each municipality, he said, was a fief: "People live as slaves, and their children are born slaves generation after generation."[15]

Additional local problems were identified in a study by the Empresa Geotécnica reported in July 1983. Focusing on fourteen peripheral neighborhoods, the study characterized Juazeiro as a pole of migration. Some people, it found, had gravitated to the city in pursuit of a better life, others because they had been pushed off their small parcels of land. Of this population some 15 percent had lived in Juazeiro less than a year, 26 percent less than two years. One in eight had come from the interior of the

13 Interview with Ermi Ferrari Magalhães, Juazeiro, July 25, 1983. Ermi favored the sale because he felt it would eliminate the bureaucracy and corruption associated with a state enterprise.

14 Don José Rodrigues de Sousa, "Entrevista," *Caminhar Juntos* 73 (November 1982): 2.

15 See a detailed summary of the problems in a paper distributed by the diocese, "Relatório das atividades da diocese: visão geral da diocese de Juazeiro, Ba" (Juazeiro, 1981), mimeographed copy. These problems are also documented in Conselho Pastoral Diocesano, "Documento dos sindicatos dos trabalhadores rurais sobre a secas," *Caminhar Juntos* 75 (January 1983): 8–9, and "II Assembleia Geral dos Trabalhadores Rurais da Diocese de Juazeiro," *Caminhar Juntos* 72 (October 1982): 1–10.

municipality, some having been displaced by large agricultural projects and some seeking schools for their children. Some 84 percent were unemployed; 69 percent had a monthly family income of less than $60; 63 percent were illiterate. Potable water was unavailable to many homes.[16]

These concerns had been reflected in community debate in the decade between my visits. A bitter contest for political control had characterized the November 15, 1972, elections. The victor in the mayoral race had been Durval Barbosa da Cunha by 41 votes over Arnaldo Vieira do Nascimento (Table 11.1). Arnaldo, running on the Aliança Renovadora Nacional $(ARENA)_1$ ticket, had been backed by Américo Tanuri and the opposition MDB. Durval, of $ARENA_2$, had been supported by local merchants Flávio Silva and Niator Sampaio Dantas and the Vianas, although the activity of the latter had been limited.[17] The Movimento Democrático Brasileiro (MDB) had failed to elect any councilmen, but Américo's $ARENA_1$ faction had gained a majority on the council; Raimundo Medrado da Silva, Manoel Faustino da Silva, Alvaro Correia da Silva, and Orlando Pontes were reelected, and Orlando had been named president. Raimundo Medrado Primo (who had received the most votes), Ivan Amorim, Durval Vicente de Lima, and José Rodrigues de Lima had been reelected on the $ARENA_2$ slate. Newcomers had included two young journalists, Herbet Mouze of $ARENA_2$ and Paganini Nobre Mota of $ARENA_1$; one of the alternates, José Gabriel Maia, had accused Paganini of illegal campaign activities, without result.[18]

The elections of November 1974 had demonstrated the strength of the Viana faction in Juazeiro; Senate candidate Luiz Viana Filho had received 7,856 votes in contrast to Clemens Sampaio's 6,414 and Jutahy Magalhães's 472. Votes for federal deputy had gone to three elected candidates from Bahia: Lomanto Júnior, 4,849, Prisco Viana, 1,873, and Manoel Novais, 751. Votes for elected state deputies had gone to Raulino Queiroz, 4,943; Ana Olivera (ARENA), 2,647; and Otoniel Queiroz (MDB), 1,936.[19]

16 "Os números de Juazeiro," *Jornal de Juazeiro* (July 15–22, 1983): 3. One reason frequently suggested for these problems is need for more support at local levels. In August 1983 São Paulo Governor Franco Montoro joined with mayors of municipalities throughout his state to sign a letter demanding a redistribution of tax monies and more autonomy for municipalities. Pernambuco Senator Marco Maciel was pushing a constitutional ammendment in Congress. Their concern reflected a nationwide problem that was recognized by politicians but not the military government. See "A 'Carta dos Municípios,' " *Folha de São Paulo* (August 23, 1983).

17 State Deputy Ana Oliveira, for example, was not permitted to speak at political rallies because she was unpopular. Letter to Ronald H. Chilcote from Padre Mansueto de Lavor, Recife, August 1973.

18 "Vereador não perde mandato," *Tribuna do Povo* 13 (August 11, 1973): 1.

19 *Rivale* 3 (November 23–24, 1974): 1.

Table 11.1. *Juazeiro municipal elections, 1972–82*

	November 15, 1972	November 15, 1976	November 15, 1982
Mayor			
Durval Barbosa da Cunha ($ARENA_2$)	6,879		
Arnaldo Vieira de Nascimento ($ARENA_1$)	6,838	16,589	
Francisco Etelvir Dantas[a] ($ARENA_2$)		10,587	
Alberto Gasper (MDB_1)		483	
Ivan Lima (MDB_2)		249	
Jorge Khoury (PDS_1)			14,240
Joseph Bandeira (PDS_2)			11,533
João Oliveira (PDS_3)			2,281
Edilson Monteiro (PMDB)			4,974
Municipal Council			
Raimundo Medrado Primo[a] ($ARENA_2$)	1,316		
Raimundo Medrado da Silva[a] ($ARENA_1$; PDS_1)	1,161	1,347	1,691
Herbet Mouze Rodrigues ($ARENA_2$; PDS_1)	1,106	827	1,411
Ivan de Araújo Amorim[a] ($ARENA_2$)	1,084		
Paganini Nobre Mota ($Arena_1$)	879	1,497	
Durval Vicente de Lima ($ARENA_2$)	614		
Manoel Faustino da Silva ($ARENA_1$)	605		
Antônio Carlos Chaves ($ARENA_1$)	597	782	
José Rodrigues Lima[a] ($ARENA_2$)	539		
Alvaro Correia da Silva[a] ($ARENA_1$)	524	803	
Geraldo Francisco da Silva ($ARENA_1$)	497	1,238	
Francisco Xavier Souza ($ARENA_2$)	477		
Orlando Pontes de Nascimento ($ARENA_1$)	448		
João Oliveira ($ARENA_2$)		2,736	
João Macário de Oliveira (PDS_2)		1,279	1,250
Amadeus Damásio		843	
João Medrado da Silva		829	

Table 11.1.(cont.)

	November 15, 1972	November 15, 1976	November 15, 1982
Municipal Council			
Lúcia Carmen Sobreira (PDS_1)		806	1,021
Jorge de Souza Duarte		791	
Helena Araújo Pinheiro		787	
Pedro Alcântara (PDS_1)			1,731
Gilson Borges (PDS_1)			1,434
Manuel Raimundo (PDS_1)			1,191
José Priminho (PDS_1)			870
Samuel Nascimento (PDS_2)			1,571
Ademar Gonçalves (PDS_2)			1,141
Geraldo Silva (PDS_2)			935
Moaníton Lopes (PMDB)			936
Paulo Cesar (PMDB)			820

[a]Member of ruling class, 1971.

Sources: O Farol 58 (November 30, 1972): 11; *O Farol* 62 (December 11, 1976): 11; *Rivale* 10 (November 26, 1982).

In the municipal elections of November 15, 1976, Arnaldo Vieira de Nascimento had been elected by a wide margin over Etelvir Dantas, while the MDB candidates, divided between two factions, had received less than 3 percent of the votes. João Oliveira of the $ARENA_2$ faction (aligned with Viana interests) had received the most votes, while the $ARENA_1$ had maintained a bare majority in the council by reelecting Raimundo Medrado da Silva, Paganini Nobre Mota, Antônio Carlos Chaves, Alvaro Correia da Silva, and Geraldo Francisco da Silva. Despite their victory, the $ARENA_1$ faction had charged corruption and irregularities, but their allegations had never been substantiated.[20] In an early interview, the new mayor had attributed the problems of the city to a lack of infrastructure and capital. His priorities, he said, were in education, health, social assistance, agriculture, roads, and aqueducts in the interior. Asked to explain the significance of the campaign slogan "O povo no poder" (The People in Power), he had responded that he was "a poor candidate tied to the poorest elements of the population and wanted to deal with their problems."[21]

20 "ARENA 1 requer impugnação do último pleito," *Rivale* 5 (December 5, 1976): 1.

21 Arnaldo Vieira do Nascimento. "Entrevista com o novo prefeito," *Rivale* 5 (January 30, 1977): 3. A review of the previous municipal administration is in Durval Barbosa da Cunha, "Mensagem a Câmara de Vereadores-administração Durval Barbosa da Cunha," *Rivale* 5 (January 30, 1977); a review of Arnaldo's administration is in Amadeus Damásio, "Juazeiro: progresso e fraternidade," *Rivale* 10 (July 15, 1982): 7.

In the elections of November 1978, Juazeiro had given its votes to Lomanto Júnior (13,207) for senator and to Leur Lomanto (5,274) and Prisco Viana (3,188) for federal deputy; they had been elected to office, while former mayor Durval Barbosa, with 4,918 local votes, had failed to gather sufficient statewide support. Local votes had been divided among five local candidates for the state Assembly: Etelvir Dantas (10,690), Joseph Bandeira (5,365), Raulino Queiroz (4,996), Ana Oliveira (542), and Paganini Nobre Mota (406). Only Etelvir, with 27,979 votes statewide, and Raulino, with 13,433, had been elected. Making a political comeback, Etelvir[22] had replaced Ana Oliveira, who had begun her career in Juazeiro as a councilperson in 1934 and since 1959 had served five terms in the Assembly.

Politics during the early 1980s revolved around the group of young university graduates who in 1970 had organized the Association of University Students of Juazeiro in an effort to stimulate change. They were concerned about political apathy and the failure of local authorities to support culture. Principal participants in this group were Jorge Khoury, Joseph Bandeira, and Paganini Nobre Mota.[23]

By this time the government had abolished the old parties and instituted a multiparty system designed to divide the omnipresent opposition. The ARENA had become the Partido Democrático Social (PDS), and a group of moderate conservatives had left it to form the Partido Popular (PP). The MDB had become the Partido do Movimento Democrático Brasileiro (PMDB), and in early 1982 the PP had joined it. Other parties were the Partido Trabalhista Brasileiro (PTB), founded by Getúlio Vargas and now under the leadership of his niece, Ivette Vargas; the Partido Democrático Trabalhista (PDT), an offshoot of the PTB under the popular Leonel Brizola; and the Partido Trabalhista (PT), a socialist party under the leadership of Luís Inácio da Silva, or Lula, known for his leadership of the São Paulo metallurgical workers' strikes in the late 1970s.

The elections of November 15, 1982, focused largely on three factions within the government PDS party. The PMDB was able to present opposition candidates, and the PT, with the support of some workers' organizations and the discreet backing of progressive elements in the church, was in the process of organization. Attention centered on the convention of the PDS in Juazeiro on July 25, 1982. Jorge Khoury, the favorite, and his running mate Antônio Carlos Tanuri (son of Américo) emerged with 35 votes among the sixty-two delegates, while Joseph Bandeira obtained 19 votes. According to the system of proportional representation, Khoury

22 Etelvir identified himself as an accountant, industrialist, merchant, farmer, and rancher. A long list of his business interests and positions on corporate boards and civic organizations appeared in *Rivale* 7 (July 15, 1978).

23 See "Reactivação da AUJ foi discutida em Juazeiro," *A Tarde* (July 27, 1983).

was permitted to run a slate of twenty-one candidates for municipal council and his opponents, Bandeira and João Oliveira, six and twelve candidates respectively. Khoury, representing the PDS_1 faction, was backed by Arnaldo Vieira, Bandeira and the PDS_2 by Etelvir Dantas, and Oliveira and PDS_3 by Prisco Viana.[24] Although there were rumors of a possible alliance between the Bandeira and Oliveira factions, they were committed to separate campaigns.[25] The PMDB was united behind the candidacy of local dentist Edilson Monteiro and nineteen candidates for the municipal council.[26]

The elections resulted in victory for the PDS_1 faction; Jorge Khoury won easily over Bandeira (14,240 votes to 11,533), and João Oliveira trailed with 2,281 votes; Monteiro received 4,974 votes. Khoury's faction elected seven councilpersons to four for the Bandeira faction and two for the PMDB. Only Raimundo Medrado da Silva and Herbet Mouze were returned to office, and altogether only four former councilpersons were elected. Established politicians Amadeus Damásio and Jorge Duarte, the latter president of the PDS, were defeated.

Juazeiro gave 70 percent of its votes to Luiz Viana Filho, who was reelected to the Senate. Etelvir received a good share of the votes in a successful attempt to take a seat as federal deputy. All eight local candidates for the state Assembly failed to win a seat, a consequence of Juazeiro's partisanship and divisiveness.[27]

In an interview following his victory, Khoury promised not to compromise his administration by showing favoritism to special-interest groups or individuals. His principal objective, he said, would be to improve life for the people in the interior, solve problems in the Salitre Valley, build roads to facilitate agricultural production, and improve salaries and working conditions for teachers. Within the city he desired to complete proj-

24 This allocation of candidates among the three factions resulted in a dispute, forcing the convention to suspend its activities for three days in order to clarify the position of the Dantas faction. See "Etelvir esmagado em Juazeiro," *A Tarde* (July 26, 1982); "Em Juazeiro o PDS não conclui convenção," *A Tarde* (July 28, 1982); and "Política vence primeiro grande teste e complica grupo adversário," *Jornal de Juazeiro* (July 28–30, 1982): 6. Oliviera's representation was the result of support by the PDS Executive Committee at the state level, an indication of Viana influence; see "Partidos fazem convenção no domingo em Juazeiro," *A Tarde* (July 22, 1982).

25 Impressions based on interviews with the three PDS candidates during the convention, Juazeiro, July 25, 1983.

26 Interview with Edilson Monteiro, Juazeiro, July 27, 1983.

27 See editorial "Exito não se explica, o fracasso não se justifica," *Rivale* 10 (November 26, 1982): 3. *Rivale* editor Ermi Ferrari, a strong supporter of Khoury and secretary in his administration, criticized the tactics and the absurd use of propaganda and money of the PDS_2 faction; see "Eleição em Juazeiro, lição á aprender," *Rivale* 10 (November 26, 1982): 3. In 1981 Ermi had helped form and was the secretary of the local PP; the national PP was a splinter group of the ARENA that later merged with the PMDB, although Ermi chose to remain in the mainstream of Juazeiro politics; see *Rivale* 9 (August 15, 1981): 1.

ects in process, give priority to sport and culture, and improve health services.[28]

When I interviewed Mayor Khoury, eight months later, he mentioned his surprise at having lost in the interior and attributed it to his inexperience and to old-style politics. He had pledged, he said, to open politics to the democratic process. He referred to the five-year municipal plan that he was about to present to the council, which dealt with the problems he had mentioned earlier. Asked about his relations with Bishop Dom José Rodrigues de Souza, who was attracting national attention with his concern over the drought and the consequences of the construction of the Sobradinho Dam, Khoury said that he was attempting to work with the bishop, whom he considered knowledgeable, committed, well traveled, and representative of a new generation.[29]

Pluralism in politics was to some extent responsible for the continuing influence of the Vianas that was occasionally evident in the local press. Town historian Walter Dourado had recently recounted the founding of nearby Casa Nova by Colonel José Manuel Viana and called attention to the hundredth anniversary of the birth of Adolfo Viana,[30] while Bahian deputy Prisco Viana, a distant relative, affirmed his support for João Oliviera, candidate for mayor in 1982.[31] In an interview with former Governor and now Senator Luiz Viana Filho, I attempted to explore the past and present influence of the family in the region. It had been his father, Luiz Viana (oldest son of José Manuel Viana), who had ordered troops to nearby Canudos to quell Antônio Conselheiro in the late nineteenth century. A product of the sertão, Luiz Viana had made sure his children received higher education. At the turn of the century the family had lived in Casa Nova and Juazeiro, where they had dominated political life. Luiz Viana Filho had been born in Paris and lived most of his life in Salvador, though he had spent some time in Casa Nova. Alfredo Vianna, former mayor of Juazeiro, was his cousin. Another cousin, Adolfo Viana de Castro, was mayor of Casa Nova.[32]

Luiz Viana Filho had attended law school in Bahia and begun his professional career as a journalist. In 1934 he had been elected federal deputy in opposition to the government of Getúlio Vargas. During the

28 "Entrevista do novo prefeito," *Rivale* 10 (November 26, 1982): 3.

29 Interview with Jorge Khoury, Juazeiro, July 26, 1983. For biographical details, see "Dr. Jorge Khoury candidato a prefeito," *Rivale* 10 (January 30, 1982): 1.

30 Interview with Walter Dourado, Juazeiro, July 29, 1982. See Walter Dourado, "Casa Nova – origem, formação, desenvolvimento e transformação," *Rivale* 5 (May 1, 1976): supplement, p, 3; and his "Dr. Adolfo Viana: centenário de nascimento," *Rivale* 5 (May 1, 1976): 1.

31 Prisco Viana, "Participarei ativamente das eleições municipais de Juazeiro," *Rivale* 10 (April 7, 1982): 1

32 Interview, Luiz Viana Filho, Salvador, July 23, 1982.

late 1930s he had taught law and history at the Federal University of Bahia. In 1945 he had been elected federal deputy to the Constituent Assembly, a post he had held until entering the Castelo Branco government as minister of justice. He had been governor of Bahia from 1967 to 1971 and senator thereafter.[33] During his term as governor, he said, he had implemented many projects in Juazeiro, including the construction of the port, a hotel, a hospital, schools, and an industrial park. He had supported João Oliveira for mayor, and his connections in Juazeiro included state deputy Ana Oliveira, former mayor Alfredo Vianna, a cousin, José Carvalho Vianna, and engineer Alipio Viana. Pointing out that many local politicans were hostile to him, he said that the family no longer had much influence in Juazeiro. He admitted, however, that his ties to the Coelhos were close and that, with their ranches and enterprises in Bahia, they were influential.

Although Luiz Viana Filho supported the government party and the policies of the dictatorship, he took a political stand on the growing gap between the poverty of the Northeast and the relative prosperity of the industrialized Center-South. He regretted the decline of the area since 1970.[34] A major speech to the Senate focused on education in the Northeast, especially the problem of illiteracy: "The sad reality is that the states of the North and Northeast do not have the resources to educate. We remain in a vicious circle, a terrible vicious circle. Being poor, the people cannot become educated, and not being educated, they remain poor."[35]

This concern for the poor contrasts sharply with the view of the Vianas expressed by the diocese of Juazeiro: "The violence of the Vianas is longstanding. . . . Important positions are instruments of control over local politics. . . . When corruption is exposed, the dominant group hides it. Those who think and act are pressured and persecuted without pity. The majority of the people live in the shadow of the Vianas."[36] The diocese implicated the Viana family, with its ties to the Castros and the Bragas, in a 1980 attempt to displace fifty-three families and 351 persons in the municipality of Riacho Grande through the illegal sale of their land to the Empresa Camaragibe. Thugs with machine guns would have ousted them

33 Like his contemporary, Nilo Coelho, Luiz Viana Filho became president of the Senate (1979–80). He was the author of a biography of Castelo Branco (*O governo Castelo Branco*, 2d ed. [Rio de Janeiro: Livraria José Olympio Editora, 1975]), as well as studies of Rui Barbosa and Joaquim Nabuco. Twelve boxes of his correspondence during his tenure with the Castelo Branco government are deposited in the Arquivo Nacional in Rio.

34 Speech summarized in "Brazil: No Miracle in These Parts," *Latin America* 9 (October 24, 1975): 330.

35 Luiz Viana Filho, *Educação no norte e no norteste: discurso proferido no Senado Federal, em 28 de maio 1982)* (Brasília, 1982), p. 11. See also "Senador solicita apoio para a educação no NE," *A Tarde* (July 27, 1982).

36 "Violência política em Casa Nova-BA," *Caminhar Juntos* 78 (April 1983): 6–7.

had it not been for the intervention of the diocese. Members of the Viana family involved in the incident included Maria da Luz Viana de Castro, Carmen Viana Castro Braga, Coleta dos Santos Castro, and Laura Sodré Viana. Two years later the Vianas had enclosed the area of Fazenda Santarém and attempted to incorporate the adjoining land and ousted nineteen families of the town of Alagoinhas.[37]

Petrolina reexamined

The municipal population of Petrolina was 104,094 by 1980 and was growing at more than 5 percent annually. Census data showed 17 industrial firms employing 1,357 persons and 4,670 agricultural units incorporating 16,382 persons. Despite an increase in numbers of schools and teachers, 55.5 percent of the population was illiterate.[38] Petrolina appeared much as it had a decade earlier. There were some new buildings, and others had been renovated. For political reasons a new radio station, Emissora do Grande Rio, had been established by the Coelhos to compete with the progressive Emissora Rural.

In 1981 the cinema had closed briefly because the government requirement that half the films shown be national in origin was untenable to the diocese, which considered many of them immoral and substandard in quality.[39] Television had reached the area by 1972, the Museum of the Sertão had been inaugurated by Geraldo Coelho in 1976, and a School of Administrative Sciences had been established. *O Sertão* had closed in 1972, but *O Farol* continued to publish, and two newpapers appeared in anticipation of the November 15, 1982, elections.

Padre Mansueto de Lavor, a state legislator with the intention of running for Congress, had founded the monthly *Tribuna do Sertão,* which featured news of Petrolina and the Pernambuco interior. In its September 1981 issue, Petrolina's respected judge Possídio de Nascimento Coelho offered a brief history of the municipality;[40] journalist Elisabet Gonçalves Moreira reviewed its cultural advances but suggested that much more was needed;[41] the local bookdealer Joaquim Florêncio Coelho attributed the development of Petrolina to the leadership of Bishop Dom Malan and argued that development under the "local oligarchy" of the Coelhos was distorted by poor planning. For example, he said, the new industrial park

37 Ibid, pp. 6–9.

38 Data from the Instituto Brasileiro de Geografia e Estatística (IBGE), Petrolina, July 27, 1983.

39 *Tribuna do Sertão* 1, no. 6 (July 1981): 5.

40 Possídio do Nascimento Coelho, "Comemoração e convivência histórica," *Jornal de Petrolina* 1, no. 18 (September 1981): 5.

41 Elisabet Gonçalves Moreira, "Muito se fez, muito resta fazer," *Jornal de Petrolina* 1, no. 18 (September 1981): 11.

was located in an area frequently flooded by the São Francisco River; there was little financial support for new industry or for relocation of existing industry, and small and medium-sized commercial businesses lacked direction. He deplored the deficiencies in public transportation, the lack of sanitary facilities for all but the most privileged, and public works of little benefit such as a library without books and a port without service.[42]

At the same time, Antônio Carlos Teixeira Moura (related by marriage to the Coelho family) had founded the biweekly *Jornal de Petrolina*, presumably with the intent of supporting Coelho candidates in the forthcoming electoral campaign. Its editor, Elisabet Gonçalves Moreira, emphasized that the newspaper would be "independent, embracing both tradition and change," but also "creative and critical, with emphasis on our area and issues."[43] The paper covered the progress of the municipal government and the visit to the area of senators Nilo Coelho and Marcos Freire. Commenting on the latter, Elisabet noted in one editorial that such visits had little impact: "Conversing with them, interviewing them, we note that all speak of assuming responsibility. . . . The power that they represent . . . seems incoherent. They frequently contradict themselves and never accept responsibility for failure. They take on the struggle for new and old causes, always expressed with demagogic speeches . . . unfulfilled promises. An eternal vicious cycle in the structure of our political roots."[44]

Most of the persons I had interviewed earlier were still active and conspicuous. Cid Carvalho now concentrated on writing poetry, Yeda Nogueira had departed for a school administration position in Recife, and Bishop Dom Campelo had retired to Salvador. The latter's successor, Dom Geraldo Andrade Ponte, was discreet and politically moderate in contrast with Bishop Dom José Rodrigues de Souza in Juazeiro, but he had begun to analyze the city's socioeconomic problems. He was arguing that Christians must participate in politics, thereby committing themselves to the struggle for social justice and citizens' rights, and that the existing system

42 Joaquim Florêncio Coelho, "Progresso a todo custo," *Tribuna do Sertão* 1, no. 18 (September 1981): 6–7.

43 Elisabet Gonçalves Moreira, "Um jornal que se apresenta," *Jornal de Petrolina* 1, no. 1 (January 1, 1981): 2. She identified the tradition of journalism, including *O Trabalho*. founded by Colonel Clementino Souza Barros as Petrolina's first newspaper; *O Comercio*. in 1913 by João Batista de Aragão; and *O Farol* on September 10, 1915. In addition, there were *O Alicate* of Antônio de Santa Padilha, the student paper *O Escrinio* of Araci Braga, *O Cristo Rei* of the diocese, and others.

44 Elisabet Gonçalves Moreira, "Assumindo responsibilidade," *Jornal de Petrolina* 1, no. 4 (February 1981): 2. Among the visiting dignitaries were President Figueiredo, Interior Minister Andreazza, and Federal Deputy Osvaldo Coelho. About this time Nilo Coelho arrived in Petrolina to speak of his accomplishments, in particular his recent election as party leader in the Senate. He reiterated his pride in Petrolina, his love for the Northeast, and his dedication to public life on behalf of rich and poor alike (poor implying the Northeast, and Petrolina in particular); see Nilo Coelho, "Senador recebe homenagem," *Jornal de Petrolina* 1, no. 5 (March 1981): 3.

must be changed by peaceful means. One observer noted "tenuous relations between the local power and the church" and concluded that the eminently traditional and hegemonic position of "our city shows signs of change in its political structure."[45]

National attention upon Petrolina was evident in the visits of various military presidents – Emílio Garrastazú Médici in 1972, Ernesto Geisel in 1978, and João Figueiredo in 1980 in connection with various government projects that reinforced its infrastructure. Government agencies in Petrolina included the Companhia de Desenvolvimento do Vale do São Francisco (CODEVASF), subordinate to the Superintendência do Desenvolvimento do Nordeste (SUDENE), and the Centro de Pesquisa Agropecuária do Trópico Semi-Arido, a research center. Federal, state, and municipal funds were mobilized around a municipal development plan launched in 1977 with the aim of integrating resources with production, expanding agroindustrial activities and exports, consolidating and expanding commerce, and increasing employment, especially for lower-income families.

It had been politics as ususal in the municipal elections of November 15, 1972, as the ARENA party swept into power without opposition (Table 11.2). Maintaining the tight rein characteristic of his leadership in the previous administration, Geraldo de Souza Coelho had steered his cohorts through four years without serious political confrontation. His main emphasis had been attracting outside capital investment in a number of public works projects.

The 1974 elections had generally represented a defeat for the national government as the international petroleum crisis and political discontent at home combined to undermine the "economic miracle." Thereafter the military had found it necessary to promote its legitimacy through a policy of relaxation of the repressive national-security state and eventually the strategy known as *abertura,* or "opening" in the direction of permitting an opposition full political participation. In Petrolina, Marcos Freire had received 5,573 votes en route to victory in his senatorial race; João Cleofas, the ARENA candidate, had received 7,693, but the strong MDB showing had been a surprise and a signal to the opposition that the Coelho hegemony could be challenged.[46]

José Walter Lubarino had mobilized the opposition to the Coelhos in 1976. He had been active in student politics both in Petrolina and in law school in Recife. In 1974, together with Rui Amorim and others, he had organized the MDB and helped Marcos Freire win a majority of votes in

45 Elisabet Gonçalves Moreira, "Igreja toma posição," *Jornal de Petrolina* 1, no. 15 (August 1981): 2.

46 "Surpreendente vitória da oposição," *O Farol* 60 (November 21, 1974): 1. Honório Rocha had received 7,394 votes to hold his seat as a representative in the state legislature.

Table 11.2. *Petrolina municipal elections, 1972–82*

	November 15, 1972	November 15, 1976	November 15, 1982
Mayor			
Geraldo de Souza Coelho[a] (ARENA)	10,065		
Diniz de Sá Cavalcanti[a] (ARENA)		12,255	
José Walter Lubarino[a] (MDB)		5,641	
Augusto de Souza Coelho[a] (PDS)			19,642
Joaquim Florêncio Coelho (PMDB)			10,418
Municipal Council			
Augusto de Souza Coelho[a] (ARENA)	2,263		
Eurico de Sá Cavalcanti (ARENA–PDS)	2,110	2,182	1,956
Geraldo Teixeira Coelho (ARENA, MDB, PMDB)	1,483	1,098	1,756
Laureano Alves Correia (ARENA)	1,331		
Jeconias José dos Santos (ARENA)	825	989	
Joaquim Coelho de Amorim (ARENA)	798		
Clenicio Souza (ARENA)	678		
Simão Amorim Durando[a] (ARENA)		1,447	
Emmanuel Alfrío Nunes Brandão (ARENA)		1,337	
Juarez Coelho Amorim (ARENA–PDS)		1,220	1,330
Miguel Antônio Amorim (ARENA)		1,209	1,134
José Olímpio Rodrigues (ARENA)		1,126	
Rui Amorim (MDB)		657	
Maria Laura de Araújo Falcão (ARENA)		975	
Mário Pereira Lima (ARENA–PDS)		921	1,153
Ranilson Brandão Ramos (PDS)			2,074
José Walter Lubarino[a] (PMDB)			1,807

Table 11.2.*(cont.)*

	November 15, 1972	November 15, 1976	November 15, 1982
Municipal Council			
Francisco de Alencar Lima (PDS)			1,508
Maria Maga Liberatino Silva (PDS)			1,473
José Wilson de Souza Araújo (PMDB)			1,276
José Nisaldo Vasconcelos (PDS)			1,215
Júlio José Torres dos Santos (PMDB)			795

[a]Members of ruling class, 1971.

Sources: O Farol, 58 (November 30, 1972): 1; 62 (December 11, 1976): 1; *Rivale* 10 (November 26, 1982), "Tribuna Regional Eleitoral de Pernambuco, Eleções de 15.11. 1982," Recife, December 1982. Vote totals checked with Cartório Eleitoral Petrolina, September.

the city. Two years later his candidacy and threat to the political hegemony of the Coelhos had persuaded them to rally behind Diniz Cavalcanti, a popular figure whose candidacy for mayor had initially divided the ARENA into two factions, only one of them favorable to the Coelhos. The campaign had been lively, including one rally in which an angry Paulo Coelho had dispersed the crowd with a pistol shot.[47] José Walter had garnered nearly a third of the 18,000 votes, and Rui Amorim had won a council seat.[48] Geraldo Teixeira Coelho (not related to the former mayor), originally (in 1972) elected to the council as a candidate of the ARENA, had later switch to the MDB. This meant that it now had two seats and created an effective opposition for the first time since the Coelhos had assumed power. Geraldo was a lawyer who had been active as a student leader, and his victory in 1972 had represented a concerted effort on the part of students in Petrolina to acquire representation in local government. Apparently never endorsed by the Coelhos, he had gradually gained respect among voters and within the council, which had elected him president in 1978. Resentful of Coelho paternalism and always feel-

47 Carlos Alberto Menezes, "Carta-denúncia enviada às autorídades," *Diário de Pernambuco* (January 3, 1975): 5. See also "Governo ve fraude política em banco oficial de Recife," *Diário de Pernambuco* (December 31, 1974), for details implicating eight politicians in irregularities in the November elections. Included in the list were Felipe Coelho, no relative but a political ally of the Coelho family.

48 Interview, José Walter Lubarino, Petrolina, July 27, 1983.

ing himself an outsider, Geraldo had changed his party allegiance soon thereafter.[49]

The elections of November 15, 1978, had produced victories for Nilo Coelho in the Senate and Osvaldo Coelho in the Chamber. In Petrolina, Nilo had received 14,125 votes to 6,217 for MDB candidate Jarbas Vasconcelos and 364 for ARENA candidate Cid Sampaio. At the state level, the two ARENA candidates had been able to combine their votes, allowing Nilo, with the most votes, to capture the seat even though each had received considerably fewer votes than Jarbas.[50] Again at the state level, Honório Rocha had been reelected with the support of 9,401 Petrolina votes but soon thereafter had joined the cabinet of newly named Governor Marco Antônio Maciel, then a Coelho confidant.[51] José Ramos, the former Coelho lawyer, had received only 340 votes in Petrolina but had been reelected to the Assembly. When Maciel and his vice governor both resigned in early 1982 to run for other offices, Ramos, who as president of the Assembly was next in line, became governor, thereby preserving the traditional Coelho links to Pernambuco politics.[52] Despite their success, the Coelhos had been rudely shocked by the victory of Padre Mansueto de Lavor, the former director of the Emissora Rural and now legal counsel for the diocese. In Petrolina Mansueto had received 4,914 votes, considerably fewer than Rocha, but his strength elsewhere in the interior had given him a seat in the Assembly.

Fearful of opposition advances and desirous of manipulating the abertura to its own advantage, the national government had postponed the 1980 municipal elections until 1982, allowing Diniz Cavalcanti to remain in office six years. The accomplishments of his administration, according to the mayor, included improved street lighting, road paving, and the building of a recreational area, a public market, a public library, and other works.[53]

Commenting on the forthcoming elections, Mansueto predicted that the PMDB would present a strong candidate to an electorate that no longer had to depend on the choice of a single political group. He refused to answer whether he would run for mayor on the grounds that such a choice rested with his political party. Nor would he acknowledge the

49 Interview, Geraldo Teixeira Coelho, Petrolina, July 26, 1983.

50 The opposition alleged that many votes were fraudulent, especially in the interior, where Coelho was strongly supported. Interview, Pedro Mansueto de Lavor, July 30, 1982.

51 *O Farol* 64 (March 23, 1979): 1. The electoral results were reported in *O Farol* 64 (November 30, 1978): 1.

52 In May 1982 Governor Ramos returned to Petrolina; see *O Farol* 67 (May 31, 1982): 4.

53 Interview, Diniz Cavalcanti, Petrolina, July 28, 1982. Also see Diniz de Sá Cavalcanti, "Administração Diniz Cavalcanti: tres anos de governo," *O Farol* 65 (February 29, 1980): 1; and Cid Carvalho, "Diniz cumpre mandato municipal," *Jornal de Petrolina* 1, no. 3 (February 1981): 5.

partisan support of the local diocese, arguing that he had no responsibilities other than to serve as legal counsel and, furthermore, that his own political involvement was within the spirit of the Church's concern with problems of people. Why is it, he inquired, that priests active in the government party were considered virtuous whereas others, like himself, who favored the opposition were characterized as politicians of the worst type?[54]

In July the PMDB announced its candidates. Mansueto would run for a federal seat in the Chamber and Councilman Rui Amorim would run for the state legislature. Joaquim Florêncio Coelho would be candidate for mayor while Geraldo Teixeira Coelho would seek reelection on the municipal council. Neither was directly related to the dominant Coelho family.

Meanwhile, the Coelho family was preparing its own candidates, Augusto de Souza Coelho for mayor and Fernando Bezerra de Souza Coelho for state deputy. The latter, son of Paulo, had emerged as president of CODESF and of the recently established Fundação do Ensino Superior do Vale do São Francisco, the higher-education nucleus established in Petrolina through the efforts of Deputy Osvaldo Coelho.[55]

At this point irregularities in higher education became a political issue with the appointment of Fernando Bezerra de Souza Coelho and the naming by the mayor of João Veiga Leitão and Alexandre José Coelho de Macêdo (the latter the nephew of Nilo Coelho and the mayor's son-in-law) as director and vice director of the Faculdade de Administração. The PMDB protested these appointments, alleging that they were based on ties to local power rather than educational merit, and charged that professors were being hired illegally and that the admissions process was being manipulated. The party demanded a return to legal procedures and selection of directors from among the six licensed instructors rather than among unqualified persons recruited outside the school.[56]

54 Antônio Carlos Moura, "Deputado fala sobre sucessão municipal," *Jornal de Petrolina* 1, no. 7 (April 1981): 3. Interview with Deputy Mansueto de Lavor. Two weeks later Moura interviewed Mayor Diniz Cavalcanti as to who his successor might be and initiated his interview with reference to Mansueto as "the almost certain candidate of the opposition for mayor"; see Antônio Carlos Moura, "Diniz fala sobre seu sucessor," *Jornal de Petrolina* 1, no. 8 (April 1981): 3.

55 In an interview, Fernando Coelho elaborated on the possibility of eventually establishing a Universidade do São Francisco in the area; see Antônio Carlos Moura, "Ensino superior," *Jornal de Petrolina* 1, no. 13 (July 1981): 3. The *Jornal de Petrolina* frequently published a column of CODESF news under Fernando's name in an obvious effort to build his prestige within the community.

56 José Walter Lubarino was probably the best qualified among the staff, but his selection was "impractical" because he was a member of the opposition; see Elisabet Gonçalves Moreira, "Arranjos políticos," *Jornal de Petrolina* 1, no. 11 (June 1981): 2, for details and analysis. The MDB protest was published as "MDB apresenta nota de protesta," *Jornal de Petrolina* 1, no. 12 (June 1981): 3.

Throughout the Northeast, the PDS emerged victorious in most elections at the national, state, and local levels, while the PMDB won in nine states, including São Paulo and Minas Gerais, and the PDT in Rio de Janeiro. Marcos Freire lost his bid for the governorship of Pernambuco but picked up more than a third of the votes in Petrolina. Cid Sampaio, who had helped Nilo Coelho to power and now belonged to the PMDB, lost the senate seat to Marco Maciel.[57] Both Osvaldo Coelho (PDS) and Mansueto de Lavor (PMDB) won seats in the Chamber of Deputies, with Fernando Bezerra de Souza Coelho (PDS) winning (and thereafter emerging as the leader of the majority party) and Rui Amorim (PMDB) losing in their bids for seats in the state legislature.

Despite a strong race by PMDB candidate Joaquim Florêncio Coelho, the municipal elections brought Augusto Coelho and Simão Durando to power as mayor and vice mayor. Four PMDB candidates won seats on the municipal council, however. The campaign was vigorous, the opposition charging the Coelhos with having contrived to remove judges in order to impede the supervision of the elections and with irregularities and fraud in the balloting and ballot counting.[58] The opposition was further at a disadvantage because of its lack of financial resources in the face of Coelho tactics such as defacing of murals and propaganda, the use of hundreds of cars to transport voters to the polls, and the buying of votes. Even the threat of violence was at issue when José Mauro (Zeco), apparently in league with the Coelhos, attempted to break up a large rally by force. Disarmed of his revolver, he claimed that he had "matters to settle" with Mansueto.[59]

The Coelho dynasty in the early 1980s is described in the regional press as controlling a "republic" that embraced not only Petrolina but also the neighboring municipalities of Orocó, Santa Maria de Boa Vista, Afrânio, and Cabrobó – an area larger than Lebanon.[60] "Coelho country" is portrayed as a vast feudal domain ruled by Nilo Coelho and a hundred-

57 As ARENA runner-up to Coelho in the 1978 senatorial elections, Sampaio had remained an alternate even though subsequently he shifted to the PMDB; thus, in November 1983 he succeeded to the Senate seat after Nilo died of complications from heart surgery.

58 During July 1983 I examined a hundred or so receipts signed by or in the name of Mayor Diniz Cavalcanti. One receipt, for 350 cruzeiros, was dated July 18, 1978, in payment for a marriage license and registration of a birth. Another, undated but written and signed by Diniz, stated: "I authorize the provision of certificates for this old woman, with payment by me." These examples show how public funds are allocated paternalistically to ensure votes at election time.

59 Leticia Lins, "Pemedebistas desarmam alfaiate," *Diário de Pernambuco* (October 3, 1982). This report states that the revolver was kept by a retired police officer and not turned over to the police, that Petrolina police did not assist in the matter, and that violence was prevented by the PMDB's own voluntary security people.

60 Geneton Morães Neto, "A república sertaneja dos Coelhos," *Diário de Pernambuco* (December 3, 1978): D-4 and 5.

member family that in 1976 elected five mayors and thirty-seven of the area's forty-five municipal councilpersons. "Our predominance is natural," Augusto Coelho explains: "We are a numerous group of 10 brothers and sisters, 53 sons and daughters, and 35 nephews and nieces. If one has political influence, why give a position to an adversary?"[61] The press points to the fact that many local features have been given the family name: a school named for Colonel Clementino, an avenue for Nilo, and neighborhoods for Eduardo, a son of Nilo who died at seven years of age, and Gercino, a deceased brother. It notes further that school and hospital administrators and the heads of social clubs, civic organizations, and even the Sindicato Rural de Petrolina tend to be Coelhos and that no state or federal project can function without Coelho approval. (Often cited as an example of the latter is the Coelhos' blocking of the national welfare and social security agency from establishing a local office.)

Political paternalism is revealed in an interview with Maria Liberalina Silva, known as Maria Maga, owner of a downtown bar and for thirty years loyal to Coelho interests. She explained that in 1951 Osvaldo Coelho had assisted her in purchasing a new sewing machine: "He helped me. I was captivated. I never voted against them." A popular figure, she represented hundreds of votes for the Coelhos. Once, she recounted, she was arrested for building an illegal wall to keep cars from parking in front of her bar; the following day Paulo Coelho had his lawyer solve the problem with the construction of some pillars and compensation for the wall torn down. When she then demanded the resignation of the police chief, he was transferred to another town.[62] Ultimately she was rewarded with a seat on the municipal council. Running on the PDS ticket, she received 1,473 votes in the 1982 election.

In addition to exercising political control, the Coelhos maintained an economic network of five industries, an export firm, three supermarkets, two automobile agencies, a construction business, and a radio station. They had ranches in Petrolina and vacant land in the city and along the river as well as large expanses of land in Pará and Piauí. The Exportadora Coelho had purchased two large parcels of land in Pará, one of 19,500 hectares in the name of Silvio Roberto de Morães Coelho (a nephew of Nilo) and the Boa Esperança ranch and the other of 2,143 hectares in the hands of Osvaldo Coelho. Boa Esperança had acquired another parcel of 2,311 hectares.[63] The economic and political influence of the Coelhos in Bahia had recently been the subject of an investigation by the state legislature.

61 José Maria de Andrade, "O país dos Coelhos," *Veja* (February 25, 1981): 18–19.

62 Morães Neto, "Republica sertaneja," p. D-4.

63 Victor Asselin, *Grilagem: corrupção e violência em terras do Carajás* (Petrópolis: Editora Vozes with the Comissão Pastoral da Terra [CAT], 1982), p. 155.

A rancher from the area told me that the family had invested substantial capital in agriculture.[64] Two areas of Bahia, including three municipalities, were under Coelho control. One was the municipality of Guanambí, where Nilo Morães Coelho (a nephew of Nilo Coelho) was mayor and owner of large *fazendas* and an agriculture firm, Rural Nordeste S.A., with holdings of some 200,000 hectares in cattle and crops. Nilo was the son of Gercino de Souza Coelho, who had married into the Morães family of the area. Assuming control of the local government in the 1982 elections, he had also managed to obtain representation at the state level through the election of Raimundo José Sobrera, a native of Petrolina who some years ago had been sent by the Coelhos to work as a technician on their ranches. Nilo had apparently acquired his holdings systematically by the allegedly unethical but legal means common to large ranches in the area and through contacts and credits granted by SUDENE. His influence extended beyond Guanambí to nearby municipalities, including Maranda and Itapora. According to my source, the rise of Coelho influence in Guanambí had coincided with that of PDS politician Luiz Viana Filho and had been opposed by the former Governor Antônio Carlos Magalhães. In the municipalities of Cotejipe and Brejolândia, Osvaldo Coelho was responsible for family holdings known as Nova Terra Alimentos S.A., with about 60,000 hectares of grazing land, and Brojalândia S.A. with 30,000 hectares. The Coelhos also owned a distributorship of agricultural equipment in Barreiras, a regional economic center. In addition to the considerable influence of Osvaldo and Nilo Coelho at the federal level, the family worked through Bahian federal deputy Prisco Viana, who was distantly related to Luiz Viana Filho.

Queried about their dominant role in Petrolina, the Coelhos responded by citing their accomplishments. They had been responsible, they said, for bringing electric power to the area, and Colonel Clementino had been the largest private stockholder in the Companhia Hidroelétrica do São Francisco (CHESF). They had attracted important politicians and foreign capitalists to the area; in 1972 Rodman Rockefeller and a group of U.S. businessmen had visited the Bebedouro project and dined with Josefa Coelho, who traditionally opened her home to dignitaries.[65] Geraldo Coelho had implemented a development plan during his term as mayor and constructed the new public market.[66] Osvaldo Coelho had appealed to fellow deputies to incorporate the Northeast into national economic devel-

64 Interview, Brasília, September 17, 1983.

65 "Missão Rockefeller em Petrolina," *O Farol* 62 (January 30, 1972): 1, and "Rockefeller: 'Bebedouro está transformando humildes agricultores em homens productivos,' " *O Farol* 62 (March 23, 1977): 1.

66 Geraldo de Souza Coelho, "Desenvolvimento urbano de Petrolina," *O Farol* 62 (March 23, 1977): 1.

opment plans.[67] All this progress had made Petrolina "one of the most developed municipalities in the Northeast."[68]

Scholars of "colonelism" such as Maria Isaura Pereira de Queiroz have seen it as declining in the face of urbanization and industrialization. Maria Auxiliadora Ferraz da Sá argues, in contrast, that colonelism tends to persist in the Northeast, although in an altered form.[69] Maria Cristina Leal de Serejo agrees, pointing out that colonelism has been sustained by commercial activity and, further, that the agricultural change in the area, rather than undermining the influence of the new colonels, has increased it.[70] In the new colonelism, merchant capital combines with state and sometimes industrial capital to transform some traditional relations of production while at the same time permitting the strengthening and expansion of the influence of the dominant families and classes.

Cracks were, however, beginning to appear in the Coelho edifice. The rise of a political opposition would seem to be no serious threat, but what I discovered in 1982 and 1983 was widespread resentment to the political style that had characterized Coelho control over three decades. Paternalism, manipulation, and repression were increasingly seen as incompatible with bourgeois and petty-bourgeois interests in the era of abertura. Those not directly dependent on the Coelhos were joining the opposition. The problem for the opposition was mobilization of the popular classes, workers and farmers, who resisted breaking their traditional ties. When, against his family designs, Fernando Coelho joined the PMDB and successfully ran for federal deputy in 1986, a fissure within the Coelho family was also apparent.

Public works in the name of progress were increasingly seen as ill adapted to local needs. The public market, located outside the city, was inaccessible to many. The bridge extension in front of the Hotel do Grande Rio was branded an "intrusion" into the city. The Sobradinho Dam had brought an end to much of the transport and commerce on the river, and small farmers along its banks were finding themselves unable to adjust to the arbitrary fluctuations in water flow. The Coelho industries,

67 Osvaldo de Souza Coelho, "Discurso pronunciado na Câmara dos Deputados a 26 de maio, pelo representante de Pernambuco . . . ," *O Farol* 64 (June 26, 1979): 1, 4.

68 "Petrolina: primeiro lugar em desenvolvimento no estado," *O Farol* 60 (April 11, 1975): 1. Based on a report in *Diário de Pernambuco* (April 5, 1975).

69 Maria Auxiliadora Ferraz da Sá, *Dos velhos aos novos coronéis: um estudo da redefinições do coronelismo* (Recife: Pimes, 1974). A master's thesis, cited by Tereza Cristina Leal de Serejo, "Coroneis sem patente: a modernização conservadora no sertão pernambucano" (Niterói: Master's thesis, Universidade Federal Fluminense, 1979).

70 Serejo, "Coroneis," p. 186. She was able to determine (p. 207) the extent of the Coelho clientele through the *compadrio* (relations maintained as the godfather of children of other families): José Coelho, more than 100; Nilo, between 10 and 20; Augusto, 25; Adalberto, 20; Paulo, 10; Osvaldo, 50. (Geraldo refused to give a figure.)

while providing employment for thousands, also impacted the local environment with air and water pollution. Smoke from the factories was sometimes a problem. Chemicals from the new tanning factory were being dumped into the São Francisco, threatening villages and farms, while the stench of the factory often reached the town.

The continuity of Coelho rule was also open to question. Most Coelhos now resided in Salvador and Recife, apparently in the belief that these areas offered their children better opportunities. When asked if and when she might return to Petrolina, the wife of Paulo Coelho responded that that would be possible only after her children had been educated in Salvador.[71] The political fortunes of the family rested on their economic base. The Coelho empire had traditionally been premised on commercial activity, and although some Coelho capital had been invested in local industry and projects, a large share of it had stemmed from intricate financial arrangements, especially loans and credits with state and federal agencies and banks. Coelho industries dominated the region, but the political opposition questioned their viability without fiscal incentives provided by public entities. In 1981 the industries had reported a loss. The real condition of the Coelho enterprise was unknown, but an internal report prepared several years earlier had revealed serious deficiencies.[72]

According to their consultants, the industries' problem was "fundamentally structural in that the administrative apparatus is not responding with the efficiency the circumstances call for, perhaps because of lack of preparation at the managerial and supervisorial levels – failure to delegate power or to define executive objectives."[73] The report recommended that family and political ties not be considered in appointments to managerial positions. In the past, it had found, incompetent administrators had "burned" good ones; especially weak had been the managers in accounting, administration, sales, personnel, and general services. For example, one client, which accounted for 42 percent of all sales, had been capable, because of its practice of delaying payments, of threatening the financial situation of the firm. Further, the report criticized the lack of clarity of the chain of administrative command and the tendency to draw funds for the purchase of raw materials from high-interest bank loans rather than corporate capital. A financial analysis had shown a substantial increase in the past decade in the long-term debt along with a rapid growth of capital. Details of profit and loss had revealed five of thirteen products in the red and four others barely profitable, permitting the firm to show an overall profit of

71 Lizette Bezerra Coelho, interview in *Jornal de Petrolina* 1, no. 15 (August 1981): 7.

72 "Relatório apresentado por técnicos de empressa para os diretores das Indústrias Coelho, S.A." (Petrolina, May 1977), 76pp. This is an unpublished report. In addition, I saw documents revealing delays in payments of debts.

73 "Relatório," p. 1.

Table 11.3. *Financial positions of various Coelho firms (thousands of cruzeiros), March 31, 1977*

Firm	Date founded	Type of activity	Debt	Credit
Exportadora Coelho S.A.	February 6, 1953	Commerce	18,130	
Construtora Coelho S.A.	February 6, 1953	Construction	2,040	
Somassa S.A.	December 19, 1953	Biscuits, macaroni	11	
Imobiliária de Terrenos Rurais (ITRUL)	January 11, 1962	Real estate	691	
Petrolina Veículos Ltda (PETROVEL)	January 2, 1965	Volkswagen dealership	86	
Pasto Bons Ltda	March 29, 1966	Cattle raising		21
Transportadora Grande Rio	May 17, 1971	Transport	16	
Novaterra Alimentos S.A.	June 19, 1971	Cattle raising	238	
Maquinas e Veículos Ltda (MAVEL)	May 2, 1975	Mercedes Benz dealership		187
Curtume Moderno S.A.	November 18, 1975	Tanning factory	267	
Brejo Velho Alimentos	June 4, 1976	Cattle raising	37	
Fazenda Riacho C do Tijucucu	?	Cattle raising		59
Fazenda Bela Vista	?	Cattle raising	239	
Total			21,755	267

Source: "Relatório," p. 75. Not included in the table are Mecanização Agrícola do Vale Ltda (MAVALE), providing agricultural mechanical services, founded July 19, 1976; Cantina Sobrado Ltda., a commercial firm specializing in agricultural merchandise, founded August 5, 1967; and Itaparica Veículos Ltda (ITAVEL), which sold vehicles and was founded October 6, 1976.

9.8 percent. Among the report's conclusions had been a warning that allowing large amounts of credit to be dispersed among interrelated firms was likely to undermine central operations. In the balance sheet of Table 11.3, the dependence of Exportadora Coelho on Indústrias Coelho S.A. (ICSA) is clear, because it was drawing 83 percent of available credit. While providing ICSA with much of its raw material, Exportadora was also a liability, because it usually fell behind in payment of its debts, necessitating that ICSA make available its own funds. In turn, this practice made it difficult for ICSA to pay wages and taxes.

In Petrolina the Coelhos were viewed with trepidation and treated with respect, outsiders withheld respect but acknowledged their power. Politically, Nilo Coelho aligned himself with the military dictatorship. He supported General Figueiredo for the presidency. He opposed amnesty for political exiles, claiming the "political crimes cannot be forgiven." He favored restraint of the press during electoral campaigns, and he believed that "nowhere in the world is there a press as free as the Brazilian press."[74] Figueiredo favored Nilo as majority-party leader in the Senate, a post he accepted early in 1981. During the 1982 elections there were rumors of differences between Nilo and Figueiredo, but this was likely attributable to anxiety over his party's losing if it remained too close to the government.

A year later Nilo was favoring *queremismo,* a movement to reelect Figueiredo in 1985.[75] One reason for this was the possibility of his emerging as the vice-presidential nominee on the ticket of either Mário Andreazza or Paulo Maluf, the two PDS candidates favored to succeed Figueiredo. In any event, he would preside over the electoral college that would vote on the matter.[76]

When Nilo was elected president of the Senate in February 1983, the press described him as "a man of contrasts . . . like a colonel of the Northeast with a hard look, clumsy in speech, but capable of compassion." He was known for his "insolence" with technocrats and for never initiating a legislative bill. His colleagues often criticized him for "inarticulate leadership."[77] In May 1981 he had irritated the military and received the applause of the opposition during a speech in the Senate. When it was suggested by an advisor to General Golbery do Couto e Silva that he revise his speech, he replied: "I am not here to defend generals; I only defend the President."[78]

His greatest moment of glory may have been his permitting the opposition to vote down Bill 2024, which limited salary adjustments in accordance with demands of the International Monetary Fund (IMF). Pressured by labor leaders, students, and others who packed the congressional gallery, he refused to follow the direction of the government and his party to suspend the session. He explained:

> I am not the president of the Congress of the PDS. I am President of the Congress of Brazil. . . . I have the votes of all parties and I have to honor that mandate. I do not have to respond because the leader of my party had decided against the question of order. . . . I have 34 years of public life. I come from a suffering land. . . . My commitment is to the people.[79]

74 Morães Neto, "República sertaneja," p. D-5.

75 "Nilo diz que tese tem apoio," *Jornal do Brazil* (August 2, 1983). Queremismo (literally "I want myself") was a movement that pushed for the reelection of Getúlio Vargas during the early 1950s.

76 *Correio Brasiliense* (September 18, 1983).

77 Dilze Teixeira, "Nilo é um homem de contrastes," *Jornal do Brasil* (February 3, 1983).

78 "Coelho condena o terror e acaba chamuscado," *Veja* (May 13, 1981): 23.

79 "No último mandato, a culminancia," *O Globo* (November 18, 1983).

Figueiredo wrote the PDS leadership: "Nilo said he spoke more against the government than Juruna (a PDT deputy who had criticized the government). The next time I see him, I want to hear this from him personally."[80] Three weeks after the speech, Nilo suffered a heart attack, and in November he died of complications from heart surgery. Press accounts were sympathetic.[81]

Despite his leadership in the Senate, Nilo was not a member of his party's executive committee. His campaign for federal deputy during the early 1960s had received the support of the right-wing Instituto Brasileiro de Ação Democrático (IBAD), a front organization through which the Central Intelligence Agency participated in the overthrow of João Goulart.[82]

When he was elected to the Senate in 1978, the opposition alleged fraudulent voting,[83] and later ten SUDENE employees were reportedly dismissed for helping divert 24 million cruzeiros as a "stimulus" to his candidacy.[84] In 1981 he was photographed voting both for himself and for an absent senator (common practice in the old ARENA but usually arranged in advance through the party leadership) and was quoted as saying, "We cannot lose electoral power anywhere."[85] This act was bitterly denounced in a Recife editorial as "obscene" and "immoral": "The legislative process has been degraded to a practice without conscience."[86]

Nilo was not alone among Coelhos charged with illicit activities. His brother Osvaldo was implicated in the Mandioca scandal, involving officials of the Banco do Brasil and high officials of Floresta in the Pernambucan sertão. The case received national attention when the public prosecutor was murdered.[87] Eventually six of the seven persons on trial

80 *Veja* (October 19, 1983): 40.

81 See "Morte de Nilo Coelho causa consternação no Congresso," *Diário de Pernambuco* (November 10, 1983): part 1, p. 2; "Cerimónia do adeus: Nilo Coelho é enterrado em Petrolina e Moacyr Dalla se elege para a presidência do Senado," *Veja* (November 16, 1983): 39–41.

82 See René Armand Dreifuss, *1964: a conquista do estado, ação política poder e golpe de classes*, 3d ed. (Petrópolis: Editora Vozes, 1981), p. 344.

83 "Deu ARENA: Nilo Coelho ganha, sob acusação de fraude," *Veja* (November 29, 1978): 28.

84 Júlio Cezar Garcia et al., "Mar de lama," *Movimento* (November 11–20, 1978 [supplement]): 25. Information from *Folha de São Paulo* (August 4, 1981).

85 "Crime ao piano: líder do PDS vota duas vezes e xinga o fotógrafo," *Veja* (July 8, 1981): 24.

86 "Má informação e mau serviço," *Diário de Pernambuco* (July 11, 1981): p. A-3.

87 Marcos Ciranio, *O escândalo da mandioca e a morte do procurador*, (Recife: Calandra Editorial, 1982), p. 13. Also see José Carlos de Assis, *A chave do tesouro: anatomia dos escândalos financeiros, Brazil 1874–1983* (Rio de Janeiro: Editora Paz e Terra, 1983), pp. 231–252; and Carlos Garcia, "A plantação de dinheiro ou se preferirem: o escândalo da mandioca," *Jornal de Tarde* (August 15, 1983): 18. Joaquim Florêncio de Coelho alleged that "80 percent of the money in this scandal found its way to Petrolina," but hard evidence was difficult to uncover. Interview, Petrolina, July 25, 1983.

were sent to prison.[88] During the proceedings there was reference to the confession of the former manager of the Banco do Brasil branch in Floresta that he had attended a meeting at the home of Osvaldo Coelho in Petrolina at which Osvaldo had promised to contact other politicians and resolved the problem. The bank's director of commercial credit was José Aristófanes Pereira, who had served Nilo in his governorship as president of the Banco Estadual de Desenvolvimento in Pernambuco and had the strong support of the Coelhos. After the assassination, Pereira was suspended from his job.[89]

New leadership and demands for an opening

For nearly a generation there had been little significant opposition to Coelho hegemony, yet by the 1980s dynamic and committed persons were making an impression on Petrolina. Especially impressive were Padre Mansueto de Lavor and Joaquim Florêncio Coelho. In Juazeiro Mayor Khoury exemplified the hope of a new generation, trained in outside universities, that had returned to confront traditional partisan disputes and to bring about some constructive change. However, it was doubtful whether he would accomplish more than his predecessors. Bishop Dom José Rodrigues de Souza took the struggle directly to the people and challenged authorities at all levels.

As an advocate of democratic participation, Mansueto often used his radio station to analyze community problems and demand a new society capable of meeting the needs of the masses. His pronouncements became the basis of a campaign to undermine the hegemony of the Coelho family.[90] Mansueto also served as a link between the church and the rural unions it supported in Petrolina and neighboring municipalities. In early 1975 Mansueto had offered his prognosis for the region: "Among developments was the industrial boom in Juazeiro with Agrovale; Cica-Norte, Tomate do Brasil, and the Sobradinho Dam; the relative stagnation of Petrolina; and the tendency of the Coelho political power to fragment which will be demonstrated in the municipal elections within two years."[91] In 1976 he had formally joined the opposition MDB and had been active in the party's campaign to elect José Walter Lubarino mayor of Petrolina. Two years later he had successfully run for state deputy, generat-

88 "Raizes amargas: 'escândalo da Mandioca' leva seis a prisão," *Veja* (October 19, 1983): 44.

89 Luiz Ricardo Leitão, "Começa no Recife o jurí do procurado," *Folha de São Paulo* (October 6, 1983).

90 In addition to radio broadcasts, Mansueto began to write; see, for example, Mansueto de Lavor, "Petrolina: a terra dos impossiveis," *O Farol* 59 (July 10, 1974): 1, quotation and summary of an article originally published in the Sunday edition of *Diário de Pernambuco* (June 23, 1974).

91 Letter to Ronald H. Chilcote, Recife, January 6, 1975.

ing most of his support in Petrolina and the sertão. These victories represented the first serious political challenge to Coelho control over the area.

Mansueto was an active and respected leader in the Assembly. Two speeches, one dealing with a national issue and the other with international concerns, were representative of his visionary approach to politics and his desire to make himself visible at the national level. In the first, Mansueto attacked legislation dealing with the regulation of land by the military, presumably to bring justice to the countryside, after the 1964 coup. Contrary to what had been promised, he said, "an explosive situation" existed in the Brazilian agrarian sector; the agrarian reform had "completely failed," resulting in "15 years of frustration for Brazilian rural workers."[92] In the second, Mansueto criticized the activities of the Trilateral Commission, which he saw as having been established "for the maintenance and expansion of the capitalist system." He went on to describe the devastating effect of foreign investment on national resources, in particular in the Amazon, and to express concern over the impact of nuclear power plants in Brazil. Linking these developments to the visit to Petrolina of German Chancellor Helmut Schmidt, Mansueto concluded that exports from Petrolina to German markets did not benefit "the true rural workers of the sertão," who suffered from price manipulation and disadvantages caused by the dominance of certain local export firms. "Only the representatives of the groups that monopolize the exports have access to the Chancellor: it would be only fair for him to hear also from those who produce the exportable raw materials."[93]

In 1982 Mansueto ran for a seat in the Federal Chamber of Deputies, emerging as the PMDB's fifth highest vote recipient in Pernambuco. He wasted no time in apprising Governor Ramos and the Pernambucan authorities of his concern for the *sertanejo,* accusing the PDS and the government of abandoning the people of the interior: "One day after the election, the water trucks were withdrawn from the area. There were cases in which the provision of milk was interrupted by some municipal governments."[94]

In Congress Mansueto attacked government interference in university affairs that resulted in lower standards of research and loss of academic autonomy.[95] He pledged solidarity with the popular church and the progressive bishops who favored elimination of corruption and exploitation,

92 Pedro Mansueto de Lavor, "Discurso pronunciado pelo Deputado Mansueto de Lavor, Estatuto da Terra," *Diário Oficial* (Recife) (December 7, 1979).

93 Pedro Mansueto de Lavor, "Discurso," *Diário Oficial* (Recife) (May 1, 1979).

94 "Deputado do PMDB acusa o Governo de Pernambuco de tirar agua de sertanejo," *Jornal do Brazil* (December 2, 1982): 3.

95 Pedro Mansueto de Lavor, "Discurso, 23 de marzo de 1983" (Brasília: Câmara dos Deputados, 1983), 5pp., typescript.

political participation, and restoration of dignity to the people.[96] He also manifested his solidarity with Bishop Dom José Rodrigues de Souza of Juazeiro against attacks by the latifundistas and political chiefs of the São Francisco Valley.[97] He stood firmly behind the labor movement, insisting on workers' rights.[98] He elaborated on the problems of rural workers and farmers in the Northeast and the ineptness of government agencies despite an abundance of allocated resources.[99] He showed how the government concessions to the IMF ignored the plight of 38 million marginalized people in the Northeast. The official approach to the problems of the Northeast was unjust, he believed: "First, we have to reject the economic and political model. . . . we have to struggle for a constitution, with a juridical, social, and economic order that reflects the will of the people. . . . Second, the government must show . . . that the Northeast is a national question."[100]

Mansueto addressed the problems of the São Francisco Valley as follows: "History shows us that the system of man's domination of the São Francisco has not changed much. . . . Today the CHESF arbitrarily uses police force against farmers of the region without making social and cultural concessions."[101] He went on to develop an extensive analysis of the causes and consequences of the region's problems.[102] In his report, presented to a congressional commission investigating the Northeast, he objected to federal government interference in local affairs as producing poverty, soil erosion, and displacement of people. Five thousand people in the slum known as Papelão lived in misery and isolation, victims of the Sobradinho. Government-sponsored irrigation projects such as the Bebedouro were experiencing difficulties: Participants complained that productivity had declined because of the increasing salinity of the soil; that taxes were arbitrarily withheld from sales of their products without receipts; that

96 Pedro Mansueto de Lavor, "Discurso, 27 de junho de 1983" (Brasília: Câmara dos Deputados, 1983), 2pp., typescript.

97 Pedro Mansueto de Lavor, "Discurso, 25 de março de 1983" (Brasília: Câmara dos Deputados, 1983), 2pp., typescript.

98 Pedro Mansueto de Lavor, "Discurso, 3 de junho de 1983" (Brasília: Câmara dos Deputados, 1983), 4pp., typescript.

99 Pedro Mansueto de Lavor, "Discurso, 8 de agôsto de 1983" (Brasília: Câmara dos Deputados, 1983), 2pp., typescript. Also, "Discurso de 18 de abril de 1983" (Brasília: Câmara dos Deputados, 1983), 3pp., typescript.

100 Pedro Mansueto de Lavor, "Discurso, 13 de junho de 1983," *Diário do Congresso Nacional*. section 1 (June 1983): 6020.

101 Pedro Mansueto de Lavor, "Discurso de relatório da CPI – cheias do Rio São Francisco" (Brasília: Câmara dos Deputados, March 14, 1983), 6pp., typescript.

102 Pedro Mansueto de Lavor, "Depoimento" (Brasília: Comissão Parlamentar de Inquérito Destinada a Investigar as Causas e Consequências das Cheias do Rio São Francisco, Câmara dos Deputados, June 11, 1981), 90pp. Published as *Rio São Francisco: um depoimento* (Brasília: Centro de Documentação e Informação, Câmara dos Deputados, 1983).

they had received no title to their land; and that large parts of the project had been turned over to large firms. Mansueto pointed to the pollution of the river, the result of waste dumping by industry: "In reality, the São Francisco is a river of tears reflecting the suffering of the people who live along its banks and the exploitation of which it is victim."[103] He tied corruption to politics: "All this distortion and corruption is related to the political programs and the electoral interests of the government. . . . plans of assistance to victims of drought and floods are designed to strengthen the hand of government and ensure electoral success."[104] Eventually Mansueto's visibility and success in raising consciousness about the sertão resulted in his election to the Senate in 1986.

Joaquim Florêncio Coelho, still a student in economics at the Universidade Federal de Pernambuco in Recife during my early research in Petrolina, had subsequently worked for Indústrias Coelho as an administrative and economic advisor. On July 7, 1977, he had resigned over internal differences, and thereafter he had established a bookstore with the hope of it becoming a cultural center. He had also joined the opposition to the Coelho family and committed himself to exposing corruption and raising the political consciousness of the common people.

He had begun by unsuccessfully opposing a move by the Coelhos to gain majority control of the telephone company, Companhia de Melhoramentos do São Francisco (COMESF). This firm had been founded by 471 individuals and organizations in Petrolina and Juazeiro;[105] they had subsequently relinquished half their stock to the Bahian and Pernambucan state telephone companies in order to interface with the national and international telephone system. The Coelhos had aggregated about 15 percent of the remaining shares. They had then charged Alexandre José Coelho de Macêdo with obtaining proxies from the stockholders and, once these were in hand, convened a meeting and voted to increase the number of shares, thereby making it possible for them to purchase and control a majority of the stock.[106] Without any hope of reversing this action, Joaquim had protested it in a nine-point letter.[107]

On September 5, 1980, Joaquim had denounced on the Emissora Rural the collapse a day earlier of the public market, then being built by the Construtora Coelho with funds from the World Bank. On September 11, Joaquim and PMDB councilman Geraldo Teixeira Coelho had filed a

103 Ibid., p. 36.

104 Ibid., p. 48.

105 Companhia Telefónica do São Francisco, "Relação nominal dos acionistas e ações ordinárias em 31-08-78" (Juazeiro, September 25, 1978).

106 "Ata da Assembleia Geral Extraordinária da Companhia de Melhoramento do São Francisco – COMESF, realizada na dia 23 de Janeiro de 1980" (Juazeiro, 1980), 8pp., manuscript.

107 Joaquim Florêncio Coelho, letter to COMESF, Petrolina, June 9, 1980, 2pp.

formal complaint in court. Immediately the lawyers for Indústrias Coelho had accused Joaquim of lying. On behalf of the complaints, lawyer Mansueto de Lavor had rebutted these charges in court on November 3.[108] During the interim a commission of three construction engineers had visited Petrolina at the request of the court and offered its findings: Four pillars had failed because of the way the steel structure had been mounted, and tests showed defects in the concrete.[109] Clearly, Construtora Coelho was at fault, but the case was closed by the judge on August 21, 1981. Joaquim had succeeded in alerting the public and placing responsibility on the Coelhos, but he had been unable to generate any public response to the engineers' findings.[110]

Joaquim's activism sometimes extended into the interior. In one instance he alleged abuse of power by the local "political chief" and councilmember José Olimpia Rodriguez in his district of Dormentes. Subsequently, a petition with three hundred signatures was sent to the municipal attorney demanding that Rodriguez and two relatives desist from threats and pressures upon local residents.[111]

About this time Joaquim announced his candidacy for mayor, described in one partisan account as "a break out of the electoral corral."[112] Believing that the people were already politically conscious, Joaquim argued that the church, under its first bishop, Dom Malan, was responsible for the real development of Petrolina and that the local oligarchy had succeeded in molding itself to the needs of capitalism while maintaining the colonelist system as a means of continuing in power. His particular concern was the commercial sector, especially small and medium-sized businesses, which were increasingly isolated by the oligarchy and in need of credits and

108 Among the court documents consulted are the Construtora Coelho response in Petrolina, Cartório de Primeiro Oficio, no. 5405/80; the response by Mansueto de Lavor, "Razões dos agravantes," November 3, 1980, Processo No. 5405/80, Petrolina, Cartório do Primeiro Oficio; and the hand-written minutes of the case in Petrolina, Cartório de Segundo Oficio, November 3, 1980.

109 Janus de Freitas Mota, Antônio de Paula Lopes, and Paulo Fernando Lopes Ferreira, "A acidente ocorido na construção de Centro de Abastecimento de Petrolina" (Recife: Empressa de Obras de Pernambuco, November 18, 1980), 12pp., typescript with a cover letter by Juarez Gambetta Tavares Barreto Filho, November 19, 1980, DPR-No. 269/80.

110 Joaquim sent documents and telegrams to local newspapers and radio stations in Petrolina, Juazeiro, and Recife as well as to important politicians. He received telegrams from Jarbas Vasconcelos, acknowledging receipt, and from PMDB Senator Marcos Freire, who obtained an opinion from legal counsel to the Federal Senate; see letter of Dr. Luiz Fernando Lapagese, in response to the request of Marcos Freire and to the request of Joaquim Florêncio Coelho of October 18, 1981, with a copy of the evaluation of the Assessoria do Senado Federal signed by Pedro Cavalcante d'Albuquerque Neto, OF/SF/ASSES-115/81, Brasília, November 30, 1981, a cover letter plus four pages suggesting how to pursue the matter legally.

111 Petition to Promotor Público de Petrolina, November 5, 1981, 9pp., including signatures.

112 "Petrolina escolhe futuro prefeito," *Tribuna do Sertão* 2, no. 10 (December 1981): 2.

support.[113] He also addressed the needs of workers, expressing a desire to resolve their problems by involving them directly in self-help projects rather than allowing a small group of rich and powerful men to decide their destiny. He criticized the traditional practice of buying votes: "To pay for a favor with a vote is a negative and old attitude, not worthy of the conscientious voter . . . who should choose the candidate who struggles for a Christian objective, whose behavior recognizes a man's value as a human being and not as an object to be manipulated by the powerful people of the time."[114]

In an interview published in January 1982, he referred to the repressive role of the dominant class and its political machine: "I do not have much money nor economic power, but I have an understanding of administration, justice, and dignity." He went on to identify the major problems of the municipality: lack of schools in the rural areas and public works such as the port and a restaurant and beach along the São Francisco River that do not benefit the public, when money could have been spent for more important projects.[115]

Joaquim presented ideas for the development of Petrolina. Acknowledging the low level of resources available to the municipality, he believed that through decentralization of power and decision making and with the democratic participation of people at all levels many problems could be solved. Instead of constructing new hospitals, the municipality could allocate resources to physicians to attend to health needs in the poor districts and outlying areas. Rather than building new schools, it could concentrate on the purchase of books and paper and the use of popular methods of education. To contend with the monopolization of public transportation, a new bus company offering lower fares could be organized and ferryboat transportation between Juazeiro and Petrolina could be encouraged. Culture could be stimulated through popular events designed to educate those residing in the periphery.[116] Day care centers and recreation areas could be established. Simplified sewage systems manageable by the people at minimal cost could be built in the poorer areas.[117]

Once the campaign had ended, Joaquim felt he had become more sensitive to the problems and needs of the people and vowed to continue

113 Joaquim Florêncio Coelho, "Progresso a tudo custo," *Tribuna do Sertão* 1, no. 8 (September 1981): 6.

114 See the campaign literature, Comitê Pró-Candidatura de Joaquim, "PMDB-caminho certo para o povo" (Petrolina, 1982), 2pp.; and "Receba de quem puder e vote em quem quiser" (Petrolina, 1982).

115 Ivan Brito, "Joaquim: em preto e branco," *Jornal de Petrolina* 2 (January 1982): 3.

116 A theme stressed by Elisabet Gonçalves Moreira, "Incentivos artísticos," *Jornal de Petrolina* 1, no. 12 (June 1981): 2.

117 Interview, Joaquim Florêncio Coelho, July 23, 1983.

his effort to dislodge the Coelhos from power. When the municipal government of Augusto Coelho imposed a 795 percent tax increase on his bookstore, he suspected reprisals. Carrying his case to the municipal council, he appealed for a reversal of this decision, arguing his rights and the unconstitutionality of the tax increase: "It is not only our firm that is being forced by the municipal government to pay exorbitant taxes but all merchants and businessmen, many of them lacking the means to defend themselves because they are not familiar with their true rights."[118]

Dom José Rodrigues de Souza, from his position of authority and prestige, envisioned his role as that of counciliator and activist in behalf of the popular church and the oppressed. As conciliator he was willing to work with others in an incessant search for solutions to the social and economic problems of the community. As activist he confronted those who ruled – politicians, businessmen, and bureaucrats – and exposed their favoritism, incompetence, and lack of responsibility.

Dom José mounted a campaign against the dominant families in his diocese, the Brazilian dictatorship, and the evils of capitalism and imperialism. Knowledgeable and well organized, he mobilized competent people to work with the church-based communities and the rural workers' unions. He communicated to these groups through the monthly newsletter *Caminhar Juntos* and to the community at large through his weekly programs on the Emissora Rural and Rádio Juazeiro.[119]

Dom José placed his crusade in historical perspective. Understanding of history, he believed, allowed for reflection on the past and present. His radio programs and analyses in the diocese's newsletter focused on Indian revolts, workers' protests, and black struggles, especially during the sixteenth century, when Palmares was established as a refuge for renegade slaves. He interpreted the case of Antônio Conselheiro and Canudos not as a rebellion of fanatics, but as a conscientious, courageous, and organized struggle for land and for a new egalitarian society: "Antônio Conselheiro was not a fanatic, but emerged in the history of Brazil as an authentic product of its contradictions and as a leader of a poor and exploited people who desired to live peacefully in a more humane and happier society." He contrasted the activity of Conselheiro to the role of the governor at the

118 Petition to Câmara de Vereadores de Petrolina, April 20, 1983, 3pp. Attached letter of February 17, 1983, to Augusto de Souza Coelho, mayor of Petrolina, and a response from Samuel Silveira de Freitas, Petrolina, March 9, 1983, 2pp.

119 In addition to the base communities and workers' union, the diocese sponsored research teams to study regional problems. Among the groups whose reports appeared in the newsletter were the Associação dos Moradores, the Movimento Estudantil, the Comissão das Mulheres, the Movimento Negro Unificando, and the local PT party.

time, Luiz Viana, the "ancestor of the political chiefs of Casa Nova."[120] He also recalled the movement of Pau de Colher, which had emerged in Casa Nova in 1938 after the destruction of Caldeirão in Ceará. Some of the leaders of Caldeirão had fled to the fazenda Pau Colher, where a "popular Catholicism " was practiced under José Senhorinho. The religious movement had soon become a well-organized social one. Alarmed local authorities had called in troops, who had attacked the fazenda and killed 157 of its inhabitants. Dom José felt that Pau de Colher symbolized "the dream of a society based on a new economic organization that continues among us."[121]

Dom José felt that *cangaceiros,* or social bandits, like Antônio Silvino and Lampião were "not the product of an evil being, but the result of a socioeconomic–political structure in which they lived." They were "cruel, ferocious, and perverse because their society was profoundly unjust. The cangaçeiro was the product of a conjuncture of the Northeast in its particular time of cyclical droughts, economic crisis, unemployment, and hunger."[122]

His newsletter also published a piece on Padre Cícero in which two impressions emerge: "On the one hand, a man of profound creativity, lover of peace and justice, a great counselor and zealous defender of the faithful. On the other hand, a man of great courage and firm decisions, able to understand the moment of action, and inevitably violent without losing the sensitivity of a saintly man."[123]

For Dom José these historical movements symbolized hope for a better world. Change, however, would require raising the people's consciousness about the structure of society: "Brazil is structured so that the poor become poorer and the rich richer. We call this savage capitalism: The wealthy are organized to dominate and the poor do not have the conscience and organization to liberate themselves." A pyramid best depicts this structure. At the top one finds "the capitalism that dominates us, government that does nothing, bad administration. They want to stay in power. They do not want the poor to learn." At the bottom "the poor are afraid. They choose incompetent people. Through their votes they maintain the

120 Quotes in *Caminhar Juntos* 82 (August 1983): 1–4. The bishop expressed concern over the formation of a group, Casa Nova, Trabalho, União (CNTU), which was trying to influence the poor and counter the diocese's activities by alleging that a new Pau de Colher was emergent in Casa Nova. The cardinal from Salvador, Dom Avelar Brandão Vilela, was reportedly concerned over Dom José Rodrigues's celebration of Mass in memory of Conselheiro and Canudos; see "Missa ao herege: Igreja biana reabilita as vítimas de Canudos," *Veja* (August 8, 1984): 65–66.

121 *Caminhar Juntos* 82 (August 1983): 1–4.

122 *Caminhar Juntos* 82 (August 1983): 6.

123 Bento Salviano da Silva with João Acioly Pães, "Duas comemorações do Padre Cícero," *Caminhar Juntos* 88 (February 1984): 6–7.

domination. They do not understand the parties, they lack unity and organization."[124]

The severe drought that lasted from 1978 to 1983 provided the occasion for concrete criticism of authorities at all levels. The World Bank was providing Juazeiro with loans to assist in the construction of health clinics, a water system, and recreational facilities, but the outlying rural areas were little affected. Furthermore, nothing was being done to help the 20,000 unemployed or to deal with the problem of hunger. Mayor Khoury and other politicians could take credit for these projects and talk optimistically, but in reality they lacked funds to deal directly with the problems of the people. Further, the bank loans called attention to Brazilian dependence on the world economy.[125] When asked if he agreed with President Figueiredo's claim that the nation's problems were fundamentally international, Dom José criticized him for "insisting that our economy is a consequence of the recessive international conjuncture" and declared that "the truth of the government cannot be separated from the reality of the Brazilian people."[126] He drew an analogy between the suffering of the people and the pain experienced by the president after his operation for a coronary bypass: "The life of the president was saved by the skin of his teeth. His arteries were 95 percent obstructed. For many years Brazil has felt the same pain in its chest, with its arteries almost completely obstructed. Of the 120 million Brazilians, 10 million are very rich and 100 million poor, with 60 million starving every day. There are 32 million illiterates. . . . In Juazeiro there are 10,000 young people without schools."[127]

After the November 1982 elections Dom José reminded PDS politicians that their victory had been largely achieved in the Northeast – that they were, in effect, the Partido dos Nordestinos and the people were awaiting the fulfillment of their promises.[128] A few months earlier he had strongly attacked the authorities for not dealing with the consequences of the regional drought. In particular, he had pointed out that the minimum wage was insufficient to support a family. He referred to the threatened invasion by hunger victims seeking food in nearby Remanso.[129] Comparing the Northeast drought to the floods in the south of the country, he noted that 241 municipalities and 252,000 persons were affected in the

124 "O porque dos problemas que aligem os trabalhadores," *Caminhar Juntos* 72 (October 1982): 2.

125 Interview, Dom José Rodrigues de Souza, Juazeiro, July 27, 1982.

126 "Entrevista D. José Rodrigues de Souza," *Caminhar Juntos* 78 (April 1983): 1.

127 Dom José Rodrigues de Souza, speech on his program "Semeanado a verdade," Emissora Rural de Petrolina, July 22, 1983.

128 Dom José Rodrigues de Souza, "Semeando a verdade," Emissora Rural de Petrolina, December 3, 1982, in *Caminhar Juntos* 75 (January 1983): 1.

129 "Bispo volta a criticar duramente as autoridades," *A Tarde* (July 14, 1983).

South, while 1,054 municipalities, or 85 percent of the region, and 21 million persons were suffering in the Northeast. He chastised authorities for devoting so little attention to the North and for their excuse that nothing could be done in the Northeast because the problems were fundamentally structural.[130] He lamented that hunger was tearing families apart and pointed to the 200,000 victims of the drought residing in the seven municipalities of his diocese.[131]

These efforts to raise consciousness among the people sometimes resulted in violence. Although the Sobradinho Dam had created one of the world's largest artificial lakes, downstream from the reservoir the drought was affecting small farmers, who generally did not benefit from irrigation. When two large ranchers installed electric pumps on the Rio Salitre, a tributary of the São Francisco that runs through Juazeiro, the small farmers in the area lost a major source of water. In response, they cut the wires of the pumps and, when confronted with arms, killed the ranchers. The incident prompted right-wing forces aligned with former Bahian governor Antônio Carlos Magalhães to blame the bishop for the violence. A series of false reports, published in the *Correio da Bahia,* exclaimed "Bishop Calls for Armed Struggle in Juazeiro" and "Bishop Leads Slaughter."[132] Another headline announced "Mayor of Juazeiro Also Accuses the Bishop," an apparent attempt to sour relations between the bishop and Mayor Khoury, who was aligned with Governor João Durval, an opponent of Magalhães. Khoury immediately affirmed his support for the bishop, who in turn exposed the whole affair.[133]

In 1981 the governor, reacting to the bishop's having linked him with the Viana–Castro–Braga group in the takeover attempt mentioned earlier, had attacked Dom José for the publication of a pamphlet urging people to exercise their right to vote and participate in politics. The pamphlet had described politics in terms of the struggle for liberation – mobilization through base communities, unions, cooperatives, and popular movements in pursuit of justice and the common good. Politics, it had continued, could be a way of deceiving, oppressing, and exploiting the people unless they were actively involved in it themselves. It had gone on to describe the popular revolts of Brazilian history and to characterize the existing political parties' attempts to relate to the people. The PDS, it said, tended to

130 "Bispo de Juazeiro revela: a desgraça da seca e maior que a desgraça das enchentes do Sul," *A Tarde* (July 25, 1983).

131 "Bispo lamenta desagregação dos nordestinos," *Folha de São Paulo* (August 15, 1983).

132 For details, see Juan de Onís, "Sprinkle of Hope Falls on Five-Year Drought," *Los Angeles Times* (March 25, 1984): part I. Also César Boaventura, "Prefeito de Juazeiro também acusa o bispo," *Correio de Bahia* (February 15, 1984): 8.

133 Dom José Rodrigues de Souza, "Bispo fala sobre as mortes do Vale do Solitre e violência da seca," *Caminhar Juntos* 89 (March 1984): 13–14.

praise government projects such as the Sobradinho Dam and irrigation schemes to promise the people money, clothes, and other favors; sometimes it resorted to threats and lies. In contrast, the PT was depicted as a party that organized rural and urban workers so that they could understand and participate in politics.[134] The distribution of the pamphlet had provoked reaction among conservatives. Graffiti had appeared on the doors of the church, labeling the bishop a communist, and on the walls of buildings, demanding death to communist priests.[135] Unknown persons had invaded his rectory in 1981 while he was absent. On August 31, Governor Magalhães had attacked the bishop on the Globo television network.[136] In response, 25,139 persons had signed a petition expressing solidarity with Dom José and affirming that the political pamphlet was in line with the encyclicals of Pope John Paul II, the positions of the Conferência Nacional dos Bispos do Brasil (CNBB), and the desires of the people.[137] Opposition PMDB Deputy Roque Aras of Bahia had denounced the authorities, including Governor Magalhães, Bahian senators, and the federal police, for sustaining such a "cruel crime" against the bishop, and he had carried his complaints, together with documentation, to the Brazilian Congress.[138]

On the evening of September 9, 1982, in the midst of the electoral campaign, a pamphlet calling for violence and armed struggle was widely distributed throughout Juazeiro. Entitled "Red Clergy" and depicting a cross and a sickle, the pamphlet ended with the names of five bishops and the forged signature of Dom Josē. Its contents associated the clergy with the PT and called for violence and armed struggle on behalf of rural and urban workers:

> Let's agitate, invade, and take some of the lands that belong to God and all of us. . . . Our motto is an eye for an eye, a tooth for a tooth. Our objective for you, workers, is to bring down the rich and powerful and destroy the military dictatorship.[139]

134 *Política: a luta de um povo*, preface by Dom José Rodrigues de Souza (Juazeiro: Diocese of Juazeiro, June 8, 1981), 46p. Other pamphlets later appeared, including *Como Votar* in 1982 and *Cartilha da Saúde* in 1984. Also a book analyzing poverty; see Equipe de Pastoral de Diocese de Juazeiro, *O povo descobre a sociedade: "capitalismo x socialismo." subsídio para reflexões de CEBS* (São Paulo: Edições Paulinas, 1984).

135 Interview with Dom José Rodrigues de Souza, Juazeiro, July 23, 1983. The bishop showed me his photograph album, compiled on September 13, 1981, which depicted the graffiti.

136 See *Jornal da Bahia* (September 2, 1981).

137 "Manifesto dos Cristãos de Juazeiro, BA" (Juazeiro, September 8, 1981).

138 Roque Aras, *A besta-fera contra a igreja* (Brasília: Centro de Documentação e Informação, 1981). 49p.

139 The pamphlet was typical of false documents distributed against the church throughout Brazil. The pamphlet, *Clero Vermelho*, signed by Dom José Rodrigues de Souza, was undated, mimeographed, and three pages in length. Dom José's response on Rádio Juazeiro, September 10, 1982, was reprinted in *Caminhar Juntos* 72 (October 1982): 13–15.

These incidents served to direct national attention to Dom José's activities. His efforts intensified and became more radical. In the middle of 1983 Paulo Freire was invited to discuss an educational program for the diocese. Freire was renowned for his literacy program in the Northeast prior to the coup of 1964, and his methods, endorsed by the United Nations Educational, Scientific, and Cultural Organization (UNESCO), were also applied in Chile under the Allende government and in Nicaragua after the overthrow of Anastasio Somoza. Both Freire and his son-in-law, economist Ladislau Dowbar, had served as consultants to the revolutionary government of Guiné-Bissau.[140]

Politics past and present

I have shown that in Juazeiro participation in decisions was diffused among competing groups of power holders, whereas in Petrolina participation was concentrated and direct, especially among members of the Coelho family, who operated in the center of community affairs and determined the outcome of decisions. My study revealed these patterns of participation through the tracing of relationships based on blood, marriage, friendship, and other social ties. Historically, a few families dominated these communities. In Petrolina, the Coelhos had established hegemony over politics and the economy in the mid-1950s. In Juazeiro, economic leadership had since 1945 tended to be exercised by businessmen from other parts of the region who maintained commercial interests in town while holding agricultural property outside. A patrimonial order, employing patronage and cooptation, had permeated the political economy in periods of military dictatorship and of parliamentary democracy alike.

Advanced capitalist societies may have a well-defined bourgeoisie, a petty bourgeoisie, an intermediate class of professionals and managers, a working class, and a peasant class. In Juazeiro and Petrolina these classes were not fully developed, although it was clear that a ruling bourgeoisie or dominant class existed and tended to own and control the means of production by using its economic power to control politics and society. This class had not traditionally been allied with the monopolistic and foreign bourgeoisies that reside outside Juazeiro and Petrolina. Generally, it did not include the large owners of industry and banking capital or agrarian capitalists, who use machinery and pay salaries to workers. Only the Coelhos were involved in these activities, in Petrolina and elsewhere. The ruling class thus reflected traditional merchant capital and the emerging

140 Freire's visit was fully documented in *Caminhar Juntos* 79 (May 1983): 1–2, and Dowbar's writings and ideas took up a full issue of the newsletter; see no. 80 (June 1983). For a sympathetic interview with Dom José, see Elieser César, "D. José Rodrigues: o povo deve ser o sujeito da história," *Jornal da Bahia* (April 1–2, 1984).

capitalism of the region and was composed of owners of commercial firms and a few local industries, some professionals and small merchants, and some traditional landowners whose estates lay idle or in the hands of an administrator who exploited tenant farmers and sharecroppers.

Juazeiro and Petrolina were closely linked to each other, their respective states, the federal government, and local, national, and international capital. A paternalistic bureaucracy and divisions within the polity contributed to Juazeiro's reliance on the outside world and failure to promote any substantial capitalist development. In contrast, dominance of a patriarchy with power concentrated in a single family conduced to closer ties between Petrolina and the outside world, resulting in a break with the traditional dependence upon Juazeiro as a commercial center and some evidence of capitalist accumulation. This finding suggests that where the ruling order of a traditional community in the backlands tends to be cohesive, some form of capitalist accumulation may take place, whereas factionalism within the ruling class may be accompanied by a lack of development. Among the consequences of development, however, may be domination and repression, loss of individual rights, and resort to patronage in an attempt to quell the antagonism of the population at large.

The indirect election of Luiz Viana Filho and Nilo Coelho to the govenorships of Bahia and Pernambuco in 1966 was facilitated by electoral procedures implemented by the military after the 1964 coup. Subsequently, each man became senator and president of the Senate. Because their families had ruled in Juazeiro and Petrolina, it could be assumed that these municipalities, long neglected by past state and federal administrations, might benefit from their governorships. Petrolina clearly profited from Nilo's tenure; Juazeiro received no special attention because the Viana family no longer had any political or economic interests there. However, candidates favored by the family did find themselves at an advantage in election for mayor and municipal council.

My research showed that as power was consolidated under military rule at the national level, the state intruded into local affairs in both municipalities. Although the autonomy of the local municipality would appear to have been threatened by these changes, mayors were still perceived by the people as the most visible elected officials. The mayors and vice mayors who had served since 1945 tended to be members of the power structure, the upper echelon of the ruling class. Professionally, most of them were prominent businessmen and ranchers, and in Petrolina many were associated with Coelho interests. I concluded that the prestige of the office might relate to recognition of the incumbent's position in the community. Power was also associated with the position of mayor because of patronage in the form of rewards, the awarding of contracts, and the granting of favors. In return, the mayor watched over the interests of the ruling class.

Municipal councilmembers represented the ruling classes but were not usually top power holders. They were businessmen, farmers, professionals, and bureaucrats. My early research revealed that the ruling class attached little significance to the affairs of the municipal council except when issues of government manipulation or corruption were introduced by the opposition. Throughout the period of my study, rivalry was evident in Juazeiro both between government and opposition parties and between factions of the government party. In Petrolina councilmembers aggregated within the government party around Coelho interests.

Prior to 1964, three prominent national parties were active in Juazeiro and Petrolina. The splintering of the multiparty system often necessitated coalitions. After 1964 the government party came to prevail as electoral opposition disappeared in Petrolina; only a handful of opposition candidates managed to win council seats. Thus, the parties both prior to and after 1964 functioned as institutions through which the paternalism of the ruling class was extended to city and countryside. Where consolidation of local political power within a single party was possible, this ensured not only political stability but a regional basis for negotiating with state and national bosses for favors and assistance. Where power was diffused among party factions, as in Juazeiro, there was less consensus on an agenda in dealings with officials at the state and national levels. In both cases, however, the federal government exercised its influence through the government party at the local level.

Municipal administration in Juazeiro was based primarily on patronage. For example, the municipality provided minimal salaries to rural teachers who were assigned to ranches and farms whose owners' support was counted on in elections. Patronage also was evident in Petrolina, even though the administration appeared more orderly and efficient than that of the neighboring municipality. Patronage ensured the continuity of the traditional political system in accordance with interests of the ruling class. The local administration was, however, subject to decisions made outside the community. Because state and federal governments were reluctant to provide municipalities with sufficient resources to meet local needs, aggressive lobbying and pressure had to be carried on at those levels. Federal and state agencies traditionally were placed in Juazeiro, and after the emergence of the Coelhos additional services were established in Petrolina. Thus battalions of soldiers in Juazeiro and Petrolina ensured security and stability and also represented new resources from the outside. With the introduction of fiscal surveillance at the local level, it became necessary for the ruling class to influence the appointment of personnel to state and federal tax agencies. These agencies were tied to local interests in various ways; for example, sometimes tax inspectors could be counted on to pressure opponents of ruling-family and class control. At time of elections, judges could ensure results in favor of ruling interests.

Perhaps the most interesting development was what appears to be a decline of Coelho influence in Petrolina, the center of their family empire. The opposition warned that Nilo's death would mean political change by the 1986 elections. Their challenge in the elections of 1976, 1978, and 1982 showed that they could contend with the hegemony of the Coelhos and even elect some candidates to public office. They focused on exposing political manipulation, raising consciousness, and mobilizing the population to participate freely. This opened the way for the emergence of popular movements – neighborhood associations, urban and rural unions. ecclesiastical base communities, and so on. Professionals in the bourgeoisie – lawyers, doctors, and teachers – joined the opposition, although small merchants generally remained tied to the Coelhos. The elements loosely defined as the ruling classes were breaking up. The small ruling center was intact, but Coelho interests were diffused throughout several Northeast states. They thus represented a new class,[141] symbolically held together by Dona Josefa, the matriarch of the family. Most of them resided in Recife and Salvador, and few of the children of the Coelho brothers appeared either interested in assuming the legacy of political and economic power or competent to do so. There was evidence, however, of dissension between the brothers over the succession of their sons to leadership in the community and the family business. Other sertanejo families had split apart, for example, the Bezerras of Ouricurí in the 1978 elections, after the family matriarch passed away. More ominous was a possible victory by the opposition in future elections, for a change in Pernambucan political leadership might undermine Coelho influence at all levels of the state administration, including health, education, banking, taxing, and possibly the police.

141 Pedro Mansueto de Lavor suggested the Coelhos represented "a new class." Interview, Brasília, September 17, 1983.

12

State intervention and the prospects for capitalist accumulation

Three days of discussions and debate during a visit to Juazeiro in May 1983 convinced economist Ladislaw Dowbar that the area's economy was breaking with its traditional structure. Although traces of the old economy – for example, artisan work – were evident, capitalism had taken hold. Capitalist development in the region had been stimulated by government incentives and credits, especially to multinational firms. Thus it was erroneous, he said, to speak of precapitalism in a system that had been capitalist for some time. Capitalism had absorbed various economic formations, in part because the *sertão* was historically tied to the export economy and international markets. At the same time, he noted the absence of any democratic structures of participation. The people had little control over what was happening to the land. Water for irrigation was monopolized and unavailable to small farmers, and development projects were not being implemented for the people. The structure of local power consisted of traditional families who were now familiar with the financial apparatus – how to work with the government and obtain credits – but largely dependent on the state machinery.[1]

The Northeast is of interest to students of capitalist development like Dowbar because, as Celso Furtado reminds us, it remains a dependency of the Center-South of the country, its autonomy relinquished and its capital drained by commercial activity and official pricing policy: "The Northeast is the face of Brazil which transmits with brutal clarity the suffering of her people. . . . The Northeast shows us all the malformations of our development. . . . if Brazil is to overcome underdevelopment it must not continue to ignore the Northeast."[2] In particular, the sertão suffered, historically, from cycles of growth and decline; from discrepancies between the advancing coastal economy and that of the rural interior, the consequences

1 Interview with Ladislaw Dowbar, São Paulo, September 1, 1983.

2 Celso Furtado, "O significado real do Nordeste no atual quadro do país," *Novos Estudos* 1 (December 1981): 13. A detailed analysis of the region's problems is Conferência Nacional dos Bispos do Brazil, *Nordeste desafio à missão de igreja no Brasil* (São Paulo: Edições Paulinas, August 31, 1984).

of the exploitative practices of dominant families and ruling classes; and from disequilibrium in income and capital investment, which has interfered with the process of capitalist accumulation and the penetration and reproduction of capital in the sertão.

My study revealed that not all these views were shared by the inhabitants of Juazeiro and Petrolina. There were indeed references in the press and in books to the dependent relationship of the communities to the state capitals, the federal government, and the international political economy. More than half of the persons I interviewed believed that capitalist imperialism and foreign ideological and cultural influences had negatively affected Brazil. Although a willingness to tolerate foreign influence was expressed by men who profited from close contacts with foreign firms and were identifiable in the upper strata of the power structure, many respondents were not sensitive to issues of outside influence because national and international firms had not penetrated deeply into the local economy, where merchant capital was predominant. This was especially true in Petrolina, where the perspectives of most people were shaped by the activities of the Coelhos. In Juazeiro, people were disturbed by outside control over local production, marketing, and the distribution and importing of capital goods. They worried about the competitive advantage of outside firms over local enterprise. There was concern over government controls and regulations on the marketing of agricultural products. Many felt that outside influences had limited local development and advocated autonomy and local control so that capitalism might prosper unimpeded.

Nearly half of the respondents defined development in terms of growth and progress. A large majority in Juazeiro said they would relinquish a salary increase, be willing to pay higher taxes, and give up material possessions in order to ensure that Brazil advance economically, whereas those in Petrolina tended to reject such sacrifices. This finding confirmed my impression that work toward a common goal and sharing in material progress represented the general sentiment in Juazeiro, whereas emphasis on individual endeavor was essential to the outlook of those in Petrolina. These contrasting attitudes suggest that, although most community leaders were traditional and conservative, some had the cosmopolitan outlook of an emerging bourgeois society whose economic base was agricultural and commercial activity linked to the capitalist world. Power holders believed that protection of property rights was essential, but they also expressed allegiance to values of togetherness and equality that were associated with respect for family, church, and community. Some were committed to community over family and expressed progressive sentiments regarding taxation and distribution of profits according to productive work. In Juazeiro, in particular, there was strong support for community services and a belief that competitive capitalism, individualism, and greed had not yet taken hold.

The people I interviewed were strongly patriotic and nationalistic and supported authority, control, and centralization of power. Most in Juazeiro felt that there was national unity in Brazil; those in Petrolina did not share this view. The ruling classes considered nationalism an ideological stimulus for political development in the sense of opening up greater political participation. They also believed that nationalism affects economic development through demands for distribution of goods to all, defense of natural resources, and opposition to foreign penetration. Most respondents were interested in governmental affairs, but they ranked national and state affairs as more important than local – probably because of the historical ties to the state and federal agencies located in Juazeiro and to the benefits to Petrolina of Coelho influences at the state and national level. The rise of the Coelhos had brought public funds and an effort to build an infrastructure for capitalist development. Under Governor Nilo Coelho a road was completed from Recife to Petrolina, and power was extended to farming areas and towns along the São Francisco. Petrolina benefited from a new sewage system; expansion of hospital services and education; the construction of a tourist hotel, a new port, and a bus depot; the introduction of television; and other projects. Integration of the interior and the coastal economy was now a possibility, and the prospects for combining local and outside capital were enhanced. The revitalization of Petrolina's economy also pointed to the possibility of closer economic ties with Juazeiro.

My study has been concerned with how these changes and outside capital affected patterns of rule and capitalist accumulation. Bank managers did not appear in the power structure, nor were they active in community affairs. They were rotated from area to area every few years so as to ensure that their ties would not lead to favoritism or illicit dealings, but they exercised some control over the interior economy through approval or disapproval of loans. The local merchant usually exercised little influence in the financial sector unless he established branches in Recife and Salvador, a practice initiated by the Coelhos. Generally, short-term commercial credit was available through private banks, whereas long-term credits through state banks and government agencies were obtainable for medium-sized and large agricultural and industrial producers.

Rivalries between families and traditional differences between the towns had interfered with efforts to integrate the regional economy. Commerce was the major economic activity, dominated since the turn of the century by Juazeiro merchants whose ties to Salvador ensured their influence over regional markets. Aggressive tactics and links to Recife allowed the Coelhos to assume control over most commerce in Petrolina and the neighboring municipalities. With hegemony over the local economy, they sought credit, fiscal incentives, and other financial arrangements from government. This alliance of private enterprise with state capital allowed the family to build the area's major industry. At the same time, a few families, including the Coelhos, controlled most of the land, although livestock production was only a secondary activity for them because of droughts and other difficulties and their agricultural interests were mainly in the more productive areas of Bahia. Small farms along the river and experimental cooperatives sponsored by the government produced citrus, vegetables, and other crops for regional consumption, but hopes for a prosperous agricultural belt were dependent on government plans to expand irrigation and investment.

The intervention of the state in the region, usually bolstered by international credits, affected traditional patterns of living. For example, with the construction of the Sobradinho Dam, small farmers along the banks of the São Francisco could no longer count on the natural flow of water, fisherman experienced difficulty navigating the lake, and boatmen could no longer carry goods up and down the river. State policy favored corporations to the detriment of small producers on cooperative farms such as Bebedouro. Further, the state was primarily interested in attracting outside national and multinational capital to the region; local capital was rarely incorporated into these ventures. Thus, various local classes, including the rural and urban petty bourgeoisie, the commercial bourgeoisie, and rural workers had some common ground for criticism of activities directed by the state.[3]

The Sobradinho: problems in the name of progress

> Casa Nova of the "noble man" who govern Bahia; Petrolina of the "Quelés" who want to turn it into a kingdom.
>
> Juazeiro the "crossroad" the best of the Velho Chico; the artists turn the city into the "Princess of the São Francisco."[4]

3 After the collapse of the economic "miracle" in 1974, a debate ensued over the government's role in controlling prices, expanding public ownership, and intervention in the economy. Silvia Raw says that three-fifths of state firms known to exist in 1975 were established after the military intervention of 1964. She cites former Planning Minister Roberto de Oliveira Campos's assertion that "Great Britain is a crypto-capitalist country with socialist rhetoric and Brazil a crypto-socialist country with capitalist rhetoric" (from *Visão* [October 3, 1977]: 47) as an example of the antistate perception that prevailed among the Brazilian bourgeoisie. She shows how the campaign against *estatização* shifted from a focus on the efficiency of state enterprises and unfair competition with the private sector to their inefficiency and bureaucratization. See Raw, "State-Owned Enterprises in Brazil: 1964–1980," revision of paper presented to the Meetings of the Latin American Studies Association (Mexico City, September 29–October 1, 1983). After 1980 the bourgeois opposition to the regime expressed concern over state favoritism to politically committed private firms; such ties were undermined in states such as Rio de Janeiro and São Paulo after the opposition won elections in 1982.

4 Anonymous poem in Wilson Dias da Silva, *Os remeiros do São Francisco* (Juazeiro, 1983), p. 21.

Such images of grandeur reflect a traditional vision of the São Francisco Valley. After the coup of 1964, however, Brazilian planners imposed their own vision upon the valley. They planned a series of hydroelectric projects to provide the infrastructure for national development. Little consideration was given to their ecological consequences until the *abertura* of the early 1980s. The dam at Itaipú along the border with Paraguay created a lake that covered forever the famous Sete Quedas, or Seven Falls, on the Paraná River, one of the wonders of the world.[5] The construction of the Sobradinho Dam on the São Francisco, inaugurated on May 28, 1978, contributed to a rapidly increasing foreign debt that approached $100 billion by 1984. Brazil found itself squeezed between the demands of the international financial community, which insisted on repayment, and internal economic measures that severely limited salary adjustments in the face of an inflation that exceeded 200 percent annually.

Expectations of the Sobradinho Dam were high at the outset.[6] Petrolina historian Antônio Padilha saw it as solving the traditional problem of the rise and fall of the São Francisco in response to rain and drought.[7] Pernambucan politician Marco Maciel spoke of the benefits irrigation and power would bring to the region.[8] The movement to build the dam at Sobradinho, however, had been more than a local effort. It was a response to the demand for solutions to recurrent drought and to the international petroleum crisis that had undermined the Brazilian "miracle." Droughts together with expulsion of people from their land made life nearly intolerable in the interior, while the illusion of prosperity in the coastal cities attracted the *sertanejo*. Because migration to the coast created new urban problems, the dam was envisioned as a means of keeping people in the interior and attracting others to it. Indeed, the population was projected in one report to reach 200,000 inhabitants in Juazeiro and 700,000 in Petrolina by the end of the century.[9]

Construction began in 1973, and it soon became apparent that the dam would bring dramatic changes. Located 40 kilometers to the south of Juazeiro, it was to have a reservoir extending 350 kilometers to the town of Xique Xique, with a width varying from 15 to 40 kilometers – one of the largest artificial lakes in the world.[10] The project brought affluent

5 For a critical view of the inundation of the Sete Quedas, see Luís Carlos Pagnozzi, "Sete quedas," *O Estado de Paraná* (August 21, 1982).

6 Eunápio Peltier de Queiroz, "A barragem do Sobradinho," *Rivale* 1 (November 12, 1972): 3.

7 Antônio de Santana Padilha, "A seca do São Francisco," *O Farol* 59 (September 7, 1973): 1.

8 Marco Maciel, "Irrigação, electrificação e a barragem de Sobradinho," *O Farol* 59 (September 7, 1973): 1, 4.

9 "O ciclo das águas," *Veja* (October 11, 1978): 70–72.

10 CHESF provides visitors with overwhelming information; for example, the lake inundated an area of 4,214 square kilometers with 34.1 billion square meters of water. Visit to Sobradinho, July 27, 1982.

executives and technicians to the region. The Coelhos began to manage real estate in response to the increased demand for land and the construction of homes. Petrolina's water system, proudly inaugrated in 1967 with the expectation that it would meet needs until the year 2000, began to be seen as insufficient. With thousands of workers being attracted to the construction site and to the nearby copper project in Juazeiro, Petrolina mayor Diniz de Sá Cavalcanti saw the region's future as a struggle of unknown dimensions: "We'll probably become sleeping quarters for all these people."[11] The reservoir was to inundate the municipalities of Casa Nova, Sento Sé, Remanso, and Pilão Arcado, along with dozens of towns and farms. Nearly 12,000 families, or 72,000 persons, would be displaced, and $70 million had been allocated for compensation and reconstruction of the municipalities. The ruling families in these areas appeared satisfied,[12] and President Geisel said that the project would benefit everyone.[13] An internal Companhia Hidroelétrica do São Francisco (CHESF) report was less optimistic, warning that the poor and underdeveloped region would experience "profound social problems." It saw people as being faced with a "dramatic imposition" from above in the name of progress; having had little choice, they needed to be offered new means of living no worse than before.[14]

Early cries of alarm emanated from the diocese as local priests called upon the people to demand a home and lot of equal value, payment of moving expenses, and a year's subsistence.[15] The Superintendência do Desenvolvimento do Nordeste (SUDENE) criticized the lack of coordination among various federal agencies and called for measures to avoid a regional economic crisis, including boats for transportation, emergency services, and recreation sites along the lake. There was concern for the goods brought down the river from cities such as Xique Xique and Bom Jesus da Lapa because winds on the lake would prevent navigation by most existing transport.[16]

One of the last persons to leave Pilão Arcado was the town jailer, Félix Teixeira de Medeiro "Filoco," who commented that the move represented "the end of the world" prophesized by Antônio Conselheiro a century earlier.[17] When a farmer named Ezequiel asked for his parcel of land, a

11 "O ciclo das águas," p. 72.

12 "Sobradinho, ano 1: Remanso-Pilão Arcado-Sento Sé-Casa Nova," *Rivale* 3 (June 22–23, 1974): supplement of reports.

13 *Jornal da Bahia* (December 15, 1973).

14 Report of Eunápio Peltier de Queiroz, CHESF director of construction, June 14, 1972: summarized in Dom José Rodrigues de Souza, "Depoimento na CPI das enchentes do Rio São Francisco (1978, 1979 e 1980) na Câmara Federal," *Vozes* 75 (September 1981): 506.

15 Padre João, "Desterro amargo: carta ao povo de Pilão Arcado" (Pilão Arcado, 1974).

16 "SUDENE reconhece que Sobradinho causará prejuizos," *O Farol* 62 (December 11, 1976): 1.

17 "O ciclo das águas," p. 72.

CHESF official responded that it was in the cemetery. Four families of Altaneira resisted the threats of the tractors of three firms under contract with the CHESF. In Remanso the first 12 families were moved in September 1976 but were left sick and without food, water, electricity, and sanitation. In Casa Nova, João José de Souza committed suicide as the rising water approached his small farm.[18]

Although unemployment was high in nearby Juazeiro, most workers employed by CHESF came from outside the municipality. They were settled in three towns: Santana for technicians, São Francisco for skilled workers, and São Joaquim for unskilled laborers and the unemployed. The "free town" of São Joaquim arose in 1972 when CHESF distributed the first lots to employees of firms under contract. In late 1980, the Juazeiro diocese reported that 2,695 families, or 13,878 persons, from 16 states resided in São Joaquim. Of this total, 1,305 families desired to remain, 679 wanted to leave, and the rest were undecided. There were then 542 unemployed workers, but by the end of 1981, when work on the dam was to terminate, most would be without work. A climate of insecurity, marked by poverty, begging, prostitution, and violence, prevailed.[19]

With the dam and reservoir in place, navigation suffered drastically. Of eighty-four motor boats, fifty-six were deactivated, and the wood-burning paddlewheel steamboats no longer moved up and down the river. Previously, hundreds of thousands of tourists had been attracted to the riverboats, but now winds and high waves on the lake made movement between Juazeiro and Pirapora impossible.[20]

Unanticipated were the floods of the late 1970s. Rains in Minas Gerais and maintenance of the lake at a high level caused floods along the river as far as Juazeiro. In response to a CHESF official's attempt to explain the unanticipated water levels as "an act of God," a Petrolina poet and long-time resident recalled the similar consequences of the floods of 1919, 1926, 1949, and 1960 and concluded that "the level of the lake was kept too high without any apparent reason."[21] Bishop Dom José Rodrigues explained that the water level had been kept high in anticipation of President Geisel's arrival to inaugurate the lock that permits passage of boats, and he accused the CHESF of incompetence and irresponsibility. The floods affected 800 homes and 4,689 persons, mostly in the poor neighborhoods of Juazeiro. Damage to homes in Petrolina and to farms

18 Incidents reported in the Bahian press and cited in Rodrigues de Souza, "Depoimento," pp. 508–510. This report cites hundreds of complaints.

19 Research by Lúcia Helena Soares Viana, October–December 1980; results reported in Rodrigues de Souza, "Depoimento," p. 521.

20 Dias da Silva, *Os remeiros do São Francisco*, p. 39.

21 R. J. Sampaio, "Sobradinho – barragem, alagamento e imprevisto," *O Farol* 64 (February 23, 1979): 1.

and homes along the river was extensive. The rising floodwaters inundated the newly constructed farms and homes along the margins of the lake.[22]

Complaints were voiced by other authorities and persisted into the 1980s. Moacyr dos Santos, editor and reporter for the *Jornal de Juazeiro,* criticized the planning, the abrupt and unsatisfactory relocation of thousands of families, the pressures on the people and the failure to consult them, the unsatisfactory compensation, the flooding, the disease, the backwardness of agriculture, the difficulties for fishermen, and the loss of culture and history for the people who were displaced.[23] Federal Deputy Mansueto objected to the indiscriminate release of water to ensure a constant flow of power, resulting in difficulties for farmers along the riverbanks, who in the past had planted their crops in accordance with anticipated seasonal and climatic variations. He lamented that navigation and traditional trade along the river had come to a standstill. He recalled the sentiments of historians, poets, and novelists who had called the São Francisco "the most Brazilian of all rivers, reflecting in its waters the sentiments, dramas, and problems of the Brazilian people." The river, he said, would never be the same again. Further, the dam had been built solely for the purpose of producing hydroelectric power, not to contain floods: "These floods are manipulated by the opening and closing of the dam, in other words, they are floods administered according to criteria that do not consider the livelihood and interests of the people of the region."[24]

A study group formed by the Juazeiro diocese found fishermen complaining of not being able to make a profit and expressing concern over the risk to their lives and over exploitation. Their problems included lack of credit, perilously small motorless boats, and limited medical service. Many had given up fishing for lack of fish, a consequence of changing conditions (temperature, plant life, and pollution) in the Sobradinho reservoir.[25]

In June 1982, 1,650 people from the municipality of Curaçá and 600 from Juazeiro signed a petition protesting the misery caused by the dam. They complained that their once fertile lands were now covered with salt,

22 Rodrigues de Souza, "Depoimento," p. 531. In an interview in Juazeiro, November 5, 1984, and his report, Dom José showed problems caused by the continuing drought and the lowering of the water level. See his "A situação dos pobre agricultores, pecuaristas e pesquisadores nas bordas do Lago Sobradinho e poluição no vale do São Francisco," *Caminhar Juntos* 96 (October 1984): 1–8.

23 Interview, Moacyr dos Santos, Juazeiro, July 25, 1982.

24 Interview with Pedro Mansueto de Lavor, Juazeiro, August 3, 1982. Quotation from speech to the Pernambucan Legislative Assembly, Recife, March 26, 1980, *Diário Oficial* (Recife) (March 27, 1980).

25 Celito Kestering, "Situação dos pescadores do Lago do Sobradinho," *Caminhar Juntos* 61 (November 1981): 6–11.

sand, and other matter, and that people living below the dam could not support themselves. They asked for irrigation projects and land above the dam, power for those residing along the riverbanks, compensation for damage caused by the floods, and amnesty for those unable to pay their debts.[26]

In his analysis of the situation, Paulo Henrique Ribeiro Sandroni advanced the hypothesis that the dissolution of noncapitalist forms of production is dependent upon the differences between noncapitalist and capitalist productivity. The building of a large dam to provide power to the large centers of the Northeast had resulted in the displacement of tens of thousands of peasants; while they had been paid for their destroyed lands, ultimately they had become more impoverished. The dam had not been constructed to benefit the farmers of the region, because it was not used as a means of flood control. Thus, in the name of progress, these peasants had become more backward, and their ability to subsist had been undermined. Changes were immediately apparent and increasing because of the purchase by private enterprise of lands close to the river, which isolated other parcels, thus reducing their value and prompting their owners to sell. Many peasants had been *foreiros*, small noncapitalist renters; once dislocated and given new lands, they had become small producers. Their situation was worse than before because of the arbitrary and unpredictable release of water from the dam. Lacking resources and technical assistance, they were also vulnerable to takeover of their land by large capitalist agricultural cooperatives in the south of the country. Their secondary activity, fishing, was precluded by the large lake behind the dam and the strong winds that prevented navigation of their small boats. Of the 1,343 parcels given to peasants, only a quarter were prepared for planting and 10 percent actually cultivated. Of 192 parcels distributed in Santana and 52 in São Luiz, 80 percent and 50 percent, respectively, had been sold, most of them to the Cooperativa Agrícola Atibaiense or to small merchants and professionals from Juazeiro and Petrolina. Thus the land quickly passed to medium-sized and large capitalist agrarian enterprises. The Cooperativa purchased its land in 1979 and 1980 and was therefore able to control access to the river water and isolate other farmers, forcing them to sell at low prices. The disorganization and destruction of the productive base of the small farmers along the São Francisco River resulted in a substantial reduction of local agricultural production. A farmer had to give up his traditional ways and use new technology and irrigation to survive. Most were unable to do this for lack of financial resources and therefore sold their lands, either to become proletarians or to take up nonagricultural

26 "Grito dos ribeirinhos do S. Francisco, abaixo da Barragem de Sobradinho," *Caminhar Juntos* 69 (June 30, 1982): 10.

activities without proletarianizing themselves; some rented land as *parceiros* or became salaried workers on the land of their renters.[27]

The agrarian question

In the period before 1945 there was a tendency to describe the backwardness of the area in terms of lack of technology, the result of the power of the traditional colonels and oligarchs and their organization of the relations of production. The agrarian ruling class controlled not only the political economy but also the state agencies established to alleviate problems. While these conditions changed during the populist period from 1945 to 1964 as a bourgeoisie emerged in urban centers and peasants, particularly in sugarcane areas, were proletarianized and politicized, life in the sertão continued as before. The small working class was unable to mobilize itself, and peasant farmers tended to work for subsistence. Politically, the masses continued to be manipulated by the vote for a favor, compromise, or patron, preferring to exchange something of little value for material advantage. During this period there were demands to expropriate the latifundios, divide land among the peasants, and implement agrarian reform. In some parts of the Northeast, such as Pernambuco, agrarian reform became a major objective of the populist movement, but its impact was minimal in the sertão.

Abdias Vilar de Carvalho has suggested that interest in the Northeast before 1964 was attributable to the drought of 1958 and recognition of the disparity between the region and the prosperous Center-South: "The great drought showed in a drastic way the misery in which a great part of the Northeast's population lives."[28] According to Carvalho, political platforms and electoral campaigns between 1958 and 1962 employed such phrases as "structural dualism," "development of underdevelopment," and "internal colonialism." A new social consciousness had emerged that was related to the drought, the agrarian structure, and the underdevelopment of the region.

After 1964 the military government suppressed the popular movement and devoted itself to solving agrarian problems in terms of the Land Statute of November 30, 1964. The regime promoted a policy of increased capitalization of agriculture through an alliance of the industrial bourgeoisie and landowners: "Eliminating previous proposals to alter the agrarian structure, the state now assumed the role of controlling all agrarian reform

27 See Paulo Henrique Ribeiro Sandroni, "Sobradinho: sertão e diferenciação" (São Paulo: Master's thesis, Pontifícia Universidade Católica de São Paulo, 1982).

28 Abdias Vilar de Carvalho, "A questão nordeste no estado nacional," *Temas de Ciências Humanas* 7 (1980): 106.

initiative and ensuring the cohesion of the dominant classes."[29] The state was to "modernize" agriculture through the introduction of technology, the provision of incentives to agricultural and agroindustrial enterprises, and the restructuring of commerce and credit: "The state orients, provides incentives, and intervenes directly in order to orient the primary sector to the new needs of monopolistic financial capitalism and to diminish the important social tensions in the countryside."[30]

In the period 1978 to 1983, the Northeast suffered another disastrous drought, and the disparities between wealthy landowners and the rest of the rural population became more conspicuous. Drought victims desperate for work and subsistence resorted to the sacking of warehouses near Fortaleza and Recife. In Canindé, 5,000 raided a local warehouse after only 800 of them had been given assistance by the local authorities. Similar incidents were reported in Crato.[31] Nine hundred raided a warehouse in São José de Belmonte, in the sertão of Pernambuco, and 2,000 invaded a food distribution center in Aguas Belas.[32] The mayor of the town Euclides da Cunha characterized the drought as worse than the one described in *Os Sertões*. (Ironically, Canudos had been submerged in a reservoir constructed for a nearby irrigation project.)[33] Although Petrolina had access to water from the São Francisco, the interior of the municipality suffered, and a solar distiller with a capacity of 1,500 liters daily was installed to distill brackish water.[34]

Although some excellent reporting by Brazilian journalists offered insight into the problems,[35] the dimensions of the drought could not easily be described. Many politicians blamed the government for failure to

29 Ibid., p. 111.

30 Ibid., p. 112. Among the agencies established to carry out these objectives were the Instituto Nacional de Colonização e Reforma Agrária (INCRA), Empresa Brasileira de Pesquisas Agropecuária (EMBRAPA), Empresa Brasileira de Assistência Técnica e Extensão Rural (EMBRATER), Programa de Redistribuição de Terras e do Estímulo a Agro-Indústria do Norte e do Nordeste (PROTERRA), Programa de Desenvolvimento de Áreas Integradas do Nordeste (POLO-NORDESTE), Programa de Transformação e Fortalecimento da Economia Semi-Árida (Projecto SERTANEJO), and Fundo de Assistência ao Trabalhador Rural (FUNRURAL).

31 Newspaper accounts in *Folha de São Paulo* (August 16, 1983) and summarized in "Romaria de saques," *Veja* (August 24, 1983): 29–30.

32 "Flagelados voltam a saquear em Pernambuco," *A Tarde* (July 22, 1982); "Águas Belas sofre saque de camponês," *Diário de Pernambuco* (July 29, 1983). A day after the Águas Belas incident, the mayor, his secretary, and a local dentist were wounded in an assassination attempt; while the crime appeared not be related to the sacking events, it reflected the tension and violence in the area.

33 "Seca em Canudos relembra o drama de *Os Sertões*," *Folha de São Paulo* (August 16, 1983).

34 "Distilador solar é uma opção," *Diário de Pernambuco* (July 28, 1983).

35 See "Os sertões do nordeste morrem de sede," *Veja* (March 18, 1981): 44–52; "A tortura da seca," *Veja* (August 17, 1983): 56–66; and "Diante da seca, só fantasias," *Isto é* (August 10, 1983): 28–39.

allocate adequate resources and for poor planning.[36] During June and July 1983 floods devastated the southern states of Paraná and Santa Catarina, and the nation rallied to their aid. In the course of these events, millions of suffering Northeasterners were forgotten until the clamor of local politicians and the presentation of desperate scenarios on national television refocused attention on an area many people in the Center-South probably perferred to forget. Once evidence of starving families and dying children became conspicuous, it turned into a national problem. Philosopher Marilena Chauí labeled it a "scandal of hunger and unemployment."[37] Ceará Governor Gonzaga Mota warned that lack of water and food would bring hundreds of thousands of drought victims to Fortaleza, doubling the slum population by the end of the year. Promised government money had not arrived, water supplies in the state capital were at a low point, and authorities were panic-stricken. The commander of the military police was not responsive to demands for support in the interior because "he feared a general assault on Fortaleza."[38] In Petrolina, journalist Elisabet Moreira questioned whether the problem was one of God or man. Critical of electoral pacts, disastrous inflation, unemployment, urban violence, and the financial and social disorder, she implicated "decisions from above implemented without consultation" and "planning as a technique of intervention and social control which can only strengthen the power and hegemony of ruling elites." Cuts in funds, delays in projects, postponing of definitive solutions showed that "it was not only God who forgot the Northeast."[39]

In the face of drought, social inequality, and widening differences between ruling and popular classes, official descriptions of the Northeast emphasized the accomplishments of the government. Interior Minister Mário Andreazza, favored by President Figuereido as his successor, showed that in 1979 the drought had affected 513 of 1,416 municipalities in the area, and that number had increased to 1,000 by August 1983. Anxious to show the government's positive influence, he claimed that the number of people with homes had increased from 9 to 24 million; 83,000 kilometers of roads had been built, improved, or maintained; and 1.5 million hectares of land had been brought under cultivation. This progress, he argued, was due to government planning and fiscal stimulus to private enterprise. Although admitting that these measures could not overcome drought and poverty, he continued, "When there is a tie between the state and private initiative, the

36 See excerpts from interview with Filemon Matos and Genebaldo Correira, "PMDB acusa governo de manipular seca e fome," *A Tarde* (July 27, 1983).

37 Marilena Chauí, "O escândalo da fome e do desemprego," *Folha de São Paulo* (September 5, 1983).

38 Edmundo Maia, "Fortaleza teme chegada de flagelados," *Folha de São Paulo* (August 28, 1983): 24.

39 Elisabet Gonçalves Moreira, "Seca no sertão, problema de Deus ou do homem," *Jornal de Petrolina* 1, no. 6 (March 1982): 2.

results are always positive and reflect directly on the improvement of quality of life. . . . fiscal incentives are the principal instrument for the continuing process of industrialization in the Northeast."[40]

Despite its rhetoric, the government effort was not altogether positive in its effects. After nearly two decades of intervention, government policies had preserved and even enhanced the monopolization of private lands. Rural credits benefited large rural properties and agrarian industry to the detriment of the small farmer. Consequently, the availability of new technology and capital had led to what Brazilian specialists call "conservative modernization" of rural areas, resulting in a greater concentration of large landed estates and an alliance between agriculture and industry. Industry had allied itself with agriculture by providing insecticides, machinery, and seeds, while the multinationals invested capital and technology. The state had provided incentives to private enterprise, encouraged colonization, and facilitated the gradual rationalization of capitalism in rural areas.[41] Cooperation between the state and private enterprise clearly had not met the requirements of most people. The drought exposed the need for a restructuring of agriculture, which had declined for all but a privileged few even during the period of the "economic miracle" from 1967 to 1973 and after 1978, when the agrarian question became a government priority.[42]

The 1975 census revealed that, with arable land at a premium, there

40 Mário David Andreazza, "A seca e a ação do governo federal no Nordeste," and "Nordeste: porque incentivar sua industrialização," *Folha do Povo* (September 3 and 4, 1983). Contrast these impressions with the pessimistic account of Raymundo Faoro, "O Nordeste inacabado," *Senhor* 128 (August 31, 1983): 32. In the debate over the drought, the dry Northeast was compared to the prospering desert areas of Israel, to which four hundred Brazilian Jews had emigrated. There, water supplies were less plentiful than in the São Francisco Valley. See Rubens Rodrigues dos Santos, "Israel, um exemplo para o Nordeste," *O Estado de São Paulo* (September 25, 1983). This edition contained an article by Ana Lígia Petrone, "Desde 1959, um projeto para acabar com a seca," which described the proposal of engineer Pedro Coutinho to divert water from the Tocantins River and definitively resolve the problem of drought. Another proposal, under study in Congress, called for irrigation of 1.6 million hectares through the diversion of water from the São Francisco toward Fortaleza and Natal; see Comissão de Estudos e Referente à Transposição de Águas do Rio São Francisco para a Regiões Semi-Áridas do Nordeste (CESAN), "Projeto de derivação de água do Rio São Francisco para o semi-árido nordestino" (Brasília: Departamento Nacional de Obras de Saneamento, August 1983).

41 The consequences of agricultural "modernization" are described by Marcus Cunha as a "greater opening of the economy to the outside; concentration of income; acceleration of industrial development; and reformulation of the financial system and stimulants for the concentration of capital." See Cunha's "A reforma agrária," *Reforma Agrária: Boletim da Associação Brasileira de Reforma Agrária* 11 (July–August 1981): 11–12.

42 Citing the work of economist Ignacio Rangel, José Graziano da Silva warns that the agrarian question must not be confused with the agricultural question. Agricultural production must keep pace with the needs of industrialization; otherwise crisis will ensue. If agriculture frees labor or restricts the access of labor in industrial expansion, then an agrarian crisis is likely to occur. See Silva's *O que é questão agrária*, 5th ed. (São Paulo: Brasiliense, 1982), pp. 10–11.

Table 12.1. *Distribution of irrigation projects, São Francisco River basin*

Project	Year	Location	Total area (hectares)	Area for enterprise (hectares)	Area for farmers (hectares)
Bebedouro	1968	Petrolina	2,000	800	1,000
Mandacarú	1972	Juazeiro	370		370
Maniçoba	1975	Juazeiro	4,655	2,600	2,000
Tourão	1976	Juazeiro	10,473	11,000	
Massangano (Nilo Coelho)	1982	Petrolina	22,000	8,000	12,000

Source: CODEVASF.

were 2.5 million small producers on 8 million hectares of land and 50,000 large producers on 150 million hectares. As large producers expanded their holdings, thousands of small landowners, renters, sharecroppers, and others were leaving their land and migrating to cities in search of a new way of life. This acceleration of the urbanization process prompted the government to seek ways of encouraging farmers to remain in the interior. First, work forces were formed to provide temporary employment and income to drought victims. Second, and more ambitious, a series of colonization and irrigation schemes was initiated.

During the decade of the seventies, irrigation policy was implemented by the Companhia de Desenvolvimento do Vale do São Francisco (CODEVASF), with headquarters in Brasília and a regional office in Petrolina.[43] The principal objective of CODEVASF was the implementation of irrigation projects. This involved the acquisition of land and the building of roads, housing, and other facilities for cooperatives of small farmers or large private agricultural enterprises. Table 12.1 shows the projects in Juazeiro and Petrolina. These irrigation projects were conceived partly as a means of attracting small farmers and organizing them into cooperatives, thus providing a basis of employment and retention of work force in the interior. However, after fifteen years of activity, only 307 settlers were working the land, including 105 at Bebedouro, 49 at Mandacarú, and 153 at Maniçoba. It was projected that eventually Massangano would attract 30,000 farmers and serve as a brake on emigration, but cuts in government funds delayed its implementation and by 1983 there was little evidence of activity.[44] The government offered state credit and encouraged

43 The Superintendência do Vale do São Francisco (SUVALE) had become CODEVASF in 1975.

44 João Veiga, "Projeto Massangano: obra abandonada," *Jornal de Petrolina* 1, no. 2 (January 17, 1981): 4.

private enterprise to organize projects: Thus Agrovale (7,000 hectares), Alfanor (4,000 hectares), and Cica-Norte (500 hectares) established themselves in the area. With the aid of a processing plant in Juazeiro, credit ties to small farmers, and production on land in Maniçoba, Cica-Norte monopolized the market for tomatoes. At Tourão, Agrovale, and Alfanor, sugarcane was produced for distillation into alcohol. At Bebedouro three firms (backed by Belgian, U.S., and Pernambucan capital) leased land for fifteen years.[45] Massangano was similar to Bebedouro, with 40 percent of the land planned for small and medium-sized enterprise.

Clearly, CODEVASF preferred private enterprise. Critics suggested that the policy of concessions to small and medium-sized enterprise left Coelho influence in the area untouched. Manoel Correia de Andrade was strongly critical of the results: "CODEVASF works slowly, and the number of settlers, in a society with many landless workers, is insignificant, even smaller than the number of expropriated owners; it is expropriating land and encouraging emigration of small producers while benefiting small and medium firms that use wage labor in the area." Developmental policy, he argued, should not be oriented to profit: "Profit pure and simple should not and cannot be the principal goal of the state."[46] He concluded that the state, in its application of large capital and technology, was "modernizing" the area without promoting its social development; the people should participate in the planning and implementation of rural programs in opposition to the interests of the ruling classes.

An important issue was access to the means of production, particularly land and water, for the rural worker. One government report insisted that "the restructuring of land tenure and the guarantee of access to land and water constitute the first and principal condition for changing the conditions of poverty and subordination in which the great majority of small producers and their families find themselves."[47] Poverty and its "manifestations of hunger, begging, slums, cultural and social marginalization, insecurity, and violence" affected the 4.6 million regional rural workers who received the minimum wage or less. Whereas in 1965 those receiving the minimum had to work 87 hours to provide for their food, in 1980 it took them 179 hours. Structural problems included unequal and concentrated land ownership, lack of water, credit limitations, and the tendency

45 Settlers at Bebedouro complained of such problems as salinization and low soil productivity, tax increases on water, and lack of rules over ownership of cultivated areas, according to *Tribuna do Sertão* 1, no. 3 (February 1981): 5.

46 Manuel Correia de Andrade, *Tradição e mudança: a organização do espaço rural e urbano na área de irrigação do submédio São Francisco* (Rio de Janeiro: Zahar Editores, 1982), pp. 106–107.

47 Projeto Nordeste, Grupo IV-Regional, "Programa de apoio ao pequeno produtor rural do Nordeste" (Salvador, October 1983), 2: 208.

for public agencies to ignore the small producer while favoring medium-sized and large producers.[48]

In 1982 the Projeto Nordeste was conceived as a new plan to boost agricultural productivity in the Northeast. Financing of the fifteen-year, $12 billion project would be through the World Bank and the federal government. An initial study involving 300 technicians, including national and foreign consultants of public and private entities, concluded that previous governmental intervention had not solved such problems as poverty, regional inequalities, concentration of income and land, backwardness in the agricultural sector, and inadequacies in education, health, and credit. Although significant changes had occurred in the economy, particularly the industrial and service sectors, most traditional activities had been abandoned in favor of the production of intermediate goods and durable consumer goods. Agriculture had declined after 1960 to the point that basic production of foodstuffs could not satisfy the needs of an expanding population. Regional growth fell in all sectors beginning in 1980 and was further affected by the drought. Despite the desire of the government to accelerate rural and regional development and to improve living conditions, income had become increasingly concentrated in a small portion of the population, and small rural producers had suffered.[49] The study also determined that the large number of projects in the region had led to a multiplicity and overlapping of bureaucratic activities, poor coordination, and incompatibility between projects and problems.[50]

The second phase of the project involved the formulation of a global strategy for the agricultural sector, giving priority to the small farmer. This was to involve state coordination of landholdings, irrigation, credit, technology, market, and community activities. During the first of three five-year stages the plan was designed to reach 600,000 families and

48 Projeto Nordeste, Grupo IV-Regional, "Programa," vol. 1.

49 Ibid., pp. 166–167.

50 Government efforts to stimulate development in the Northeast were evident in the Directive Plans from 1961 to 1970 and the three National Plans of Development after 1971. In addition, a host of projects were initiated in the Northeast: the POLO-NORDESTE, established October 1974 with the objective of modernizing agricultural activities; Programa Especial de Apoio ao Desenvolvimento da Região Semi-Árida do Nordeste (Projeto Sertanejo), founded August 1976 to assist small and medium-sized cattle producers; Programa Especial de Apoio às Populações Pobres das Zonas Canavieiras do Nordeste (PROCANOR), established April 1980 with the intent of assisting poor peoples in sugar-producing areas; Programa de Aproveitamento de Recursos Hídricos do Nordeste (PROHIDRO), created in September 1979 to promote water projects in semiarid and arid areas; and Programa de Desenvolvimento da Agroindústria do Nordeste, initiated in May 1974 to stimulate agroindustrial activities. These activities are described in *Projeto Nordeste: concepção básica*. Preliminary Version (Recife: Superintendência do Desenvolvimento de Nordeste and other government agencies, April 1984), pp. 83–104.

employ 1.8 million; over the fifteen years it was expected to affect 2 million families and employ 6 million persons.

In a scorching critique, Deputy Mansueto noted that while the project acknowledged the failure of past government policy in the Northeast, it did not mention the essential political reasons for that failure: "the domination and exploitation of economic elites who use political power against the majority of people, principally against urban and rural workers and small farmers. . . . the proponents of this government action are part of the dominant minority." He argued that the alarming poverty of the Northeast was due not to the incapacity of its people or to its climate but to the activities of the dominant classes and their "methods of paternalism, violence, corruption, and electoral fraud." Although the project called for "participatory planning," he said, in reality it reflected the interests of the elites in power and national and international economic–financial forces. No real restructuring of land tenure was addressed, yet the data showed that most food was produced and most rural workers (80 percent) were found on farms of less than 50 hectares. Ideologically the project reflected international financial capitalism; in keeping with imperialism, the World Bank would make all the important decisions. Mansueto saw little hope for this project unless it were implemented by a democratic government with the power to alter existing political and social structures and allow the participation of the people.[51]

Agrarian reform remained an untried approach to the resolution of the agrarian crisis of the 1980s. If large estates were divided among small farmers, the development of capitalist relations of production would put an end to traditional agriculture. In the context of the general economic crisis, a coalition of forces emerged to pressure for real agrarian reform.[52] Such reform was endorsed by the Third National Congress of the Confederação Nacional dos Trabalhadores na Agricultura (CONTAG) in

51 Pedro Mansueto de Lavor, "A democracia é fundamental para alcançar soluções permanentes," *Voz da Unidade* 210 (July 21–27, 1984): 8–9. Mansueto's criticism was in line with sentiments about the drought expressed in a letter to the author: "This problem is worsening each day, and one can foresee at any moment a social convulsion. The situation in the country, from an economic and social point of view, is terrible. The IMF is determining the direction of our political economy in a way that protects the interests of the bankers and leaves the people in a precarious state. Unemployment is alarming. Industries and other enterprise are shutting down. We are living in a period of hard recession." Letter of December 22, 1983, Brasília.

52 The coalition included the Confederação dos Trabalhadores da Agricultura (CONTAG), Comissão Pastoral de Terra (CPT), Conselho Indigenista Missionário (CIMI), Conferência Nacional de Bispos do Brasil (CNBB), Associação Brasileira de Reforma Agrária (ABRA), and the Instituto Brasileiro de Análises Sociais e Econômicas (IBASE). Jointly they sponsored the National Campaign for Agrarian Reform; see their *Campanha Nacional pela Reforma Agrária* (Rio de Janeiro: Editora Codecri, April 1983).

1979 and by the Conferência Nacional da Classe Trabalhadora (CONCLAT) in 1981 and 1983.

Tradition or transition?

In the politics of Juazeiro and Petrolina, the transition from dictatorship to parliamentary democracy after World War II and during the late 1970s and early 1980s was accompanied by the rise of an opposition. Throughout the period, politics in Juazeiro were dispersed among many parties or factions, whereas in Petrolina family groups worked through parties until the hegemony of the Coelhos was established, again in 1976, and thereafter when an opposition emerged.

There was also a transition from family to class rule although the Coelhos were able to ally with the bourgeosie without abandoning their family base of power. The old system of colonelism had emerged during the ninteenth century when a patrimonial and bureaucratized state, confronted with centrifugal tendencies, had extended its authority into outlying areas by allowing local control through a national guard and the conferring of military rank on landowners and local chiefs. During the Old Republic, influential landowners had negotiated with these local chiefs to form coalitions, sometimes led by a dominant family, that assumed control of the state and electoral machinery. During the New State, colonelism had persisted in the face of the Vargas regime's attempts to centralize power at the national level. After 1945 colonelism remained, somewhat residually in most regions, and families like the Coelhos adapted it to the new conditions of urban development, industrialization, and migration. The emergence of a new colonelism was characterized by the dominance of the ruling family over mercantile interests and the investment of merchant capital together with state credits in new industry, usually tied to the processing and maintenance of agricultural products. Thus the new colonelism was represented by the dominant family in alliance with bourgeois elements. This bloc manipulated a dependent and political public, expending resources and extending services and favors to ensure its allegiance at election time.[53] After the coup of 1964 the new colonels consolidated their position and in Petrolina went unchallenged until 1976. In Juazeiro there was a decline of family rule before 1964, and the emerging ruling class comprised commercial and petty-bourgeois interests operating at a low level of development of the forces of production.

Goodman and Redclift's study of the agrarian transition is helpful for

53 A helpful source that analyzes these economic and political links is Antônio Otávio Cintra, "Traditional Brazilian Politics: An Interpretation of Relations between Center and Periphery," pp. 127–166 in Neuma Aguiar, ed. *The Structure of Brazilian Development* (New Brunswick, N.J.: Transaction Books, 1979).

understanding the change that has taken place in the sertão. They describe the transition as a process through which a predominantly peasant agriculture is transformed into one dominated by a rural proletariat.[54] They address the problem of how to characterize small agricultural commodity producers when their real subsumption to capital is incomplete – that is, when producers retain possession of their means of production and exercise some control over the immediate labor process so that they are not dependent on the wage form for their reproduction. They show that the emergence of classes of rural capitalists and free landless workers is not always evident in the capitalist development of agriculture. They examine various relations of production in agriculture, including landlord payments to workers in cash rather than land when the value of land increases; mechanization and emphasis on cash cropping; and situations in which peasants obtain land and work it independently of the landlord. These distinctions are relevant to an understanding of the uneven process of capitalist development that characterizes agriculture in the contemporary Northeast. Capitalist enterprise has reached certain areas, including Juazeiro and Petrolina, yet noncapitalist family labor forms of production, such as small owner-producers, sharecroppers, and small tenants, predominate.

State agricultural policy has been instrumental in this process. Before 1964 the drive toward urban industrialization was based on the diversion of agricultural surpluses to the urban sector. This was a period of import substitution, involving protectionist tariffs, discretionary restrictions on imports, and multiple exchange rates that favored industrial imports and capital goods. The 1964 coup destroyed the nationalist elements that favored such a policy, disenfranchised the working class, implemented repressive wage policies, centralized the state, restructured industrial and financial capital, and allowed the internationalization of capital in much of the economy. Since 1964 there has been strong state intervention through credit policy and practice in an effort to expand productivity in agriculture

54 Goodman and Redclift characterize capitalist agriculture in industrial societies as involving more specialized and more diversified production than under precapitalist conditions. Specialization, technology, and closer articulation with the market all lead to concentration of production in fewer and larger units, increase in size of farms, and decline in number of workers. They show that peasant farming in Europe survives in combination with other activities. They question the position of Marx (*Eighteenth Brumaire)* that the peasantry should disappear with the emergence of capital and its hold on family producers. They turn to Lenin's reformulation of this position and show that the full development of capitalist forces was dependent on resolution of the agrarian question in Europe, where agriculture had to generate a surplus to make industrialization possible, and in Russia, where Lenin emphasized the diversified role of the peasantry in the development of the home market. This led to consideration of a possible alliance between the peasantry and the industrial proletariat and to the idea that some segments of the peasantry can resist proletarianization. See David Goodman and Michael Redclift, *From Peasant to Proletarian: Capitalist Development and Agrarian Transistion* (New York: St. Martins, 1982), chap. 1.

by transforming large landed property into large agricultural enterprise: "Modern techniques thus are diffused by credit and fiscal policies which subsidize the cost of capital, both for current production outlays and long-term investment."[55]

Traditionally merchant capital in the sertão has drawn resources from the banking system and profited from the disparity of subsidized official credit rates. Goodman and Redclift refer to usurer capital controlled by traditional agents such as landowners, local traders, shopkeepers, and crop-processing firms in small-scale agriculture. Because large producers often take on these merchant-usurer activities to ensure their dominance over marketing and distribution channels, the distinction between traditional merchant-usurer capital and modern commercial capital is not always clear:

> Nevertheless, we can generalize with some accuracy and say that "antediluvian" forms of merchant-usurer capital are concentrated in small-scale peasant agriculture. In contrast, the production of export crops and raw materials is financed in formal credit markets and distribution is controlled by large commercial capitals, agro-industry, producers' cooperatives and state agencies.[56]

Noncapitalist forms of labor exploitation such as sharecropping are reproduced. The owner has a commercial hold over his tenants and appropriates surplus in the form of interest payments on advances to cover subsistence needs and input purchases. The landowner becomes a merchant by parceling out his land and then appropriating surplus in the sphere of circulation: "The forms and relations of production in North Eastern agriculture continue to exhibit great complexity and intra-regional diversity, providing ample scope for the activities of traditional merchant-usurer capital."[57]

This analysis illuminates the complex relationships among state, merchants, landowners, and various types of agricultural producers. Goodman and Redclift propose that a bourgeois revolution similar to that of Europe was avoided by an alliance between the rising industrial bourgeoisie and the rural landed classes, a consequence of state control of agricultural pricing. Brazilian agriculture illustrates "diverse, frequently discontinuous, processes of capitalist differentiation, regional variations in their intensity and the heterogeneous relations between small proprietors, rural

55 Ibid., p. 145. My discussion is drawn from their excellent analysis of changes in Brazilian agriculture. For analysis of this modernization process in the state of São Paulo, see José Graziano da Silva with Barbara A. Kohl, "Capitalist 'Modernization' and Employment in Brazilian Agriculture, 1960–1975: The Case of the State of São Paulo," *Latin American Perspectives* 11 (winter 1984): 117–136.

56 Goodman and Redclift, *From Peasant to Proletarian*, p. 154.

57 Ibid., p. 158.

workers and various forms of capital. . . . it is misleading to ascribe a unilinear development to the capitalist transformation of agriculture, which crystallizes into a class of rural capitalist and free rural proletariat."[58] They conclude that although there is evidence of an agrarian transition as some agriculture is industrialized and integrated into the reproduction of productive capital, "this movement is marked by discontinuities and seemingly contradictory patterns which maintain, even recreate noncapitalist relations of labor exploitation and forms of production."[59] On the basis of my study, I would add that while there is evidence of an agrarian transition in some parts of Brazil, particularly the more developed state of São Paulo, the transformation of traditional social relations of production has not yet occurred in the sertão. The capitalist wage form does not yet predominate in rural areas of Juazeiro and Petrolina. The recent efforts of the World Bank, in conjunction with the Brazilian government, to transform peasants into small independent landowning producers are unlikely to succeed without profound agrarian reform. The outcome will probably favor the traditional landowners and merchant-usurers instead. Nor is it clear, however, that the traditional agricultural producers will become a rural proletariat. Thus the prognosis for agriculture in the sertão is uncertain.

The Brazilian population was growing at close to 3 percent annually in the 1960s and 2.4 percent in the 1970s. These rates were exceeded by the explosion of population in Juazeiro and Petrolina, where hundreds of thousands were expected to live by the end of the century. Given limited municipal autonomy and resources, the provision of services to the rapidly increasing population was becoming a major problem. This problem was aggravated by the drought and the attraction of Juazeiro and Petrolina for many families who could no longer survive in the barren sertão. The state's strategy of providing funds and projects to absorb some of the growing labor force and retain people in the area was only partially successful. Construction of the Sobradinho Dam attracted labor from outside the area and left it to survive without an adequate infrastructure to meet basic human needs. The irrigation projects attracted small farmers from outside rather than incorporating local people. The planning, outside capital, and credits did create some employment for the local work force, along with the appearance of development and growth. The powerful and wealthy enriched themselves through contractual and credit arrangements. At the same time, the projects provided a structural façade that tended to obscure real problems.

The projects introduced into the region brought local power holders

58 Ibid., p. 181.
59 Ibid., pp. 183–184.

both prestige and economic advantage. Enterprise from the Center-South constituted little political threat, because its managers lacked political power. The accompanying increase in jobs in the area represented potential votes among the lower-income people who were incorporated into the local political machinery. Thus the participation of the state in local development projects, designed to relieve pressure on the coastal urban areas, tended also to reinforce the position of the local ruling class. In this process the state was pervasive: "Planning does not represent the presence of a mediating state but the reverse, the presence of a state enveloped by the most advanced forms of the reproduction of capital in order to impose a tendency toward harmony or . . . national integration."[60] Essential to issues of autonomy and capitalist accumulation was how the local ruling class related to the state and national and multinational capital, for it was clear that the full development of productive forces in the region had yet to be achieved and the transition of capitalism, while underway, was not yet complete.

60 Tereza Cristina Leal de Serejo, "Coronéis sem patente: a modernização conservadora no sertão pernambuco" (Niterói: Masters thesis, Instituto de Ciências Humanas e Filosofia, Centro de Estudos Gerais, Universidade Federal Fluminense, 1979), pp. 179–180.

Appendix

QUESTIONNAIRE

We are social scientists from the University of California, Riverside, undertaking a scientific study of leadership in six communities of Latin America. Your answers will be confidential and kept anonymous, including your name and the name of your community.

1. Who is the most important person?
    1. This community
    2. Neighboring community

2. If a project were before the community that required a decision by a group of leaders - leaders that nearly everyone would accept - which ten would you accept? (Show list 1 and have respondent mark an "x" before ten names.)

3. Do you belong to any important civic clubs or any organizations of which the others are members? (Show list 2 and have respondent mark an "x" before each organization.)

4. Have you worked in a committee with any of the persons on the list? (Record name of committee - formal or informal - and the persons on each committee.)

    Committee   Persons from list on committee

5. Which persons (on list or otherwise) might you call upon for advice? (Record each person and type of advice.)
    1. Local government
    2. Business and economics
    3. School matters

5a. If a project were before the community that required a decision by a group of leaders - leaders that nearly everyone would accept - which ten would you accept? (Please mark an "x" before each of ten names on the list below.)

5b. Do you belong to any important civic clubs or any organizations of which the others are members? (Please mark an "x" before each organization below.)

6. We would like to know how well you know the persons on the list. Please indicate your relationship with each person. [See illustration following question 7 to see how responses were charted.]

   A. Code: 1. A relative by blood or marriage (Show master list again.)

   B. Code: 2. A person with whom respondent seeks special counsel - see question 5 (Code later.)

   C. Code: 3. Very close personal relationship
   4. Knows socially - may or may not have high regard but knows personally and well
   5. Knows very little and has few contacts
   6. Heard of name but cannot describe how person functions in community

   8. Does not know
   9. Refused to answer

7. In your opinion how does each person on the list function in relation to community projects? (Read each name again and obtain evaluation of one of the following.)

   Code: 1. Very actively involved
   2. Actively involved but limited by personal problems, inability to lead or administrate - has good intentions
   3. More or less involved (generally with projects relating to vocation or business)
   4. Not involved

   8. No information
   9. Refused to respond

Portion of the chart used to code responses for questions 6 and 7:

(6) A	B	C	NAME OF PERSON	(7)

8. Now we would like to know your impressions and perspectives of economic life in the community as well as economic leaders and influentials. (Direct response to each of the following sectors. Probe with relevant questions but assess respondent's attitude according to code below. List additional comments.)

   <u>Economic perspectives</u>
   1. Commercial sector
   2. Industrial sector
   3. Agricultural sector

   Code: 1. Strongly positive
   2. Positive with reservations
   3. Neutral
   4. Slightly negative
   5. Strongly negative

   8. No opinion
   9. Refused to respond

   <u>Economic leadership</u>

   Code: 1. Very strong (active, aggressive, capable)
   2. Potential (strong, significant, capable)
   3. Weak
   4. No leadership

   8. No opinion
   9. Refused to respond

   <u>Economic development perspectives</u>

   Code: 1. Strongly positive
   2. Positive with reservations
   3. Neutral
   4. Slightly negative
   5. Strongly negative

   8. No opinion
   9. Refused to respond

9. Now we would like to know your impressions and perspectives of political life in the community as well as political leaders? (Probe

for direct response to each of the following sectors. Ask relevant questions and code. List additional comments.)

Political perspectives (the political life, style)

Code: 1. Strongly positive
2. Positive with reservations
3. Neutral
4. Slightly negative
5. Strongly negative

8. No opinion
9. Refused to respond

Political leadership

Code: 1. Very strong (active, aggressive, capable)
2. Potential (strong, significant, capable)
3. Weak
4. No leadership

8. No opinion
9. Refused to respond

Political development (political opposition, decision making, participation)

Code: 1. Strongly positive
2. Positive with reservations
3. Neutral
4. Slightly negative
5. Strongly negative

8. No opinion
9. Refused to respond

Part I Municipal Problems

10. We are going to examine some issues or problems that have been more or less resolved during the past ten years. Did you participate in decisions that may have resolved some of those problems; and specifically how did you participate (e.g., personally, through a

political party, a special committee, or some other organization). (Show list 3 and note complete response.)

Problem or decision

1. Industry
2. Roads
3. Tourism
4. Sewage
5. Border traffic
6. Schools
7. Housing
8. Development of agriculture
9. Health and construction of hospitals
10. Water supply
11. University
12. Urban planning
13. Local transportation
14. Fishing

A. Degree of participation.

Code:
1. Very much involved (officially or indirectly influenced outcome)
2. Involved but not decisively
3. Slightly involved (indirectly)

8. Does not know issue
9. Refused to respond
0. Not involved

B. Manner of participation.

Code:
1. Personal interest
2. Through special committee
3. Through politics (party or person)
4. Through organization
5. Other (not clear)
6. Two of above
7. Three or more of above
8. No opinion
9. No response
0. Not involved

Part II Attitudinal

A. <u>POWER, DECISION MAKING, AND COMMUNITY PERSPECTIVES</u>

11. Generally speaking, how important are the following groups in making the key decisions on important policies in the community:

1. Mayor
2. City council
3. Out-of-town companies
4. Largest firms
5. Leading civic organizations
6. Banks and insurance companies
7. Businessmen
8. Voters
9. Labor leaders
10. Neighborhood committees
11. State officials
12. Federal officials

Code: 1. Very important
2. Not so important
3. Unimportant

8. No opinion
9. Refused to respond

11a. Generally speaking, which group is the most important?

12. Which three civic, fraternal, or social organizations are most influential in the making of important decisions affecting the whole community? (Show list 4.)

13. Which of the following statements do you think best applies to each of the following? (Show list 5.)

1. Church officials
2. School officials
3. Municipal officials
4. State officials
5. Federal officials

Code: 1. They do pretty much what the citizens want.
2. They do what some of the more influential people want.
3. They do not pay much attention to what the people want but tend to do what they themselves think best.

8. Did not know
9. Refused to respond

14. If you were concerned about a local community problem and contacted the appropriate local officials, how do you think they would react? Which of the following statements best describes the way the officials in each group would respond to you? (Show list 6.)

    1. Municipal officials
    2. Out-of-town company officials
    3. Officials of the largest firms
    4. Officials of leading civic organizations
    5. Officials of banks and insurance companies
    6. Businessmen
    7. Labor officials
    8. Officials of public services

    Code: 1. They would try to understand my problem and do what they could about it.
    2. They would listen to me but would try to avoid doing anything - would pass the buck.
    3. They would ignore me or would dismiss me as soon as they could.
    4. They would say that decisions are made at the top and that it would not be possible to make them here.

    8. No opinion
    9. Refused to respond

14a. Have you ever had this kind of experience?

    Code: 1. Yes
    2. No

    8. Do not know

14b. (If response to item 14a is "yes")
With which of the listed officials or groups of officials did you have this experience? (Code as above.)

15. In general, how do you feel about living in this community?

    Code: 1. An excellent community to live in
    2. A very good community to live in
    3. A good community to live in

4. Not a very good community to live in
5. A poor community to live in

8. No opinion
9. Refused to respond

16. How would you rate this community for each of the following and why?

    1. Opportunity for economic advancement
    2. Schools
    3. Availability of adequate housing
    4. Community spirit or attitude of people toward the community or people's pride in the community
    5. Willingness of people to undertake and support action to meet community needs and problems
    6. Friendliness of people
    7. Responsiveness of city government to people's wishes
    8. Community spirit of the big companies

    Code: 1. Excellent
    2. Very good
    3. Not very good
    4. Poor

    8. No opinion
    9. Refused to respond

17. Dimensions of decision making relating to community issues.

    Issues (problems and needs) addressed included:
    Infrastructure: electric (power and light), rural (electricity), street (construction and maintenance), planning for development, industry, agricultural development, credits/loans
    Welfare services: unemployment, poverty/hunger, social security, housing, recreation
    Health services: medical, sewage, water supply and treatment
    Education: primary, secondary, college, adult
    Other: electoral participation, immigration (rural to urban), emmigration (to coast), foreign influences, other

1. Is an issue identifiable in experience of respondent/community (over past ten years)?

   Code: 1. Yes
   2. No

   9. Does not know or refused to respond

2. Issue for respondent is:

   Code: 1. Central to interests
   2. Peripheral
   3. Not important

3. Issue for community is:

   Code: 1. Central to interests
   2. Peripheral
   3. Not important

4. Effective action is:

   Code: 1. Possible
   2. Impossible

   9. Does not know or refused to respond

5. Issue should be resolved at:

   Code: 1. Local level
   2. State level
   3. Federal level

6. In evaluating issue resolution, respondent is:

   Code: 1. Very satisfied
   2. Somewhat satisfied
   3. Somewhat dissatisfied
   4. Very dissatisfied
   5. Undecided

   (Respondents were also asked to describe their perspectives of what the issues are.)

17a. Of the following issues which three do you believe have been the most important for the community during the past ten years? (Show list 7.)

B. IDEOLOGY: DEVELOPMENT AND LOCAL, NATIONAL, AND INTERNATIONAL PERSPECTIVES

18. Given below are statements on various social problems about which we all have beliefs, opinions, and attitudes. We all think differently about each matter. There are no right and wrong answers. Please respond to each of the items as follows: Strongly agree, agree, disagree, or strongly disagree. Respond to each statement as best you can. Do not spend too much time on any one statement; try to respond and then go on. Don't go back once you have marked a statement. (Show list 8.)

1. Large fortunes should be taxed fairly heavily over and above income taxes.
2. Society should quickly throw out old ideas and traditions and adopt new thinking and customs.
3. If civilization is to survive, there must be a turning back to religion.
4. To ensure adequate care of the sick, we need to change radically the present system of privately controlled medical care.
5. A first consideration in any society is the protection of property rights.
6. Municipal ownership and management of utilities leads to bureaucracy and inefficiency.
7. Municipal aid for the construction of schools is long overdue, and should be instituted as a permanent policy.
8. Our present economic system should be reformed so that profits are replaced by reimbursements for useful work.
9. Municipal laws and regulations should be such as first to ensure the prosperity of business since the prosperity of all depends on the prosperity of business.
10. The well-being of the community depends mainly on its private industry and business.
11. All individuals who are intellectually capable of benefiting from it should get university education at public expense if necessary.

12. True democracy is limited because of the special privileges enjoyed by private business and industry.
13. There should be no municipal interference with business and trade.
14. Some sort of religious education should be given in public schools.
15. Unemployment insurance is an inalienable right of the working man.
16. Individuals with the ability and foresight to earn and accumulate wealth should have the right to enjoy that wealth without government interference and regulations.
17. Most communities are good enough as they are without starting any new community improvement programs.
18. This used to be a better community to live in.
19. The home and the church should have all the responsibility for preparing young people for marriage and parenthood.
20. The responsibility for older people should be confined to themselves and their families instead of the community.
21. Schools in most communities are good enough as they are.
22. Too much time is usually spent on the planning phases of community projects.
23. Adult education is not necessary as a part of the local school program.
24. Only physicians should have the responsibility for the health program in the community.
25. The spiritual needs of the citizens are not adequately met by the churches.
26. While it grows, a community need not provide additional recreation facilities.
27. In general, church members are better citizens.
28. The social needs of the citizens are the responsibility of themselves and their families and not of the community.
29. No community improvement program should be carried on that is injurious to a business.
30. The first and major responsibility of each citizen should be to earn dollars for his own pocket.
31. What is good for the community is good for me.
32. Each one should handle his own business as he pleases and let the other businessmen handle theirs as they please.
33. A community would get along better if each one would mind his own business and others take care of theirs.
34. Each of us can make real progress only when the group as a whole makes progress.

35. The good citizens encourage the widespread circulation of all news including that which may be unfavorable to them and their organizations.
36. A citizen should join only those organizations that will promote his own interests.
37. Everyone is out for himself at the expense of everyone else.
38. Unions are necessary for the workers.
39. The main responsibility for keeping the community clean is up to the city officials.
40. Community improvements are fine if they don't increase taxes.
41. A progressive community must provide adequate recreational facilities.
42. Government officials should get public sentiment before acting on major projects.
43. A good citizen should be willing to assume leadership in a civic improvement organization.
44. Progress can best be accomplished by having only a few people involved.
45. Community improvement should be the concern of only a few leaders in the community.
46. Living conditions in a community should be improved.
47. Improving slum areas is a waste of money.
48. The paved streets and roads in most communities are good enough.
49. The sewage system of a community must be expanded as it grows even though it requires increasing taxes.
50. Modern methods and equipment should be provided for all phases of city government.

Code:
1. Strongly agree
2. Agree
3. Disagree
4. Strongly disagree
5. Indecisive or neutral

8. No opinion
9. Refused to respond

18a. I would be interested in learning what you think of the relationship between the political and economic sectors of this community.

1. Degree of cooperation

Code: 1. Excessive
2. Enough cooperation
3. Need more cooperation
4. Cooperation not necessary

8. No opinion
9. Refused to respond

2. Degree of dominance

Code: 1. Economic sector dominates political sector
2. Political dominates economic
3. Each sector autonomous or exerts influence equally
4. Other

8. No opinion
9. Refused to respond

Local-Cosmopolitan

19. Indicate your response to the following: (Show list 8.)

1. The most rewarding organizations a person can belong to are local clubs and associations rather than large nationwide organizations.
2. National and international happenings rarely seem as interesting as events that occur right in the local community in which one lives.
3. While newcomers to the community are probably capable people, when it comes to choosing a person for a responsible position in the community, I prefer a person whose family is well established in the community.
4. The local community constitutes the strength of the country.
5. I have greater respect for a man who is well established in his local community than a man who is widely known in his field but who has no local roots.

Code: 1. Strongly agree
2. Agree
3. Disagree
4. Strongly disagree

5. Indecisive or neutral

8. No opinion
9. Refused to respond

20. (Screening question) Some people seem to think about what's going on in government most of the time, whether there's an election or not. Others are not that interested. How frequently do you follow what's going on in government?

Code: 1. Most of the time
2. Some of the time
3. Only now and then
4. Hardly at all

8. No opinion
9. Refused to respond

21. (Not asked to those giving the "hardly at all" response to the previous question.)

1. Which of these do you follow most closely?
2. Which do you follow least (read three remaining)?
3. Of the other two (read), which ones do you follow most closely?
4. Residual rank.

Code: 1. International affairs
2. National affairs
3. State affairs
4. Municipal (city) affairs

22. Since every person has different degrees of confidence in the various levels of government, I would like to know in which level do you have most confidence:

Code: 1. International
2. National
3. State
4. Municipal

Patriotism

23. I am going to read you some statements and would like you to indicate for each statement whether you strongly agree, agree, disagree, strongly disagree. (Show list 8.)

    1. No duties (responsibilities) are more important than duties (responsibilities) toward one's own country.
    2. This nation's frontiers should be open to all those who wish to settle here.
    3. When a national government is incompetent, the use of force to remove it can be justified.
    4. A nation ought to be willing to give up its independence and submit to the authority of a world government.
    5. One should always show greater loyalties to the president and the government than to a national political party.
    6. All human beings are equally important. No person from the nation is of more value than any person from any other country.
    7. Our nation ought to support the establishment of a world government that could solve international disputes.
    8. The defense of our nation can never justify the taking of another human life.
    9. One should show greater loyalty toward humanity than toward (name of country) as a nation.

    Code: 1. Strongly agree
    2. Agree
    3. Disagree
    4. Strongly disagree
    5. Indecisive or neutral

    8. No opinion
    9. Refused to respond

Developmental Nationalism

24. What are the most notable characteristics of the people (three characteristics):

25. How much national unity exists in Brazil?

Code: 1. Much
2. Sufficient
3. Little
4. None

8. No opinion
9. Refused to respond

25a. (If answer above is little or none, continue.) In your opinion what are the obstacles that impede the realization of national unity?

Code: 8. No opinion
9. Refused to respond

26. Following are some statements which might describe characteristics of national unity. Please indicate if you strongly agree, agree, disagree, or strongly disagree with each:

1. A single language (Portuguese)
2. A single territory (Brazil)
3. The heritage of customs and traditions
4. Symbols of national experience, such as the flag, anthem, etc.
5. Institutional solidarity, including a single government
6. Autonomy (of nation from outside influence)
7. Self-determination (from outside)
8. Common consciousness of nation among its citizens
9. Creed of loyalty among the nation's citizens
10. Justice for all

Code: 1. Strongly agree
2. Agree
3. Disagree
4. Strongly disagree

8. No opinion
9. Refused to respond

27. Could you briefly describe what development means to you?

Code: (coded after interview)
0. Progress and growth

1. Culture and education
2. Stability and peace
3. Opportunity for all
4. Technology
5. Infrastructure
6. Change in the perspective or mentality of the people
7. Total participation of the people
8. Centralized planning by government
9. Other (specify)

28. Following are more statements about activities the national government might undertake in an effort to achieve development and national unity. Please indicate if you strongly agree, agree, disagree, or strongly disagree. (Show list 8.)

Political:

1. Decisions should be based on popular acceptance and the will of the people.
2. The party system should involve the masses.
3. A free press and radio should be maintained.
4. The vote should be given to all Brazilians.
5. Services should be expanded to provide for the needs of all the people.
6. A vocal opposition should be encouraged and tolerated.
7. The government should build support for its actions by propagating its ideology.
8. Stability and democratic order should be maintained.
9. Bureaucracy should be made efficient and honest.

Economic:

10. Consumption should be limited to the needs of the people (luxury items eliminated).
11. The government should assume control of all industry.
12. The land tenure system should be reformed so as to allocate land to all those who need it.
13. The government should control all rents and the value of housing.
14. Protective tariffs should be established.
15. The government should build infrastructure (roads, power, transport, etc.).
16. The tax structure should be reformed so as to allocate income more evenly among all people.
17. Credit for business, commerce, and agriculture should be made available to all.

18. The government should control all natural resources.
19. Foreign enterprise should be nationalized.
20. There should be trade with all nations (Western as well as socialist).
21. All iron and steel firms should be nationalized.
22. All public utilities should be nationalized.

Social:

23. Racial barriers should be eliminated.
24. Allegiance for the collective society should replace dependence on the family.
25. A classless society should be established.
26. Religion should be deemphasized as a national value.
27. Paternalism should be eliminated.
28. Medical service should be provided to all.
29. Housing should be provided to all.
30. Food for all should be provided.

Cultural:

31. Educational facilities should be expanded so as to allow all to attend school freely, from elementary to higher education.
32. National values should be enhanced; local values should be downgraded.
33. National values should be enhanced; regional and state values should be downgraded.
34. National values should be enhanced; foreign values should be downgraded.

Psychological:

35. There should be an emphasis on allegiance, and pride in nationality.
36. There should be consciousness of national identity.
37. There should be motivation, will, and commitment to national objectives.

Code:
1. Strongly agree
2. Agree
3. Disagree
4. Strongly disagree
5. Indecisive or neutral

8. No opinion
9. Refused to respond

C. <u>DEPENDENCY AND UNDERDEVELOPMENT</u>

29. To continue I am going to mention some sacrifices which perhaps would be necessary in order that Brazil could advance economically in the next few years. Would you sacrifice the following or not?

    1. Salary increases
    2. Paying larger taxes
    3. Automobile or television
    4. Spending less on a vacation or luxury goods

    Code: 1. Would not sacrifice
    2. Would sacrifice

    8. No opinion
    9. Refused to respond

30. Do you believe that there exists foreign influences which are detrimental to what happens in the country today?

    Code: 1. Yes
    2. No

    8. No opinion
    9. Refused to respond

(If the response to 30 is affirmative, continue to 31.)

31. Could you mention, in order of importance, two of the most important foreign influences that have hurt the country? And two that you consider beneficial?

    Two that have been detrimental?

    Two that have been beneficial?

32. Other persons have mentioned that economic development in this community is impeded by certain problems. How do you feel about the following - are they detrimental to local development? (Show list 9.)

    1 Increasing outside control over the economy of the community:
    1. Yes 2. No Type of dependence
    (Probe cause of dependence.)

2. Outside control of local production:
   1. Yes 2. No Type of dependence
   (Probe cause of dependence.)

3. Outside control of local marketing and distribution:
   1. Yes 2. No Type of dependence
   (Probe cause of dependence.)

4. Outside control of patents and licenses:
   1. Yes 2. No Type of dependence
   (Probe cause of dependence.)

5. Increasing competitive advantages for outside firms over local firms:
   1. Yes 2. No Type of dependence
   (Probe cause of dependence.)

6. Outflow of capital, especially profits:
   1. Yes 2. No Type of dependence
   (Probe cause of dependence.)

7. Export of specialized products thus limiting market and availability of these products within the community:
   1. Yes 2. No Type of dependence
   (Probe cause of dependence.)

8. Introduction of outside technology without regard to size or composition of the local labor market, resulting in unemployment (and restriction of market):
   1. Yes 2. No Type of dependence
   (Probe cause of dependence.)

9. Lack of local industry and consequently an increased dependence on imports:
   1. Yes 2. No Type of dependence
   (Probe cause of dependence.)

10. Outside introduction of managerial class, especially in the public sector, thus undercutting local initiative in economic development:
    1. Yes 2. No Type of dependence
    (Probe cause of dependence.)

Code: 1. Yes
2. No

8. No opinion
9. Refused to respond

List 9: 0. Dependence on the neighboring city
1. Dependence on the province (state)
2. Dependence on a neighboring province
3. Dependence on the national government
4. Dependence on commerce or industry in another part of the country
5. Dependence outside the country
6. Dependence explained by local happenings and factors (an external factor not identified by respondent)
7. Other
8. Does not know
9. No response (to yes above)

33. What are your perspectives on the proposed development of copper deposits by Anaconda. Detrimental or beneficial to the local economy?

Code: 1. Detrimental
2. Beneficial

8. Did not know
9. Refused to respond

D. MOBILIZATION (Participation, Recruitment, Aggregation)

34. The citizen has many rights. Which are, in your opinion, the most important? Place in order the following items, giving 1 to the most important, 2 to the next in importance, and so on until reaching 4.

Are there any items that presently are not guaranteed for all Brazilians?

	Order	Limited
1. Equality	______	______
2. An effective voice in the political process	______	______

3. Free education for all ______ ______
4. Access to the social services of the nation ______ ______

35. People speak of the obligations that they owe to their country. In your opinion what are the obligations that every man owes his country. (Take down full response - probe for individual responses.)

35a. Which in your opinion are most important? Order with 1 given to the most important obligation, 2 for the next important, and so on until 4.

35b. Which obligations are not being met by Brazilians today?

	Order	Limited
1. Vote	______	______
2. Try to understand and keep informed about governmental affairs, read about them, etc.	______	______
3. Participate in public and political activities, discuss politics, express one's opinion	______	______
4. Obey the laws, respect authority	______	______
5. Love one's country, be loyal and respectful, speak well of it, represent it well in other countries	______	______
6. Pay taxes	______	______
7. Defend the country, serve in armed forces if needed	______	______
8. Do one's job right, raise children properly, be upright, responsible in personal life	______	______
9. Be honest, moral, work to better the nation (Code this only if nothing more specific mentioned.)	______	______
10. Other	______	______

36. Many people I have talked with have said that they have trouble understanding political and governmental affairs. Which of the reasons on the list best explains why this happens? (Hand list.)

Code: 1. The problems are too complex.
2. People don't care and don't try.
3. Those in power don't help people to understand.

4. Other (specify)

8. No opinion

37. One sometimes hears that some people or groups have so much influence on the way the government is run that the interests of the majority are ignored. Do you agree or disagree that this is so?

Code: 1. Agree
2. Partially agree
3. Disagree
4. Other

8. No opinion

38. We know that the ordinary person has many problems that take his time. In view of this, what part do you think the ordinary person ought to play in the local affairs of his town? (If needed) What specifically ought he to do? (Take down full response.)

Code: 1. Nothing
2. Take part in local government, participate in governmental groups, organizations, committees
3. Take part in nongovernmental groups and organizations dealing with local affairs - community betterment groups, charitable activities
4. Take part in political parties
5. Take part in church and religious matters
6. Try to understand and keep informed
7. Do job well, take care of family, be upright and responsible in one's personal life
8. Just take an interest in local affairs (Code this if only an interest in local affairs mentioned, but nothing more specific.)
9. Vote
10. Other (specify)

11. No opinion
12. Refused to respond

39. Suppose that a regulation was being considered by the local government which you considered very unjust or harmful, what do

you think you would do? (If needed.) Anything else? (Take down full response.)

Code: 1. Nothing
2. Work through informal, unorganized groups, friends, and get friends to write letters, sign petitions
3. Work through political party
4. Work through other formal, organized group (church, etc.)
5. As individual, talk to, contact councilmen, etc.
6. Consult a lawyer
7. Vote
8. Take action, protest, appeal, maintain dialogue (no specific indication of action to be taken)
9. No opinion
0. Other

39a. If you made an effort to change this regulation, how likely is it that you would succeed?

Code: 1. Very likely
2. Moderately likely
3. Somewhat unlikely
4. Not at all likely - impossible
5. Likely only if others joined in

8. No opinion
9. Refused to respond

39b. If such a situation arose, how likely is it that you would actually do something about it? (Code as above.)

40. Suppose a regulation was being considered by the state assembly which you considered unjust or harmful, what would you do? (If needed.) Anything else? (Take down full response.)

Code: 1. Nothing
2. Work through informal, unorganized groups, friends, and get friends to write letters, sign petitions
3. Work through political party
4. Work through other formal, organized group (church, etc.)
5. As individual, talk to, contact councilmen, etc.

6. Consult a lawyer
7. Vote
8. Take action, protest, appeal, maintain dialogue (no specific indication of action to be taken)
9. No opinion
0. Other

40a. If you made an effort to change this law, how likely is it that you would succeed?

Code:[12] 1. Very likely
2. Moderately likely
3. Somewhat unlikely
4. Not at all likely - impossible
5. Likely only if others joined in

8. No opinion
9. Refused to respond

40b. If such a situation arose, how likely is it that you would actually do something about it? (Code as above.)

40c. Have you ever done anything to try and influence an act of the state assembly?

Code: 1 Often
2. Once or twice, a few times
3. Never

9. Refused to respond

41. Suppose a regulation was being considered by the national congress which you considered unjust or harmful, what would you do? (If needed.) Anything else? (Take down full response.)

Code: 1. Nothing
2. Work through informal, unorganized groups, friends, and get friends to write letters, sign petitions
3. Work through political party
4. Work through other formal, organized group (church, etc.)
5. As individual, talk to, contact councilmen, etc.
6. Consult a lawyer

7. Vote
8. Take action, protest, appeal, maintain dialogue (no specific indication of action to be taken)
9. No opinion
0. Other

41a. If you made an effort to change this law, how likely is it that you would succeed?

Code: 1. Very likely
2. Moderately likely
3. Somewhat unlikely
4. Not at all likely - impossible
5. Likely only if others joined in

8. No opinion
9. Refused to respond

41b. If such a situation arose, how likely is it that you would actually do something about it? (Code as above.)

41c. Have you ever done anything to try and influence an act of congress?

Code: 1. Often
2. Once or twice, a few times
3. Never

9. Refused to respond

42. Supposed that several persons were trying to influence a government decision. Here is a list of things they might do. Which of these approaches do you think would be the most effective? Least effective? (Show list 10.)

Code: 1. None
2. Working through personal and family connections
3. Getting people interested - forming a group
4. Working through a political party
5. Organizing a protest demonstration
6. Other (specify)

8. Do not know

a - most effective
b - least effective

Awareness of politics (Related to socialization section below)

43. Public issues often arise that are complex and hard to understand. Suppose such an issue arose which might affect your own way of life, but you did not understand this issue fully. What would you do to find out more about it? (If only one answer given) Is there anything else?
(Code under general or particular categories below depending on whether or not respondent has something particular in mind. Respondent's score can then be tallied by adding up the points for categories coded.)

1. Talk to (particular) people from daily life - friends, neighbors, relatives, fellow workers, etc. (1 point)
2. Talk to or write to (particular) government or political party official - representative, government agency (3 points)
3. Talk or write to (particular) specialists or experts not in government or political party - a newspaper editor, a lawyer, an official of an organization (2 points)
4. Talk or write (general) - no particular person mentioned (1 point)
5. Read about it (general) - read newspapers, magazines, but not particular magazines (1 point)
6. Read about in (particular) source - source named (3 points)
7. Listen to radio and/or television (general - no particular station or program mentioned) (1 points)
8. Listen to radio and/or television (particular) (3 points)
9. Attend meetings (general) - not specified (l point)
10. Attend meetings (particular) - specific (3 points)
11. Other (1 point)
12. Nothing (0 points)

43a. Tally total points for 43:

1. One
2. Two
3. Three
4. Four
5. Five
6. Six

7. Seven
8. Eight
9. Nine
10. Ten or more
11. None

44. Do you follow the accounts of political and governmental affairs - would you say you follow them regularly, from time to time, or never?

    Code: 1. Regularly
    2. From time to time
    3. Never
    4. Other

    9. Did not respond

44a. What about newspapers. Do you listen to or read or discuss the accounts or items? (Code as above.)

44b. What about radio or television? Do you listen to or discuss the accounts or items? (Code as above.)

44c. What about magazines? Do you read or discuss the accounts or items? (Code as above.)

44d. What about talking about public affairs to other people? Do you talk with others or discuss the accounts or items? (Code as above.)

E. <u>SOCIALIZATION AND POLITICAL SOCIALIZATION</u>

45. We are interested in how decisions are made in your family, say when you were 16. Here's a list of ways of making family decisions. (Show list 11.)

    Code: 1. Generally father made the decision
    2. Generally mother made the decision
    3. Both parents acted together

4. Each parent acted individually
5. Other

9. Don't know
0. Inappropriate (for example, doesn't have parents)

45a. How does this compare with your present family in general? How are decisions made in your family now? (Show list 11.) (Code as above.)

45b. What about deciding on how to vote? (Show list 11.) (Code as above.)

46. When your parents made decisions affecting you, say when you were 16, how well did you think they understood your needs?

Code: 1. Very well
2. Fairly well
3. Not so well
4. Not at all
5. Other

8. Don't know, cannot remember
9. No response
0. Inappropriate

47. How much influence do you remember having in family decisions affecting yourself?

Code: 1. Much influence
2. Some
3. None at all

8. Don't recall or don't know
9. No response
0. Inappropriate

48. Were you satisfied or dissatisfied with the amount of influence you had in family decisions when you were 16?

Code: 1. Satisfied
2. Dissatisfied
3. Other

8. Don't know
9. No response
0. Inappropriate

49. When you were growing up, do you remember how interested your father was in public affairs and politics?

Code: 1. Very much interested
2. Somewhat interested
3. Didn't pay much attention

8. Don't recall or don't know
9. No response
0. Inappropriate

49a. During that time, do you remember how interested your mother was in public affairs and politics? (Code as above.)

50. Do you and your (wife) (husband) ever talk about any kind of public affairs and politics, that is, anything having to do with local, state, national, or international affairs?

Code: 1. Yes
2. No

9. Did not respond
0. Inappropriate
(If yes, continue)

50a. Do you happen to recall which kind of public affairs and politics you have talked about recently? (Note response.)

Code: 1. Politics and religion
2. Politics and economics, developmental policies
3. How politics affects family affairs
4. Voting, elections
5. Ideology
6. Administration
7. Politics and youth, education
8. Other (specify)
9. Does not know (If no response to "yes" response in 50, code as 8 or "other.")

0. Inappropriate

50b. When you disagree on politics, what is it usually about? (Note response.)

Code: 1. Local politics, local government, local administration
2. Provincial (state) politics
3. National (federal) politics
4. Elections in general (succession)
5. Paternalism and politics
6. International politics

8. Other (specify)
9. Does not know (If no response to "yes" response in 50b, code as 8 or "other.")

51. In general, how much voice do you think children of 16 should have in family decisions?

Code: 1. Great deal
2. Some
3. Little
4. None
5. Other

8. Don't know
9. No response

52. What kinds of hopes do you have for your (son) (daughter) (children) as to what they will be doing during the next three or four years? (Note response.)

Code: 1. That they be cultured, integral, educated
2. That they be leaders
3. That they be prepared to undertake a profession
4. That they receive a university education
5. That they work for the betterment of the country
6. That they be good citizens

8. Other (specify)
9. No response
0. Inappropriate

53. Do you remember how much time was spent in your school in studying current events and the government of the country?

Code: 1. A lot
2. Some, but can't remember how much
3. A little
4. None
5. Other
6. Don't know, don't remember

54. Here is a list of things that children may be taught in school. Which was stressed the most in your school? (Show list 12.)

Code: 1. Have faith in leaders
2. Obey the law
3. Know how the government is run
4. Love your country
5. Other

8. Don't know, don't remember
9. No response
0. Inappropriate

55. In some schools the children are encouraged to discuss and debate political and social issues and to make up their own minds. How was it in your school? How much chance did the children have to express their opinion?

Code: 1. A lot
2. Some
3. None
4. Other

8. Don't know, don't remember
9. No response
0. Inappropriate

56. What about your teachers? How interested were they in you as an individual?

Code: 1. A lot of interest
2. Some interest
3. Depended on teacher

4. None
5. Other

8. Don't know, don't remember
9. No response
0. Inappropriate

57. If you felt you had been treated unfairly in some way or disagreed with something the teacher had said, did you feel free to talk to the teacher about it?

Code: 1. Felt free
2. A bit uneasy
3. Better not to talk to the teacher
4. Other

8. Don't know, can't remember
9. No response
0. Inappropriate

58. Are you satisfied with the education that you received?

Code: 1. Yes
2. No

8. No opinion, did not know
9. Refused to respond
0. Inappropriate

59. Which do you consider should be the principal task of education? (Read.)

Code: 1. Create a national spirit in youth
2. Prepare youth to be good citizens
3. Prepare youth professionally and technically
4. Form cultured men
5. Other (specify)

8. Does not know
9. Refused to respond
0. Inappropriate

60. Approximately, what do you believe ought to be the minimum education that the majority of youth today should have?

Code: 1. None
2. Read and write
3. Primary
4. Vocational and technical
5. Secondary and normal
6. University

8. Did not know
9. Refused to respond
0. Inappropriate

61. Which school do you consider better, public or private?

Code: 1. Public
2. Private
3. Indifferent

8. Does not know, no opinion
9. Did not respond
0. Inappropriate

62. Are your children in public or private school?

Code: 1. Public
2. Private
3. Both

8. Does not know
9. Did not respond
0. Inappropriate

63. Which do you consider to be worse for your children, that their teachers be severe or too tolerant?

Code: 1. Very severe
2. Too tolerant (lax)
3. Neither severe nor tolerant
4. Other

8. Does not know

9. Did not respond
0. Inappropriate

64. Are there important things about which you and your (son) (daughter) disagree?

Code: 1. Yes
2. No

8. Does not know
9. Did not respond
0. Inappropriate
(If "yes" answer to 64, continue.)

64a. What sorts of things do you disagree about with your children? (Note response.)

Code: 1. Obsession of parents with traditional customs
2. Economic affairs, commerce, etc.
3. Education, studies
4. Politics: the government, etc.
5. Youth: its liberties, excessive life, and social orientations (manner of dress, dance, etc.)
6. Family problems, personal matters
7. Religion
8. Other (Specify)
9. Does not know (no response to a "yes" response in 64, coded as 8 or "other.")
0. Inappropriate

65. Has your (son) (daughter) ever been taught or told things in any of (his) (her) classes at school that you didn't like?

Code: 1. Yes
2. No

8. Does not know
9. Did not respond
0. Inappropriate
(If "yes" answer to 65, continue.)

65a. What kinds of things didn't you like? (Note response.)

Code: 1. Sex education
2. The behavior of the professor (his punishment of students, failure to understand)
3. Religious matters
4. Ideology
5. Vices practiced among the students
6. Behavior of the students - their disobedience and manner of treating other persons
7. Economic and social interpretations
8. Other
9. Does not know (no response to a "yes" in 65, coded as 8 or "other")
0. Inappropriate

66. Do you recall if anything else has happened during the last two or three years that made you upset or concerned about the high school your (son) (daughter) attends?

Code: 1. Yes
2. No

8. Does not know
9. Did not respond
0. Inappropriate
(If "yes" answer to 66, continue.)

66a. What upset you, for example? (Note response.)

Code: 1. Sex education
2. The behavior of the professor (his punishment of students, failure to understand)
3. Religious matters
4. Ideology
5. Vices practiced among the students
6. Behavior of the students - their disobedience and manner of treating other persons
7. Economic and social interpretations
8. Other
9. Does not know (no response to a "yes" in 65, coded as 8 or "other")
0. Inappropriate

67. Do you believe that your (son) (daughter) should study politics and government in school?

    Code: 1. Yes
    2. No

    8. Does not know
    9. Did not respond
    0. Inappropriate

68. Some persons I have talked with say that violence and conflict are characteristics of the culture of the sertão. How do you feel about that?

    Code: 1. Agree
    2. Disagree
    3. Other

    8. Do not know

68a. (If agree) How do you explain that?

69. Some historical violence has in fact taken place in this region. I would like to identify several events and ask you if you have heard of them. (If familiar, ask to elaborate on significance of the event for the local area.)

    1. Palmares
    2. Social banditry (Lampião)
    3. Canudos (O Conselheiro)
    4. Padre Cícero of Juàzeiro do Norte
    5. Labor disputes of early 1960s
    6. Peasant organizations of 1960s (peasant leagues, etc.)
    7. Other (specify)

    Code: 1. Familiar (can give details)
    2. Have heard of (but cannot explain significance or give details)
    3. Does not recognize

    9. Did not respond

Interview Evaluation

Part III. Biographical Data

Place ____________ Case Number ____________
Interviewer ________________________
Time Start ____________ Time Finish ____________
Time Elapsed ____________
Morning ________ Afternoon ________ Evening ________
Date of Interview ________________________
Number of callbacks ________
Interview quality (limit to three problems)

1. No major problems, respondent cooperative.
2. Respondent at first reluctant, but satisfactory interview and all responses obtained.
3. Respondent reluctant and several responses not obtained.
4. Respondent encountered difficulty with questions due to personal problems (physical defect, for example).
5. Interviewer failed to ask two or more questions.
6. Order of questions altered to facilitate interview.
7. Interview marred by interruptions or presence of other persons.
8. Tape recording marred by noise, weak batteries.

70. Respondent's Name ________________________
(First) (Last)
71. Address ____________ 71a. Telephone ________
72. Sex: M ( ) F ( )
73. Place of Birth ____________ 73a. Date of Birth ________
(City) (State) (Day) (Mo) (Yr)
74. Marital Status ____________
(M, S, W, D)
75. If married, widowed, divorced, number of children ________

Children	Name	Sex	Age	Marital Status	Education Level	Present School	Residence
1.							
2.							
3. (etc)							

76.

	Sex	Age	Marital Status	Education Level	Principal Occupation	Place of Birth	Place of Residence
Father							
Mother							
Brothers							
Sisters							

Total ______

77. Did your mother have to work to support the family?
If yes, why?

78. Where did you study?

	Place	Name of School	Level or Degree Obtained	Type of Study
Primary				
Secondary				
Vocational				
University				
Other				

79. Please indicate your jobs since you left school (chronological order).

	Occupation	Name of Firm	Place	Dates From To	Why Left
1.					
2.					
3.					

80. How long have you lived in this community?

81. Counting rents, salary, and other income, could you select one of the following categories that represents your family's total income before taxes for last year?

Code: 1. $5,000 or less or $96 per week
2. $5,001 to $6,900 or $96 to $135 a week
3. $7,000 to $9,900 or $135 to $193 a week
4. $10,000 to $14,999 or $193 to $289 a week
5. $15,000 and over a year or more than $289 a week

82. What is your religious affiliation, if any?

    Code: 1. Catholic
    2. Protestant (Specify)
    3. Jewish
    4. Other (Specify)
    5. None

83. What has been your political affiliation since 1945? Specify.

	Organization	Date From To	Committees	Official Post
1.				
2.				
3.				

84. Have you occupied any government post? If yes, specify post and dates held.

85. Is this dwelling owned by you or are you renting?

    Code: 1. Owned or being bought
    2. Rented

    8. Don't know
    9. No response

86. Most people are accustomed to identifying themselves with groups or social classes. I am going to read you three lists of groups and ask you to identify with one of the categories in each list.

    A. Code: 1. The rich
    2. The modest average
    3. The poor
    4. None

    8. Don't know
    9. Refused to respond

    B. Code: 1. Upper class
    2. Middle class
    3. Lower class
    4. None

8. Do not know
9. Refused to respond

C. Code: 1. Upper bourgeoisie
2. Lower bourgeoisie
3. Proletariat
4. None

8. Do not know
9. Refused to respond

87. Do you ordinarily take vacations each year?
If yes, where are they usually spent?

Code: 1. Locale of residence
2. Capital of country
3. United States

6. Other (Specify)

8. Does not spend vacation in any particular place
9. Refused to respond

88. We would like to know if you have contact with businessmen and/or governmental agencies.

If contact with businessmen, which? (Probe for local, state, national, international)

If contact with government agencies, which?

89. Are you in favor of maintaining these contacts?
If yes, why?

90. Do you have contact with foreign firms or foreign agencies?

For foreign firms, if yes, which?

For foreign agencies, if yes, which?

91. Now we need to know something about organizations you have belonged to during the past five years - such as groups connected with schools, church, political clubs, civic clubs, social clubs, and

so forth. (Specifically ask for: school organizations; union organizations; clubs and social organizations; cultural organizations; religious organizations; political clubs and organizations other than parties; veterans and patriotic organizations.)

Name of Organization	Type Local	Type Nat'l	Type Intern	% Attendance last year Yes	% Attendance last year %	% Attendance last year No	Financial contrib. last year Yes	Financial contrib. last year No	Officer last 5 years Yes	Officer last 5 years No	Which Pos. Held?
1.	1	2	3	1		2	1	2	1	2	
2.	1	2	3	1		2	1	2	1	2	
3.	1	2	3	1		2	1	2	1	2	
4.	1	2	3	1		2	1	2	1	2	
5.	1	2	3	1		2	1	2	1	2	
6.	1	2	3	1		2	1	2	1	2	
7.	1	2	3	1		2	1	2	1	2	
8.	1	2	3	1		2	1	2	1	2	
9.	1	2	3	1		2	1	2	1	2	
10.	1	2	3	1		2	1	2	1	2	
Total Organization	___	___	___	___		___	___	___	___	___	

91a. Why are these clubs and organizations important to you?

92. Which are the three principal socioeconomic problems facing the community at this time?

93. Could you comment briefly on interrelations between the communities, their problems and perspectives for solution of problems?

Bibliography

Following are major sources used in preparation of this book. Because most sources are cited in the footnotes, the emphasis is on monographs and a few important documents. Excluded are obscure, inaccessible documents that are cited in the text and notes. Only significant periodical articles are included, generally from academic journals in Brazil and elsewhere. I relied heavily on certain periodicals which are cited in the text rather than herein, including *O Farol* (1915–87) and *Rivale* (1973–82); *O Sertão* (1950–72), *Tribuna do Sertão* (1981–82), and *Jornal de Petrolina* (1981–82) complete archives of which I was able to consult. I also looked at partial runs of other local newspapers, including *O Algodão* (1978–80), *Correio do São Francisco* (1903–12), *O Echo* (1930), *Cidade de Joazeiro* (1896), *Tribuna do São Francisco* (November 1970), *Jornal de Juazeiro* (1981–83), *Tribuna do Povo* (1973), *Caminhar Juntos* (1982–88). While I was in the field I read *Jornal do Commercio* and *Diário de Pernambuco* of Recife; *A Tarde* and *Jornal da Bahia* of Salvador; *Folha de Sõa Paulo* and *Estado de São Paulo;* and *Jornal do Brasil* of Rio de Janeiro. I reviewed *Visão* and *Veja* from 1970 through 1984 and *Istoé* for most of this period. The more useful of my hundreds of interviews are cited in the footnotes.

Abouchar, Alan. "The Performance of the Berkeley Program in Brazil: Comment," *Economic Development and Cultural Change* 20 (April 1974): 503–506.

Adams, Richard N. "Political Power and Social Structures," in *The Politics of Conformity in Latin America,* ed. Claudio Veliz. London: Oxford University Press, 1967, pp. 15–42.

"Power and Domains," *América Latin* 9 (April–June 1966): 3–21.

Adrian, Charles R. "Local Politics, " in *International Encyclopedia of the Social Sciences,* vol. 9. New York: Macmillan/Free Press, 1968, pp. 459–464.

Agger, Robert E., Daniel Goldrich, and Bert E. Swanson. *The Rulers and the Ruled: Political Power and Impotence in American Communities.* New York: John Wiley, 1964.

Aguiar, Neuma. "Impact of Industrialization on Women's Work Roles in Northeast Brazil," *Studies in Comparative International Development* 10 (Summer 1975): 78–94.

The Structure of Brazilian Development. New Brunswick, N.J.: Transaction Books, 1979.

Album histórico e ilustrado de Petrolina. Petrolina: Gráfica Petrolina, September 1948.

Albuquerque, Ulysses Lins de. *Un sertanejo e o sertão.* Rio de Janeiro: Livraria José Olympio Editora, 1957.

Alford, Robert R. "The Comparative Study of Urban Politics," in *Urban Research and Policy Planning*, ed. Leo F. Schnore and Henry Fagin. Beverly Hills, Calif.: Sage Publications, 1967, pp. 263–302.

Almond, Gabriel A., and Sidney Verba. *The Civic Culture: Political Attitudes and Democracy in Five Nations*. Princeton: Princeton University Press, 1963.

Alves, Márcio Moreira. *A Grain of Mustard Seed: The Awakening of the Brazilian Revolution*. Garden City, N.Y.: Doubleday Anchor Press, 1973.

Andrade, José Maria de. "O país dos Coelhos," *Veja* (February 25, 1981), 18–19.

Andrade, Manoel Correia de. *Espaço, polarização e desenvolvimento: a teoria dos polos de desenvolvimento e a realidade nordestina*. Recife: Centro Regional de Administração Municipal, 1967.

"Produção de energia e modernização do Vale do São Francisco," *Revista de Economia Política* 4 (January–March 1984): 43–55.

A terra e o homem no nordeste. São Paulo: Editorial Brasiliense, 1963.

Tradição e mudança: a organização do espaço rural e urbano na área de irrigação do submédio São Francisco. Rio de Janeiro: Zahar Editores, 1982.

Anselmo, Otacilio. *Padre Cícero: mito e realidade*. Rio de Janeiro: Editora Civilização Brasileira, 1968.

Apolinário, Olivá. *Mesa posta*. Petrolina: Editora Universitária da Universidade Federal de Pernambuco, 1978.

Apter, David E., ed. *Ideology and discontent*. New York: Free Press of Glencoe, 1964.

Aras, Roque. *A besta-fera contra a igreja*. Brasília: Centro de Documentação e Informação, 1981.

Arraes, Miguel. *Brazil: The People and the Power*. Baltimore: Penguin Books, 1972.

Asselin, Victor. *Grilagem: corrupção e violência em terras do Carajás*. Petrópolis: Editora Vozes with the Comissão Pastoral da Terra (CAT), 1982.

Assis, José Carlos de. *A chave do tesouro: anatomia dos escândalos financeiros, Brasil 1874–1983*. Rio de Janeiro: Editora Paz e Terra, 1983.

Azevedo, Aroldo de. *Regiões e paisagens do Brasil*, 2d ed. São Paulo: Companhia Editora Nacional, 1954.

Bachrach, Peter, and Morton S. Baratz. "Two Faces of Power," *American Political Science Review* 56 (December 1962): 947–952.

Baer, Werner. *Industrialization and Economic Development in Brazil*. Homewood, Ill.: Richard D. Irwin, 1965.

Baer, Werner, and Andrea Maneschi. "Import-Substitution, Stagnation, and Structural Change: An Interpretation of the Brazilian Case," *The Journal of Developing Areas* 5 (January 1971): 117–192.

Baer, Werner, Richard Newfarmer, and Thomas Trebat. "On State Capitalism in Brazil: Some New Issues and Questions," *Inter-American Economic Affairs* 30 (Winter 1976): 69–91.

Baltzell, E. Digby. *Philadelphia Gentlemen: The Making of a National Upper Class*. New York: Free Press, 1958.

Banco do Nordeste do Brasil. *Petrolina-Juazeiro: aspectos sócio-econômicos e área de influência comercial*. Fortaleza: Banco do Nordeste do Brasil, 1968.

Banco do Nordeste do Brasil, Departamento de Estudos Econômicos do Nordeste. *Recursos e necessidades do nordeste*. Recife: Banco do Nordeste do Brasil, 1964.

Bandeira, Joseph Wallace Faria, et al. *E nós, para onde vamos? Crónica de integração do São Francisco*, 2 vols. Juazeiro: Prefeitura Municipal, Secretaria de Educação e Cultura, 1974 and 1977.

Barroso, Gustavo. *Ao som da viola (Folklore)*. Rio de Janeiro: Livraria Editora Leite Ribeiro, 1921.

Segredos e revelações da história do Brasil, 2d ed. Rio de Janeiro: Edições O Cruzeiro, 1961.

Barth, Ernest A. T., and Stuart D. Johnson. "Community Power and a Typology of Social Issues," *Social Forces* 38 (October 1959): 29–32.

Bastide, Roger. *Brasil, terra de contrastes*, 2d ed. São Paulo: Corpo e Alma do Brasil, Difusão Européia do Livro, 1964.

Bell, Daniel. *The End of Ideology: On the Exhaustion of Political Ideas in the Fifties*. New York: Collier Books, 1962.

Bendix, Reinhard. *Max Weber: An Intellectual Portrait*. Garden City, N.Y.: Doubleday Anchor, 1962.

Blondel, Jean. *As condições da vida política no estado da Paraíba*. Rio de Janeiro: Fundação Getúlio Vargas, 1957.

Bonilla, Frank, and José A. Silva Michelena, eds. *A Strategy for Research on Social Policy*. Cambridge, Mass.: MIT Press, 1967.

Booth, David A., and Charles R. Adrian. "Power Structure and Community Change: A Replication Study of Community A," *Midwest Journal of Political Science* 6 (August 1962): 277–296.

Boschi, Renato Raul. *Elites industriais e democracia: hegemonia burguesa e mudança política no Brasil*. Rio de Janeiro: Edições Graal, 1979.

Bottomore, Thomas B. *Elites and Society*. New York: Basic Books, 1964.

Bouchardet, Joanny. *Sêccas e irrigação: solução scientífica e radical do problema nordestino brasileiro, geralmente intitulado 'O problema do Norte.'* Rio Branco, Minas Gerais: Officinas Graphs. da Papelaria Império, 1938.

Brito, P. Saturnino Rodrigues de. *As sêccas do norte*. Recife: Imprensa Industrial, 1913.

Bursztyn, Marcel. *O poder dos donos: planejamento e clientelismo no Nordeste*. Pretropólis: Editora Vozes com CNPq, 1984.

Calmon, Pedro. *História da fundação da Bahia*. Salvador: Museu do Estado (Publication No. 9), 1949.

História do Brasil na poesia do povo. Rio de Janeiro: Editora A Noite, n.d.

Cameron, David R. "Toward a Theory of Political Mobilization," *Journal of Politics* 36 (February 1974): 138–171.

Campos, Renato Carneiro. *Ideologia dos poetas populares de Nordeste*. Recife: Centro Regional de Pesquisas Educacionais do Recife, 1959.

Cardoso, Fernando Henrique. *Cuestiones de sociología del desarrollo de América Latina*. Santiago: Colección Imagem de América Latina (3), Editorial Universitária, 1968.

Empresariado industrial e desenvolvimento econômico no Brasil. São Paulo: Difel, 1972.

and Enzo Faletto. *Dependency and Development in Latin America*, trans. Marjory Mattingly Urquidi. Berkeley: University of California Press, 1979.

Cardoso, Vicente Licinio. *À margem da história do Brasil (Livro póstumo)*. São Paulo: Companhia Editora Nacional, 1933.

Carli, Gileno de. *Política de desenvolvimento do nordeste*. Recife: Universidade de Pernambuco, 1971.

Carneiro, Edison. *O quilombo dos Palmares, 1630–1695*. São Paulo: Editora Brasiliense Limitada, 1947.

Carvalho, Abdias Vilar de. "A questão nordeste no estado nacional," *Temas de Ciências Humanas* 7 (1980): 99–113.

Carvalho, José Murilo de. "Political Elites and State Building: The Case of Nineteenth-Century Brazil." *Comparative Studies in Society and History* 24 (July 1982): 378–399.

Carvalho, Orlando M. *O rio da unidade nacional: o São Francisco*. São Paulo: Companhia Editora Nacional, 1937.

Cascudo, Luís da Câmara. *Vaqueiros e cantadores: folclore poético do sertão de Pernambuco, Paraíba, Rio Grande do Norte e Ceará*. Rio de Janeiro: Tecnoprint Gráfica, 1963.

Casimir, Jean. "De la sociología regional a la acción política (un ejemplo latinoamericano)." Unpublished manuscript based on the 1966 study of the Centro Latinoamericano de Pesquisas em Ciências Sociais, 1969.

Castro, Josué de. *Death in the Northeast.* New York: Random House, 1966.

Cavarozzi, Marcelo. "Elementos para una caracterización del capitalismo oligárquico," mimeographed copy. Buenos Aires: Documentos CEDES-CLACSO (12), Centro de Estudios de Estado y Sociedad, June 1978.

Centro Latinoamericano de Pesquisas em Ciências Sociais. "Juazeiro e Petrolina, um polo de crescimento?" Rio de Janeiro: Centro Latinoamericano de Pesquisas em Ciências Sociais, 1967.

Chacón, Vamireh, "Burocracia e desenvolvimento," *Boletim do Instituto Joaquim Nabuco de Pesquisas Sociais* 9 (1960): 45–55.

Chandler, Billy Jaynes. *The Feitosas and the Sertão dos Inhamuns: The History of a Family and a Community in Northeast Brazil: 1700–1930.* Gainesville: University of Florida Press, 1972.

Chilcote, Ronald H. "Dependency: A Critical Assessment of the Literature," *Latin American Perspectives* 1 (Spring 1974): 4–29.

"Issues of Theory in Dependency and Marxism," *Latin American Perspectives* 8 (Summer–Fall 1981): 3–16.

"The Politics of Conflict in the Popular Poetry of Northeast Brazil," *Journal of Latin American Lore* 5, no. 2 (Winter 1979): 205–231.

Chilcote, Ronald H., ed. *Protest and Resistance in Angola and Brazil: Comparative Studies.* Berkeley and Los Angeles: University of California Press, 1972.

Chilcote, Ronald H., and Joel Edelstein, eds. *Latin America: The Struggle with Dependency and Beyond.* Cambridge, Mass.: Schenkman Publishing Company, 1974.

Chilcote, Ronald H., and Roy Goldman. "Status Quo and Reform Attitudes of Backlands High School Students of Dominant Class Parents in Brazil, Chile, and Mexico," *International Journal of Comparative Sociology* 16, nos. 1–2 (1975): 37–50.

Chilcote, Ronald H., and Timothy F. Harding. "Introduction," *Latin American Perspectives* 6 (Fall 1979): 2–15.

Christiansen, B. *Attitudes toward Foreign Affairs as a Function of Personality.* Oslo: Oslo University Press, 1959.

Cintra, Antônio Otávio. "Traditional Brazilian Politics: An Interpretation of Relations between Center and Periphery," in *The Structure of Brazilian Development,* ed. Neuma Aguiar. New Brunswick, N. J.: Transaction Books, 1979, pp. 127–166.

Ciranio, Marcos. *O escândalo da mandioca e a morte do procurador.* Recife: Calandra Editorial, 1982.

Cohen, D. L. "The Concept of Charisma and the Analysis of Leadership," *Political Science* 20 (September 1972): 299–305.

Comissão de Desenvolvimento Econômico de São Francisco. *Petrolina–Juazeiro, centro regional do baixo médio São Francisco.* Rio de Janeiro: Etas, Alejandro Solari, Engenheiros Consultores, 1969?

Comissão Pastoral de Saúde. Diocese de Juazeiro. *Cartilha da Saúde.* Juazeiro, Bahia: Diocese de Juazeiro, 1984.

Comissão Pastoral da Terra. Diocese de Juazeiro. *Como votar?* Juazeiro, Bahia: Diocese de Juazeiro, 1982.

Confederação dos Trabalhadores da Agricultura et al. *Campanha Nacional pela Reforma Agrária.* Rio de Janeiro: Editora Codecri, April 1983.

Conferência Nacional dos Bispos do Brasil. *Nordeste desafio à missão da igreja no Brasil.* São Paulo: Edições Paulinas, August 31, 1984.

Corradi, Juan. "Cultural Dependence and the Sociology of Knowledge: The Latin American Case," *International Journal of Contemporary Sociology* 8 (January 1971): 35–55.

Cunha, Euclides da. *Rebellion in the Backlands (os Sertões).* Chicago: University of Chicago Press, 1944.

Cunha, João Fernandes da. *Memória histórica de Juazeiro,* 2d ed. Juazeiro, 1978.

Cunha, José Guilherme da. *Esquina do Badu.* Juazeiro, Bahia, 1984?

Cunniff, Roger L. "Regional Image and Social Change in Northeast Brazil," *Journal of Inter-American Studies and World Affairs* 15 (August 1973): 363–373.

Cússa, Regina. *Re-Vista: Velha poesia nova.* Juazeiro: Juazeirenses Amigos da Cultura, 1978.

Dahl, Robert A. "A Critique of the Ruling Elite Model," *American Political Science Review* 52 (June 1958): 463–469.

Who Governs? Democracy and Power in an American City. New Haven: Yale University Press, 1961.

Daland, Robert T. *Brazilian Planning: Development Politics and Administration.* Chapel Hill: University of North Carolina Press, 1967.

D'Antonio, William V., and William H. Form. *Influentials in Two Border Cities: A Study in Community Decision-Making"* Notre Dame, Ind.: University of Notre Dame, 1965.

Della Cava, Ralph. *Miracle at Joazeiro.* New York: Columbia University Press, 1970.

Diamantino, Pedro. *Juazeiro de minha infância: memórias.* Rio de Janeiro: Imprensa Nacional, 1959.

Dias, Gentil Martins. "New Patterns of Domination in Rural Brazil: A Case Study of Agriculture in the Brazilian Northeast," *Economic Development and Cultural Change* 27 (October 1978): 169–182.

Dias, Wilson. *História da imprensa Juazeirense.* Juazeiro: Gráfica Santa Inez, 1982.

Diniz, Eli. *Empresário, estado e capitalismo no Brasil, 1930–1945.* Rio de Janeiro: Paz e Terra, 1978.

Domhoff, G. William. *The Powers That Be: Processes of Ruling Class Domination in America.* New York: Vintage Books, 1978.

Who Really Rules? New Haven and Community Power Reexamined. New Brunswick, N. J.: Transaction Books, 1978.

Dourado, Walter. *Juazeiro da Bahia à luz da história: Esboço histórico e descriçáo dos fatos conexos da colônia à república.* Juazeiro, Bahia, May 9, 1983.

Pequena história da navegação no Rio São Francisco. Salvador: Editora Beneditina, 1973.

Drake, George F. *Elites and Voluntary Associations: A Study of Community Power in Manizales, Colombia.* Madison: Land Tenure Center, University of Wisconsin, 1970.

Dreifuss, René Armand. *1964: a conquista do estado, ação política, poder e golpe de classes,* 3d ed. Petropólis: Editora Vozes, 1981.

Duque, J. G. *Solo e água no polígono das sêcas.* Fortaleza: Tipografia Minerva, 1949.

Dye, David R., and Carlos Eduardo de Souza e Silva. "A Perspective on the Brazilian State." *Latin American Research Review* 14 (Winter 1979): 81–98.

Dye, Thomas R. "The Local–Cosmopolitan Dimension and the Study of Urban Politics," *Social Forces* 41 (1966): 239–246.

Who's Running America? Englewood Cliffs, N. J.: Prentice-Hall, 1976.

Dye, Thomas R., and John W. Pickering. "Government and Corporate Elites: Convergence and Differentiation," *Journal of Politics* 36 (November 1974): 900–925.

Edelman, Murray. *The Symbolic Uses of Politics.* Champaign: University of Illinois Press, 1967.

Edinger, Lewis J., and Donald D. Searing. "Social Background in Elite Analysis: A Methodological Inquiry," *American Political Science Review* 61 (June 1967): 428–445.

Equipe de Pastoral de Diocese de Juazeiro. *O povo descobre a sociedade: "capitalismo x socialismo," subsídio para reflexões de CEBS.* São Paulo: Edições Paulinas, 1984.

Erickson, Kenneth. *The Brazilian Corporate State and Working-Class Politics.* Berkeley: University of California Press, 1977.

Evans, Peter. *Dependent Development: The Alliance of Multinational, State, and Local Capital in Brazil.* Princeton: Princeton University Press, 1979.

Fagan, Richard R. "Charismatic Authority and Leadership of Fidel Castro," *Western Political Quarterly* 18 (June 1965): 275–284.

Fagan, Richard R., and William S. Tuohy. *Politics and Privilege in a Mexican City.* Stanford: Stanford University Press, 1972.

Faoro, Raymundo. *Os donos do poder: formação do patronato político brasileiro.* Rio de Janeiro: Editora Globo, 1958. 2d. ed., 2 vols., 1975.

Fields, Gary S. "Who Benefits from Economic Development? – A Reexamination of Brazilian Growth in the 1960s," *American Economic Review* 67 (September 1977): 570–582.

Fishlow, Albert. "Brazilian Development in Long Term Perspective," *American Economic Review* 120 (May 1980): 102–112.

"Brazil's Economic Miracle." *The World Today* 19 (November 1973): 474–481.

Flynn, Peter. "Brazil: Authoritarianism and Class Control," *Journal of Latin American Studies* 6 (November 1974): 315–333.

Fox, Douglas M. "Methods within Methods: The Case of Community Power Studies," *Western Political Quarterly* 24 (March 1971): 5–11.

Fox, Jonathan. "Has Brazil Moved toward State Capitalism," *Latin American Perspectives* 7 (Winter 1980): 64–86.

Frank, André Gunder. *Capitalism and Underdevelopment in Latin America: Historical Studies of Chile and Brazil.* New York: Monthly Review Press, 1967.

Freeman, Linton C., Thomas J. Fararo, Warner Bloomberg, Jr., and Morris H. Sunshine. "Locating Leaders in Local Communities: A Comparison of Some Alternative Approaches," *American Sociological Review* 28 (October 1963): 791–798.

Freire, Marcos. *Papel da SUDENE na problemática do nordeste: Discurso proferido na sessão de 5 de maio de 1971.* Brasília: Departamento de Imprensa Nacional, 1971.

Freyre, Gilberto. *The Masters and the Slaves (Casa Grande e Senzala): A Study in the Development of Brazilian Civilization.* New York: Alfred A. Knopf, 1964.

Friedrich, Paul. "A Mexican Cacicazgo," *Ethnology* 4 (April 1965): 190–209.

Frey, Frederick W. *The Turkish Political Elite.* Cambridge, Mass: MIT Press, 1965.

Furtado, Celso. "Adventures of a Brazilian Economist," *International Social Science Journal* 25, nos. 1–2 (1973): 28–38.

"Brazil: What Kind of Revolution?" *Foreign Affairs* 41 (April 1963): 526–535.

Development and Underdevelopment, trans. Ricardo W. de Aguiar and Eric Charles Drysdale. Berkeley and Los Angeles: University of California Press, 1964.

Economic Growth of Brazil: A Survey from Colonial to Modern Times. Berkeley and Los Angeles: University of California Press, 1963.

Formação econômica do Brasil. Rio de Janeiro: Editora Fundo de Cultura, 1961.

A Operação Nordeste. Rio de Janeiro: Instituto Superior de Estudos Brasileiros, 1959.

Perspectivas da economia brasileira. Rio de Janeiro: Instituto Superior de Estudos Brasileiros, 1958.

"O significado real do Nordeste no atual quadro do país." *Novos Estudos* 1 (December 1981): 13–16.

Gilbert, Claire W. "Communities, Power Structures and Research Bias," *Polity* 4 (Winter 1972): 218–235.

Gitlin, Todd. "Local Pluralism as Theory and Ideology," *Studies on the Left* 5 (1965): 21–45.

Goodman, D. D. "The Brazilian Economic 'Miracle' and Regional Policy: Some Evidence from the Urban Northeast," *Journal of Latin American Studies* 8 (May 1976): 1–27.

Goodman, David and Michael Redclift. *From Peasant to Proletarian: Capitalist Development and Agrarian Transition.* New York: St. Martins, 1982.
Gottdienner, M. *The Decline of Urban Politics: Political Theory and the Crisis of the Local State.* Beverly Hills, Calif.: Sage Publications, 1987.
Graham, Lawrence S. *Civil Service Reform in Brazil: Principles versus Practice.* Austin: University of Texas Press, 1968.
Graham, R. B. Cunningham. *A Brazilian Mystic, Being the Life and Miracles of Antônio Conselheiro.* London: William Heinemann, 1920.
Graziano, Luigi, ed. "Political Clientelism and Comparative Perspectives," *International Political Science Review* 4, no. 4 (1983): 421–556.
Greenstein, Fred I. "Political Socialization," in *International Encyclopedia of Social Sciences,* vol. 15. New York: Macmillan/Free Press, 1968, pp. 551–555.
Gueiros, Optato. *Lampião: memórias de um oficial ex-comandante de forças volantes,* 2d ed. São Paulo: Linográfica Editora, 1952.
Halliday, Fred, and Maxine Molyneux. "Brazil: The Underside of the Miracle," *Ramparts* 12 (April 1974): 14–20.
Hawley, Willis D., and Fredrick M. Wirt, eds. *The Search for Community Power.* Englewood Cliffs, N.J.: Prentice-Hall, 1968.
Hillman, Jimmye S. "Economic Development and the Brazilian Northeast: What is Economic Development?" *Inter-American Economic Affairs* (Summer 1956): 79–96.
Hirschman, Albert O. *Journeys toward Progress: Studies of Economic Policy-making in Latin American.* New York: The Twentieth Century Fund, 1963.
"Policy Making and Policy Analysis in Latin American – A Return Journey," *Political Sciences* 6 (December 1975): 385–402.
Hobsbawn, Eric. *Primitive Rebels: Studies in Archaic Forms of Social Movements in the 19th and 20th Centuries.* Manchester, England: University of Manchester Press, 1959.
Hoskin, Gary. "Power Structure in a Venezuelan Town: The Case of San Cristóbal," in *Case Studies in Social Power,* ed. Hans-Dieter Evers. Leiden: Brill, 1969, pp. 28–47.
Huddle, Donald L. "Review Article: Essays on the Economy of Brazil: The Berkeley Group," *Economic Development and Cultural Change* 2 (April 1972): 560–574.
Hunter, Floyd. *Community Power Structure: A Study of Decision Makers.* New York: Doubleday Anchor Books, 1963.
Huntington, Samuel P. *Political Order in Changing Societies.* New Haven: Yale University Press, 1968.
Political Participation in Democratic Countries. Cambridge, Mass.: Harvard University Press, 1976.
Iutakea, Sugiyama. "Social Stratification Research in Latin America," *Latin American Research Review* 1 (Fall 1965): 7–21.
Janotti, Maria de Lourdes M. *O coronelismo: uma política de compromissos.* São Paulo: Tudo é História (13), Editora Brasiliense, 1981.
Juazeiro. [Salvador?]: Banco do Nordeste do Brasil, [1982?].
Juazeiro–ano 100, lances de sua história. Juazeiro: Empresa Graphica da Bahia, [1978?].
Julião, Francisco. *Que são as Ligas Camponesas?* Rio de Janeiro: Cadernos do Povo (1), Editora Civilização Brasileira, 1962.
Kaplan, Stephen S., and Norman C. Bonsor. "Did United States Aid Really Help Brazilian Development? The Perspective of a Quarter-Century," *Inter-American Economic Affairs* 27 (Winter 1973): 25–46.
Kelsey, Vera. *Seven Keys to Brazil.* New York: Funk and Wagnalls, 1941.
Kesselman, Mark, and Donald Rosenthal. *Local Power and Comparative Politics.* Beverly Hills, Calif.: Sage Professional Papers in Comparative Politics (01–049), 1974.

Klapp, Orrin E., and Vincent L. Padgett. "Power and Decision-Making in a Mexican Border City," *American Journal of Sociology* 65 (January 1960): 400–406.

Kuznesof, Elizabeth Anne. "Brazilian Urban History: An Evaluation," *Latin American Research Review* 17 (1982): 263–275.

Lacerda, Carlos. *Desafio e promessa: O rio São Francisco,* 2d ed. Rio de Janeiro: Distribuidora Record, 1965.

Laclau, Ernesto. "Feudalism and Capitalism in Latin America," *New Left Review* 67 (May–June 1971): 19–38.

Lamare, Judith Lynch. "Causal v. Contextual Analysis: A Case Study of Brazilian Local Political Participation," *Western Political Quarterly* 27 (March 1974): 117–142.

Lambert, Jacques. *Os dois brasis,* São Paulo: Companhia Editora Nacional, 1967.

LaPalombara, Joseph. "Decline of Ideology: A Dissent and an Interpretation," *American Political Science Review* 60 (March 1966): 5–16.

Laumann, Edward O., and Franz Urban Pappi. "New Directions in the Study of Community Elites," *American Sociological Review* 38 (April 1973): 212–230.

Leal, Victor Nunes. *Coronelismo, enxada e voto: o município e o regime representativo no Brasil.* Rio de Janeiro: Livraria Forense, 1949. 2d ed. with note by Basílio de Magalhães preface by Barbosa Lima Sobrinho. São Paulo: Alfa-Omega, 1975.

Coronelismo: The Municipality and Representative Government in Brazil, trans. June Henfrey New York: Cambridge University Press, 1977.

Leeds, Anthony. "Brazilian Careers and Social Structure: An Evolutionary Model and Case History," *American Anthropologist* 6: (1964): 1321–1347.

Levine, Robert. *Pernambuco in the Brazilian Federation, 1889–1937.* Stanford: Stanford University, 1978.

Lewin, Linda, *Politics and Parentela in Paraíba: A Case Study of Family-Based Oligarchy in Brazil.* Princeton: Princeton University Press, 1987.

Lima, Estácio de. *O mundo estranho dos cangaceiros: ensaio biosociológico.* Salvador: Editora Itapoã, 1965.

Lima, Heitor Ferreira. "Problemas do Nordeste," *Revista Brasiliense* 17 (May–June 1958): 13–33.

"Soluções para os problemas do Nordeste," *Revista Brasiliense* 34 (March–April 1961): 8–22.

Loewenstein, Karl. *Brazil under Vargas.* New York: Macmillan, 1942.

Lopes, Juarez R. B. "Some Basic Developments in Brazilian Politics and Society," in *New Perspectives of Brazil,* ed. Eric N. Baklanoff. Nashville: Vanderbilt University Press, 1966, p. 59–77.

Lowry, Ritchie P. *Who's Running This Town?* New York: Harper Torchbook, 1968.

Lundberg, George A., and Margaret Lawsing. "The Sociography of Some Community Relations," *American Sociological Review* 2 (1937): 318–335.

Lynd, Robert S., and Helen Merrell Lynd. *Middletown: A Study in Contemporary American Culture.* New York: Harcourt, Brace and World 1929.

Middletown in Transition: A Study in Cultural Conflicts. New York: Harcourt, Brace, and World 1937.

Mannheim, Karl. *Ideology and Utopia: An Introduction to the Sociology of Knowledge,* trans. Louis Wirth and Edward Shills. New York: Harcourt, Brace, and World, 1936.

Mansueto do Lavor, Pedro. "A democracia é fundamental para alcancar soluções permanentes," *Voz da Unidade* 210 (July 21–27, 1984): 8–9.

"Depoimento." Brasília: Comissão Parlamentar de Inquérito Destinada a Investigar as Causas e Consequências das Cheias do Rio São Francisco, Câmara dos Deputados, June 11, 1981.

Rio São Francisco: um depoimento. Brasília: Centro de Documentação, e Informação, Câmara dos Deputados, 1983.

"Verdades que a história esconde," *Jornal de Brasília* (August 12, 1984). Interview with Marlene Anna Galeazzi.

Marini, Ruy Mauro. *Dialéctica de la dependencia,* 2d ed. Mexico City: Ediciones Era, 1974.

"Dependencia y subimperialismo en América Latina," *Cultura en México,* supplement to *Siempre* 1030 (March 21, 1973): v–vii. Interview with Luis Angeles.

"Las razones del neodesarrollismo (respuesta a F. H. Cardoso y J. Serra)," *Revista Mexicana de Sociología* 40 (1978): 57–106.

Subdesarrollo y revolución. Mexico City: Siglo Veintiuno Editores, 1969.

Martins, Luciano. *Pouvoir et développment économique.* Paris: Editions Anthropos, 1976.

Marx, Karl. *The German Ideology,* ed. by C. J. Arthur. New York: International Publishers, 1973.

Marx, Karl, and Frederick Engels. *Selected Works in Two Volumes.* Moscow: Foreign Language Publishing House, 1958.

Marzouk, M. S. "The Brazilian Economy: Trends and Prospects," *Orbis* 18 (Spring 1974): 277–291.

McDonough, Peter. *Power and Ideology in Brazil.* Princeton: Princeton University Press, 1981.

McDonough, Peter, and Amaury de Souza. "Perceptions of Development Strategies in the Brazilian Elite." Paper presented at the American Political Science Association Annual Meeting, September 1–7, 1977, Washington, D. C.

Meade, Teresa. "The Transition to Capitalism in Brazil: Notes on a Third Road." *Latin American Perspectives* 5 (Summer 1978): 7–26.

Medeiros, Carlos Bastos de, et al. *Estruturas dos processos produtivo e administrativo do setor agropecuário em Pernambuco.* Recife: Secretaria de Coordenação Geral, Conselho de Desenvolvimento de Pernambuco, 1970.

Mello, Diogo Lordello de. *Problemas institucionais do município.* Rio de Janeiro: Instituto Brasileiro de Administração Municipal, 1965.

Melo, M. Rodrigues de. *Patriarcas e carreiros: influência do coronel e do carro de boi na sociedade rural do Nordeste,* 2d ed. Rio de Janeiro: Irmãos Pongetti Editores, 1954.

Melo, Mário Lacerda de. *Paisagens do Nordeste em Pernambuco e Paraíba.* Rio de Janeiro: Conselho Nacional de Geografia, 1958.

Merton, Robert K. *Social Theory and Social Structure.* New York: Free Press, 1957.

"O milagre de Pernambuco," *A Manchete* 992 (April 24, 1971): 109–113.

Miliband, Ralph, "Poulantzas and the Capitalist State." *New Left Review* 82 (November–December 1973); 83–92.

The State in Capitalist Society. New York: Basic Books, 1969.

Miller, Delbert C. *International Community Power Structure: Comparative Studies in Four World Cities.* Bloomington: Indiana University Press, 1970.

Mills, C. Wright. *The Power Elite.* New York: Oxford University Press, 1956.

Miranda, Agenor Augusto de. *O Rio São Francisco: como base do desenvolvimento econômico do nosso vasto interior.* São Paulo: Companhia Editora Nacional, 1936.

Moniz, Edmundo. *Canudos: a luta pela terra,* 2d ed. São Paulo: Global Editoral, 1982.

"Canudos: o suicídio literário de Vargas Llosa," Encontros com a Civilização Brasileira 29 (1982): 7–20.

Guerra social de Canudos. Rio de Janeiro: Editora Civilização Brasileira, 1978.

Moore, Barrington, Jr. "Notes on the Process of Acquiring Power." *World Politics* 8 (October 1955): 1–19.

Social Origins of Dictatorship and Democracy. Boston: Beacon Press, 1966.

Moore, Stanley W. *The Critique of Capitalist Democracy: An Introduction to the Theory of the State in Marx, Engels, and Lenin.* New York: Paine-Whitman, 1957.

Morães Neto, Geneton. "A república sertaneja dos Coelhos," *Diário de Pernambuco* (December 3, 1978): D–4 and 5.

Morley, Samuel A., and Gordon W. Smith. "The Choice of Technology: Multinational Firms in Brazil," *Economic Development and Cultural Change* 25 (January 1977): 239–264.

Morse, Richard M. "Recent Research on Latin American Urbanization: A Selective Survey with Commentary," *Latin American Research Review* 1 (Fall 1975): 35–74.

"Trends and Issues in Latin American Urban Research, 1965–1970," parts 1 and 2, *Latin American Research Review* 6 (Spring 1971): 3–52 and (Summer 1971): 19–75.

Mota, Janus de Freitas, Antônio de Paula Lopes, and Paulo Fernando Lopes Ferreira. "O acidente ocorrido na construção do Centro de Abastecimento de Petrolina." Recife: Empresa de Obras de Pernambuco, November 18, 1980.

Mota, Leonardo. *Violeiros do Norte.* Fortaleza: Imprensa Universitária do Ceará, 1962.

Nettle, J. P. *Political Mobilization.* New York: Basic Books, 1967.

Nichols, David. "Ruling Class as a Scientific Concept," *Review of Radical Political Economics* 4 (Fall 1972): 35–69.

Ocampo, José Fernando. *Dominio de clase en la ciudad colombiana.* Medellín: Oveja Negra, 1972.

Ogliastri U., Enrique. "Elites, Class, Power and Social Consciousness in the Economic Development of a Colombian City: Bucaramanga." Chicago: Ph.D. Dissertation, Northwestern University, 1973.

Oliveira, Algae Lima. *Lampião, cangaço no nordeste.* Rio de Janeiro: Edição O Cruzeiro, 1970.

Oliveira, Franklin de. *Euclydes: a espada e a letra.* Rio de Janeiro: Editora Paz e Terra, 1983.

Oliveira, Francisco de. *Elegia para uma re(li)gião: SUDENE, Nordeste, Planejamento e conflito de classes.* Rio de Janeiro: Editora Paz e Terra, 1977.

Oliveira, Rosália de Araújo, Ronald H. Chilcote, and Padre Pedro Mansueto de Lavor. "Estudo sôbre a juventude em dois bairros de Petrolina." Petrolina: CEMIC, 1971.

Padilha, Antônio de Santana. *Album de Saudações.* Petrolina, 1964.

Corre um rio de lágrimas (contos). Recife: Coleção Concórida, 1965.

Pedro e Lina. Romance. Recife, 1980

Petrolina no tempo, no espaço, na vez. Recife: Centro de Estudos de História Municipal/FIAM, Biblioteca Pernambucana de História Municipal (10), 1982.

"Petrolina – súmula histórica, cronológica do seu passado político, religioso, social, administrativo e cultural." Unpublished manuscript.

Ribeiril do São Francisco. Recife, 1970.

Superfície (versos). Bahia, 1967.

Page, Joseph A. *The Revolution That Never Was: Northeast Brazil, 1955–1964.* New York: Grossman Publishers, 1972.

Palmeira, Moacir. "Nordeste: mudanças políticas no século XX," *Cadernos Brasileiros* 37 (September–October 1966): 67–78.

Pang, Eul Soo. *Bahia in the First Brazilian Republic: Coronelismo and Oligarchs, 1889–1934.* Gainesville: University Presses of Florida, 1979.

Pardal, Paulo. *Carancas do São Francisco.* Rio de Janeiro: Serviço de Documentação Geral da Marinha, 1974. Also Rio de Janeiro: Ministério da Educação e Cultura, 1979.

Pedro II, Dom. *Diário de uma viagem ao Norte do Brazil.* Salvador: Progresso, 1959.

Peña, Félix Gerardo Tamayo. "Survey of the San Francisco River Basin." Petrolina: Food and Agriculture Organization, United Nations, February 1969.

Pernambuco. Secretaria de Planejamento, Fundação de Desenvolvimento Municipal do

Interior de Pernambuco (FIAM) and Prefeitura Municipal de Petrolina. *Plano diretor de desenvolvimento urbano de Petrolina.* Recife, June 1977.

Perroux, F. *L'économie du XXème siècle,* 2d ed. Paris: Presses Universitaires de France, 1964.

Perrucci, Robert, and Marc Pilisuk. "Leaders and Ruling Elites: The Interorganizational Bases of Community Power," *American Sociological Review* 35 (December 1970): 1040–1057.

Petrolina. Câmara dos Vereadores. "Livro de Atas," 1947–1982.

Petrolina, Cartório Eleitoral da 83a Zona Eleitoral de Pernambuco. "Livro de Atas," 1947–1982.

Pierson, Donald. *O Homem no Vale do São Francisco,* 3 vols. Rio de Janeiro: Superintendência do Vale do São Francisco, 1972.

Pinto, L. A. Costa. *Lutas de famílias no Brasil: introdução ao seu estudo.* São Paulo: Companhia Editora Nacional, 1949.

Política: a luta de em povo. Preface by Dom José Rodrigues de Souza. Juazeiro: Diocese of Juazeiro, June 8, 1981.

Portes, Alejandro, and John Walton. *Urban Latin America: The Political Condition from Above and Below.* Austin: University of Texas Press, 1976.

Poulantzas, Nicos. "The Problem of the Capitalist State," *New Left Review* 58 (November–December 1969): 67–78.

Prado Júnior, Caio. *The Colonial Background of Modern Brazil,* trans. Suzette Macedo. Berkeley and Los Angeles: University of California Press, 1969.

A revolução brasileira. São Paulo: Editora Brasiliense, 1966.

Prata, Ranulfo. *Lampião, documentário.* São Paulo: Linográfica Editora, 1953.

Presthus, Robert. *Men at the Top: A Study in Community Power.* New York: Oxford University Press, 1964.

"Primeiro Congresso Eucarístico de Petrolina," *Revista do 1º* Congresso Eucarístico de Petrolina 1 (October 1948).

Projeto Nordeste: concepção básica, Preliminary Version. Recife: Superintendência do Desenvolvimento de Nordeste and other agencies, April 1984. In addition, there are several series of reports by four study groups formed in 1982. I consulted Projeto Nordeste Coordenação Executiva, Grupo 1, "Propôsta de política de desenvolvimento regional para o Nordeste," Relatório Preliminar, Recife, September 1983. Also Projeto Nordeste, Grupo 4–Regional, "Programa de apoio ao pequeno produtor rural do Nordeste," Salvador October 1983. 2 vols.

Putnam, Robert D. "Studying Elite Political Culture: The Case of 'Ideology,' " *American Political Science Review* 65 (September 1971): 651–681.

Queiroz, Maria Isaura Pereira de. *O mandonismo local na vida política brasileira (da colônia à primeira república: ensaio de sociologia política).* São Paulo, 1969.

Queiroz, Maria Isaura Pereira de, ed. *Estudos de sociologia e história.* São Paulo: Editora Anhembi, 1957.

Quixabeira. *Porque voto em Nilo Coelho.* Caruarú, 1978. Pamphlet of social poetry.

Rabinowitz, Francine F. "Sound and Fury Signifying Nothing? A Review of Community Power Research in Latin America," *Urban Affairs Quarterly* 3 (March 1968): 111–122.

Raw, Silvia. "State-Owned Enterprises in Brazil: 1964–1980." Revision of paper presented to the Meetings of the Latin American Studies Association, Mexico City, September 29–October 1, 1983.

Ribeiro, Edson. *Juazeiro na esteira do tempo: Juazeiro–Bahia, suas origens, sua política administrativa e social.* Salvador: Editora Mensageiro da Fé, 1968.

Richardson, Ivan L. "Municipal Government in Brazil: The Financial Dimension," *Journal of Comparative Administration* 1 (1969): 321–343.

Ridings, Eugene W., Jr. "Business, Nationality and Dependency in Late Nineteenth Century Brazil," *Journal of Latin American Studies* 14 (May 1982): 55–96.

"The Merchant Elite and the Development of Brazil: The Case of Bahia during the Empire," *Journal of Inter-American Studies and World Affairs* 15 (August 1973): 335–353.

Robinson, John B., Jerrold G. Rusk, and Kendra B. Head. *Measures of Political Attitudes.* Ann Arbor, Mich.: Survey Research Center, Institute for Social Research, 1968.

Robock, Stefan H. *Brazil's Developing Northeast: A Study of Regional Planning and Foreign Aid.* Washington, D.C.: Brookings Institution, 1963.

"Recent Economic Trends in Northeast Brazil." *Inter-American Economic Affairs* 16 (Winter 1962): 65–89.

Rodrigues, Nina. *Os africanos no Brasil.* São Paulo: Companhia Editora Nacional, 1932.

Rodrigues de Souza, Dom José. "Depoimento na CPI das Enchentes do Rio São Francisco (1978, 1979 e 1980) na Câmara Federal." Brasília, May 7, 1981.

Roett, Riorden. *Brazil: Politics in a Patrimonial Society.* Boston: Allyn and Bacon, 1972.

The Politics of Foreign Aid in the Brazilian Northeast. Nashville: Vanderbilt University Press, 1972.

Ruhl, J. Mark. "Social Mobilization and Political Instability in Latin America: A Text of Huntington's Theory," *Inter-American Economic Affairs* 29 (Autumn 1975): 3–21.

Russi, Peter. "Community Decision Making," *Administrative Science Quarterly* 1 (March 1957): 438–439.

Sá, Maria Auxiliadora Ferraz. *Dos velhos aos novos coronéis: um estudo das redefinições do coronelismo.* Recife: Pimes, 1974.

Sampaio, Nelson de Souza. *O diálogo democrático na Bahia.* Belo Horizonte: Edições RBEP, 1960.

Sampaio, Yony. "The Population Question in Northeast Brazil: Its Economic and Ideological Dimensions: Comment," *Economic Development and Cultural Change* 24 (January 1976): 413–414. Reply by Herman E. Daly, pp. 415–416.

Sandroni, Paulo Henrique Ribeiro. "Sobradinho: sertão e diferenciação." São Paulo: Master's thesis, Pontificia Universidade Católica de São Paulo, 1982.

Santos, Theotônio dos. "The Concept of Social Classes," *Science and Society* 34 (Summer 1970): 166–193.

Socialismo o fascismo: dilema latinoamericano. Santiago: Colección América Nueva, Editorial Prensa Latinoamericana, 1969.

"The Structure of Dependence," *American Economic Review* 60 (May 1970): 231–236.

Schmitter, Philippe C. *Interest Conflict and Political Change in Brazil.* Stanford, Calif.: Stanford University Press, 1971.

Schneider, Ronald M. *The Political System of Brazil: Emergence of a "Modernizing" Authoritarian Regime, 1964–1970.* New York: Columbia University Press, 1971.

Schwartzman, Simon. "Representação e cooptação política no Brasil," *Dados* 7(1970): 9–41.

Searing, Donald D. "Models and Images of Man and Society in Leadership Theory," *The Journal of Politics* 31 (February 1969): 3–31.

Serejo, Tereza Cristina Leal de. "Coronéis sem patente: a modernização conservadora no sertão pernambucano." Niterói: Master's thesis, Instituto de Ciências Humanas e Filosofia, Centro de Estudos Gerais, Universidade Federal Fluminense, 1979.

Shaw, M., and J. Wright. *Scales for the Measurement of Attitudes.* New York: McGraw-Hill, 1967.

Sherwood, Frank P. *Institutionalizing the Grass Roots in Brazil: A Study in Comparative Local Government.* San Francisco: Chandler, 1967.

Silva, José Graziano da. *O que é questão agrária?*, 5th ed. São Paulo: Coleção Primeiros Passos, Editora Brasiliense, 1982.

Silva, José Graziano da, with Barbara A. Kohl. "Capitalist 'Modernization' and Employment in Brazilian Agriculture, 1960–1975: The Case of the State of São Paulo," *Latin American Perspectives* 11 (Winter 1984): 117–136.

Silva, Manoel Pacífico da. *Queremos reforma agrária*. Alagôa Grande, May 12, 1971.

Silva, Wilson Dias da. *Os remeiros de São Francisco*. Juazeiro, 1983.

Silvert, Kalman H., ed. *Expectant Peoples: Nationalism and Development*. New York: Random House, 1963.

"Leadership Formation and Modernization in Latin America," *Journal of International Affairs* 20, no. 2 (1966): 318–331.

Singer, Paul. "A política das classes dominantes," in *Política e revolução social no Brasil*, ed. Octávio Ianni et al. Rio de Janeiro: Editora Civilização Brasileira, 1965, p. 72–78.

Sobrinho, Barbosa Lima. "A Bahia e o Rio São Francisco," *Revista do Instituto Archeológico Histórico e Geográphico Pernambuco* 30, nos. 143–146 (1930): 127–174.

Pernambuco e o São Francisco. Recife: Imprenta Oficial, 1929.

Souza, Alírio Fernando Barbosa de. "O coronelismo no Médio São Francisco (um estudo de poder local)." Salvador: Master's Thesis, Universidade Federal da Bahia, 1973.

Souza, Amaury de. "The Cangaço and the Politics of Violence in Northeast Brasil," in *Protest and Resistance in Angola and Brazil: Comparative Studies*, ed. Ronald H. Chilcote. Berkeley and Los Angeles: University of California Press, 1972, pp. 109–131.

Souza, Herbet, and Carlos A. Afonso. *The Role of the State in the Capitalist Development in Brazil: The Fiscal Crisis of the Brazilian State*. Toronto: Brazilian Studies 7, 1975.

Souza, Izabel Marques de. *Penitentes. Uma chama de fé*. Juazeiro: Biblioteca Pública, 1978.

Stepan, Alfred. *The Military in Politics: Changing Patterns in Brazil*. Princeton: Princeton University Press, 1971.

Stepan, Alfred ed. *Authoritarian Brazil: Origins, Policies, and Future*. New Haven: Yale University Press, 1973.

Stein, Stanley J., and Barbara H. Stein. *The Colonial Heritage of Latin America, Essays on Economic Dependence in Perspective*. New York: Oxford University Press, 1970.

Sternberg, Hilgard O'Reilly. "Aspectos da sêca de 1951, no Ceará," *Revista Brasileira de Geografia* 13 (July–September 1951): 327–369.

"Não existe ainda um plano para o problema das sêcas," *Boletim Geográfico* 16 (May–June 1958): 377–384.

"Sêca: causas e soluções," *Boletim Geográfico* 16 (September–October 1958): 638–643.

Superintendência do Desenvolvimento do Nordeste, Departamento de Recursos Naturais. *Projeto Cobre. O que é e o que pretende*. Recife: Departamento de Recursos Naturais, 1967.

Sweezy, Paul M., and Maurice Dobb et al. eds. *The Transition from Feudalism to Capitalism*. London: Verso Edition, 1978.

Taylor, John G. *From Modernization to Modes of Production: A Critique of the Sociologues of Development and Underdevelopment*. New York: Macmillan, 1979.

Ugalde, Antonio. "A Decision Model for the Study of Public Bureaucracies," *Policy Sciences* 4 (1973): 75–84.

Power and Conflict in a Mexican Community: A Study of Political Integration. Albuquerque: University of New Mexico Press, 1970.

Valenzuela, Arturo. *Political Brokers in Chile: Local Government in a Centralized Polity*. Durham, N.C.: Duke University Press, 1977.

Vargas Llosa, Mario. *A guerra do fim do mundo, a saga de Antônio Conselheiro na maior aventura literária de nosso tempo*. Rio de Janeiro: Editora Francisco Alves, 1982.

Viana Filho, Luiz *O governo Castelo Branco,* 2d ed. Rio de Janeiro: Livraria José Olympio Editora, 1975.

Vianna, Francisco José Oliveira. *Instituições políticas brasileiras,* vol. 1. São Paulo: Livraria José Olympio Editora, 1949.

Recenseamento realizado em 1 de setembro de 1920. Rio de Janeiro, 1922.

Vidal, Ademar. "Os movimentos nordestinos de emigração," *Cultura Política* 3 (January 1943): 51–56.

Vieira, Maria Sulamita de A. "As formas de agricultura no nordeste e suas relações com a modelo econômico do pacto colonial," *Revista de Ciências Sociais* 10, nos. 1–2 (1979): 159–196.

Vilaça, Marcos Vinicius and Roberto Cavalcanti de Albuquerque. *Coronel, coronéis.* Rio de Janeiro: Tempo Brasileiro, 1965.

Walton, John. *Elites and Economic Development: Comparative Studies on the Political Economy of Latin American Cities.* Austin: Institute of Latin American Studies, University of Texas, 1977.

"From the Cities to Systems: Recent Research on Latin American Urbanization," *Latin American Research Review* 14, no. 1 (1979): 159–169.

"Structures and Artifact: The Current Status of Research on Community Power Structure," *American Journal of Sociology* 71 (January 1966): 430–438.

Wanderley, Maria de Nazareth. *Mudanças e tensões sociais no meio rural de Pernambuco.* Recife: Secretaria de Coordenação Geral, Conselho de Desenvolvimento de Pernambuco, 1970.

Warner, W. Lloyd, and Paul S. Lunt. *The Status System of a Modern Community.* New Haven: Yale University Press, 1942.

Weber, Max. *The Theory of Social and Economic Organization.* Glencoe, Ill.: Free Press, 1964.

Welsh, William A. "Methodological Problems in the Study of Political Leadership in Latin America." Mimeographed copy. Iowa City: Laboratory for Political Research, University of Iowa, October 1969.

Whiteford, Andrew H. *Two Cities of Latin America: A Comparative Description of Social Classes.* New York: Doubleday, 1964.

Wolfinger, Raymond E. "Nondecisions and the Study of Local Politics," *American Political Science Review* 65 (December 1971): 1063–108.

"Reputation and Reality in the Study of 'Community Power,' " *American Sociological Review* 25 (October 1960): 636–644.

Wright, Erik Olin. "Varieties of Marxist Conceptions of Class Structure," *Politics and Society,* 9, no. 3 (1980): 299–322.

Zeitlin, Maurice, and Richard Earl Ratcliff. "Research Methods for the Analysis of the Internal Structure of Dominant Classes: The Case of Landlords and Capitalists in Chile," *Latin American Research Review* 10 (Fall 1975): 5–61.

Zeitlin, Maurice, W. Lawrence Newman, and Richard Earl Ratcliff. "Class Segments: Agrarian Property and Political Leadership in the Capitalist Class of Chile," *American Sociological Review* 41 (December 1976): 1006–1029.

Zweig, Stefan. *Brazil, Land of the Future.* New York: Viking Press, 1942.

Index

CAMBRIDGE LATIN AMERICAN STUDIES

3 Peter Calvert. *The Mexican Revolution 1910–1914: The Diplomacy of Anglo-American Conflict*
8 Celso Furtado. *Economic Development of Latin America: Historical Background and Contemporary Problems*
10 D. A. Brading. *Miners and Merchants in Bourbon Mexico, 1763–1810*
15 P. J. Bakewell. *Silver Mining and Society in Colonial Mexico, Zacatecas, 1564–1700*
22 James Lockhart and Enrique Otté. *Letters and People of the Spanish Indies: The Sixteenth Century*
24 Jean A. Meyer. *The Cristero Rebellion: The Mexican People between Church and State, 1926–1929*
31 Charles F. Nunn. *Foreign Immigrants in Early Bourbon Mexico, 1700–1760*
32 D. A. Brading. *Haciendas and Ranchos in the Mexican Bajio*
34 David Nicholls. *From Dessalines to Duvalier: Race, Color, and National Independence in Haiti*
35 Jonathan C. Brown. *A Socioeconomic History of Argentina, 1776–1860*
36 Marco Palacios. *Coffee in Colombia, 1850–1970: An Economic, Social, and Political History*
37 David Murray. *Odious Commerce: Britain, Spain, and the Abolition of the Cuban Slave Trade*
38 D. A. Brading. *Caudillo and Peasant in the Mexican Revolution*
39 Joe Foweraker. *The Struggle for Land: A Political Economy of the Pioneer Frontier in Brazil from 1930 to the Present Day*
40 George Philip. *Oil and Politics in Latin America: Nationalist Movements and State Companies*
41 Noble David Cook. *Demographic Collapse: Indian Peru, 1520–1620*
42 Gilbert M. Joseph. *Revolution from Without: Yucatan, Mexico, and the United States, 1880–1924*
43 B. S. McBeth. *Juan Vicente Gomez and the Oil Companies in Venezuela, 1908–1935*
44 J. A. Offner. *Law and Politics in Aztec Texcoco*
45 Thomas J. Trebat. *Brazil's State-Owned Enterprises: A Case Study of the State as Entrepreneur*
46 James Lockhart and Stuart B. Schwartz. *Early Latin America: A History of Colonial Spanish America and Brazil*
47 Adolfo Figueroa. *Capitalist Development and the Peasant Economy in Peru*
48 Norman Long and Bryan Roberts. *Miners, Peasants, and Entrepreneurs: Regional Development in the Central Highlands of Peru*
49 Ian Roxborough. *Unions and Politics in Mexico: The Case of the Automobile Industry*
50 Alan Gilbert and Peter Ward. *Housing, the State, and the Poor: Policy and Practice in Three Latin American Cities*
51 Jean Stubbs. *Tobacco on the Periphery: A Case Study in Cuban Labor History, 1860–1958*
52 Stuart B. Schwartz. *Sugar Plantations in the Formation of Brazilian Society: Bahia, 1550–1835*
53 Richard J. Walter. *The Province of Buenos Aires and Argentine Politics, 1912–1945*
54 Alan Knight. *The Mexican Revolution, vol 1: Porfirians, Liberals, and Peasants*
55 Alan Knight. *The Mexican Revolution, vol. 2: Counter-Revolution and Reconstruction*
56 P. Michael McKinley. *Pre-Revolutionary Caracas: Politics, Economy, and Society, 1777–1811*
57 Adriaan C. van Oss. *Catholic Colonialism: A Parish History of Guatemala, 1524–1821*
58 Leon Zamosc. *The Agrarian Question and the Peasant Movement in Colombia: Struggles of the National Peasant Association, 1967–1981*
59 Brian R. Hamnett. *Roots of Insurgency: Mexican Regions, 1750–1824*
60 Manuel Caballero. *Latin America and the Comintern, 1919–1943*
61 Inga Clendinnen. *Ambivalent Conquests: Maya and Spaniard in Yucatan, 1517–1570*
62 Jeffrey D. Needell. *A Tropical Belle Epoque: Elite Culture and Society in Turn-of-the-Century Rio de Janeiro*
63 Victor Bulmer-Thomas. *The Political Economy of Central America since 1920*
64 Daniel James. *Resistance and Integration: Peronism and the Argentine Working Class, 1946–1976*

65 Bill Albert. *South America and the First World War: The Impact of the War on Brazil, Argentina, Peru, and Chile*
66 Jonathan Hartlyn. *The Politics of Coalition Rule in Colombia*
67 Charles H. Wood and José Alberto Magno de Carvalho. *The Demography of Inequality in Brazil*
68 Sandra Lauderdale Graham. *House and Street: The Domestic World of Servants and Masters in Nineteenth-Century Rio de Janeiro*